READINGS IN CRIMINOLOGY

READINGS IN CRIMINOLOGY

Editors

Dr. R. Thilagaraj
Dr. S. Latha

GYAN

ISBN: 978-81-212-1144-4

Price: ₹ 1195

First Published 2014

Published by
Gyan Publishing House
23, Main Ansari Road
Daryaganj, New Delhi-110002
Phones: 23282060, 23261060
Fax: 91-11-23285914
E-mail: books@gyanbooks.com

Laser Typesetting: Quick Media, Delhi

Printed at: Chawla Offset Printers, Delhi

Cataloging in Publication Data--DK
Courtesy: D.K. Agencies (P) Ltd. <docinfo@dkagencies.com>

Readings in criminology / editors, R. Thilagaraj, S. Latha.
p. cm.
Contributed articles.
Includes bibliographical references and index.
ISBN 9788121211444

1. Criminology--India. I. Thilagaraj, R. II. Latha, S., 1975-

DDC 364.54 23

Contents

Foreword

Chriminology as a discipline has multiple dimensions. Dr. R. Thilagaraj and Dr. S. Latha have rendered a timely service to this continuously emerging discipline by bringing up this collection of papers.

As an administrator with 42 years of experience of public administration, I had to face issues relating to crime and tackle them hut I never had an opportunity to study criminology as a discipline. The readings compiled in this book have been so imaginatively selected that they provoke thoughts on the many aspects and dimensions of criminology.

Dr. Mridul Srivastava's paper 'Critical perspectives in criminological developments in India' is a good starting point. Dr. Srivastava observes, 'Although contemporary definitions vary in the exact words used, there is considerable consensus that criminology involves the application of the scientific method to the study of variation in criminal law, the causes of crime, and reactions to crime. This combination of method and substance evolved over lime with the expectation for a scientific methodology in place by the late 19th century and acceptance of the broad, tripartite, substantive focus established by the middle of the 20th century. Criminology is an inter-disciplinary field of study, involving scholars and practitioners representing a wide range of behavioural and social sciences as well as numerous natural sciences.'

The sin qua non for any sustainable, peaceful and progressive society is the prevalence of the rule of law. It is this rule oflaw which distinguishes a civilized society from anarchy. In recent times some states in India which were economically backward and lagging behind in all parameters of development were known collectively as 'BIMARU' states. (Bihar, Madhya Pradesh, Rajasthan and Uttar Pradesh). It was known that in one of the states—Bihar-the rule of law hardly prevailed. From the late nineties it had become a place where critics said was the rule feature of this scene is that the entries from India in this However, criminology as subject of teaching in India has a history of more than fifty years. The perception of even learned people about criminology in this nation are quite vague andmisplaced. This requires a systematics stock taking.

After all certain places and groups have been widely associated with cirminals. Mafias have their history in southern Italy, especially near Sicily. The Triads of Hong Kong and Macau in China are confined to certain parts of that country. Japan has its Yakuza gangs. In our own country certain tribes and castes got branded as criminal tribes by the British because historically the harshness of climate and lack of opportunities for agriculture and cultivation forced these unfortunate people to become marauding bandits. It is not surprising that thugs and pindaris were well known in our country before the British under Lord William Bentick subdued them. The Roma in Europe today face similar problems as migrants.

Many a time cultural values may male the problem intractable. The British in India had to come 10 a son of armed truce with the tribes of the North West Frontier and North East India. Even today the United Slates is facing the problem of culture and crime in the context of terrorism in the Af-Pak border. That brings us to a totally recent dimension of crime in the form of terrorism. Criminal action gets protection, behind tlte mask of religion or protection of one's culture.

At this stage it may be worthwhile to recall the basic purpose of study of criminology. It has at least three objectives. To begin with at a minimum any state within its jurisdiction, Saw and order, Understanding the dynamic appropriate strategies and policies.

Secondly a deeper insight into the criminal mind can help to create an environment where crime cannot or does not flourish, When Rudy Guilliani was the mayor of New York, he successfully implemented the policy of zero tolerance of crime. In this effort he was greatly aided by the vision and drive of his police chief Sadden, He came up with the counter intuitive insight of the broken window theory. The common perception would be that one should focus on large crimes to effectively check crime but the broken window theory makes this perception stand on its head of the jungle. Private, caste based armies (senas) flourished which challenged the functioning of the police in the state. In the coal belt mafia regimes dominated. Kidnapping for ransom had become a cottage industry.

Fortunately things have taken a turn for the better in recnt times. The basic rule of law has been established and minimum needs of the people for infrastructure like power, roads and drinking water (*bijli, sadak, pani*) have been provided. The Chief Minister, Nitish Kumar, has been widely hailed nationwide for this remarkable and eminently welcome development not surprisingly, he has recently won the election for another term very convincingly.

In face Bihar can provide an excellent case study for ihe multiple dimensions of criminology in the Indian context.

Any violation of the law is crime, The study of this phenomenon as to why people violate the law opens many avenues far investigation. We can focus on the individual who breaks the law. We can also focus on society as a whole and look upon crime as a social phenomenon. The focus on the individual criminal would lead to the study of psychology of the criminal and leads us to the question, 'is there anything like the criminal mind?' Enquiring into the nimd can be done by focusing on the behaviour following Freud and his school of thought. Alternatively we can look at the physical or biological basis from the point of view of me genes and DNA. At one time aggressive behaviour was linked with an extra Y chromosome.

Solutions to tackle the problem of crime can follow the physical approach of biology or the behavioural approach of psychology. It is the physical approach that led to the 19th century theories of Lombroso and pseudo-sciences like phrenology.

Alternatively as Dr. Srivastava points out sociology can provide a better approach. This in turn brings us to the issue of the culture specific approach to crime.

Dr. G.S. Bajpai's paper 'Criminology in India—status and scope' highlights an interesting point. 'Criminology is now too visible, One click of "criminology" on any search engine on Internet would pour in well over fifty thousand entries. This abundantly signifies the fact that the growth of criminology as discipline and profession has grown noticebly in the recent past. The dismal Suppose an urehin throws a stone and breaks a window in a well maintained building, if it is not immediately repaired and action taken against the person causing the damage, very soon the broken window becomes an open invitation for others to have a go at breaking the remaining windows. The neighbourhood can very soon become a criminal one. Badden began by focusing on graffiti in suburban trains and prompt action to punish the vandals had a dramatic impact on the overall crime situation. Thirdly study of crime helps to frame appropriate laws to punish crime and thus deter it.

At the same time we must not forget that, the challenge for students of criminology and enforcers of the laws against crime, it is endless. Every new technology or new sphere of activity creates its own set of fresh crime. Oscar Wilde pointed out with great insight that the thief is after all the artist, the policeman only a critic.

The explosive growth of technology and the internet has opened up a totally new area of crime-cybercrime. [refer Dr. S. Latha's paper "Cyber crimes, information security and cyber fornsics"].

It is therefore necessary for police and law enforcement agencies to be eternally vigilant. In medicine prevention is better than cure. In engineering we have the concept of predictive, preventive and breakdown maintenance. Breakdown maintenance is the last option.

Each of the papers in this selection covers the psychological or sociological dimensions of criminology. The need for developing India specific disciplines is very essential.

Incidentally, they also give a glimpse of the dynamic of how a multi-dimensional discipline like criminology develops.

First comes the study of the process through action research. [Fefer Dr. Prateep Phillip "Intervention in social work for crime prevention". And from this follows the philosophy [Refer Hema Hargovan "Restorative justice in South Africa". In physical research, every hypothesis has to be validated against ampirical results of experiments.

Each of the papers in this collection falls into one of these categories of the exciting process of knowledge creation. Dr. Thailagaraj and Dr. Latha must be congratulated for coming up with a bunch of thought provoking papers which are exciting and can act as catalysts for speeding up the growth of criminology as a discipline in India.

I wish this publication all success.

N. Vittal

Preface

Readings in Criminology is a collection of articles contributed by Scholars in Criminology and Criminal Justice Administration. There has been a long due for such publications since most of the Countries brought light the developments in Criminology in their own countries. Though Criminology as an Inter-Disciplinary subject had been introduced in 1960s in the Universities and a lot had been done on Criminological Research by way of Ph.D Dissertations and Research Projects, very little was brought to light. This book is an attempt to unravel the developments of Criminology in India. Though this book is just a beginning, it has salient features of bringing together the Criminological Research and writings at various forums.

There are three articles exclusively on the developments of Criminology in India depicting the current position, future perspective and teaching methods in Criminology by Prof. Balraj Chauhan, Dr. Madhava Somasundaram and Dr. Mridul Srivastava. These Scholars explained in detail from all dimensions in certain core issues. Dr. Sarada, a Senior Police Officer in his article on Criminal Justice Reforms emphasises the need for reforms in Law Enforcement, Judiciary and Corrections keeping in mind the needs and sufferings of a common man in the society. Similarly, Dr. Prateep, another Police Officer specialized in Community Policing dwells upon the Crime Prevention through the Intervention of Social Work. The article of Prof. Mark Brown, Australia deals with the contemporary approach to the Psychology of Crime, Law and Justice. Dr. K. Rama Subramaniam, an expert in the field of Cyber Crime and Information Security explains in detail the management of Cyber Crime from a governance approach. The problems of Vulnerable Groups such as the Children, Women and Elder persons are analyzed in detail by Dr. R. Thilagaraj, Dr. R. Shankar, Mr. Afzal and Abdul Latif, Dr. Priyamvadha and Sowmya. Papers on Transborder Terrorism by Mr. Prabhakar and Victims of Terrorism by Dr. Arvind Tiwari critically examine terrorism from various perspectives. Dr. Syed traces the development of Alcoholics Anonymous and methods of treatment of Drug Addicts. Prof. Mehraj Uddin from Kashmir University critically analyses the position of Judicial Activism in India. The need for Cyber Forensics in India is explained in detail by Dr. S. Latha and various forms of Cyber Crimes by Mr. Deepak Rao.

R. Thilagaraj, S. Latha

List of Contributors

R. Thilagaraj. Professor and Head, Department of Criminology, University of Madras, Chennai 600 005 and Chairman, Indian Society of Criminology.

Sowmya, K. UGC-Junior Research Fellow, Department of Criminology, University of Madras.

Dr. S. Latha. Assistant Professor and Head i/c, School of Criminology and Criminal Justice, Tamil Nadu Open University, Chennai 600 005 and Secretary, Indian Society of Criminology, *E*-Mail: lathasubramanian@gmail.com

Surbhi Dayal. Visiting Research Scholar (Commonwealth Scholar from JNU, New Delhi), School of Oriental and African Studies, University of London, London, UK "The transformation of *Kanjar* women: From Traditional Entertainers to Dance Bar Girls".

Balraj Chauhan. Vice-Chancellor, Dr. Ram Manohar Lohiya National Law University, Lucknow.

Lecture delivered during the 32nd All India Criminology Conference after receiving the ISC – Kumarappa Reckless Award.

S.M. Afzal Qadri. Professor, Dept. of Law, University of Kashmir, Srinagar, 190006 (India).

Abdul Latif Wani. Professor, Dept. of Law, University of Kashmir, Srinagar, 190006 (India).

Arvind Tiwari. Professor and Chairperson, Centre for Socio-legal studies, Human Rights, School of Social Sciences, Tata Institue of Social Sciences, Deonar, Mumbai-400 088, India. Email ID: tiwari_a@tiss.edu.

G.S. Bajpai. Professor and Chairperson, Centre for Civil and Criminal Justice Administration, National Law Institute University, Bhopal (M.P.), India.

Hema Hargovan. Dr. Hema Hargovan [BA (Law) Hons-Criminology, LLB, LLM, Ph.D—Criminology] is an Advocate of the High Court of South Africa and a Lecture in the Criminology Programme, School of Sociology and Social Studies, University of Kwa-Zulu-Natal, South Africa.

P. Madhava Soma Sundaram. Head, Department of Criminology and Criminal Justice, Manonmaniam Sundaranar University, Tirunelveli, India.

Mark Brown. School of Social and Political Sciences, University of Melbourne, Australia. mark.brown@unimelb.edu.au.

Mridul Srivastava. Assistant Registrar, Dr. Ram Manohar Lohiya National Law University, Lucknow.

Prateep V. Philip. Inspector General of Police, Tamil Nadu.

K. Rama Subramaniam. CEO, Valiant Technologies, Chennai and Adjunct Professor, Department of Criminology, University of Madras, rama@valiant-technologies.com.

M. Srinivasan. Associate Professor, Department of Criminology, University of Madras.

R. Shankar. Professor and Head, Dept. of Sociology, Bharathidasan University, Tiruchirappalli-620 024, Tamil Nadu.

S. Vedapurieswaran. Research Scholar, Dept. of Sociology, Bharathidasan University, Tiruchirappalli-620 024, Tamil Nadu.

Syed Umarhathab. Assistant Professor, Department of Criminology and Criminal Justice, Manonmaniam Sundaranar University, Tirunelveli. E-mail: drsyedumar@gmail.com

S. Ramdoss. Assistant Professor, Department of Criminology, University of Madras. Chennai 600 005.

M. Priyamvadha. Assistant Professor, Department of Criminology, University of Madras, Chennai.

G. Deepak Raj Rao. Research Scholar, Department of Criminology, University of Madras.

Mehraj Uddin. Head, Department of Law, University of Kashmir Hazratbal, Srinagar-6.

M.D. Allen Selva Kumar. Assistant Professor, Dept of Criminology and Police Administration, J.H.A. Agarsen College, Madhavaram, Chennai-60.

E. Prabhakaran. Assistant Professor, Department of Defence and Strategic Studies, University of Madras, Chennai-600 005.

1

CORRECTIONAL SUBSTITUTES TO PUNISHMENT: COMMUNITY BASED CORRECTION

R. Thilagaraj

Community based corrections have grown out of the belief that imprisonment does not represent as an effective device for reformation of offenders. Research studies on impact of institutional corrections proved that such institutions have deleterious effects on the personality of the convicts instead of rehabilitating them. The alternative suggested by Criminologists is Community Based Corrections. The rationale underlying this assertion is that correction is basically the task of building or rebuilding the solid ties between the offender and the community, integrating or reintegrating him into the mainstream of social life through restoration of family ties, providing employment and education, and security a place for the offender in the routine functioning of the society. Hence various methods of community based corrections have been developed and significant. Among them are probation and parole.

PROBATION

Definition

Probation is a community-based non-institutional method of treatment of offenders. Probation is defined in the Standard Probation Act of 1955 as a "procedure unaer which a defendant found guilty of crime upon verdict or plea, is released by the court, without imprisonment subject to condition imposed by the or plea, is released by the court". The American Bar Association defines probation as "a sentence not authority in the sentencing court to modify the conditions of sentence or to re-sentence the offender if he violates the conditions."

The report of the Advisory Committee on penal Institutions, probation and parole to the national commission on law, observance and enforcement defines probation as "a process of treatment, prescribed by the court for persons convicted of offences against the law, during which the individual an probation lives in the community and regulates his own life under conditions imposed by the court and is subject to supervision by a probation officer".

Development of Probation

The origin of probation was not the result of a deliberate creative, legislative or judicial act, but rather of a gradual growth, an almost unconscious modification of existing legal practices. Some authorities trace the roots of production to the middle ages when such devices as the 'benefit of clergy', 'judicial reprive' and 'recognizance', made it possible either to avoid or at least to postpone punishment. Through these devices an attempt was made to avoid the mechanical application of the harsh and cruel precepts of rigorous, repressive criminal law. These Anglo-American judicial expedients can be treated as direct precursors of probation as it is known today

The origin of probation in the sense as we understand it today can probably be attributed most aptly to the work of John Augustus, Boston, USA in 1841. He was the first to invent the system which he termed probation - of selection and supervision of referable offenders in the criminal court. Not only did Augustus initiate probation service by bailing out offenders, working with them and returning with them to court to attest to their reformation but he also set several precedents that are part of probation practice today.

Following the death of Augusts in 1859, his work was continued by other voluntary workers with almost same spirit as that of Augustus. Probation came to be regulated by statute for the first time in 1878, when Massachusetts passed a law providing for the appointment of a paid probation officer for the city of Boston. The scheme was subsequently adopted by other States in USA. Today, an overwhelming majority of criminal offenders in the US serve their sentence in the community and probation is widely used as a method of community based correction. Research studies in United States also proved beyond doubt that probation has been successful and it could achieve the objective of correction i.e. re-assimilation of offender into the main stream of social life.

Like John Augusts in America, England had Mathew Davenport hill, a lawyer by profession and social worker by choice, who practiced probation with the help of humanitarian judges. In England probation received statutory recognition in 1970 with the enactment of probation of offenders act, 1907. Under this law a probationer could be released either before the imposition of sentence or before the execution of sentence. Probation as a community based treatment of offenders is extensively used in different parts of the world. In most countries it is mandatory for juvenile offenders. Since 1948 probation has been included as a priority item in the subjects to be dealt with by the United Nations. In 1950, the international group of experts on the prevention of Crime and Treatment of offenders at its second in 1951 urged all government to give favourable consideration to the adoption and development of Probation as a major instrument of criminal policy.

In India, Probation received statutory recognition for the first time in 1898 through section 562 of the Criminal procedure committing trivial offences punishable with a sentence of not more than two years of imprisonment could be released on Probation. The scope of this section was extended with the amendment of the code in 1923. It was provided that first offenders committing offences on admonition. Suitable first offenders aged below 21 and women when not liable to be punished with death or transportation for life, and adult males above the age of 21 when not punishable with a term of imprisonment exceeding 7 years could be released on probation of good conduct. But no machinery had been provided to the courts for ascertaining the facts regarding the conduct and character of the offender and also to supervise the probationers.

In 1931, the government of India prepared draft Probation of Offenders Bill and circulated it to the then provincial governments for their views. However, the Bill could not be processed due to pre-occupations of the provincial governments. Later, the government of India in 1943, informed the local governments to enact suitable laws on the lines of the draft bill. The provinces enacted probation laws on the lines of the provisions contained in section 562 of the old code. These laws assumed great importance because they introduced for the first time provisions regarding pre-sentence enquiry, report of probation officer, super vision by paid and voluntary probation officer and compensation for injury caused to any person vicinal governments lacked infirmity and many states did not have a probation law at all. On the initiative of Dr. Reckless, an eminent criminologist and UN expert, a probation conference was held in Bombay in 1952. the conference discussed the possibility of enacting an All India probation act and prepared the draft bill for the same. The dream of the central legislation of probation was materialised in 1958. The central act called probation of offenders act, 1958 and it was enforced through out the country. Today, probation of offenders act, 1958 is a progressive legislation in the administration of criminal justice in India.

Probation of Offenders Act

In India, as a special law, the probation of offenders act, 1958 is a comprehensive piece of legislation governing the power of courts to release offenders after due admonition and probation, administration of probation and the role of probation officers including their powers and duties. The state governments also framed their respective Probation of Offenders rules to provide guidelines for the probation department for the effective implementation of the act. Though there are provisions under section 360 and 361 of Cr. P.C., their scope is limited and they are unable to achieve the objectives of community based corrections in a real sense and hence, is the areas where the provisions of the probation of offenders act are applicable, section 360 of the code of criminal procedures ceases to apply.

The provision contained under sections of the probation of offenders act empowers the court to release an offender after due admonition. It is significant to note that the release of an offender after due admonition is a discretionary measure depending upon the satisfaction of court and cannot be claimed as a matter of right. The discretion of the court, shall however, depend on the following considerations:

(I) That there is no previous conviction proved against the offender, and that

(II) The offender is found guilty of having committed any one of the following offences,

(*a*) Theft under section, 379, 380 and 381 IPC.

(*b*) Dishonest misappropriation under section 404 IPC

(*c*) Cheating under section 420 IPC

(*d*) Any offence punishable with imprisonment for not more than two years or with fine or with both under the Indian penal Code or any other law.

(III) The court is of the opinion that having regard to the circumstances of the case including the nature of the offence and the character of the offender, it is expedient to release him on probation.

The Probation of Offenders Act, 1958 in the words of Justice Subba Rao, Former chief justice of India, "is a milestone in the progress of the modern liberal trend of reform in the field of penology". It is the result of recognition of the doctrine that the object of criminal law is more to reform the individual offender that to punish him. Sections 4 and 6 of the Act are the vital provisions which empower courts to consider and release offenders on probation. Under section 4 of the Act a court is empowered to release an offender who is found guilty of having committed an offence not punishable with death or imprisonment for life. The necessary condition prescribed us that the court should form the view that "having regard to the circumstances of the case including nature of the offence and the character of the offender it is expedient to release him on probation". The offender is released with or without sureties, to appear and receive sentence when called upon during such period not exceeding three years. The court is also bound to take into consideration, the report, if any, of the probation officer concerned in the case. Court also has the discretion if it is of the opinion that "in the interests of the offender and of the public it is expedient" to pass a supervision order directing the offender to remain under the supervision of a probation officer.

Section 6 of the Probation of Offenders Act deals with offenders under the age of 21 years. This section prohibits a court from sentencing to imprisonment of offenders below 21 years of age, unless the offence is one punishable with life imprisonment or death; or when the court is satisfied that, "having regard to the circumstances of the case including nature of offence and the character of the offender", he should not be released on probation. This section also mandates that the court when imposes a sentence of imprisonment on such offender should record its reasons. The court is also for the above purpose empowered to call for a report from a probation officer and consider the report and take into consideration any other available information relating to the character and physical and mental condition of the offender. Age of the offender is a major consideration which has influenced the decision on the application of probation.

Policy Evolved by Courts

Administration of probation to an offender is a judicial function and is a part of the sentence process. While taking decision to grant probation the discretion exercised by the court is scientific and burden-some. In this context the Supreme Court has observed in Ved Pariahs Vs State of Haryana that "sentencing an accused person is sensitive exercise of discretion and not a routine or mechanical prescription acting on a hunch .. .. .. The social background and the personal factors of the crime order are very relevant although in practice criminal courts have rarely paid attention to the social milieu or the personal circumstances of the offender".

The discretion rested on the court has to be exercised on the basis of careful application and consideration of personal factors, family background, age and circumstances of each offender. For this purpose, the probation officer conduct an in-depth study of each case and submit a re-sentence investigation report to the court prior to decision making. The sentencing judge considers his personality, age, education family background. Socio-economic conditions of the offender, previous conviction, peer group relations, neighborhood conditions, probability of reformation in the community and various other factor which are relevant to consider him to release on probation. On an analysis of the decisions of the Supreme Court, the following variables emerged which to a large extent have influenced, the lower courts to take a decision in favour of releasing an offender on probation. They are viz; (i) Age of the offender (ii) Time frame of the proceedings (iii) Previous convictions and (iv) Type of the offender.

Age of the offender is a major consideration which has influenced the decision of the application of probation. Section 6 of the probation of offenders Act lays down an injunction on the courts not to impose a sentence on imprisonment on person who are below 21 years of the age, except for the offences punishable with imprisonment for a life or death. Section 6 has been constructed liberally by courts so that its operation may be effective and beneficial to young offenders who are prone to more easily to be led astray by influence of bad company. The attitude of the Supreme Court is reflected in the following observation Masarullah-Vs. State, state of Tamil Nadu.

> "Here is a young man. He is serving. He comes from lower middle class, but respectable family having an atmosphere of educational culture. In his formative impressionable years he comes under the undesirable influence of movies, eulogising crime and showing criminal as a daring person. This young man falls a prey and a victim. He emulates his move hero.Laten psycho-pathetic back ground lead him astray. Therefore, having regard to the nature of the offences, the character of the offender and the attendant and surrounding circumstances as recalled in the report of the probation officer and being influenced by the modern -trend of reclamation of the offender rather than condemnation this is a preeminently fit case to grant the benefit of modern enological approach as enacted in the Act"

Generally, courts are more inclined to grant probation to offenders who are aged either below 25 years or above 50 years.

A long period of litigation is a circumstance, which courts have taken into account before granting probation. In Ved Prakash-Vs-State of Haryana when the accused was a young person, his parents were alive and he had a wife and children to maintain, the supreme court took those factors into consideration and released him on probation on the ground that the long period of litigation and the little period of imprisonment already undergone by him had become sufficient deterrent. Similarly when a matter came to the court after 10 years and the accused had faced protracted criminal proceedings; the court even though found the accused guilty directed his release on probation

Even though section 4 or 6 of the Probation of Offenders Act does not impose any prohibition on releasing an offender who has previous conviction courts are normally reluctant to release an offender who has conviction. When the offender is a first offender the tendency is more to release him in probation when other circumstances do not warrant against such release.

Nature of the offence is one of the major factors, which influences the decision of court in releasing the offenders on probation. Probation is normally granted for the offences under Indian Penal Code, which are not of serious nature. In several cases courts have released offenders who have committed theft, misappropriation, or cheating, where the amount involved is small and the offender is willing to refund the amount courts have granted probation. In case of minor offences under the Excise Act or Probation Acts the tendency of the courts is to release the offender on probation. However, in cases where the offences are committed with premeditation, or when it is against weaker section of the society of where the offender as in one case is an "abominable culprit who had shown sufficient expertise in the art of abduction and seduction and sale of girls to others" the courts have refused to grant probation.

The American Law Institute evolved useful guidelines for probation policy, the following grounds, while not controlling the discretion of the court, shall be accorded weight in favour of withholding sentence of imprisonment :-

(*a*) The defendant's criminal conduct neither caused not threatened serious harm;

(*b*) The defendant did not contemplate that his criminal conduct would cause or threaten serious harm;

(*c*) The defendant acted under a strong provocation;

(*d*) There were substantial grounds tending to excuse or justify the defendant's criminal conduct, though failing to establish a defense;

(*e*) The victim of the defendant's criminal conduct induced or facilitated its commission;

(*f*) The defendant has compensated or will compensate the victim of his criminal conduct for the damage or injury sustained;

(*g*) The defendant has no history of prior delinquency of criminal activity or has led a law-abiding life for a substantial period of time before the commission of the present crime;

(*h*) The defendant's criminal conduct was the result of circumstances unlikely to recur;

(*i*) The character and attitude of the defendant indicate that he is unlikely to cmmit another crime

(*j*) The defendant is particularly likely to respond affirmatively to probation treatment;

(*k*) The imprisonment of the defendant will entail excessive hardship to himself or his dependants.

Judiciary and Probation

The judiciary plays a pivotal role in the implementation of a comprehensive probation programme. In fact, no correctional programme can be successful without the active correctional of the judiciary. The sentencing decisions taken by magistrates and judges occupy a central place in the penal process because of their direct and indirect influences upon the subsequent implementation of the penal measures imposed upon convicted offenders. Magistrates and judges possess wide discretionary powers in the choice of sentence.

Probation means the conditional suspension of imposition of sentenced by court in carefully selected cases. The judiciary has to realise that in a large number of cases, commission of an offence is the result of sociological, psychological and situational factors. No one is a born criminal but he is made by the society. It should also be kept in mind while dispensing justice that each sage has a past and every sinner has a future and probation is based on this fundamental philosophy. The enforcement of probation offender Act 1958 in all the major states of the country had raised the hope that probation would become an integral part of criminal justice administration and shall be treated as an import mode of dealing with certain types of offenders. An evaluation of probation system by Prof. Srivastava revealed that the courts. Particularly at the lower level, are generally less inclined to grant probation in many cases. Many of the judges and magistrates still think of probation as a leniency and are not mentally prepared to lean on the side of judicial liberalism. It has also been observed that some judges and magistrates avoid probation because it often necessitates calling for the report of probation officer, which means certain delay in disposing of the case. Justice Sadasivan's observation lends credence to this assertion, "it is seen from the Administrative Reports of some states that Magistrates are evincing a tendency to avoid recourse to statutory provisions of the probation of offenders Act, mainly because it leads to a long drawn delay". The common tendency amount such magistrates and judges is to short circuit the delay and resort to traditional methods of sentencing dispositions. These are some of the unpalatable facts which most judges and magistrates would not like to admit in public.

The low-key response of the judiciary towards the liberal use of Probation of Offenders Act is evident from the fact that the number of those getting probation is far less than those who are sent to prisons. The total number of convictions by different courts all over the country would reveal that at large number of such convicted cases could have been released on probation. Statistics from various states in India show that probation does not account for even ten per cent of convicted cases in majority of cases, whereas 63 per cent of the cases are released on probation in United States. The overcrowding in Indian prisons is primarily because of the fact that court makes lesser use of probation and sentence a majority for imprisonment. Justice S.M. Sikri, the then Chief Justice of India remarked, "the law seems adequate. But is it enough to pass a law and say that probation is a good thing? Not only should the serious student and probation officers be convinced of the advantages but the judiciary and the bar must also become its votaries. Sentencing functions best when the judge demonstrates an understanding of individualised treatment which means that the sentence must take into account the offenders needs".

Truly speaking, no conscious efforts have been made at any stage in India for the professional development of judiciary in the progressive correctional concepts and practices. Magistrates and judges are appointed by the government from among the members of the bar at district level. The academic courses leading to a law degree at the universities in India do not include probation and other non-institutional methods of offenders. As a result, most of the practicing lawyers are not aware of probation and the provisions of the probation of offenders Act. However, this lacuna can be removed by introducing in service training courses at the initial stage of recruitment of judicial personnel. This aspect has so long been lost sight of.

Role of Probation Officer

The key to effective probation system lies in the quality of the probation officer who implements the probation system. The qualities needed for effective work with criminal offenders are more human than academic. It is, of course, imperative to have a fundamental grounding in the behavioural sciences. In addition the probation officer must be aware of the resources in the community. But, more important than any of these is a deep genuine sensitivity to the needs of those in trouble and accompany commitment to be of service to humanity. The two primary functions of the probation officer are investigation and supervision.

The investigation is the preliminary assessment of a convicted individual to determine the appropriate treatment.

The pre sentence investigation report forms an integral part of the decision making process of court. The report focuses attention on socio-economic and personality aspects of the individual. The report analyses the circumstances and nature of the offences. In the opinion of Hoffmon, the necessary components of such a report are those facts, "well documented", which may help to answer two questions—will the offender's continued presence in the community constitute a danger? Are his mental and emotional equipment, habits, family situation, and physical condition are such that he can profit by probation? In fact, the probation officer's report to the court does not aim to proving either guilt or the innocence of the person. But, its is helping the judge to help the offender for the reformation. The objective of the pre sentence report is to facilitate a just disposition by presiding judge.

The second main phase of probation work, supervision, has a dual aspect. In the first place there is the authoritarian frame of reference within which the probationer must be controlled.

He is expected and required by the court to stay in the community unless permission is granted to go elsewhere; he is supposed to work regularly, report periodically to the probation officer, support his family, and stay away from ad associates, gambling resorts and places of questionable character. The judge, in ordering a sentence suspended, can also order any special condition to be followed, such as staying away from a certain place. The term of probation is set by law. It can be for the length of the sentence that was suspended or for a specific period. Good practice seems to disfavour carrying persons on probation for long periods of time, since super vision may become a deteriorating experience and a social handicap. It is much better for the law to leave it up to the probation officer to determine when a person has obtained the maximum benefit from his supervision and when he is ready for release from it.

It is the duty of the probation officer to use discretion in judging when the conduct of a probationer warrants citing him for court hearing for possible revocation of probation. How much leeway should be probationer, considering the protection of society and the rehabilitation of the offender, is a delicate question? If the case seems to be deteriorating beyond the power of the probation office and cooperating community agencies and resources to cope with the situation, the officer is obligated to cite.

When a probationer is a violator of probation conditions, it is up to the judge to either terminate probation or continue it. In the authoritarian role, officer is acting as a protector of society.

Secondly supervision affords the probation office an opportunity to develop a constructive relationship with the probationer and to work out with him a plan that will lead to more satisfactory and acceptable level of adjustment. In this capacity, the probation officer plays the role of friendly counselor and guide. He needs to encourage, interpret, and implant suggestions. In this role also the probation officer is a leader, executive, and a social therapist. He must know how active to be at any particular stage. Usually, in a case that is moving normally toward improved adjustment, the probation officer is much more active at the beginning of the period of supervision than at the end, when contacts can taper off. Cases handled under supervision can often be classified into those that need very little help and attention, and those that require active attention but do not respond. The latter is the troublesome case who makes at best a marginal adjustment of gravitates toward failure on probation.

The dual aspect of probation supervision can be integrated. The guidance phase dovetails with the authoritarian frame and can fit into this frame without the relationship of officer and probationer being impaired. However, at times of crisis authority can be brought to the fore and appropriate action taken for the safety of society. With proper initial interpretation and continual reinterpretation, the probation officer can play the dual role of authoritarian, protector and counselor or guide.

Parole

Parole is a release procedure. The offender, after having served a part of his sentence in a correctional institution, is released according to law from the prison or reformatory. It differs from Probation in that the later is a suspended sentence; the offender is not sent to a correctional institution but is allowed to remain under restricted liberty in the community during good behaviour. In the instance of parole, the offender has been committed to prison, has served part of his sentence, become eligible under law for release, is found by the parole board to release on parole, is released from prison and remains in the community under restricted liberty during good conduct. Hence, Parole is a correctional device through which am offender, after serving less than his total sentence, is conditionally released from a penal facility, under active supervision, with social reintegration as the final objective.

Conceptually, parole can notes conditional release granted to prisoner who has served a part of his sentence in a penal institution but in India, the term is being generally used for the award of temporary release of prisoners during the period of their imprisonment, synonymous with furlough, ticket of leave, emergency release etc., however, the objective behind the system of parole as internationally understood, is realised in this country through the review of sentences undertaken in accordance with the special enactments, rules or orders formulated by the State Governments. Such premature release which technically imply parole, are often known as prisoner's release on probation in certain states.

The Code of Criminal Procedure under section 432 provides that when any person has been sentenced to punishment for an offence, the appropriate Government may, at any time without conditions or upon any conditions which the person concerned accepts, suspend the execution of his sentence or remit the whole or any part of the punishment to which he has been sentenced. The provision further contains that the appropriate Government may by general rules or special orders, give directions as to the suspension of sentences and the conditions on which petitions should be presented and dealt with while the states of Haryana, Madhya Pradesh, Punjab and Uttar Pradesh are exercising these powers within the framework of special Acts enacted for the purpose, other states have formulated special rules or orders to regulate premature release of prisoners. It has, however, been observed that the conditions and procedures governing the review of sentences. and the premature release of prisoner lack uniformity and standardisation of approach.

Release of prisoner prematurely either on specified conditions or unconditionally is prevalent in almost all countries and such premature release is generally termed 'parole'. Premature release is an accepted mode of incentive to a prisoner as it saves him from the extra period of incarceration which, on the one hand is not require for his reformation and on the other may be counter productive. It reinstitutes and offenders in the society prior to the expiry, of his sentence in recognition of his good conduct and responsiveness to correctional treatment. This system of premature release drives the blind, mechanical aspects out of the 'execution of fixed sentences and renders help to the offender for smooth integration into the community. It has been strongly recommended by All India Committee on Jail Reforms (1983) that the system of premature release should be used for more numbers of eligible offenders and it should be organised and administered in par with the parole system in other countries.

Gudelines on Premature Release of the Prisoners

1. The relevant provisions in regard to the suspension and remission of sentence is contained in section 432 of the criminal procedure which reads as follows:

"Power to suspend or remit sentences:

(I) When any person has been sentenced to punishment for an offence, the appropriate government may, at any time, without conditions or upon any condition which the person sentenced accepts, suspend the execution of his sentence or remit the whole or any part of the punishment to which he has been sentenced.

(II) Whenever an application is made to the appropriate government for the suspension or remission of a sentence the appropriate government may require the presiding judge of the court before or by which the conviction was had or confirmed, to state his opinion as to whether the application should be granted or refused, together with his reasons for such of the trial or of such record thereof as exists.

(III) If any condition on which a sentence has been suspended or remitted is, in the opinion of the appropriate government, not fulfilled, the appropriate government may cancel the suspension or remission, and thereupon the person in whose favour the sentence has been suspended or remitted may, if at large, be arrested by any police officer, without warrant and remanded to undergo the unexpired portion of the sentence.

(IV) The condition on which a sentence is suspended or remitted under this section may be one to be fulfilled by the person in whose favour the sentence is suspended or remitted, or one independent of his will.

(V) The appropriate government may, be general rules or special orders, give direction as to the suspension of sentences and the conditions on which petitions should be presented and dealt with: Provide that in the case of any sentence (other than a sentence of fine) passed on a male person above the age of eighteen years, no such petition by any other person on his behalf shall be entertained, unless the person sentenced is in jail, and

(*a*) where such petition is made by the person sentenced, it is presented through the officer in charge of the jail; or

(*b*) where such petition is made by any other person, it contains a declaration that the person sentenced is in jail.

(VI) The provisions of the above sub-sections shall also apply to any order passed by a criminal court under any section of this code or of any other law which restricts the liberty of any person or imposed any liability upon him or his property,

(VII) In this section and in section 433, the expression 'appropriate government' means:

(*a*) in cases where the sentence is for an offence against, or the order referred to in sub-section(6) is passed under, any law relating to a matter to which the executive power of the union extends, the central government;

(*b*) in other cases, the government of the state within which the offender is sentenced or the said order is passed."

1.1 The above power of remission of sentences under section 432 is circumscribed by the provision of 433A which reads as under:

"Restriction on powers of remission or commutation in certain cases-notwithstanding anything contained in section 432, where a sentence of imprisonment for life is imposed on conviction or person for an offence for which death is one of the punishments provided by laws, or when sentence of death imposed on a person has been commuted under section 433 into one of imprisonment for life, such person shall not be released from prison unless he had served at least fourteen years of imprisonment."

2. Composition of the State Sentence Review Boards

Each shall constitute a Review Board for the review of sentence awarded to a prisoner for recommending his premature release in appropriate cases. The review board shall be permanent body having the following constitutions:

Minister in-charge jail department,

Principal Secretary—Home,

Principal Secretary in-charge of jail affairs law and order—Chairman

Judicial Secretary—Member

A district and session judge nominated by the high court—Member

Chief Probation Officer—Member

A senior police officer nominated by the DG of Police not below the rank of IG of Police—Member

Inspector General of Prisons—Member

The recommendations of the sentence review board shall not be invalid merely by reason of vacancy in the board or the inability of any member to attend the board meeting. The meeting the board shall not however, be held, if the quorum is less than 4 members including the chairman.

Periodicity of the Board's Meetings

The state sentence review board shall meet at least once in a quarter at the state head quarters date to be notified to members at least ten days in advance with complete agenda papers.

However, it shall be open to the chairman of the board to convene a meeting of the board may frequently as may be deemed necessary.

Eligibility for Premature Release

The following category of inmates shall be eligible to be considered for premature release by state sentence review boards.

Every convicted prisoner whether male or female undergoing sentence of life imprisonment a covered by the provisions of section 433 A Cr. P.C., shall be eligible to be considered for premature release from the prison immediately after serving out the sentence of 14 years of actual imprisonment i.e. without the remissions.

Conclusion

Research on community based corrections proved beyond doubt that they are very useful and effective in the refomation of offenders. Despite the fact that there is a Probation of Offenders Act it is very rarely applied by the members of the judiciary. As a result a good number of offenders who can be reformed through probation are unable to get the benefits of probation. Similarly premature release can be widely used for the suitable prisoners who maintained good conduct and character althrough in their prison life. The National Human Rights Commission also strongly support the use of premature release by the prison authorities for eligible prisoners.

References

- Louis P. Carney (1977), "Probation and Parole, Legal and Social Dimensions", McGraw Hill Book Co.
- Bhattacharya, K. (1986), "Probation System in India", Icianas Publications.
- Probation and Related Measures, Department of Social Affairs, United Nations, New York, 1951.
- European Seminar on Probation, Department of Social Affairs, United Nations, London, 1952.
- Practical Results and Financial Aspects of Adult Probation in Selected Contries, United Nations, New York 1954.
- AIR 1981 SC 643, 447.
- Statya Bahama Vs State of Bihar AIR 1972, SC 1554;
- Jugal Kishore Vs State of Bihar AM 1972, SC 2522,
- Moharnd Aziz Vs State of Maharashtra AIR 1972, SC 730.
- Daulat Ram Vs State of Haryana AIR 1972; SC 2434
- AIR 1983 SC 654
- AIR 1981 SC 643
- Ghanshyarn Das Vs M.C.D. AIR 1975, SC 845.
- See Khali suprce note 18 at P. 156-62, where in a number case where first offenders have been released om probation.
- Sint. Devaki Vs Tek Chand Bhatia, AIR 1979, SC 1048.
- Report of the All India Committee on jail Reforms 1980-83, Vol. 1, Ministry of Home Affairs, Government of India, pp. 243-246.
- Probation of Offenders Act.

2

AWARENESS OF THE LAWS AND REPORTING BEHAVIOUR AMONG THE VICTIMS OF EVE-TEASING—AN EMPIRICAL STUDY

Sowmya, K.

INTRODUCTION

Eve teasing is a prominent and prevalent form of harassment which women are subjected to every day. The incidents of eve-teasing have only been increasing with time. There is a huge gap between actual occurrence of eve-teasing events and the number of offences reported. We have acknowledged the troubles and problems and difficulties of women. Evidently, whatever measures that were taken are not effective. This study plans to contribute to the understanding of the present state of things regarding eve-teasing and suggest ways to reduce such incidents and also to suggest ways to improve awareness among women on laws regarding eve-teasing.

Sarika Shah Vs. The State of Tamil Nadu

It is a case where an eighteen year old young college girl viz., Sarika Shah, who was studying B.B.M II year having aspirations in her life, was teased in the public place by a group of persons, who came in a speeding auto, in the busy area of kamaraj salai in the broad day light on 18.7.1998, by pouring water on her from water packets sitting inside the auto, when Sarika Shah and her friends were proceeding to a juice shop and that, one of the accused persons also pounced over her from the speeding auto, as a result of which, she fell down and sustained head injuries and died after five days. Her untimely death was made more poignant because it happened to be on July 23, her birthday. The above act of the accused persons shows their indecent behaviour in public place towards innocent young girls and also their teasing against Sarika Shah which resulted in her unnatural death.

After this shocking incident, in fact, the government of Tamil Nadu noticed that eve-teasing in public places is a perennial problem and decided to eradicate the menace of eve-teasing as a whole and accordingly, promulgated and enacted the Tamil Nadu Prohibition of Eve-teasing Act, 1998 and it came into force on the 30th day of July, 1998.

However, even after this also, many cases were reported wherein, the victims even committed suicide due to pressures caused by Eve-Teasing and many other cases go unreported due to a number of reasons.

The Law

In legal terms, crimes against women can be studied under two headings, namely:

1. The Indian Penal Code (IPC)
2. Special and Local laws

Some of the important provisions that deal with crime against women are as follows:

Provisions in the Indian Penal Code. 1860

(*i*) Rape (Sec 376 IPC)

(*ii*) Kidnapping and Abduction for different purposes (Sec 363-373 IPC)

(*iii*) Homicide for dowry, Dowry deaths or their attempts (Sec 302/304B IPC)

(*iv*) Torture, both physical and mental (Sec 498A IPC)

(*v*) Molestation (Sec 354 IPC)

(*vi*) Sexual harassment (Sec 509 IPC)*

(*vii*) Importation of girls (up to 21 years of age) (Sec 366B IPC)

(*Referred in the past as "eve-teasing")

Provisions under Special Laws and Local Law:

(*i*) Immoral Traffic (Prevention) Act, 1986

(*ii*) Dowry Prohibition Act, 1961

(*iii*) Child Marriage Restraint (Amendment) Act, 1986

(*iv*) Indecent Representation of women (Prohibition) Act, 1986

(*v*) Commission of sati (Prevention) Act, 1987

(*vi*) Prohibition of Harassment of woman Act, 1998

Since the focus of this study is on eve-teasing it is imperative to look at three particular provisions;

1. Molestation
2. Sexual harassment
3. Prohibition of harassment of women

Out of these three provisions, the Tamil Nadu Prohibition of Harassment of women Act, 1998 deals exclusively with eve teasing.

The Tamil Nadu Prohibition of Harassment of Women Act, 1998:

Previously, the Act was called Tamil Nadu Prohibition of Eve-Teasing Act. In order to cover other types of harassment as well, the Act was amended in 2002. In this Act, unless the context otherwise requires,-

"Harassment" means any indecent conduct or act by a man which cause or is likely to cause intimidation, fear, shame or embarrassment, including abusing or causing hurt or nuisance or assault or use offeree.

Section 3 of this Act states that Harassment of women at anyplace is prohibited.

Section 4 states the penalty for harassment of women-

Whoever commits or participates in or abets harassment of women in within the precincts of any educational institution, temple or other place of worship, bus stop, road, railway station, cinema theatre, park, beach, place of festival, public service vehicle or vessel or any other place shall be punished with imprisonment for a term which may extend to three years and with fine which shall not be less than ten thousand rupees.

Statement of the problem

The present study aims at assessing the incidence and extent of harassment faced by college girls. There is a growing problem of harassment of women that is being muffled. Harassment of women does not get reported as often as it occurs. This situation creates a trend where women are constantly harassed because the perpetrators are not apprehended. Due to the less number of complaint harassment of women, the problem seems to be on the increase everyday. Therefore, there is a need to address the problem of harassment of women, awareness of the laws and reasons for their reporting behaviour.

Need and significance of the study:

The incidents of eve-teasing have only been increasing with time. There is a huge gap between actual occurrence of eve-teasing events and the number of offences reported. We have acknowledged the troubles and problems and difficulties of women. Evidently, whatever measures that were taken are not effective. This study plans to contribute to the understanding of the present state of things regarding eve-teasing and suggest ways to reduce such incidents and also to suggest ways to improve awareness among women on laws regarding eve-teasing.

We have all these laws and provisions to protect a woman from being harassed, and still, many don't report their victimisation. Is this sort of behaviour due to:

1. Lack of awareness of the laws relating to eve-teasing?

Or

2. Fear of secondary victimisation by the police and society?

In the judiciary system, "ignorance of law is not an excuse". When this concept is upheld by our judiciary, it is only logical to pose the question whether government is taking any measures to make the people aware of the laws. In the present day, the rate of awareness of one's own rights is questionable. Is it the government's duty to create awareness of laws among citizens? Now if there was awareness among the people, would the situation be any different?

With all these questions, this study's Objectives are as follows:

1. To find out the nature and extent of eve teasing faced by the victims.
2. To examine the reporting behaviour of the victims of eve-teasing.

3. To study the level of awareness among the victims of eve-teasing towards the legal provisions available to protect women.
4. To study the perception of the victims towards efficacy of the laws pertaining to eve-teasing.
5. To obtain suggestions from the victims to contain eve-teasing menace. To suggest suitable measures to control eve-teasing

Variable Studied

The following variables were studied as a part of this study,

1. Independent variables-age, educational qualification, marital status and nativity of the respondents
2. Dependent variables-nature and extent of victimisation, awareness of the laws pertaining to eve-teasing, the reporting behaviour of the respondents, suggestions.

Research Tool—Questionnaire

The Universe

The Universe of this present study is the under graduate final year college students of the Arts and Science colleges in the City of Chennai.

Sampling Method—Simple Random Sampling Method.

Sample Size

The sample size of this study is 150 college students. Fifty students from each institution mentioned above were chosen. Among the 150 samples 138 were victims of eve-teasing. The study focused only on the victims.

Main Study

After the pilot study, the main study was conducted. One hundred and fifty respondents excluding the respondents of the pilot study were asked to fill up the questionnaire.

Majo Findings of the Research

- 50 per cent of the victims very often and often face verbal forms of eve-teasing, 16 per cent of the victims very often and often face visual forms and the majority 57 per cent of the victims very often and often face Sexual forms of eve-teasing.

- 28 per cent of the victims were afraid of the eve-teasers at the time of victimisation and 31 per cent of the victims got irritated.
- Among the total victims, only 3 per cent of the victims had reported the offence to the police, the rest 97 per cent did not report the offence.
- 3 per cent of the reported cases said that the police didn't file FIR. Here the eve teaser, was caught and was let off with a mild warning and was beaten up by the police.
- 25 per cent of the victims did not report their victimisation to police due to lack of awareness, 17 per cent said fear of police and 12 per cent feels that nothing can be done. 2 per cent ignored the incident and 4 per cent said fear of parents restrained them from reporting such incidents if any. 7 per cent of the respondents took it lightly, while 9 per cent said they did not report because of social stigma attached to it. 20 per cent respondents said that they did not report the incident of victimisation due to fear of retaliation.
- Only 8 per cent of the victims from the arts group are well aware of the Tamil Nadu Prohibition of Harassment of Women Act 1998, and their awareness is obtained through the course of study. When it comes to the extent of awareness of the IPC sections relating to eve-teasing or harassment of women only 13 per cent of the victims were aware of it while 87 per cent were not aware of it.
- 59 per cent of the victims said media is their source of awareness.
- 76 per cent of the victims perceived that the laws are not effective in containing eve-teasing menace.
- 71 per cent of the victims said that they think the punishments prescribed for eve-teasing are not sufficient enough.
- 72 per cent of the respondents think that the present laws cannot prevent eve-teasing.
- 67 per cent of the respondents think that effective implementation of the existing laws can reduce eve-teasing.

- 81 per cent of the respondents think that a woman being aware of the laws would make them less vulnerable to harassment.
- 96 per cent of the respondents think that it is the duty of the Government to create awareness among women pertaining to eve-teasing.
- 91 per cent of the respondents think that the government is not effective in creating awareness regarding the laws pertaining to eve-teasing.
- 92 per cent of the respondents suggested creating awareness as the measure to control eve-teasing menace

Recommendations

In these scenarios, what are the steps needed to be taken by the government to stop or at least minimise eve-teasing?

The High Court has made the following recommendations:

- Introducing a special subject for girls and women in schools and colleges, relating to the laws of the land under which they can seek appropriate remedies from the legal forums and legal rights to which they are entitled to, such as, how to react and defend themselves in the event of any untoward incidents, viz., eve-teasing, molestation, Sexual harassment etc.
- Making them mandatory for all the schools and colleges by the experts in the field for motivating them and educating them of their rights enunciating under law so as to boost their self-confidence, self-vigilance, physical and emotional strength to react and defend themselves whenever such occasions warrants.
- Issue necessary instructions to the police authorities that whenever a girl or women approaches with such complaints, the police shall act swiftly, on the complaints of the victims without putting them in an embarrassing situation in the society and act in a friendly manner.
- The above recommendations should be implemented very effectively, as early as possible and should be in practice rather on paper.
- Along with these recommendations, I include:

- Self defence training should be given to all the girls and women in schools and colleges. "I know that they get scared if you are bold, if you get scared they will continue."
- Introducing a special subject relating to the laws not only to women but also to men so that they'll be aware of the punishment for certain act.
- "People have lost their moral values." Introducing Moral education for boys in schools to respect the modesty of women and proper guidance from the parents and teaching moral values can prevent the ethical degradation among youth.
- The public too have to be educated to rush to the aid of a girl who undergoes this and a more concrete step would be that of publishing photos of eve teasers in newspapers along with details of their unclean act.
- Since media plays such a huge role in creating awareness amongst the public, it should be made use of for creating awareness and portraying women with gumption than the usual portrayal of women as a weaker sex.
- The laws that are passed should be made effective and should be implemented more strongly.
- There is no deterrence in the offender regarding punishments for violating the morality of a woman; hence there is a need of increase in the quantum of punishment. Punishing the eve teasers in such a manner, so that none of the future eve teaser even thinks of doing so!
- There is a need to change the image and attitude of police when it conies to cases relating to eve-teasing. Every person caught eve teasing should be dealt with in all sternness and there should not be any lenience for first time offenders.
- Victims of eve-teasing should be encouraged to report the offence; victim assistance hence is very much required.

Conclusion

An out of box approach is necessary to deal with the worsening problem of eve-teasing, costing the young lives. Starting from Sarika Shah to Divya, the death of girls has been increasing day by day. So there is a need to stop these evils and protect women. Violence is directed specifically against a woman because she is a woman or affects women disproportionately and is being reduced to a state of weaker sex. The time is ripe now to give them confidence and awareness, equipping them with a sense of self-defence and security, when we are witnessing such ghastly incidents in and around, day in and day out, whereby girls and women are the most victimised, so as to face difficult and challenging situations courageously.

There is a colossal emptiness amongst the youth today when it comes to awareness of the laws or one's own rights. Mere knowledge of the existence of a law is not useful to any one at any time. They should be aware of it completely and be equipped to make use of it whenever necessary. Awareness of the laws should be given prime importance and all efforts should be taken to make it possible.

References

Ashraf, Nehal (1997)—Crime against women New Delhi: Commonwealth Publishers.

Banvasi, Prakruthi, N- Eve-Teasing Evils http://www.banwasi.com/images/etnew.jpg&imgrefurl=http://www.banwasi. com/html/etel.html (retrieved on 12.08.09)

Chowdhury, Kavitha (7 September 2007) - Fighting Eve-teasing Rights and Remedy - The Hindu.

Mohan, Vidhu and Priyadharshini, Shabham (16 August 1986) - Eve-teasing as experienced by girls—The Hindu.

Ratnavelu, A (2008)—Power of Legal Awareness 2008 Salem: Vysya College.

Sambandham, S (2007) — A Handbook of the Tamil Nadu Prohibition of Harassment of Women Act 1998.

Santoshsingh, Simer (30 Jan 2009)—"Women status in India" http://www.managementparadise.com/forums/archive/index.php-7083Q.html (retrieved on 07.08.09)

Sudhakar, S., (2003) - An Opinion Study of the Offence of Eve-Teasing Among College Students.

The Indian Penal Code http://www.indialawinfo.com/barects/ipc.html (retrieved on 02.08.09)

The Tragic Death of Divya- (11 October 2009) Maalai Malar.

Venkateshan, Radha (29 September 2007) — Make Eve-teasing cognizable Offence: law panel The Hindu.

Victims Definition http://www.osce.org/item/19292.html (retrieved on 08.08.09).

3

CYBER FORENSICS IN INDIA

S. Latha

Forensic technologies are designed to prepare and extract digital evidences. The origin of computer forensics can be traced back to a collection of intelligent tools. The primary focus of which was to address the problem of espionage. Cyber forensics can be defined as "the process of extracting information and data from computer storage media and guaranteeing its accuracy and reliability". The challenge for the forensic experts of course is actually finding this data, collecting it, preserving it, and presenting it in a manner acceptable in a court of law. Electronic evidence is fragile and can easily be modified. Also there is a challenge of destroying evidence from storage media using a variety of freeware, shareware and commercially available utility programs by the cyber criminals. When the corporate assets come under attack, or are misused, info-security professionals must be able to gather electronic evidence of such misuse and utilise that evidence to bring to justice those who misuse the technology. Cyber forensics still in India is in infant stage. With technology evolving, mutating, and changing at such a rapid pace, the rules governing the application of cyber forensics to the fields of auditing, security, and law enforcement are changing as well. Almost everyday, new techniques and procedures, are designed to provide infosecurity professionals a better means of finding electronic evidence, collecting it, preserving it, and presenting it to client management for potential use in the prosecution of cyber criminals. The anonymity provide by the Internet, and the ability for society's criminal element, to use information technology as a tool for social and financial discourse, mandates that those professionals charged with the responsibility of protecting critical infrastructure resources, have the tools to do so. The present article reviews the need for cyber forensic experts in India and the availability of educational programmes on cyber forensics in India.

The information technology can be used for destructive as well as constructive work. The fate of many ventures depends upon the intentions of the person using it. For instance, a malicious intention forwarded in the form of hacking, data theft, virus attack, etc can bring only destructive results unless and until these methods have been used for checking the authenticity, safety and security of the technological device which has been primarily relied upon and trusted for providing the security to a particular organisation. For instance, the creator of the "Sasser worm" has been hired as a "security software programmer" by a German firm, so that he can make firewalls, which will stop suspected files from entering computer systems. These methods may also be used for checking the authenticity, safety and security of one's technological device, which has been primarily relied upon and trusted for providing the security to a particular organisation. In fact, a society without protection in the form of "self help" cannot be visualised in the present electronic era. Hence there is a dire need of securing the info as an individual or institution.

Cyber Forensics

The concepts of cyber security and cyber forensics are not only interrelated but also indispensably required for the success of each other. The former secures the ICT and e-governance base whereas the latter indicates the loopholes and limitations of the adopted measures to secure the base.

The latter also becomes essential to punish the deviants so that a deterrent example can be set. There is, however, a problem regarding acquiring expertise in the latter aspect. This is so because though a computer can be secured even by a person with simple technical knowledge the ascertainment and preservation of the evidence is a tough task. For instance, one can install an anti-virus software, firewall, adjust security settings of the browser, etc but the same cannot be said about making a mirror copy of hard disk, extracting deleted files and documents, preserving logs of activities over internet, etc. Further one can understand the difficulty involved in the prosecution and presentation of a case before a court of law because it is very difficult to explain the evidence acquired to a not so techno savvy judge. The problem becomes more complicated in the absence of sufficient numbers of trained lawyers in this crucial field.

The Cyber Forensics has given new dimensions to the Cyber Criminology, Criminal laws, especially the Evidence law. Electronic evidence and their collection and presentation have posed a challenge to the investigation agencies, prosecution agencies and judiciary. The scope of Cyber Forensics is no more confined to the investigation regime only but is expanding to other segments of justice administration system as well. The justice delivery system cannot afford to take the IT revolution lightly. The significance of cyber forensics emanates from this interface of justice delivery system with the Information Technology.

Routine Activities theory was developed by Lawrence Cohen and Marcus Felson (Cohen and Felson, 1979). They state crime is normal, and just requires opportunity. For example, they attribute a rise in petty theft to the simple fact that there is now more available to steal. They say crime occurs when three things converge: the offender must be motivated, there must be a suitable target and there must be the absence of a capable guardian. A capable guardian either protects the target, or is the guardian of the offender (for example, a parent or teacher). The absence of a guardian is usually the turning point for the offender as those who are motivated to commit crime will always find suitable targets. For insider crime, the guardian is unlikely to be the electronic protection mechanisms shielding the target, such as passwords and access rights, since insiders often *already* have the necessary access rights. The guardian in this case is likely to be their manager. According to the theory, if there is an absence of that manager, then there is freedom to undertake the insider crime. The absence of the employee's manager can refer to physical absence and the employee being left alone to work, or that the manager does not understand what the employee does and so is incapable of monitoring their actions. Further it can also be inferred that in order to prevent cyber crime and guard there is a need to understand the cyber criminal's behaviour for which cyber forensics poses great importance.

The need of Cyber Forensics

The need of cyber forensics can be explained with the following criteria's:

(*a*) The traditional methods are inadequate: The law may be categorised as substantive and procedural. The substantive law fixes the liability whereas the procedural law provides the means and methods by which the substantive liability has to contended, analysed and proved. The procedural aspects providing for the guilt establishment provisions were always there but their interface with the IT has almost created a deadlock in investigative and adjudicative mechanisms. The challenges posed by IT are peculiar to contemporary society and so must be their solution. The traditional procedural mechanisms, including forensic science methods, are neither applicable nor appropriate for this situation. Thus, "cyber forensics" is the need of the hour. India is the 12th country in the world that has its own "Cyber law" (IT Act, 2000). However, most of the people of India, police, including lawyers, judges, are not aware about its existence and use. The traditional forensic methods like finger impressions, DNA testing, blood and other tests, etc play a limited role in this arena.

(*b*) The changing face of crimes and criminals: The use of Internet has changed the entire platform of crime, criminal and their prosecution. This process involves crimes like hacking, pornography, privacy violations, spamming, phishing, pharming, identity theft, cyber terrorisms, etc. The modus operendi is different that makes it very difficult to trace the culprits. This is because of the anonymous nature of Internet. Besides, certain sites are available that provides sufficient technological measures to maintain secrecy.

(*c*) Cyber crimes are different from traditional crimes.

Cyber Crime Terminology	*Conventional Crime Terminology*
Pornography	Child Abuse Pedophiles
Intellectual Property Crimes	Plagiarism
Impairing the Security of a Computer	House Breaking/ Burglary
Credit Card Frauds	Frauds in Banks
Crime Against Individual Identity	Impersonation

Though the types of crime get different nomenclature, detecting the same becomes different due to the technology involvement.

Requisites for a Cyber Forensic Professional

A Cyber Forensics professional is required to gather electronic evidence of misuse of computer networks and provide evidence in a court of law to bring the culprits to justice. A Cyber Forensics pro is sought by both public as well as private sector. In the public sector, people are mostly absorbed in law enforcement agencies like cyber crime cells, state forensics departments and central agencies like the CBI. In the private sector, it's the information that is of paramount importance for the enterprises, and so they require professionals to safeguard their data from being stolen and misused and also preserve them from hackers. Additionally, there are specialist companies that work on ethical hacking, Cyber Forensics and IT security. A budding Cyber Forensics expert can start his career as a cyber analyst or engineer for an enterprise after gaining experience and domain knowledge can proceed to niche areas in Cyber Forensics. Also, professionals can divert to freelancing and become independent security consultants.

Keeping the increasing data thefts and information breach in enterprises in mind, there is an increasing realisation worldwide for establishing internal controls and policy compliance as part of corporate governance for organisations.

There is already a lot of regulation internationally, such as the Sarbanes Oxley Act, Basel II, Patriot Act and Data Protection Act. All these require organisations to take responsibility to manage their operational risks, ensure data protection, prevent corporate fraud, and enable their storage and archive systems for e-discovery requirements, for litigation purposes. Demand for Cyber Forensics pros is already high in developed countries like the US and Europe and there is also a large demand-supply mismatch in the availability of experienced professionals.

The Indian market is also rapidly evolving in the same manner requiring information security norms and governance policies be followed by corporates in accordance with the Indian IT Act. And the demand/ supply ratio for Cyber Forensics professionals is 10:1 in India, thus, creating vast opportunities for professionals to enter this domain.

Skills Required

The field requires professionals who have specialised in gathering evidence over IT networks. This requires in-depth understanding of networking technologies, operating systems, storage and memory devices, and how various applications interact. with hardware and operating systems. Specialised forensic skills can be only built upon the above pre-requisites. The other requirement is expertise in cyber threat investigation, evidence management, legal knowledge, encryption and cryptography, and search technologies. Specialised training and experience is required to acquire these skills. The field welcomes professionals from the networking domain and those who specialise in security can also venture in this field to give their careers a new dimension. Since technologies for cyber security are fast evolving, hackers are also getting smarter and continuously developing new techniques to disrupt computer networks. A Cyber Forensics expert should have the capability to think like hackers and look for vulnerabilities in an enterprise's security.

Thus, a cyber forensic person should also have the knowledge about hacking, viruses, tracking user activity, password breaking, and experience on tools used for forensic imaging, data recovery and analysis, etc. Results or opinions obtained from cyber forensics tools like Encase and Forensic Tool Kit (FTK) are acceptable in court of law, and a cyber forensic expert never works on original media of evidence. He creates Image file of that and then follows up on the investigation on duplicate media using FTK tools.

The other facet of Cyber Forensics is the criminal litigation process, which requires the knowledge of the cyber laws and security compliance. An expert in these areas can advise companies on how to proceed with a cyber crime investigation. Also, since most Indian companies do business in the US and European countries, it's mandatory for them to comply with laws of respective countries while doing business there. Hence, the knowledge of such laws can be an advantage for a Cyber Forensics expert.

Key standard institutions offering Master's, Diploma and Certificate Programmes on Cyber Forensics

- Department of Criminology/Centre For Excellence in Cyber Forensics, University of Madras, Chennai 600 005.
- Centre of Excellence in Digital Forensics (CoEDF), Chennai. fwww.coedf.org)
- Symbiosis Society's Law College, Pune, and NALSAR University (www.nalsarpro. org)
- Indian' Institute of Information and Technology, Allahabad (www.iiita.ac.in)
- Amity Law School, Delhi, (www.amity.org)
- Department of Law, University of Delhi (www.du. ac.in)
- National Academy of Legal Studies and Research University of Law, Hyderabad-560027. (www.reachout hyderabad.com)
- Asian School of Cyber Laws, Pune (www.asianlaws. org)
- National Law School of India, University Bangalore - 72. (www.nls.ac.in)

Institute	*Certification*
University of Madras	Master's in Cyber Forensics and PG Diploma in Cyber Crime and Information Security
Centre of Excellence in Digital Forensics (CoEDF)	Master's programme in Information Security, Cyber Forensics, Diploma and Certificate programmes in cyber and digital forensics, training programmes
C-DAC, Pune	PG Diploma in Information System and Cyber Security
Encase (Guidance Software)	Encase Certified Examiner (EnCE)
Global Information Assurance Certification	Certified Forensics Analyst (GFCA)
International Society of Forensic Computer Examiners	Certified Computer Examiner
International Council of e-Commerce Consultants	Certified Ethical Hacker

Certifications

Currently, the demand curve for cyber forensics professionals is very sharp in our country while the number of experts in the field is still meager. The importance and scope of the field is visible from the fact that universities have started courses on cyber forensics, and training institutes are being set up to provide training to individuals and corporates to fight the cyber crime.

A certified Cyber Forensics expert can play a dual role, firstly as a Cyber Forensics expert in Cyber Crime Investigation (CCI) and secondly, as a Data Recovery (DR) expert in corporate sectors. It can be said that Cyber Forensics is a part of CCI. The certifications give a professional a grounding in computer ethics, evidence gathering, corporate and cyber laws, besides enhancing his IT knowledge.

Conclusion

The professionals choosing cyber forensics as a career will be highly sought after by the enterprises, government agencies for law enforcement and criminal justice, and also by the armed forces. But still there is a need for the professionals to understand information security and cyber forensics as the demand grows.

References

A Practice Guide to Computer Forensics, First Edition (Paperback) by David Benton (Author), Frank Grindstaff (Author)

Casey, Eoghan; Stellatos, Gerasimos J. (2008). "The impact of full disk encryption on digital forensics". *Operating Systems Review* 42 (3): 93-98. doi:10.1145/1368506.1368519.

Incident Response and Computer Forensics, Second Edition (Paperback) by Chris Prosise (Author), Kevin Mandia (Author), Matt Pepe (Author) "Truth is stranger than fiction..."

Praveen Dalai, "Securing cyberspace by private defence", http://cvberforensicsinindia.bloaspot.com/2006/01/securing-cyberspace-bv-private-defence.html

Praveen Dalai, "ICT strategy in India: The need of rejuvenation"

Ross, S. and Gow, A. (1999). *Digital archaeology? Rescuing Neglected or Damaged Data Resources.* Bristol and London: British Library and Joint Information Systems Committee. ISBN 1-900508-51-6.

George M. Mohay (2003).

4

"THE TRANSFORMATION OF KANJAR WOMEN: FROM TRADITIONAL ENTERTAINERS TO DANCE BAR GIRLS"

Surbhi Dayal

Introduction

This paper focuses on practice of prostitution among the *Kanjar* community in the rural areas of Alwar district in Rajasthan. It discusses the practice of prostitution among *Kanjar* women, who were traditional entertainers in the ancient period during their nomadic or semi nomadic period in the history. In particular, it sheds light on practice of prostitution by unmarried women by tradition. It makes an attempt to trace the historical linkages like their pre colonial (as entertainers), colonial (as criminal tribe) and post independence (settlements and denotified tribe) status in India. Paper tries to find out linkage between the changing technology and impact of media on the practise of prostitution, how awareness about the laws, exposure to media and changing technology changed the practice of prostitution. How all these had affected peoples perception regarding their health issues etc.

The present paper explores the changing practice of prostitution[1] among the nomadic and "ex-criminal tribe" of Rajasthan, known as *Kanjar*. The label 'ex-criminal tribes' has been used for certain nomadic and denotified tribes[2] who were earlier notified officially as the criminal tribes under the Criminal Tribes Act-1871, during the British rule, on the basis of their indulgence in criminal activities including theft, and loot (Simhadri, 1991). Prostitution was also prevalent among them. In 1947, India achieved independence and around 200 tribes or castes, which were notified as criminal tribes in British rule became free from the stigma creating qualifier "criminal" and got the status equal to other citizens of India. Therefore, they came to be known as ex-criminal tribe, denotified tribe or *Vimukata Jati* (Human Rights Feature, 2004). Time to time government, reformists tried to make a change in the situation and status of these tribes but it has not changed much yet and the stigma of being criminal once still goes with them everywhere.

Kanjar community was traditionally involved in the entertainment of kings and riches. Several historians have described the *Kanjar?*, as nomads, criminals and the ones practising prostitution. Shyamal Das (1989) considered *Kanjars, Sansis* and *Kalbelias* as forest dwellers. Tod (1929) identified the *Kanjars* as a caste engaged in the activities of dance, theft etc. Vyas (1986) observed that the *Kanjars* used to sing hereditary songs like *Meenas* and *Charans* in earlier times but later they resorted to criminal professions. Mewar Census (1941) described the Kanjars as a "sub-caste" which earned its livelihood by exhibiting its physical capabilities and begging". There are several other historical references and descriptions about the *Kanjars* as nomads, forest dwellers, beggars, keepers and hereditary singers. In contrast to the above observations, a few other scholars report that the females of a few tribal/nomad communities like the *Kanjar, Bediya, Banchada* have been indulging in prostitution traditionally, and even today are used for sexual pleasure by the rich (Mukherjee, 1989; Bedi, 1992; Gathia, 1999).

As far as the emergence of prostitution as a tradition and its association with criminal acts among the tribal groups is concerned, it has not been recorded systematically. However, the practice of prostitution as a group activity or a profession finds mention in various ancient texts and scriptures. Several historians, anthropologists and sociologists have talked about the association of some denotified tribes with the prostitution. Tod (1929), Vyas (1986), Bedi (1992) and Gathia (1999) mentioned in their studies that during the Ancient and Medieva! periods, the *Banjaras,* the *Kanjars* and other such communities who used to sing hereditary songs like *"Charans"* in earlier times, often resorted to prostitution and other criminal professions. Mukherjee(1989) observed that *Bedia, Nat, Sithoura, Nawadia, Basuka, Kanjar, Bhatu, Habura, Dehredar and Gandharp* have been accepting flesh trade as occupation for centuries. Crooke (1974) pointed out that out of ten classes of prostitutes found ordinarily in the plains of North Western India, the two *(Ranjani* and *Gandharp)* are Hindus, and other eight are the Muslims. He also revealed that the communities introduced their daughters to prostitution in ritualistic ways. Kapadia (1952) mentioned that among the *Bedars* (in Bombay), *Harnis, Kaikadis,* and *Manggarudus* caste women were often engaged in prostitution and used to offer themselves as mistresses and temporary wives. During last two decades, several researchers like Anandraj (1999), Patkar (1990), Ghosh (1991) have conducted studies on the sex workers, but these studies mainly deal with the problems related to the urban sex workers or the girls who opt prostitution because of poverty, unemployment or other compulsions.

Objectives of the Study

In the above context, the main objectives of the present paper are:

- To understand the changing practice of prostitution among *Kanjar* community.
- To study changes in standard of living occur due to the technology advancement.
- To explore and understand the impact of media exposure on the practice of prostitution.
- To understand sex-workers' awareness regarding their health issues.

Methodology

Sample Universe

This study is a descriptive and exploratory one. The data were mainly collected through interviews with the help of interview schedules, observation and case studies. Genealogical charts were also prepared.

Alwar district of Rajasthan is chosen as the area of study for two reasons:

(1) There is a large concentration of'*Kanjar* community in this district[3], and

(2) The researcher is familiar with the area as she belongs to Rajasthan.

Alwar district is situated in the north-east of Rajasthan between 27°4' and 28°4' north Latitudes and 76°7' and 77°13' east Longitude. Its greatest length from south to north is about 137 K.M. and greatest breadth from east to west is about 110 K.M. It is bounded on the north and north-east by Gurgaon (of Haryana) and Bharatpur districts, on the north-west by Mahendragarh district of Haryana, on the south-west by Jaipur and on the south by Dausa and Jaipur districts. The city is about 168 kms away from Delhi and 150 kms from Jaipur city of Rajasthan. This city connects with Bharatpur too, which is one of the famous areas for *Kanjar, Nat* and *Bediya* hamlets. Alwar city is a famous tourist place and better known for Sariska tiger sanctuary.

Unit of Analysis

Female members *of Kanjar* families engaged in prostitution, and their other family members.

Data Collection

Secondary data was obtained from government officials and old records, documents, census reports, police records, archives and research studies done by researchers in the current area. Primary data has been collected from several *Kanjar* hamlets in Alwar district of Rajasthan and several visits to dance bar girls in Mumbai.

Tracing an outline of prostitution from traditional entertainers to dance bar girls

Ancient Period

Historical records indicate that even during the medieval period dominated mainly by the Muslim rulers; *Kanjars* were among the various communities which practised prostitution as their hereditary occupation. And after the downfall of the Mughal Empires hordes of concubines, singing and dancing girls and attached women were dislodged from the privileged positions in royal places and were thrown to the streets. When faced with the economic problems, they had no choice but to take recourse to the earliest of all the trades, the sale of sex. The professional prostitutes of today like *'Bedias', 'Nats',*

'Srijwasis', 'Paturias', 'Rajdharus' and 'Dehredar' describe themselves as the descendants of women of the Mughal Courts. (Mukherjee, 1989). Records of around 1336 A.D. indicate that the dancers and prostitutes under royal patronage occupied a recognised position both economically and socially. Around 1440 A.D., prostitution was an acceptable source of revenue to the government. During Mughal rule too, prostitution had its own role. Dancing girls were also an indispensable accessory in the Maratha states. From the early days, prostitutes occupied a recognised position. In several places they lived in quarters separately established, and were granted honorary position in courts and represented an important source of state revenue.

British Period

During the British period, efforts were made to cater to the sexual needs of soldiers based in India a practice although against the British norms in the native country. In the 19th century *Chaklas* were maintained near British army cantonments. During 1883, there were around 280 prostitutes who served 11,000 soldiers in three cantonments at Ambala, Meeruth and Lucknow (Henrique, 1961). Recruitment of prostitutes for the army or general public was either from the communities traditionally engaged in the flesh trade or from among widows, unhappy wives etc. Henriques (1961) mentioned that the vocation of prostitution was traditionally accepted in some communities. He also mentioned that there were a few castes exclusively devoted to prostitution, the girls as whores and the men as pimps.

Post Independence

Post Independence period prostitution as a group or individual activity continued because of poverty and unemployment, the number of prostitutes has increased. The *Kanjar* community, who practice singing and dancing in earlier period, continue prostitution as their traditional occupation. The other modes of their livelihood had come to an end and they became dependent solely on prostitution. As the feudal system also ended post independence, they lost their job of keeping genealogies although they have their Jajman's now too but it is not much paying occupation now. Stigma of criminality is still attached with *Kanjars* they do not have access to top good jobs and the literacy rate is also very low. As a result the other occupations came to an end and prostitution became center of family economy. Researches done by several scholars show that in the earlier period *Kanjars* were traditional entertainers but in the later on *Kanjars* became dependent solely on prostitution (Mukherjee, 1989; Bedi (1992). There are journalistic and institutional reports too which published time to time and had shown *Kanjars* continuous indulgence in prostitution. These studies provide a detailed account of traffickers as brothel keepers, pimps and customers. It illustrates the operation of sex as a commercial enterprise and trade.

Given account shows that *Kanjars* were traditional entertainers earlier but due to the circumstances occurred in colonial period this tribe fallen in the list of Criminal Tribes made by Britishers. Britishers labeled around 200 Indian castes and tribes in this list though some of the tribes were not involved in any kind of criminal activity and in some tribes only a few members were involved in the criminal activity but this law made the whole communities criminal in eyes of law and people too. *Kanjar* women lived in brothels maintained by Britishers and became exclusively dependent on prostitution and this stigma of once criminal and sex-workers remain unchanged even after independence.

Linkage between the changing technology and impact of media on the practise of prostitution

The result of present study shows that *Kanjars* were earlier a nomadic tribe, used to entertain kings and riches in their nomadic state. After the independence they settled in the settlements made by government and these settlements were mainly outside the main village and near the highways. Highways are highly busy as people can reach early to their destinations. Alwar-Jaipur highway around 1500 trucks passes daily and on Alwar Delhi highway around 2000 trucks crosses daily. These truckers are out from their homes for long times so for their fulfilment of sexual needs they visit sex-workers frequently.

Due to new modes of entertainment dance bars opened in metropolitan cities. The dance bar owners tried to search women from the communities whose traditional occupation was performing dance and entertainment. There are reports in media, which focussed on the traditional entertainers (Bhattachrya, 2005), They had published several interviews too. *Kanjar* women are well fitted into dance bar girl's category, as their *Chakri* dance is famous and the most sensual one. Due to the high technology whole world is like a village, one can travel from one end to another end in few hours. Dance bar occupation is paying so much money so families and women of *Kanjar* community had nothing to fear. Dancing in bar is a highly paid occupation; they do visit their homes by fast trains, planes and taxis too. So girls started going to metropolitans. All these women and their family have access to all high technology appliances and services.

The findings of research as are follow:

- The findings suggest that none of the family living in Kachcha house, most of the houses are pakka, though there are several semi-pakka houses too.
- The findings show these houses have high technology appliances like television; DVD-CD players, fridge, washing machines and handy cams are available in abundance.
- Around half of the families own four wheelers; they run these vehicles on hire.
- People in the hamlet have their own mobiles.
- Girls dancing in dance bars outside have their own mobiles.
- When dance bar girls come to their home mostly they come by air upto Delhi or Jaipur and from their to their native place their family members accompany them in taxi.
- In Mumbai these girls live in flats on shared basis.
- They have fixed taxi walas to take them to bars.
- These girls visit beauty parlours very often; girls working as sex-workers at their native place also go to the parlours.
- Sex-workers and dance bar girls are aware about the latest fashion they colour their hairs, wear latest fashion dresses.

- Dance bar girls have their own appliances at their flats in metropolitans like TV, DVD player, washing machine, hair dryers, and hair epifators.

Media exposure

Media is publishing reports on traditional entertainers time to time. They are trying to make people aware about their rights too. As all these families have access to television these families and women are very much aware about the current world, they keep a touch on news, interact with media. Earlier they were a highly exploited category but now as they are in touch of media resources they know how much they should get paid, what are the laws for them. The current example of their awareness is case of dancing in dance bars closing by Maharashtra government. Maharashtra government banned dancing in bars which result lots of unemployment in these women. Dance Bar Girls with NGO are fighting against this on the basis of fundamental right of earning livelihood and freedom of speech. High Court had ruled down the ban as it was making right to earn livelihood inaccessible to dance bar girls. Also the ban is discrimination as it permits dance in 3 star or higher star hotels and clubs exempt form the ban. Though the Maharashtra government got stay on removing this ban dance bar girls are still fighting for the equal rights.

Awareness about Health Related Issues

Television is great source of knowledge for sex-workers. Due to media advertisements and programmes sex-workers are very cautious regarding their health. Women involve in prostitution and other related occupations are very cautious about their health; they visit the doctors frequently. Majority of the respondents consult private doctors, they never visit *neem hakeems4.* The government Health department conducts HIV/ AIDS check up camps each month for them. Most of the respondents are aware about HIV/AIDS. They have adequate knowledge about AIDS, and majority of them are aware about their vulnerability to the disease. They are aware that they are prone to get infected by HIV/AIDS in this *dhandha* and also that it is a disease which can not be treated and cured. But very few of them are aware that it is a dangerous disease and contagious too. All the respondents know that they should ask customers to use condoms as a safety measure. They feel that the use of condoms is a must not only for their own health but also for the customers' health. They believe using condoms is must in this occupation, as chances are more to get sexually transmitted diseases (STD) in *dhandha*. But still they cannot force the use of condom on customer. They request them to use that but ultimately it is their wish. Most of respondents came to know about AIDS from a local nurse and through television.

Conclusion

In the above context, it can be concluded that:

- The practice of Prostitution by tradition has changed its face with changing time, but the nature of practise as entertainers and community's economic dependence on the profession is still same.
- The standard of living is being changed positively due to the technology advancement. Most of the houses of the community are over flooded with advanced household gadgets compared to any other community and same economic status.
- T.V. is the most affective channel of media exposure on the community. The community members are aware about the happenings in the world specially related to them. But the positive aspects of media exposure like: education, in depth knowledge of health, hygiene is still to be occurred.
- Local Medical staff and Media are making them (sex-workers) aware to health issues. Although most of them are fully aware about their well being yet the knowledge is still superficial and unclear.

Notes

1. According to Indian Bare Acts, "prostitution" means the sexual exploitation or abuse of persons for commercial purposes, and the expression "prostitute" shall be construed accordingly.
2. Denotified tribes are the tribes earlier notified as criminal under C.T. Act and later denotified from that list.
3. Pandey and Singh (1998) mentioned that Kanjars are chiefly

concentrated in Malakhera and Kalsada regions of Alwar district and Bharatpur district of Rajastan.

References

Anandraj, H, (1999), Development of Children of Female Commercial Sex Workers of Vijaywada, *The Indian Journal of Social Work,* 60 (4), 553-565.

Bedi, M. S. (1992), *Protection of Women in Moral Danger,* Udaipur: Himanshu Publications.

Bhattacharya, C.S. (2005), Bias Dances Wild in Ladies' Bars, Mumbai: The Telegraph.

Crooke, W. (1975), *The Tribes and Castes of the Northern Western,* Delhi: Cosmo Publications.

Das, S. (1989), *Veer Vinod,* Jaipur: Mayank Prakashan.

Gathia, J. (1999), *Child Prostitution in India,* New Delhi: Concept Publishing.

Ghosh, S. (1991), Girl Child: A Lifetime of Deprivation and Discrimination, *Indian Journal of Social Work,* 52(1), 21-28.

Henriques, F. (1961), *Stews and Strumpets,* London: Macgibbon and Kee.

Kapadia, K. M. (1952), The Criminal Tribes in India, *Sociological Bulletin,* Vol. 1 (2), 1 GO-139.

Mewar Census (1941), *Mewar Census,* Mewar Government Press.

Mukherjee, K.K., (1989), *Flesh Trade a Report,* Ghaziabad: Gram Niyojan Kendra.

Patkar, P. (1990), Children of Prostitute: A Perspective, Paper Presented in *National Workshop on Prostitute and Their Children,* May 28-29, New Delhi.

Simhadri, Y.C. (1991), *Denotified Tribes: A Sociological Analysis,* New Delhi; Classical Publishing House.

Singh, V. and Pandcy, R.P. (1998), *Ethnobotany of Rajasthan, India,* Jodhpur: Scientific Publishers (India).

Tod, J. (1929), *Annals and Antiquities of Rajasthan,* London: Routledge and Kegan Paul. Vyas, G.B. (1986), *Mewar Ka Samajik Va Aarthik Jeevan,* Jodhpur: Printing House.

5

CHALLENGES BEFORE THE DISCIPLINE OF CRIMINAL LAW AND CRIMINOLOGY IN THE PRESENT SCENARIO AND FUTURE DIMENSIONS

Balraj Chauhan

I know not whether Laws be right,
Or whether Laws be wrong,
All that we know who lie in gaol
Is that the wall is strong;
And that each day is like a year.
A year whose days are long

Oscar Wilde

Concern about crime and the need to develop effective measures to control criminal behaviour have spurred the development of the Criminology as an academic discipline. This discipline is devoted to developing valid and reliable information that addresses the causes of crime as well as crime patterns and trends. Criminologists use scientific methods to study the nature, extent, cause, and control of criminal behaviour. Unlike many commentators, whose opinions about crime can be colored by personal experiences, biases and values, criminologists remain objective as they study crime and its consequences. The field of Criminology has gained prominence as an academic area of study due to the constant threat of crime and the social problems it represents. It focuses on the nature and extent of crime, the causes of crime, crime pattern, and crime control.

Given the fact that effectiveness of the Criminal Justice System is invariably the decisive factors as to the level of peace, harmony and stability in the society, reforms in the area of criminal jurisprudence appears to us to be the key to ensure that rule of law prevails. The widening base of market economy, globalisation, the reach and effects of giant advancements in technology coupled with hyper-active fundamentalist forces in different nooks and corner of the world have added to the challenges for the Criminal Justice apparatus of modern states, giving international dimensions to the problem. The scourge of terrorism that plagues almost every region and continent today is one of the bi-products of the above and cognate factors. It is meaningless for any country today to claim to be an island in itself, aloof of what is going on elsewhere.

What is Criminology?

Criminology is the scientific approach to studying criminal behavior. In their classic definition, Criminologists Edwin Sutherland and Donald Cressey state the following:

Criminology is the body of knowledge regarding crime as a social phenomenon. It includes within its scope the processes of making laws, of breaking laws, and of reacting toward the breaking of laws.... The objective of Criminology is the development of a body of general and verified principles and of other types of knowledge regarding this process of law, crime and treatment.

Sutherland and Cressey's definition includes the most important areas of interest to Criminologists: (1) the development of criminal law and its use to define crime; (2) the cause of law violations; (3) the methods used to control criminal behaviour. This definition also refers to the term verified principles, which implies that the scientific method should be used in studying Criminology. Criminologists use objective research methods to pose research questions (hypotheses), gather data, create theories, and test their validity. They also use every analysis of existing records, experimental designs, surveys, historical analysis, and content analysis.

Criminology is an interdisciplinary science for which relatively few academic centers grant graduate degrees. As a result, a many Criminologists have also been trained in diverse fields, most commonly sociology, but also Criminal Justice, Political Science, Psychology, Economics, and the natural sciences. Whereas for most of the twentieth century criminologists primary orientation has been sociological, today it can be viewed as an integrated approach to the study of criminal behaviour. Although it combines elements of many other fields, the primary interest of its practitioners is understanding the true nature of crime, law, and justice.

Now being a law student and having developed the interest in the field of Criminology through the channel of criminal law I can't see the discipline of Criminology in isolation and the focus must be towards the whole Criminal Justice System rather addressing only theoretical aspects of crime and criminals. Needless to say that Criminology is not a discipline to be taught in the confined walls of any college or University but it is the police, prosecution, judiciary and correctional institutions and personnel's who practice Criminology in actual sense and in their day to day life. The purpose is now more clear that how the Indian Society of Criminology is being successful in gathering all the functionaries from the whole country.

Development of the Indian Society of Criminology and its Role

In 1957, the UNESCO Report on teaching of Criminology provided required impetus to introduce this subject worldwide. This Report advocated the need of Criminology in reducing crime and develops theoretical understanding about crime not merely as judicial abstraction but as human act, a natural and social fact. In response to the report, the University of Sagar became the first University in India to have established the very first full-fledged Department of Criminology and Forensic Science in the year 1959. Before independence, Jail Training Institute was established in Lucknow and in a conference of the Inspector Generals the decision of making a Criminology Society was taken. Now almost 41 years before, in the year 1970 The Indian Society of Criminology was established to bring some positive changes in the society by developing the discipline of Criminology in India. In the memorandum of ISC six objectives were laid down.

1. to advance the study, research and application of Criminology and allied sciences for the welfare of society;
2. to promote the organisation and utilisation of criminological research, education and services;

3. to facilitate co-operation among persons and institutions interested in the study of phenomena of crime and criminal behaviour
4. to co-operate with other societies having similar or allied interests;
5. to establish local branches of the society in other centres in the country and
6. to carry on such activities as deemed necessary to promote the objects of the society.

The activities of the society includes organising:

1. Conferences
2. Periodical Symposia
3. Training Programmes
4. Public Lectures

The Journal of the Society i.e. The Indian Journal of Criminology is published from the year 1973. Till date ISC has organised 35 conferences in almost all parts of the country. **Till the year 2000 the focus was on the crime, criminals and other issues but after 2001 the focus has been shifted towards the whole Criminal Justice System**. Dignitaries like Prof. J.J. Pannakal, Justice Krishna Iyer, Justice P.N. Bhagwati, Prof. M.Z. Khan contributed as presidents in the Society and took the society to different heights of excellence.

Other luminaries who have shown the path of development of Criminolcgy in India includes Prof N.R. Madhva Menon, Dr. K. Chockalingam, Prof. D.P. Jatar, Dr. T.E. Shanmugam, Dr. S.M. Diaz, Mr. N. Pitchandi, Dr. Hira Singh, DR. S.K. Mukherji, Mr. S. Venugopal Rao, Dr. S.S. Srivastava, Justice S. Natarajan, Justice M.G. Mukherji, Mr. N.S. Saxena, Dr. M.S. Gore, Justice Venkatachalaih, Prof. B.B. Pande, Prof. S.P. Srivastava, Prof. B.N. Chattoraj, Mr. Amod K. Kant, Justice A.S. Anand, Dr. A. Sivamurthy, etc.

The second generation of Criminologists includes Dr. B.V. Trivedi, Dr. R. Thilagaraj, Prof. Mehrajjudin, Dr. Subhash C.Raina, Dr. S. Sanyal, Dr. Kiran Bedi, Dr. Jaya Tilak Guha Roy, Prof. Arvind Tiwari, Prof. G.S. Bajpai, Dr. S.Latha, Dr. Mridul Srivastava, Mr. K.A. Pamdey etc.

Another significant contribution of ISC includes the opening of local branches of ISC in other States. Now, 13 local branches of ISC are existing throughout the country.

Contemporary Issues

Globalisation has changed the institutional settings of each society of the world and some have described this process as a 'world in motion' (Inda and Rosaldo, 2002). The changes in the economic and political institutions have been noticed mostly and have become topic of discussions for economists and political scientists. The corresponding changes in law and order situation are also noticeable and gradually becoming a part of the political discourse of many South Asian countries. The fact of the matter is that the process of globalisation has changed the nature of crime and criminality. The criminals have also turned global in terms of their operations that are mostly known as 'transnational' acts or activities. Illicit drug trafficking along with human trafficking became such dominant 'transnational' activities that concerted efforts are needed to address them. Thus, we have several UN agencies to deal with these kinds of illegal transnational activities. However, for many, these issues have Western biases, "and the proclamations of global solidarity in the Western media tend to be primarily reserved for affluent global capitals and tourist resorts rather than third world cities and countries" (Aas, 2007, 283). Though migration and movement of people across the boundaries of nation-states have been with us for a long time, the issues related to transnational organised crime, human smuggling and trafficking, money laundering and transshipment of weapons for the purpose of terrorism need a global approach to be dealt with. C. Wright Mills' sociological imagination (1982) allows us to explore the causes of these deviant behaviors but for the overall comprehension, we need to move beyond the societal approach and develop a criminological and Criminal Justice approach. These problems demanded stricter regulation and control; however, we also need to study the breeding factors of crime and criminality for the development of effective intervention and prevention programs. Sociology has a long and enduring tradition of studying crime, deviance, law, morality, justice, and punishment. Durkheim, Weber, Marx, and Simmel among others in classical sociology left a great tradition of studying crime and deviance in particular and the understanding of the complexities of governance in modern societies in general. In this back-drop, we are making a case for the introduction of a new emerging science of behaviour known as Criminology and Criminal Justice in India.

The Distinction between Criminology and Criminal Justice

Although the terms Criminology and Criminal Justice are similar and people often confuse the two, there are major differences between these fields of study. Criminology explains the etiology (origin), extent, and nature of crime in society, whereas Criminal justice refers to the agencies of social control that handle criminal offenders. Whereas criminologists are mainly concerned with identifying the nature, extent, and cause of crime, criminal justice scholars describe, analyse, and explain the behaviour of the agencies of justice — police departments, courts, and correctional facilities — and identify effective methods of crime control. Because both fields are crime-related, they overlap. Criminologists must be aware of how the agencies of justice operate and how they influence crime and criminals. Criminal justice experts cannot begin to design programmes of crime prevention or rehabilitation without understanding something about the nature of crime. It is common therefore, for Criminal Justice programme to feature courses on Criminology and for Criminology courses to evaluate the agencies of justice. The tremendous interest in Criminal Justice has led to the creation of more than a thousand justice-related academic programmes; not surprisingly; these programmes are often staffed by Criminologists. These two fields not only coexist but help each other grow and develop.

The Distinction between Criminology and Deviance

Criminology is also sometimes confused with the study of deviant behaviour. However, significant distinctions can be made between these disciplines. Deviant behaviour refers to any action that departs from social norms. Under this definition, deviant behaviours fall along a broad spectrum, ranging from the most socially harmful, such as rape and murder, to the relatively inoffensive, such as joining a nudist colony.

Crime and deviance are often confused because not all crimes are deviant or unusual acts, and not all deviant acts are illegal or criminal. Therefore, to argue that all crimes are behaviours that depart from the norms of society is probably erroneous. Similarly, many deviant acts are not criminal even though they may be shocking. For example, suppose a passerby observes a person drowning and makes no effort to save that person, the general public would probably condemn the person's behaviour as callous, immoral and deviant our no legal action could be taken because citizens are not required by law to effect rescues. In sum, many criminal acts, but not all, fall within the concept of deviance. Similarly, some deviant acts, but not all, are considered crimes.

To understand the nature and purpose of law, criminologists study the process by which crimes are created from behaviour that previously were considered merely deviant. Two issues that involve deviance are of particular interest to Criminologists: How do deviant behaviours become crimes? When should crimes be legalised, making them immune to state sanction and legal punishment? The first issue involves the historical development of law. Many acts that are legally forbidden today were once considered merely unusual or deviant behaviour.

The Origins and Evaluation of Criminology

Crime is as old as human society and attention to crime can be traced back to ancient Babylon and the Code of Hammurabi. The Ten Commandments, the Christian perspective, the Hindu Laws and the Muslim Laws have all had their own way of dealing with their respective law and order situation emerging due to violations. Punishing the criminals was one of the ways to maintain social order. However, with the Enlightenment the social and intellectual reforms focused criminality differently than the religious perspectives. The Enlightenment period introduced a new way of thinking that provided an alternative to the logic of spiritual explanations. One of the major developments that came in the wake of modernisation in the West, particularly from the middle of the twentieth century, has been the emergence of the notion of Criminal Justice as a separate but highly interconnected system within the structure of governance. A separate system of criminal Justice emerged to redefine the boundaries of crime, develop new strategies of crime control and prevention, reform the traditional institutions of police, prison, and the court, and protect human rights, freedom, democracy, privacy, and justice (Maquire et. al., 2007). These institutional transformations came in the context of ideals of modernisation, renewed understanding of the science of human behaviour, and the philosophy of enlightenment. Criminology now has a strong base to provide theoretical explanations of why do people commit crimes. "For example, some scientific theories in Criminology make statements about the relationship between the certainty and severity of criminal punishments and the volume of criminal behaviors in society. Other scientific theories make statements about the relationship between biological, psychological, or social characteristics of individuals and the likelihood that those individuals will engage in criminal behaviour" (Vold et.al., 1998, 2). During the 1970s and 1980s, almost all advanced countries of the West, particularly the United States, Canada, England, France and Germany reformed their Criminal Justice Systems as an integral part of reforming their institutions and culture of governance.

Over the past couple of decades, theories of crime and punishment have blossomed in their diversity. Not only has the study of crime and punishment broadened throughout the behavioral and social sciences, but, increasingly Criminologists have adopted perspectives that are no longer grounded in "classical" versus "positivist" views of human nature and social interaction. In today's postmodern and multicultural worlds of Criminology and Criminal Justice characterised by post-structuralism, post-Marxism, post-affirmative action, and post-feminism, Criminologists from a variety of schools of thought, including but not limited to critical, constitutive, positivist, and integrative, have come to appreciate, in different and in related ways, the numerous limitations of simple or "non-integrative" theories. In short, the traditional or one-dimensional accounts, models, and explanations of crime and/or punishment that have tended to divide human beings and society into biological, cultural, psychological, or sociological entities, at best, are partially correct. At worst, these analyses are very inadequate as they typically ignore more factors than they consider.

In response to the limited range and application of most non-integrative theories of crime and punishment, more and more criminologists, theorists and non-theorists alike, are embracing integrative and/or interdisciplinary frameworks of examination. Like theories in general which have diversified in kind and approach, the same has been true of integrative theories, perhaps more so. What makes integrative theories especially appealing is that the diversification of models is liberating to the extent that they allow for a creative plurality of knowledge based frameworks. This is the case, both within and across disciplinary boundaries, as well as within and across modernist and postmodernist modes of thought. At the same time, some integrative theories focus on criminal behaviour and criminal activity, others focus on punishment and crime control, still other focus on crime, justice, and social control. Moreover, some integrative theories are formalistic and consist of propositional statements stemming from two or more theories usually within the same discipline; other integrative models or theories are less formalistic and consist of conceptualising the reciprocal or interactive relations between various levels of human motivation, social organisation, and structural relationships. Hence, when one thinks of integrative models one must realise from the beginning that there are many interpretations of what it means to be "doing" integration.

Four Modalities of Criminology

The theory and the practice of Criminology in the universities and in the applied field of Criminal Justice appear to fall broadly into three categories. Some approaches emphasise the control model, in which changes in behaviour and the objectives of practice emphasise external control, such as arrest and apprehension, custody, behaviour modification by reward and punishment, and similar control approaches. The medical model or patient model sees offenders as maladjusted or "sick" persons who need psychotherapy, casework, education, counseling, and other approaches that will help them to deal better with their environment. In the sociogenic approach, offenders are seen as products of their environment; their social and economic settings need to be improved, involving such things as change of home or neighbourhood, improving the conditions in the inner city or ghetto, and other modifications designed to improve their environment. The justice model is simply determinate sentencing to fit the seriousness of the crime without being concerned about causation or other factors. There has been no definitive study to indicate the superiority of one approach above the other. In practice, it is apparent that all four are brought to bear on the offender and the crime problem in different degrees.

The three natural origins of punishment or reaction to crime have been (1) the presence of a harsh environment with which humans nave to deal, (2) occurrence of natural disasters, and (3) religion (Newman, 1978, p. 14). Society's reaction during early times was in retribution and compensation through slavery, which as a social institution contributed much to Penology (Sellin, 1976).

Criminology emerged as a separate discipline between the eighteenth and twentieth centuries. Before the publication of Beccaria's Essay on Crimes and Punishments in 1764, crime was seen as sinful and motivated by supernatural spirits of various sorts. Between 1764 and 1883, the Classical School of Criminology prevailed, in which crime was seen as free choice and the offenders were codified in the law with appropriate punishments attached. The biological movement of the nineteenth century found expression in Criminology in Lombroso's work published in 1876, which initiated the Positive School, focusing on the offender rather than the law. Lombroso, Garofalo, and Ferri have been called the holy three of Criminology (Schafer, 1968, p. 3). All were determinists in that they held that crime was caused by factors beyond the individual's control rather than chosen through free will. Lombroso emphasised biological factors. Garofalo held that criminals suffer from inherited moral degeneracy. Ferri placed priority on social and environmental conditions, such as the neighbourhood socioeconomic levels, and proposed programs aimed at improvement of living and social conditions. The biological theories of Lombroso were discredited by the work of Goring, published in 1913, after which social, economic, and psychological causes of crime dominated the field. By the early twentieth century, Criminology had emerged as a special discipline or area of study and practice. Crime has been seen as an identification of problem areas in any society. This has led some writers to conclude that crime really creates the social order, and not the other way around, that one has to forgive one's enemies, but not before they have been hanged (Newman, 1978, p. 187). There is little grace in justice.

Growth of Criminal Justice Professionals

With the advance of reforms in criminal justice, there also began the growth and expansion of the field of Criminology, and a new group of Criminal Justice professionals. These professionals came from a variety of fields such as sociology, public administration, political science, psychology, law, and even biology and chemistry. Sociology has made the dominant impact on the rise and theoretical legitimacy of the field of Criminology. Today, criminology and Criminal Justice together is one of the most rapidly advancing areas of social and behavioural sciences (Miller et. al., 2008). Major world-class universities such as Oxford, Cambridge, Harvard, Yale, Stanford and Berkeley have established centers and programmes for Criminology and Criminal Justice.

In the United States, about thirty major universities offer doctoral programs in Criminology and Criminal Justice. Two hundred universities offer Masters in Criminology and Criminal Justice. There also exist thousands of undergraduate programmes for training a new generation of Criminal Justice Professionals. The growth of Criminology and Criminal Justice in the advanced countries has helped the growth of effective governance and effective policy-making in crime and justice areas. Similarly the contemporary global situation of national security, the crisis related to the human trafficking, cyber crime phenomenon, sophisticated money laundering schemes and the constant threat of terrorism require highly specialised trained group of professionals who will have skill, knowledge, and training to protect people. In India about 16 Universities are running the course of criminology whether full-time, part-time or self-finance. It is also included in some units of disciplines like sociology, law, political science, anthropology. Thus, across the USA we see the expansion of Criminal Justice education and training. These developments have made them able to face the challenges of crime and justice in more effective and efficient manners.

Criminology and the institutions of modern criminal justice are spreading all over the world as a result of globalisation. Similarly criminal justice problem of one society hardly remains as a problem of that particular unit. "In the emerging global (dis)order, the notion of 'society' is transformed beyond recognition by the growing trans-border flows, and can no longer preserve the illusion of being a discrete and separate entity. Consequently, one can no longer study, for example, Italy simply by looking at what happens inside its territory, but rather one needs to acknowledge the effects that distant conflicts and developments have on national crime and security concerns, and vice versa" (Aas, 2007, 286). Drug trafficking, human trafficking and corruption became global in nature and their containment must be approached globally. Is this process requiring wholesale removal of national and international borders or is it creating an environment for collaborations and cooperation? In a global economy nation states enjoy less autonomy in regulating capital and labor movements. In economy, the slogan is 'let's break the barriers,' whereas, in the field of criminal justice, the trend is towards more control and restrictions.

At the international level, many regulatory laws are passed to enhance the power of law enforcement authorities across the board (Summer, 2007). The world bodies will create more regulatory agencies as time goes on. The United Nations Convention on the Rights of the Child, have now made it possible to talk of global juvenile/youth justice (Muncie, 2005). In recent years, emphasis on global terrorism has not only framed the state's agenda, but it stands as a gateway to exert significant influence over the range of possible outputs. After 9/11 the perspective of global trend has changed significantly and the change is towards the growth of a single dominant ideology, which intends to control crime and criminal behavior by reaching over political boundaries of other suspected countries. In this kind of environment, it is important that the small and poor nations should be vigilant and be aware of the process of globalisation of criminal justice agencies and issues so that the process of globalisation should secure their national interests and reduce true threats of international terrorism. Big and small, all countries are truly interested in curbing terrorism and violence. The nature of today's terrorism is as such that it needs international cooperation to develop effective measures to contain them. As a result of this we see the growth of transnational efforts and agencies. The global expansion of criminal justice agencies made it more than important for small countries to develop their own methods and perspectives to comprehend and understand the criminal justices issues for the protection of their own interests. The science of Criminology and Criminal Justice will provide the knowledge, ability and skills that will not only help us to protect our interests it will also help us to play our required roles in shaping the future direction of forthcoming regulatory laws at the international level.

Current Crime Trends in India

According to the recent Crime in India 2007 published by National Crime Records Bureau, Ministry of Home Affairs, New Delhi there is a remarkable growth in the crime figures. One should not be astonished because as the population grows naturally the crime rate will also increase. Let us have a look on the crime figures:

Crime	*1953*	*2007*
Murder	9802	32318
Attempt to commit murder	NA	27401
C.H. not amounting to murder	NA	3644
Rape	NA	20737
Kidnapping and Abduction	5261	27561
Dacoity	5579	4579
Robbery	8407	19136
Burglary (House-Breaking)	147379	91218
Theft	256567	285043
Riots	20529	59915
Criminal Breach of Trust	NA	15531
Cheating	NA	65326
Counterfeiting	NA	2204
Arson	NA	9024
Hurt	NA	273067
Dowry Deaths	NA	8093
Molestation	NA	38734
Sexual Harassment	NA	10950
Cruelty by husband or Relatives	NA	75930
Importation of Girls	NA	61
Causing Death by Negligence	NA	86790

Other IPC Crimes	148440	829206
Total Cognisable Crimes Under IPC	601964	1989673

Crimes like murder has increased almost three and half times in the year 2007 in comparison with the figures of 1953.

Criminology and Criminal Justice in India

In India, Criminology and Criminal Justice, however, is still in their infancy. Although in one sense, criminal justice in India is as old as India. In a more modernising or in a sociological sense of institutional differentiation and integration, criminal justice in India is still very archaic in nature. In most countries of South Asia, the criminal codes and the penal institutions developed by the British colonial governments have not changed in any significant way. The institutions of police, court, and prison are still very ancient in nature and most of them are incompatible with the modern notions of human rights, freedom, justice, equality, privacy, and democracy. However, what we see today is that a new discourse for modern criminology and criminal justice has now been spreading in all Indian societies including among their policy-makers, leaders of civil societies, women groups, NGOs, and local international assistance communities. The educational institutions of India compared to Pakistan and Bangladesh is ahead in imparting criminal justice and criminology education. Gradually other universities followed and introduced the education of criminology and criminal justice.

There are five levels of teaching of Criminology in India:

(1) Independent departments of Criminology;

(2) Joint departments of Criminology and Forensic Science;

(3) Diploma Courses;

(4) Distance education courses; and

(5) Criminology in training institutions.

Role of the Discipline of Criminology and Criminologist

Regardless of their background or training, criminologists are primarily interested in studying crime and criminal behaviour.

As two noted criminologists, Marvin wolfgang and Franco Ferracuti, put it, "A criminologist is one whose professional training, occupational role, and pecuniary reward are primarily concentrated on a scientific approach to, and study and analysis of, the phenomenon of crime and criminal behaviour."

The contribution of the discipline of criminology to the study of crime and prison includes:

(1) Crime has a legal as well as sociological definition. Legally, crime is to act against law. Sociologically, crimes are conducts harmful to the society.

(2) Study of crime must be done scientifically and objectively with the use of empirical data and grounded theory.

(3) Crime can only be completely understood and effectively dealt with in cultural context. How criminals, victims and society perceived and received crime depends on cultural meaning assigned and feelings evoked.

(4) Criminals are not born evil but a product of their social environment. People are born into pre-existing roles and relationships which affect their outlook and determine their action.

(5) Prisons should not be an institution of punishment, but a place to reform offenders.

(6) Prisoners should be treated individually. Collective treatment and punishment of prisoners with uniform rule, identical policy and fixed regulation will not be effective in reforming prisoners, who suffer from different personalities, labour under disparate life circumstances, and offend in unique situations.

(7) Prisons should be staffed by social workers schooled in treatment of sick people and not prison guards specialised in the punishment of offenders.

To study the above mentioned aspects of crime, criminal and criminal justice system, the criminologists use to collect different kinds of information. They generally try to understand the following aspects:

Criminal Statistics: The subarea of criminal statistics involves measuring the amount and trends of criminal activity. How much crime occurs annually? Who commits it? When and where does it occur? Which crimes are the most serious?

Sociology of Law: The sociology of law is a subarea of criminology concerned with the role social forces play in shaping criminal law noncomitantly, the role of criminal law in shaping society. Criminologists study the history of legal thought in an effort to understand how criminal acts such as theft, rape, and murder, evolved into their present form.

Theory Construction: From the beginning, criminologists have wondered why people engage in criminal acts. Why when they know their actions can bring harsh punishment and social disapproval, do they steal, rape and murder? In short, why do people behave the way they do? Does crime have a social or an individual basis? Is it a psychological, biological, social, political, or economic phenomenon? Because criminologists bring their personal beliefs and backgrounds to bear when they study criminal behaviour, there are diverse theories of crime causation.

Criminal Behaviour Systems: The criminal behaviour systems subarea of Criminology involves research on specific criminal types and patterns: violent crime, theft crime, public order crime, organised crime, and so on. Numerous attempts have been made to describe and understand particular crime types.

Penology: The study of penology involves the correction and control of known criminal offenders. Penologists formulate strategies for crime control and then help implement these policies. Although the field of criminal justice overlaps this area, criminologists have continued their efforts to develop new crime control programmes and policies.

Victimology: Two classic criminological studies, one by Hans Von Hentig and another by Stephen Schafer, first identified the critical role of the victim in the criminal process. These authors suggested that victim behaviour is often a key determinant of crime and that victim actions may actually precipitate crime. Both Von Hentig and Schafer believe that the study of crime is not complete unless the victim's role is considered.

Future Dimensions

'Doing this or that is a morally deplorable act' — the person who enounces this proposal appreciates or evaluates human behavior. It is therefore clear that ethical concerns refer to values. For most, if not all of us, crime is amorally deplorable act; it is a morally deplorable act, because it hurts common values and our consciousness. As far as crime is defined with reference to the tradition of legal positivism and as far as it is thought as a matter of criminological research (criminology as empirical science), crime refers to norms, whereas ethics refer to values.

Law teachers have no concern for questions about the moral dimension of the law. They do not ask whether this or that legal disposition is morally deplorable or not; they have concern for the conditions under which a legal norm can be thought and be defined as valid; they study the structure of the legal system and when they question the validity of a legal disposition or a judgment, it is never with reference to morals, but always with reference to the legal system and the hierarchical order of its norms. When law teachers and lawyers talk about justice and injustice, it is always with regards to the question whether a judgment do or do not comply with precept 'nullum crimen sine lege'. 'nulla poena sine lege' both the rules of the civil or criminal procedure. Analogically a legal disposition is just if it conforms with the Constitution, it is unjust if it do not comply with the Constitution. To resume when they talk about justice then it is generally in the same way as the positivist law does. The teacher and the positive law define crime as from norms, not as from values.

And yet the same teacher or lawyer, when talking in everyday-life about justice or injustice, does not necessarily refer to this positivist-legal understanding. We have all experienced many situations and many cases where we are well disposed to qualify an act which is legally just as unjust and inversely. When the same law-teacher talks about crime as a private person, then he/she talks about crime as we all do in daily life and as some philosophers, exactly as the young Marx, have done and continue to do. All the evidence suggests that the normative and positivist definition of crime is less prominent in everyday-life crime talk than the axiological, moral one. 'Misery makes crime' – so far the quintessence of Marx's story. This slogan is the origin of the economical causes of crime in modern social theory. The paradigm has had a strong influence on criminology and, even in our times, it is very prominent in criminology.

An eminent law teacher and criminologist, Prof. N.R. Madhav Menon, in one of his article said, *"Criminal justice is the true mirror of the degree of civilisation of a society. Criminal justice in this regard includes the procedural guarantees to the accused in defending innocence, the extent to which law allows curbs on freedom, the nature and severity of punishment, the degree of victim support and witness protection, the sense of security enjoyed by the people, the nature of treatment given to inmates of jails and custodial institutions, and the scope for people convicted of crime to get back into normal social life."*

He also suggested three-fold organisation of substantive criminal law in terms of risk and severity of the harm, presupposes three different types of procedures:

1. Hard crimes (India Penal Code)
2. Correctional offences (Indian Correctional Code) and
3. Welfare/Civil offences (Indian Welfare Offences Code).

By and large, the procedure recommended is warrant trial for hard crimes, summons trial for correctional offences, and summary trial for welfare offences. In the first case, police do have power of arrest on their own, while in the second, only with warrant, and in the third, not at all. In the third category, the suggestion is to avoid police intervention altogether unless serious violence is involved.

It was Santayana (1905) who said "those who cannot remember the past are condemned to repeat it." One might also suggest that those who ignore the future are destined for a rude shock when it arrives. Of course, one of the better ways of predicting the future is to look at the present and extrapolate from it. This does not always work. About ten years ago, one might have speculated that junk mails would become a problem. So, in today's world, things can happen quickly. Moreover, there are natural disasters, wars, and economic crises, which are not always foreseeable. Each of these can impact on public safety, even on the other side of the globe.

Factors Influencing the Future Criminal Environment

Economic reforms, and the organisational changes in both public and private sectors which may be expected to accompany them, will continue to create winners and losers in society. Many of the losers, particularly those who are young and male, unskilled and uneducated, may be expected to direct their frustration internally, engaging in one or more of a variety of self-destructive behaviours, or outwardly, in the form of interpersonal violence. Some of the winners, seeking an even bigger slice of the pie, may be tempted to use illicit means.

There are a number of other potentially criminogenic factors, already visible, which are likely to persist into the new millennium. Among these are family dissolution, as well as economic pressures and other cultural forces which encourage both parents to engage in full-time employment, where they are fortunate enough to find such employment. Developments in technology have also posed new opportunities for offenders and risks for prospective victims.

Space does not permit a full exposition of the causal processes by which these factors can contribute to crime, except to suggest that they can affect the risk of victimisation as well as offending. Three examples include dwellings which are left unattended during the day, lack of appropriate male role models for young boys, and diminished parental supervision of their children's activities. One suspects that illegal drugs will continue to be immensely satisfying to those who ingest them, and immensely profitable to those who produce and distribute them. These will continue to pose challenges both to advocates of zero tolerance, and to exponents of harm minimisation.

The Increasing Complexity of Crime Control

Those who understand and appreciate the complexity of crime will recognise that the state is withdrawing from many functions altogether, and scaling down its investment in other activities, which could contribute to crime control. In the wider scheme of things, this may be beneficial. In order to maintain our standard of living in an increasingly competitive global economy, some readjustments and some sacrifices may be necessary.

What this withdrawal means is that the task of crime control, already no longer a monopoly of public sector agencies, will increasingly be shared with individual citizens, businesses, and not-for-profit organisations. The good news is that this will probably stimulate a good deal of creative thinking about crime control on everyone's part. The bad news is that the benefits of this thinking may not be shared equally across Indian society. There remains a real risk that the most disadvantaged in society will receive inadequate protection by public sector agencies, and will also be unable to afford those protective services provided by the private sector.

Look first at policing. The public regards the police as the first line of defence against crime, and finds great reassurance in a visible police presence. They will continue to do so. At the same time, global markets will continue to constrain governments, particularly in their spending. Police today are being asked to do more with less. Complicating this is the fact that police have traditionally been expected to perform many roles which are only indirectly related to crime control: duties relating to traffic, rescue, and a variety of other welfare functions. The challenge of managing increased demand with limited resources will require an unprecedented degree of resourcefulness, adaptability and entrepreneurialism on the part of police.

What trends are currently impacting criminal justice functionaries and their environment, and where will they lead?

1. Changes in organisational life

The police may continue to enjoy a monopoly on the legitimate use of force, but not a monopoly on policing. While some will lament this loss of "market share", others may see it as a golden opportunity for police to harness external resources in furtherance of their mission.

A fundamental question for the future will be the extent to which the police interact with various external institutions, such as the security departments of large companies, internet service providers, private sector specialists in such fields as forensic accounting and cryptography, or other individuals and organisations in a position to provide useful information, or to remedy circumstances which contribute to crime. One might refer to local councils, to public and private transport authorities, or public housing authorities, not to mention research institutions, which may from time to time provide useful ideas and perspectives.

One could envisage a scenario in which these various institutions operate independent of, indeed, isolated from, each other. An alternative scenario, one more likely given the continued demand for public safety in the light of finite capacity of public police, would see police working closely with these institutions.

2. Individual initiatives

The withdrawal of the state from many areas of activity has become a fact of life in nations around the world. Governments will continue to wind back on services. To the extent that they continue to provide services, these services will, as much as possible, be offered on a user-pay basis. The underlying theory behind this withdrawal lies on the three pillars of encouraging self reliance, inspiring entrepreneurial activity, and reducing public expenditures. These are all laudable values.

To be sure, individual self help can be taken too far. The history of vigilante activity around the world is a bloody one. In the United Kingdom, the recent "naming and shaming" of alleged pedophiles has caused completely innocent people, by reason of mistaken identity, to become the victims of vigilante attacks. But one may imagine how efficient and effective outcomes may be even more achievable through coordinated efforts. And crime prevention, once regarded as an intellectual backwater of criminology, has achieved considerable theoretical and operational breakthroughs, and has been enthusiastically embraced by governments around the world.

Some commercial entities may dictate or induce crime control measures on the part of their customers or suppliers, or may trade on a reputation for safety. Insurers are increasingly requiring a degree of target hardening as a condition of insuring property, or offering incentives for the adoption of security measures. Residential security is advertised as an attractive feature of some housing developments.

3. *Traditional reactions*

Alongside the diversification and innovation that will characterise future forms of crime control, some reactions to crime may be less amenable to change. The impulse to punish is deeply engrained in many, if not all of us. Although some cultures are more forgiving than others, the vengeful spirit is alive and well in India.

All else equal, one can hypothesise that a society which is secure, affluent, egalitarian and homogeneous will be less punitive than one marked by poverty, social divisions, and uncertainty. By world standards, India sits well toward the comfortable end of this continuum, but not close enough that punitive sentiments are unusual. On the contrary, Indians can expect continued "law and order" themes to dominate policy discourse in the domains of both law enforcement and sentencing.

A good deal of the business of the public police will be devoted to the time- honoured task of protecting the advantaged members of society from the symbolic and instrumental challenge by the disadvantaged; particularly in public places, where both simple disorder and more serious predatory behaviour are likely to be met with a repressive response. Those who favour simple solutions to complex problems will be pleased to note that simple solutions (most notably increased reliance on imprisonment) will continue to be advanced. Champions of simplicity will be less pleased to know that these simple solutions are not guaranteed to meet with dramatic success. What success they do achieve will come at significant financial and human cost.

An encouraging prospect is the rise of the restorative justice movement, the full development of which is yet to be seen. Meanwhile, capital punishment will emerge as an issue periodically, but because it is such a divisive issue in India.

Erosion of Freedoms

All of us would remember the advent of red light cameras and CCTV, not to mention the days when almost anyone could acquire a wide variety of firearms quickly and legally. Who would deny that there has been a gradual erosion of individual freedom. It is not difficult to foresee a range of new prohibitions, some of which have already begun to emerge. These include the proliferation of alcohol-free zones, greater police powers to search, question and disperse juveniles, and prohibitions on the carrying of knives, or other concealed weapons.

Many of these encroachments on our freedom will be facilitated by developments in technology. Already technologies of surveillance and tracking can permit identification of an individual's or a vehicle's (or any other valuable commodity's) precise location. Every move one makes on the Internet is potentially traceable. One suspects that closed circuit television and other modes of surveillance will become all but ubiquitous. Drug testing may well become a way of life in most Indian schools and workplaces. DNA sampling of criminal suspects, if not the general populace, could become commonplace.

Research and Policy

What are the implications of all the above for research and policy? Public discourse on crime will continue to generate more heat than light. It will continue to be driven more by ideology than by science. The role of researchers, and of the developers of policy, is to understand the changing environment that they are working in, and to identify promising policy opportunities when and where they can. If there is one opportunity for research and policy, it is to identify a range of alternative institutional arrangements in which criminal justice functionaries can work with and through a variety of other institutions, to deliver the best results for society as a whole. What constitutes "best results" may be in the eye of the beholder. Society should strive for those outcomes that deliver the greatest dominion—the greatest overall freedom—for the public as a whole.

More immediately, new arrangements through which criminal justice functionaries interact with non- governmental actors should be sought out or consciously designed, inventoried, and catalogued. Just as botanists of today, and their predecessors of years past, enhance our knowledge of the natural world with their efforts to describe and classify, so too should various institutional configurations and patterns of communications, integration, and other forms of interaction be regularly and comprehensively mapped. Above all, these new forms of organisational life should be analysed in terms of their viability and failure, their public accountability and the equity of their impact.

On Evaluation

Whatever initiatives are introduced to control crime, whether they be introduced by police, by other governments, or by private individuals, they should be subject to objective, independent evaluation. If society is serious about controlling crime, rather than merely achieving a warm inner glow, its policies must be subjected to rigorous evaluation. Just as no one would dream of introducing a new pharmaceutical drug to the market without determining that it is safe and effective, so too should we ensure that our crime prevention initiatives achieve their intended goals without producing harmful side effects.

If our crime control rupees are government expenditures, it seems risky indeed to toss them around without determining as precisely as possible what difference they make. Few governments today are willing to throw money at a problem without bothering to determine what they are getting in return. One might say the same about investments by non governmental institutions. Commercial organisations, at least, have the discipline of the market to attend to. But resources invested in non-profit endeavours are no less valuable. Whatever the setting, cost benefit analysis is likely to receive more attention in years to come.

On Equity in Crime Control

The benefits of future crime control endeavours will not be evenly shared across Indian society. This should come as no revelation, as some would argue that such has always been the case with regard to valued goods and services, whether law enforcement, education, or the arts. But Indians are celebrated for the "fair go", and one of the challenges faced by law enforcement agencies and crime prevention planners in private and non-profit sectors is how to avoid an even greater concentration of violence and theft in relatively less well-off communities that exist today. Perhaps to some extent, the growing privatisation of public protection may take some of the pressure off public agencies, and enable them to focus limited resources on those citizens unable to afford private protection.

The devolution of choice to the consumer of public services, by bestowing vouchers upon individuals or communities, and allowing them to purchase the services they want from the source which they prefer, might strike some as pretty drastic. But some internationally acclaimed observers of policing such as Bayley and Shearing seriously canvass the concept of security vouchers, which could be redeemed by local communities much as education vouchers can be redeemed by families in some overseas jurisdictions. "Security endowments" to particular communities can be used to purchase the kind of police or security services which the community wants, from the organisation or organisations, public or private, which they prefer.

One fundamental challenge is aggregating interests within a community which may be diverse, or even irreconcilable. If half of a community thinks alcohol abuse is the problem, and the other half thinks that alcohol is the solution to their problems, democracy can be difficult. But where there is a degree of consensus about the security needs of a community, and some protection guaranteed for minority groups, the potential for community-based solutions may exist.

Freedom-enhancing Alternatives

The gloomy scenario presented above may not be inevitable. There are strategic alternatives to more repressive policing which are based on interventions far upstream. These include developmental crime prevention, and the potential of various developmental initiatives to reduce the likelihood that ***a child will grow into an adult client of the criminal justice system***. Some of the more promising interventions involve home visits to young expectant mothers by professional visiting nurses; parenting education programs preschool enrichment programs for children from disadvantaged backgrounds; and remedial education, vocational training, and job placement for adolescents.

Incidentally, the effectiveness of these programs has been demonstrated by rigorous controlled evaluation. The importance of developmental intervention for crime prevention and indeed, these very strategies, were recognised a decade ago by the Indian Government.

Of course, the benefits of such early intervention extend far beyond crime prevention. Greater investment in the first three years of life can yield significant benefits in terms of a healthier, better educated, more productive workforce, and a nation better equipped to compete in the global economy.

Conclusion

Criminology is faced with a different kind of dilemma for the foreseeable future; including a different kind of 'aetiology' altogether that rests not on whether it is possible to specify motivations, cognition and causes of individual human behaviour; but focuses instead on the explanation of human actions with reference to their simultaneous constitution as informational and technical events. Similarly, analyses of criminal justice can no longer rest at analysis of social interests, and motivations, but must address the technological properties of the body politic, and of the institutional landscape of control, as inseparable from their form.

Significant disparities in wealth are nothing new in India. The young and disadvantaged in those societies seize their opportunities, licit or illicit, when and where they can. The more prosperous Asian nations may be experiencing a gradual erosion of the nuclear family, which, in the fullness of time, may impact adversely upon the upbringing and supervision of children. One might suggest that global influences are reducing the widespread cultural differences between nations, but are increasing the heterogeneity and stratification within nations. For the most part, this is a recipe for conflict and repression. If some of the above scenarios appear gloomy or foreboding, there are others which are more encouraging. But whatever the case, the next two decades promise to be very interesting for criminologists, and for the crime control industries.

6

CRIMES AGAINST WOMEN: LEGAL RESPONSES AND SOCIAL OBLIGATIONS

S.M. Afzal Qadri, Abdul Latif Wani

Ancient India has treated women better than her counterparts in rest of the world. She was given the status of Goddess in ancient Indian culture. But in the later Vedic period we find that the position of the woman was reduced and she was supposed to perform only one job, namely, to bring progeny for the family. She was treated as a son producing machine and a sonless woman had no value for the family. In the words of the historian Romilla Thaper there had been variations on the status of woman in the subcontinent. Aristotle treats the authority of man over woman to be natural as he is the head of the household and rules the household.

Women enjoy a unique position in every society. Despite the significant contribution made by the women in the society she has always been placed in a disadvantageous position. There has been a movement all-over the world to recognise woman's position in the society. At the global level we find that a significant contribution has been made to recognise the rights of women and remove all types of discrimination against her. The important document in this direction is Convention on Elimination of All Forms of Discrimination Against Women (CEDAW) which provides equal rights for the women. The Preamble of this document says that welfare of the world and progress of peace is possible only when maximum participation is provided to the women on equal terms with men.

These internationally recognised principles of equality and special status also find place in the Indian legal and constitutional system. The Constitution of India provides that irrespective of their sex, men and women are treated equally before law and are accorded equal protection of laws. Article 15 of the Constitution prohibits discrimination against any citizen on the grounds of religion, race, caste, sex etc. However, Article 15(3) makes a special provision enabling the State to make affirmative discriminations in favour of women. The Constitution also provides equal opportunities in the matter of public employment for all its citizens. The concern for women is also reflected in the Directive Principles of State Policy. Article 39(a) lays down that State shall direct its policy towards securing to all its citizens, men and women, equally, the right to means of livehood, while Article 39(c) ensures equal pay for equal work. Article 42 directs the State to make provision for ensuring just and humane conditions of work and maternity relief. Even the Constitution imposes a duty on the citizens of this country to give away such practices which are derogatory to the dignity and honour of the women.

But in practice the ideas provided and safeguards made in our Constitution are not applied in their true spirit. In the words of Krishna Iyer J., "the Indian woman is sad reflection on the distance between the law in book and the law in action". She has been subjected to all kinds of torture, harassment etc., and the same continues even today through the State agencies, by the members in the community and family set-up which is a manifestation of her unequal status and perception of her inferior status in the family and community.

The discrimination and violence against the woman starts even when she is in mother's womb. It continues in her day-to-day life in the shape of molestation, kidnapping, rape, demand for dowry, harassment at home and workplace. This even continues when she is divorced by her husband for one reason or the other. The other types of crimes against the women include prostitution, trafficking etc. The situation becomes more complex in respect of the State of Jammu and Kashmir which is confronted with a conflict situation where the gun has ruled supreme for about two decades and where people in general have become the victims of depression etc. It is here that this violence is the result of extraordinary situation where both the accused and the victim live and where their psyche has been greatly influenced by the prevailing uncertain situation. The main theme of this paper is to discuss the extent of this problem, legal framework designed to eradicate rising violence against this weaker section of the society, to dissect the role that the judiciary has played to make the law effective through its judgments and finally the role that the social institutions like the family, the institution of religion, educational institutions have to play and whether they have lived to the expectations of the people as a whole.

Official Data

The official data that is consolidated for the whole country by the National Crime Records Bureau (NCRB), Ministry of Home Affairs, Govt. of India and which is presented and analysed in this paper represents just a fraction of the total volume of crimes committed against the women. The main reason for the same being that most of the excesses committed against the women inside the four walls of the matrimonial home or within the office chambers are not reported because of certain social compulsions.

As per the figures made available by the NCRB a total of 185312 incidents of crime against women were reported at the national level which shows an increase of 12.5 per cent during 2007 over 2006. The table below will show the total number of crimes committed against the women during 2007:

1. Rape	20737
2. Dowry Death	8093
3. Torture	75930
4. Molestation	38734
5. Sexual Harassment	10950
6. Kidnapping and Abduction	20416
7. Importation of Girls	61
8. Dowry Prohibition Act	5623

The above figures show that the offences against women are on increase and if not controlled the problem will get complicated in the days to come.

The law prohibits discrimination against the women, but this discrimination starts with the conceiving of the child itself. Those who think that sex determination technique is used only in big cities are mistaken. In 204 districts of the country the sex ratio is very much alarming. According to the statistics more than 5 million female foetuses are destroyed every year and history is witness to this fact that in Pre-Islamic Arab society the girls were buried alive and this barbaric practice was stopped with the advent of Islam. The worst form of cruelty against the women is when society prefers the son over the girl. This son preference becomes worst when the society wants to get rid of girl foetus by use of various methods and eliminate her when she is still in mother's womb. This practice of killing a child is an offence under section 315 of the IPC. During the year 2005, a total of 96 cases were reported under section 315 of the IPC. Those who resort to this practice plead the prevalence of dowry and the ill treatment of girl child after the marriage as reason for female foeticide. This shows the bankruptcy of their mind. One more myth in the society is that since the male is the sole bread winner of the family, therefore, the woman is a liability on the society/family. The decline of the female population is due to the abortions at the early stages of pregnancy. According to the 2001 Census, the ratio for 1000 males was 927 females while as this ratio was 934 in 1981. This puts India right at the bottom of the chart internationally. In fact it fares even worse than countries like strife-wracked Nigeria (965) and neighbouring Pakistan (958). According to the report, only China with 832 girls per 1000 boys ranks below India on this dubious front. According to the Census of 2001, the ratio for Jammu and Kashmir is 900 girls for 1000 boys. The scientific and technological developments in the field of medical science have been abused by doctors all over the country to carry out the sex determination tests. But the role of society has been very positive against such scientific devices which help in the destruction of the foetus and accordingly Parliament enacted a law known as Pre-Natal Diagnostic Techniques (Regulation and Prevention of Misuse) Act, 1994 to control this problem. Even Supreme Court in *Centre for Enquiry into Health and Allied Themes (CEHAT) v. Union of India*, sharply reacted and directed the concerned authorities to strictly monitor the activities of the ultrasound diagnostic clinics to prevent illegal female foeticide. However, with no change in the mindset about females, the sex determination tests add to the already adverse situation. This is evident from the recent case decided on 7th August, 2007 in which Bombay High Court turned down the request of a couple

Vijay Kirti Sharma who had two daughters and wanted a son to create a balance in their family, to get the pre-natal test conducted, so that they could choose a male child. The Court held sex determination is not only against the spirit of the Constitution; it also insults and humiliates womanhood. The Court rightly said:

> *It is unfortunate that people should be under the influence of out dated notions regarding son versus daughter. As long as such notions exist, the girl child will be unwanted.*

In view of the directions issued by the Supreme Court in *CEHAT v. Union of India,* some changes were introduced in the law which aimed at:

(*a*) banning pre-conception sex selective techniques;

(*b*) prohibiting the techniques for sex selective abortions; and,

(*c*) using these techniques for detecting genetic abnormalities or congenital malformation.

The State of Jammu and Kashmir has its own law which is by and large same as the central legislation on the subject. But the law alone cannot control this menace in the society. It is the family, religious leaders and non-governmental organisations which have to play a vital role to control and combat this menace in the society. In Kashmir valley in the absence of any authoritative survey, no idea can be made about the extent of this crime against the society, but possibility of commission of this crime cannot be ruled out at all. There is a need that an awareness campaign is started in the society so that wherever this tendency exists that is eradicated to some extent, if not wholly.

The other crime against woman is illegal sex relations and it has been regarded as an extremely grave crime in every society. The element of use of force is an essential ingredient of almost all cases of illegal sexual relations like rape. The problem of rape has assumed high magnitude in almost all Western societies. In U. S. A., it is reported that a rape is committed every ten minutes. In India, the number of cases of rape was 20737 during the year 2007 and it has shown an increasing trend during 2003- 2007. In the State of Jammu and Kashmir, as per the data made available by the State Women's Commission, the total number of rape cases reported during 2007 was 1553, out of which 792 cases were reported from the Kashmir valley and 761 from the Jammu province.

The Valley of Kashmir has in the recent years witnessed various cases of rape and molestation allegedly committed by the security forces or by unknown gunmen. The then Chief Minister of the State is reported to have admitted on the floor of the State Legislative Assembly that only 4 per cent of these rapes are committed by the security forces. This phenomenon is not very common in the rest of the country. But the feeling among the people is that these acts/omissions are committed by those in power in order to suppress the feelings against the administration for the excesses committed by security forces against the kashmiri society. The infamous case of Kanun Poshpora in which not only young girls were molested/raped but even the elderly women were not spared is pointer to the fact that rape has become a weapon in the hands of security forces. But not a single accused was punished in that case. In other incident in the frontier district of Kupwara a girl, namely, Tabinda Gani was raped and murdered by some persons but the case has not been yet decided by the court. In the recent days, valley was shocked by the rape and murder of Asiya and Nelofar in the suburbs of the Shopian, where the police termed it as a simple case of drowning and refused to even file F.I.R under Sections 302,376 R.P.C. It was only after a massive public agitation which compelled the police to file the F.I.R. This shows the apathy of the State administration towards the poor rape victims in this country, and the Supreme Court observed:

> *Public abhorrence of the crime needs reflections through imposition of appropriate sentence by the court and pleaded for deterrent theory of punishment.*

The court has even said that the theory of reformation cannot be invoked in awarding the sentence for rape. While awarding the sentence the courts cannot forget the plight of the victim and their duty to the society. The court will have to do justice to the society as well as to the victim.

One of the worst aspects of offences related to sex is that the girls who are unemployed are lured in the prostitution on the promises of the providing jobs by those who are either in the power or purport to be very close to the State administration.

The infamous sex scandal case of the Jammu and Kashmir is an example where the top politicians, bureaucrats, security force personnel, and others were involved. The case is pending before the court of law and the people are waiting for the decision which is expected in near future. However, we cannot blame only those who are perpetrators of crime, but the family, society and others are also liable who are not keeping any kind of vigil on their daughters and allow them to be lured by these unscrupulous persons who only use them to satisfy their sexual lust taking the advantage of their ignorance and poverty.

The other crimes which are committed against women are molestation, dowry demand, harassment after marriage etc. These are some of the crimes which often confront a woman in her day-to-day life. The cases of molestation are on increase in the country. During the year 2007, a total of 38734 cases of molestation under Section 354 of the I. P. C. were reported in the country. These figures show a 5.8% variation in 2007 over 2006. This definitely is an alarming situation which shows that with the development in the society the social values and respect for the women is becoming a casualty. The State of Jammu and Kashmir is not any exception to this problem. The figures available show that a total of 3944 cases were reported in the State during 2007, out of which 2903 were reported from Kashmir province. If the figures given above by the official agencies are believed, then we can conclude that our society is fast loosing the faith in which the woman was supposed to be respected and the social activists, religious leaders and the parents will have to play a positive role. However, if this trend continues it will bring disaster to the society as a whole.

Dowry demand and harassment at the hands of the in-laws is a very serious crime against women. These crimes are often committed within the four walls of the matrimonial home and are reported only in very extreme situations. The custom of dowry is deep rooted in Indian society, but over the years it has turned into a social menace, too entrenched and diabolical to be tackled by reformers and law makers. This problem has become an alarming social evil and has resulted into the worst form of violence against the women. This fact can be established by the figures which are available for the country. These figures show that a total 8093 cases of dowry-deaths were reported in the country during the year 2007 which shows an increase of 6.2 per cent over the previous year. The State of Jammu and Kashmir is not an exception to this menace. In the year 2007, nine cases of dowry deaths were reported from the State. It is generally believed that the dowry in its original form is not bad but extortion in the name of dowry is not only bad but a curse for the whole society. In the words of a women rights activist, the dowry demand are as much related to greed as rape is to sexual satisfaction. Both are essentially forms of violence whose primary object and purpose is to degrade and victimise a woman. Though Section 304-B IPCdeals with the dowry death cases and we have the comprehensive legislation in the shape of Dowry Prohibition Act, 1961, but still the crime is going unabated. To supplement the law, section 498-A has been incorporated in the I.P.C. which deals with the cases where cruelty by the husband or relatives is the cause of dowry. Provisions of Sections 174 and 176 Cr.P.C are also available to the law enforcement agencies to deal the cases where allegation is that the death is unnatural. To protect the victims against cruelty and dowry related harassment, the Evidence Act was amended and Section 113B incorporated whereby the burden of proof is shifted to defence in case of dowry deaths. Judicial response in dowry death and other related issues is very much encouraging. The Supreme Court has advocated the ruthless action and deterrent punishment in cases of bride burning and even denied the anticipatory bail in such cases. In dowry death cases the courts must keep in mind the object of legislation. The Supreme Court in *State of Karnataka v. M.V. Manjunathe Gowda* showed its concern and observed:

> *that despite stringent laws, the evil practice of giving and taking of dowry remain unabated. On the contrary, it is menacingly on the increase. Every court must be sensitised to the enactment of the law and the purpose for which it is made by the legislature keeping in view evil practice of dowry.*

The demand for dowry is associated with other crimes which are committed against women at her matrimonial house. It includes harassment, torture and desertion. Those unfortunate women who are not in a position to fulfill the dowry demands, they are deserted by their husbands. In the State of Jammu and Kashmir this has shown an increasing trend and desertion, torture and harassment are very common in the State. The figures available with the State Women's Commission show that about 80 complaints relating to desertion, torture and harassment were received by the Commission during January 2006 to March 2008 in Kashmir province and 48 complaints of the same nature were received during the same period in Jammu province. Besides this, complaints regarding maintenance, cheating and fraud were also received by the Commission during the same period.

Conclusion

After discussing the extent of some of the crimes committed against women in the country in general and in Jammu and Kashmir in particular, it can be logically concluded that this State is not an exception so far as the crimes against women are concerned. Considering the social setup of the State, the women were respected a lot due to its religious, geographical and social structure, but now it seems that the situation is not so good. The newspaper reports are full of stories where women are treated badly at home and outside the home. They are not treated with the same dignity as our elders would do. The story of Romana's brutal killing, alleged dowry death of Farzana and the rape and murder of Nilofer and Asiya are the tip of an iceberg. There may be many more such cases which may or may not have been reported. The infamous sex scandal case is one such example. The perpetrators of all these crimes are either shielded by the State or by the society. The question that has agitated the minds of many and which needs to be answered is as to how these crimes can be stopped. The law is not the only means to control crimes against the women. The law will be the ultimate resort to do so but we in the society are bound to open our eyes and find the causes and remedies to control it.

Women empowerment is good enough, but it does not erase the limits set up by our religion and society. The free mixing of opposite sexes is to be controlled because the same is definitely in conflict with our own traditions. The administration of criminal justice is normally a challenging job and it becomes more difficult when there is minimum social support. The cases involving excesses against women should be normally investigated by the women police officers and more often they should not act as police officers but as counsellors whose aim should be to resolve the issue instead of trying to seek the conviction. Conviction should be the last resort. It should be also kept in mind that in dowry cases and in cases of Section 498-A IPC, the party should not abuse her right to take revenge from her erring husband/in laws. Here the investigating officers have to remain more vigilant as the liberty/life of an individual is at stake and the investigating officer shall not rely only on assumptions and presumptions. However, where the atrocities against the women are grave in nature and based on evidence, the investigation of such cases shall be taken up by the senior officers assisted by the female police personnel. To deal with the cases of matrimonial disputes the recommendations of 91st law Commission for establishment of family courts should be followed strictly and these courts shall be required to decide the family disputes within a stipulated time frame.

Law enforcement agencies will have to contribute a lot by helping the women to fight against crime, but challenge lies in front of women themselves who must fight against the ills by empowering themselves.

The need of the hour is to start a campaign to evolve a collective mindset of the society. For this it is necessary that everyone amongst us should change his mind and heart and to replace the hatred, greed and anger by mutual love and affection. We also need to educate the women in proper perspective and make them financially independent, inculcate both in men and women the human values so that both of them respect each other's sentiments and no one will feel that he/she is superior to others. There is a constant erosion of the basic human values of tolerance and the spirit of "live and let live." All social evils in our society will die a natural death if we all agree that everybody among us is a human being and he has to regard others also in the same way.

For this purpose, the first priority should be to start a social movement and create awareness among the masses and to inculcate in them the ideas of love, affection and respect for women at all places including their matrimonial homes. Laws alone cannot assure respect to the women, they can help in achieving the goal. However, to conclude I quote the few lines what Justice Anand has said:

> *Fight for justice by females or cry for gender equality is not fight against men. It is fight against traditions that have chained them-a fight against attitude that is ingrained in the society.*

References

Neelam Uphadya and Rekha Pandey, Women in India—Past and Present, 1990, pp. 6-7.

Bodenheimer, E., Jurisprudence (Harvard University Press), 1974, p. 8.

Article 14.

Article 16.

Article 51-A.

C.B. Muthimma v. Union of India, A.I.R. 1979 S.C. 1868.

Crime in India, NCRB (2007).

Anand, A.S., Justice for Women (Universal Law Publishing Co. Pvt. Ltd.). p. 7.

Times of India, September 8, 2007, p. 13 (Pune).

Times of India, 10 December 2006, p. 1 (Lucknow edn.) See also: Gaur, K.D., The Indian Penal Code (Universal Law Publishing Co.), 2009, pp. 571-572.

A.I.R. 2003 S.C. 3309.

Times of India, September 8, 2007, p. 13 (Pune).

A.I.R. 2003 S.C. 3309.

Annual Report (2006-2007), Jammu and Kashmir State Women's Commission, pp. 68-69.

Proceedings of the Jammu and Kashmir Legislative Assembly, statement of the then Chief Minister, Gh. Nabi Azad made on the floor of the House on 21.7.2007. See Kashmir Times Dt. 22.7.2007.

The story of Asiya and Nelofar's death is the tragic story of collapse of administration of criminal justice in the State. It is alleged that the culprits in this case are those who are supposed to administer the law. Thepolice even refused to register the FIR of rape and murder in this case. The two ladies were allegedly raped and killed by unknown persons and the whole valley observed complete shut down for about a month and after that State police registered an F.I.R. This case is also pending trial in the court.

Ranbir Penal Code (R.P.C. is the penal law applicable to the State of J & K.

State of Karnataka, v. Krishnappa (2004) 4 SCCC 75.

State of M.P. v. bala (2005) 8 SCC 01.

Crime in India (2007) NCRB, MHA, Govt. of India.

Annual Report (2006-2007), Jammu and Kashmir State Commission for Women, p. 69. In the year 2009 a young teenaged girl namely, Romana was killed by two young boys by chasing and hitting her with their vehicle in broad day light in the outskirts of Srinagar city. In the initial stage these boys tried to molest her when she was on her way to a tuition class. The molestation bid she resented and as a result she was brutally hit by the vehicle and died on the spot. The case is still pending trial in the Srinagar court.

Qadri, S.M.A., Criminology, Eastern Book Company (2009) p. 527.

Supra note 20.

Supra note 21. The year 2009 witnessed another important incident of alleged dowry related death of Farzana, a young woman who committed suicide by jumping into the river. In this case it is alleged that the victim was harassed by her in-laws for bringing less dowry.

Madhu Kishwar in Manushi, May–June 1986.

Virbhan Singh v. State of U.P., 1983 SCC (Cri)781. Also see: Sunder Singh v. State of Rajasthan, 1987 SCC (Cri)189.

(2003) 2 SCC 188.

Annual Report (2006-2007), Jammu and Kashmir State Women's Commission.

Ashok Bhan, (Dr.),Violence Against Women and Criminal Justice System, KULR (2003) p. 198.

Kundela Bala v. State of A.P., 1993 (2) SCC 684.

Anand A.S., Justice for Women, Universal Law Publishing Co. (2008) p. 49.

7

VICTIMS OF TERRORISM IN INDIA: AN OVERVIEW

Arvind Tiwari

Introduction

Terrorism is as old as the Roman Empire and it existed in some form or the other, be it the Zealots in Judea or the Assassins in the 11th to 13th century with religion being a strong motivating factor behind terrorist activities until the French Revolution. In fact, the term "terrorism" originated from Reign of Terror (Regime de la Terreur) of 1793-94. Thus, terrorism is not a new phenomenon, and yet it has become fundamentally different from anything that was known before the destruction of twin towers of the World Trade Centre in New York.

The attacks in the USA on 11 September 2001, capitulated terrorism into the international eye by their visibility, sovereignty and symbolism. The impact of this event was not just on public perceptions on terrorism; it also galvanised a powerful actor to drive the global community in the new directions in responding to terrorism. The new response emphasised the major legal elements: control of the financing of the terrorism through tighter international monetary mechanisms; and security by force, using police and military as the means to achieve this.

What is Terrorism?

Terrorism may be defined as an act of organised violence to create chaos and disorder for achieving the goals which in normal course cannot be realised within the framework of legal and constitutional institutions. It is an act of intimidation seeking to subjugate the people and the governments into acceptance of their point of views and also the methodology to propagate it. The terrorists are always in search of soft targets so as to attract world attention and make their presence felt whether the motivation is economical, political or ideological the rapid spread of violence seems to be eating the vitals of an organised social order.

The innocent citizens who may be remotely connected with terrorism or terrorist cause become the major victims of terrorist violence. The increase in terrorist violence and incidents of terrorist activities has usually been a cause of panic giving rise to fear psychosis among the people.

It is somewhat surprising that despite terrorism being recognised as a global phenomenon, attempts in the past for arriving at an internationally accepted definition of terrorism have proved futile. According to some observers, this ambivalence is primarily due to two reasons : firstly, a 'terrorist' in one country may be viewed as a 'freedom fighter' in another; secondly it is known that some States resort to or encourage various kinds of criminal acts, clandestinely, through their own agencies or hired agents to subvert or to otherwise destablise another lawfully established government or in extreme cases get important political or governmental personalities of another State assassinated. History is replete with instances of acts of this nature. Hence, there is an obvious lack of political will, if not resistance to any universally acceptable definition of terrorism.

Elements of a Comprehensive Definition

From a human rights perspective, support is most likely to coalesce around a definition that focuses on indiscriminating or targeted violence against civilians which aims to spread terror. The definition formulated by the UN High-level Panel on Threats, Challenges and Change provides a starting point, although no consensus among human rights organisations has yet emerged to support it. In its 2004 report, *A More Secure World*, the High-level Panel described terrorism as:

> Any action (....) that is intended to cause death or serious bodily harm to civilians or non-combatants, when the purpose of such act by its nature or context, is to intimidate a population or to compel a government or an international organisation to do to abstain from doing any act.

The advantage of this description is that it focuses entirely on the act, and not the actor. It excludes possible justifications related to perpetrators and their motivation, and focuses on what type of violence is used, against whom and for what purpose. Under this description, whether a situation of armed conflict exists is irrelevant. According to the High-level Panel, terrorism occurs when three qualifying conditions are present simultaneously:

- When a degree of violence is applied that is "intended to cause death or serious bodily harm".
- When the victims of the act of violence are "civilians or non-combatants",
- When the motivation of the violent act is "to intimidate a population, or to compel a Government or an international organisation to do to abstain from doing any act".

A terrorist act would have to meet all three conditions.

In formulating this description, the High-level Panel excluded from its consideration acts that were committed by states (state terrorism). Some will see in this an imbalance that benefits states which can (and do) condemn the actions of enemy combatants as "terrorist' while escaping similar stigmatisation. The description also excluded the possibility that certain acts could be considered a legitimate exercise of the right of resistance.

Terrorism as an offence does not figure in the Indian Penal Code of 1860 as amended from time to time. In India, the first special law which attempt to define terrorism was the Terrorists and Disruptive Activities (Prevention) Act, (TADA) 1987 which was followed by the Prevention of Terrorism Act 2002 (POTA). With the repeal of later in 2004, The Unlawful Activities (Prevention) Act, 1967 was amended in 2004 to include the definition of terrorist act. Section 15 states "whoever with intent to threaten unity, integrity, security or sovereignty of India or to strike terror in the people or any section of people in India or in any foreign country, does any act by using bombs, dynamite or other explosive substances or inflammable substances or firearms or other lethal weapons or poisons or noxious gases or other chemical or any other substances (whether biological, or otherwise) of a hazardous nature in such a manner as to cause, or likely to cause. death, or injuries to any person or persons or loss of, or damage to, or destruction of, property or disruption of any supplies or services essential to the life or the community in India or in any foreign country or causes damage or destruction of any property or equipment used for the defence of India or in connection with any other purposes of the Government of India, any State Government or any of their agencies, or detains any person threaten to kill in or injure such persons in order to compel the government in India or a government of a foreign country or any person to do so, or abstain from doing any act commits a terrorist act".

Terrorism: Evolution of an International Response

Anti-terrorisms measures have a long and varied history. Nationally most countries including India have some measures to deal with terrorism, and internationally, UN counter terrorism conventions date from the 1960s. As terrorism globally shifts and evolves, bilateral, cross-borders and regional instruments increasingly compliment the framework of conventions established by the United Nations.

The late 1980s saw activities emerge at a different UN level. In the Commission on Human Rights, government led by Colombia and Peru started pushing for a resolution on the threat to human rights posed by the activities of armed opposition groups. In 1990 the Commission adopted a resolution entitled "Consequences of acts of violence committed by armed group that spread terror among the population and by drug traffickers on the enjoyment of human rights". The text expressed deep concern at the "adverse effect, on the enjoyment of human rights of persistent acts of violence committed in many countries by armed group, regardless of their origin, that spread terror among the population.......". The Commission mechanisms were asked to pay attention to those acts of violence in their reports and non-governmental organisation were encouraged "to bear in mind the adverse effect, on the enjoyment of human rights, of the acts of violence committed .... By armed groups ....." Non-governmental organisations (NGOs) and some Western states opposed this trend because they feared it could redirect the attention of international bodies monitoring human rights violations. The Commission continued to pass this resolution for a number of years, but it fell short of qualifying acts of terror as human rights violence.

Between 1995 and 2004, a different type of resolution on "Human Rights and Terrorism" was passed each year. In its preambular paragraphs the resolution expressed deep concern about the "gross violations of human rights perpetrated by terrorist groups". In its operative paragraphs it went on to condemn "all acts, methods and practices of terrorism, regardless of their motivation, in all their forms and manifestations, wherever and by whomever committed, as acts aimed at the destruction of human rights, fundamentals freedoms and democracy ....". Starting in 1999 the Commission also condemned "violations of the right to live free from fear and al the right to life, liberty and security". The Sub-commission, for its part, appointed a Special Rapporteur to conduct a study on human rights and terrorism that was finalised in 2004.

It is noteworthy that whereas human rights advocates have striven to demarcate clearly in their advocacy and report, the line between "violations" of human rights committed by states, and human rights "abuses" committed by non state actors, such legal niceties have not been observed by other important human rights actors.

The said, NGOs campaigned for the creation of an independent enquiry mechanism on the promotion and protection of human rights while countering terrorism, finally established by the Commission on Human rights in 2005.

It is important to mention that the United Nations Global Counter – Terrorism Strategy was adopted by Member States on 8 September 2006. The strategy, in the form of a resolution and an annexed Plan of action, is a unique global instrument that will enhance national, regional and international efforts to counter terrorism. This is the first time that all Member States have agreed to a common strategic approach to fight terrorism, not only sending a clear message that terrorism is unacceptable in all its forms and manifestations but also resolving to take practical steps individually and collectively to prevent and combat it. Those practical steps include a wide array or measures ranging from strengthening state capacity to counter terrorist threats to better coordinating United Nations system's counter-terrorism activities. The adoption of the strategy fulfils the commitment made by world leaders at the 2005 September Summit and builds on many of the elements proposed by the Secretary-General in his 2 May 2006 report, entitled 'Uniting Against Terrorism Recommendations for a Global Counter-Terrorism Strategy'.

The plan of action includes the following **four** measures:

(i) Measures to address the conditions to the spread of terrorism, including but not limited to prolonged unresolved conflicts, dehumanisation's of victims of terrors in all its forms and manifestations, lack of rule of law and violations of human rights, ethnic, national and religious discrimination, political exclusion, socio-economic marginalisation, and lack of good governance.

(ii) Measures to prevent and combat terrorism, in particular by denying terrorists access to the means to carry out their attacks, to their targets and to the desired impact of their attacks.

(iii) Measures to build States' capacity to prevent and combat terrorism and to strengthen the role of the United Nations system in this regard.

(iv) Measures to ensure respect for human rights for all and the rule of law as the fundamental basis of the fight against terrorism, reaffirming that the promotion and protection of human right for all and the rule of law is essential to all components of the strategy, recognising that effective counter-terrorism measures and the protection of human rights are not conflicting goals, but complementary and mutually reinforcing, and stressing the need to promote and protect the rights of victims of terrorism.

Yet despite 13 International Counter Terrorism Conventions and an attempt made by UN in Security Council define the term in 2004, the International Community failed to agree on a legal definition of terrorism. This failure has allowed for the enactment of inconsistence of national definitions across the counties, many of which provide broad catch all applicable to numerous forms of unlawful conduct. The wide scope of these laws has enabled police abuse in applying them to innocent individuals, groups and actions.

In keeping with the requirement of dealing with the menace of terrorism, India has put in place a comprehensive legal infrastructure. There are several pieces of legislation of which some of them are listed below:

(i) The Unlawful Activities (Prevention) Act 1967 (as amended in 2004 and 2008)

(ii) The National Investigating Agency Act, 2008

(iii) The Code of Criminal Procedure, 1973 (Amendments in the Cr.Pc)

(iv) The Prevention of Money Laundering Act, 2002

(v) The Armed Forces (Special, Powers Act, 1967)

(vi) The National Security Act, 1980

(vii) The Arms Act, 1959

(viii) The Explosive Act, 1884

(ix) The Explosive Substance Act, 1908

(x) The India Penal Code, 1860

(xi) The Anti Hijacking Act, 1982

The Unlawful Activities (Prevention) Act, 1967

This Act was enunciated by the Indian Parliament in 1967 to make powers available to the law enforcement agencies for dealing with unlawful activities directed against the integrity and sovereignty of India. It provides for effective prevention of certain unlawful activities of individuals and associations including terrorist organisations. It extends to the whole of India.

Sec. 3 Power of the Government of India to declare an association as unlawful.

Sec. 16 Punishment for terrorist acts – death or imprisonment for life as the case may be and liable to a fine.

Sec. 17 Punishment for raising funds for terrorist acts – imprisonment for life and also liable to a fine.

Sec. 18 Punishment for conspiracy – imprisonment from five years to imprisonment for life and liable to a fine.

Sec. 19	Punishment for harbouring, etc. – imprisonment from 3 years to imprisonment for life and liable to a fine.
Sec. 33	Forfeiture of property of certain persons during trial and conviction.
Sec. 40	Offence of raising funds for a terrorist organisation – imprisonment up to fourteen years or with a fine or both.

This law was enacted to provide for more effective prevention of certain unlawful activities of individuals and association and for more matters connected with it. It empowered appropriate authorities to declare any association as 'unlawful' it, it is carrying out 'unlawful activities'. This law was comprehensively amended by the Unlawful Activities (Prevention) Amendment Act, 2004 to deal with terrorist activities. Like POTA, it defines a 'terrorist act' and also defines a 'terrorist organisation' as an organisation listed in the schedule or an organisation operating under the same name as an organisation so listed. It further provides a mechanism for forfeiture of the proceeds of terrorism apart from providing stringent punishments for terrorism related offences.

It is noteworthy to mention that although ULPA as amended in 2004 incorporates provisions regarding seizure and forfeiture of property, enhanced punishment and list of terrorist organisations, it does not provide for special courts of enhanced powers of investigation and provision regarding confessions made before police officers. However, these issues were addressed by another amendment made in the Act in 2008.

In the wake of the mayhem unleashed in Mumbai on November 26-28, 2008, by a group of 10 Pakistani terrorists, which left 173 dead and 288 injured besides substantial damage of property, the National Investigating Agency (NIA) was launched on January 1, 2009. A day earlier (December 31, 2008) the President of India had given assent to the National Investigation Act, 2008 and the Unlawful Activities (Prevention) Amendment Act, 2008.

Under the Unlawful Activities (Prevention) Act, 1967, after its amendment in 2008, an accused can be detained without trial for 180 days. This Act has defined "terror acts" to include "use of bombs dynamite, poisons or noxious gases, biological, radioactive, nuclear substances. "Punishment up to 10 years imprisonment for "aiding abetting or committing a terrorist act" has been provided. Similarly, for "funding terror activities, organisation training camps and recruiting persons for committing terror acts" the imprisonment can be up to five years. A draconian provision has also been added. It is that the "court shall presume, unless the contrary is shown, that the accused has committed the offence." The NIA will all the powers invested in it by the NIA Act, 2008 and the procedure and punishment prescribed in the Unlawful Activities (Prevention) Act, 1967, as amended in 2008, should be able to assist the Central and State Government to control terrorist activities in India and prevent a replication of the Mumbai attack.

Salient features of National Investigation Agency

- The Act for constitution of the National Investigation Agency (NIA) will be applicable to whole of India, citizens of India outside India and persons on shops and aircraft registered in India.
- Officers of the NIA will have all powers, privileges and liabilities which the police officers have in connection with investigation of any offence.
- The police officer in charge of a police station on receipt of the report of the offence shall forward it to the state government which in turn will send it to the Centre.
- If the Centre feels the offence is terror related, it shall direct the NIA for investigation.
- Provisions for transfer of investigation and trial of offences to state government with Centre's prior approval.
- NIA may investigate other offences connected with terror-related offences.
- A state government shall extend all assistance to NIA for investigation of terror-related offences.
- Provisions of the Act with regard to investigation shall not affect powers of the state government to investigate and prosecute any terror crime or other offences.
- The Centre shall constitute special courts for trial of terror-related offences.
- Special Courts may sit at any place for any of its proceedings.

- For speedy and fair trial, the Supreme Court may transfer any case pending with the special court to another special court in the same state or any other state, and the High Court may transfer such cases to any other special court within the State.
- Offences punishable with imprisonment for less that three years may be tried summarily.
- Special court to have all powers of the court of sessions under CRPC for trial of any offences under the Act.
- Proceedings to be held 'in camera' if special court deems it necessary.
- Trial to be held on day-to-day basis on all working days and to have precedence over the trail of other offences.
- State governments empowered to constitute one or more special courts.
- No appeal shall be entertained after the expiry of 90 days. Highlights of Unlawful Activities (Prevention) Amendment Bill, 2008.
- Use of bombs, dynamite, poisons or noxious gases, biological radioactive nuclear substances are terror act.
- Aiding, abetting or committing a terrorist act shall be punishable with imprisonment up to ten years.
- Funding terror activities, organising training camps and recruiting persons for committing terror acts shall be punishable with at least five years' imprisonment.
- Detention of accused upto 180 days if investigation not completed.
- No bail shall be granted if accused is not an Indian citizen and has entered the country unauthorisedly.
- No accused, if in custody, to be released on bail or his own bond.
- Court shall presume, unless contrary is shown, that accused has committed offence.

The National Security Act, 1980

The Act came into force in 1980 with a view to providing power to the Central Government and State Government to make order to detain certain persons including foreigners whose action may be prejudicial to the defence of India, security of India, prejudicial to the maintenance of public order and maintenance of supplies and services essential to the community.

Sec. 3-(3)	Detention period – in the first instance exceed three months but the State Government may, if satisfied as aforesaid that it is necessary so to do, amend such order to extend such period from time to time by any period not exceeding three months at any one time.
Sec. 9	Constitution of Advisory Boards
Sec. 11	Procedure of Advisory Boards
Sec. 13	Maximum period of detention: 12 months

Prevention of Money Laundering Act, 2002

Sec. 2	Whosoever directly or indirectly attempts to indulge or knowingly assists or knowingly is a party or is actually involve in any process or activity connected with the proceeds of crime and projecting it as untainted property shall be guilty of the offence of money laundering.
Sec. 4	Punishment for money laundering
Sec. 5&8	Deals with provisional attachment and confiscation
Sec. 19	Power of arrest
Sec. 24	Puts the burden of proof on the accused
Sec. 45	Offences cognizable, non-bailable and limitations on granting bail
Sec. 72	Provides for continuance of proceedings in the event of death or insolvency

Armed Forces (Special) Powers Act, 1967

(Salient features – without replicating the wording in the Act)

Sec. 3	The whole or any part of the country/state can be declared as a disturbed area by the central government or the governor of the state
Sec. 4	*Special powers can be utilised by any commissioned officers, non-commissioned officers, warrant officers or any other person of the equivalent rank.

*Authorises the destruction of any arms dumps, prepared or fortified positions from which armed attacks are made or likely to be made.

*Authorises arrest without warrant of any person who is suspected to have committed or likely to commit any cognizable offence. May even use such force as necessary to effect the arrest.

*Enter and search without warrant any premises suspected to be used for any illegal purposes as defined under the Act.

*Arrested person to be handed over to the officer in charge of the nearest police station with the least possible delay.

The above provisions confer sweeping powers on the members of the armed forces and since they are likely to be misused the Supreme Court of India has issued eleven commandments regulating the exercise of powers under this Act.

Terrorism in India: Contemporary Scene

India has been among the major victims of terrorism – mostly cross-border and State sponsored terrorism for our two decades. According to an estimate, India lost over 53,000 lives to terrorism over the last decade. In comparison, it lost 8,024 lives in all its wars since independence including Kargil. In other word, terror attacks in India have blown the country much more than conventional wars.

More recently in 2008, India ranked among the world's most terrorism-affected countries. On November 26 in a pivotal moment that is now called "26/11" terrorists struck at a variety of locations in Mumbai on November 26, killing atleast 183 people, including 22 foreigners, six of whom were Americans and 14 members of the police and security forces. Over 300 were injured.

All terrorist attacks stroked during last few years have certain common features. Broadly, these could be grouped into three categories:

(i) Attack on the institutions of democracy, which is the very basis of our country (by attacking Parliament, Legislative Assembly etc.) and attack on the economic system by targeting economic nerve centres (Bangalore, Ahmedabad, Surat, Jaipur, Hyderabad and Mumbai),

(ii) Attack on symbols of national pride and on security/ strategic installations (i.e. Red Fort, Military Installations and Camps, Radio stations, Hotel Taj, CST Railway Station etc.

(iii) Attack on civilians to generate terror and fear psychosis among the general populace. The attack at worshipping places to infuse sentiments and to wipe communal passions. These are designed to position the people against the government by creating a feeling of insecurity.

While holding the constitutional validity of POTA, the Supreme Court observed that "terrorist acts are meant to destabilise the nation by challenging the sovereignty and integrity, to raze the constitutional principles that we hold dear, to create a psyche of fear and anarchism among common people, to tear apart the secular fabric, to overthrow democratically elected government, to promote prejudice and bigotry, to demoralise the security forces, to thwart the economic progress and development and so on. This cannot be equated with usual law and order problem within a State. On the other hand, it is inter-state, inter-national and Cross-border in character".

In response to Mumbai attacks, the government has established a new agency, The National Investigation Agency (NIA), to create national level capability to investigate and potentially prosecute such acts. Also in response to Mumbai attacks, the government amended some existing laws to strengthen the hands of security and law enforcement agencies in fighting terrorism. Two themes have framed the public debate on the new legislation, State's rights vs. Federal power and Civil Liberties vs. Strengthening Law Enforcement Power.

An analysis of the recent terror attacks on various courts in Uttar Pradesh and 26/11 in Mumbai are evident that terrorist have no respect for the rule of law. Instances of their muzzling the judiciary, the press and other democratic institutions are many. Terrorists who violate the rights of other citizens with impunity are often the first to invoke the protection of such rights, main under Siege. What ought to be the response of the judiciary, human rights activists and NGOs on such an occasion? While we have a number of international conventions and treaties on tackling international and terrorism, what more needs to be done to translate these into concrete measures at the national level? We need to ponder over these issues and rights of victims of terrorism should be seen from this perspective.

Victims of Terrorism

Human rights advocates and organisations generally face the criticism that they fail to give adequate attention to victims' rights. This criticism takes two forms. One is a demand that human rights organisations should advocate more actively for victims' compensation. On this matter, human rights organisations would normally agree that government should compensate victims of attack, and provide restitution where this is possible. They also have a responsibility to arrest and prosecute individuals responsible for such attacks. The issue therefore is whether they give enough attention to this question.

A second more radical critique is that human right organisations are partial in their advocacy. It is argued that they focus disproportionately on the rights of detainees, and fail highlight equally the right of ordinary people to security – their right to life, to freedom of movement and to freedom from fear, which are no less fundamental to the notion of civil liberty than the rights of detainees.

The true victims of terrorism is society itself. Terrorism not only subverts the political and social climate but also threatens the economic stability of the country undermines democracy and even deprives ordinary citizens of their fundamental rights including their right to life. A spate of bomb blasts in prosperous metros has sparked off "security management" and "terror insurance cover" as the new board room buzzwords. A recent survey carried out by the Mahindra Special Service Groups showed that a majority of corporate (97 per cent) viewed security as an area of increasing priority in the future. It is estimated that a medium size corporation spends about seven crores annually on engaging the services of private security industry that is valued about ten thousand crores. The fear of terror attacks in industry and various religious institutions across Mumbai is constantly increasing. Consequently these establishments pay an annual premium of Sixty-five crores for cover against terrorism (the corresponding figure for Maharashtra is approximate two-hundred fifty crores.

Globally, there are fears of terrorists outfits laundering money and diverting them to stock markets. The Indian Government (then Finance Minister, Mr.P.Chidambaram, said in the Indian Parliament that it is keeping a watch on some people who may be involved in a case pertaining to raising money from the booming stock markets for funding terror activities. This aside, the government is also examining records of about six hundred financial transactions that it believes could be linked to terror funding and other suspicious activities in the country and the region.

It is evident from above that terrorism is impacting larger society indirectly as prices of commodities do increase due to security and terror related expenditure incurred by the companies.

Another dimension of terrorism is that the criminal justice agencies – police, prosecution, judiciary and prisons are giving much attention to terror related matters and access to justice for poor and socially excluded people is becoming bad to worse.

Rights of Victims in Indian Criminal Justice System

Victims of crime are important players in criminal justice administration both as complainant/informant and as witness for police/prosecution. Despite, the system being heavily dependent on the victims, criminal justice has been concerned with the offenders and his interests is almost subordinating or disregarding interests of victims. However, a common understanding regarding the necessity of promoting the protection and support of victims of crime developed. This development, which mainly took places in the western countries after the 1960s, can be divided into three stages: The first stage was the establishment of a system of monetary support for the victim (1960s); the second stage was the strengthening the immediate and direct support for the victim (1970s). After the second stage, there was a realisation that the victim in the criminal justice process had very few rights and the actual process sometimes victimise them a second time and this led to the third stage. The third stage has brought about the enactment of statute for the improvement of legal status of the victim and the establishment of the rights of victims (from the 1980s).

The adoption by the General Assembly of the United Nations at its 96th Plenary on November 29, 1985, of the Declaration of Basic Principles of Justice for Victims of Crime and Abuse of Power, hereafter UN Declaration) constituted an important recognition of the need to set norms and minimum standards in international law for the rights of victims of crime. The UN Declaration recognised four major components of the rights of victims of crime: (i) access to justice and fair treatment; (ii) restitution (iii) compensation (iv) rehabilitation.

(i) **Access to justice and fair treatment** – This right includes access to the mechanisms of justice and to prompt redress, right to be informed of victim's rights, right to proper assistance throughout the legal process and right to protection of privacy and safety.

(ii) **Restitution** – including return of property or payment for the harm or loss suffered; where public officials or other agents have violated criminal laws, the victims should receive restitution from the State.

(iii) **Compensation** – when compensation is not fully available from the offender or other sources, State should provide financial compensation at lest in violent crimes, resulting in bodily injury for which national funds should be established.

(iv) **Assistance** – victims should receive the necessary material, medical, psychological and social assistance through governmental, voluntary and community based means. Police, justice, health and social service personnel should receive training in this regard.

While all the above rights enshrined in the UN Declaration on the Basic Principles of Justice for Victims of Crime and Abuse of Power are applicable to all kind of victims of crime, there is a special need to distinguish the victims of terrorist violence to alleviate their sufferings in view of the increasing phenomenon of urban terrorism, and its impact of terrorism on the victims and their families, criminal justice system and the larger society.

In India, there is no comprehensive legislation for compensation to the victims of terrorism. However, Government of India, Ministry of Home Affairs (MHA), has notified a scheme entitled "Assistance to Victims of Terrorists and Communal Violence" which is being implemented with effect from April 1, 2008 (detailed scheme is annexed). The scheme provides financial assistance to the family member(s) in the event of death or permanent incapacitation of the victim in terrorist violence. The assistance would be given over and above ex-gratia or any other relief from the State government or its agencies. The salient features of the scheme are summarised below:

(i) An amount upto Rs. 3 lakhs would be given to the affected family, irrespective of the number of deaths in the family in a particular incident;

(ii) The principal amount would be deposited in a nationalised bank for lock-in period for 3 years and the interest on the above sum will be credited to the beneficiaries' saving account on quarterly basis;

(iii) A district level committee under the chairmanship of District Magistrate will identify beneficiaries;

(iv) While examining eligibility claims, the District Committee would look into the FIR, post-mortem certificate etc. for determining the rightful beneficiary/claimant;

(v) The MHA after examining the case would issue the cheque in the name of the beneficiary and this would be sent to the District Magistrate (DM) for disbursement;

(vi) In case of employment if given to any family member of a victim of terrorist violence, the family will not be entitled to assistance under this scheme;

(vii) Those permanently incapacitated, and the member of the victims killed/permanently incapacitated in the terrorist violence would be give a health card by the District Health Society funded under National Rural Health Mission, Rashtriya Arogya Nidhi, and the National Trauma Care Project. This card will provide free medical treatment for victims and their families.

An analysis of this scheme shows that the scheme is mainly based on welfare approach and not on rights based perspective. The victim does not have any right to get compensation, however, the financial assistance would depend on recommendations made by the bureaucrats, police officials and the doctors. Further, this does not include any component for other support systems such as counseling, assessment of loss/damage/property, financial expenses and other out of pocket expenses by victims and their families and also medical expenses incurred in the private hospitals. The procedure to get the financial support is very cumbersome and time consuming. The whole process gives lot of discretionary powers to the bureaucrats and therefore this will result in delay in the disbursement of the compensation to the victims. The element of corruption may also not be ruled out while awarding the compensation for the victims.

Civil Society Response for Victims of Terrorism

In response to recent terror attacks in metropolitan cities – Ahmedabad, Surat, Bangalore, Hyderabad and Mumbai (26/11), civil society organisations and concerned citizens have severely condemned and also shown solidarity with the victims and their families. In Mumbai demonstrations were organised against the political leadership for their failure to provide safety and security to the citizens. In fact "these attacks have provided grounds for the coming together of the poor and the vulnerable with the more affluent to demand greater state responsibility and accountability".

The public response to the terror attacks is a reflection of the awakening of the upper echelons of society and the media to the erosion of state responsibility to its citizens. The heightened awareness of the threat to physical security in these sections mirrors the physical, social and economic vulnerabilities faced by marginal sections every day.

The demonstrations should be seen as a wake-up call to the state to rework its agendas and actions so as to strive towards genuine achievement of its obligations to the people. Physical and economic security, and social justice have to be simultaneously addressed – merely measures to address terror will not be adequate in the absence of actions that tackle pressing issues of social justice. In addition, it is necessary for the state to recognise that the public will not longer accept moves that seek to fix the blame for terror attacks on scapegoats or that lead to disruption of peace processes with neighbouring nations. In short, the state will do well to focus to efforts on strengthening itself from within by addressing the human security of its populace in an integrated manner.

Besides demonstrations and condemnation of the political establishment, the civil society organisations have also raised money in partnership with corporate sector and concerned citizens which was provided to the victims and their families to meet medical expenses and social rehabilitation. Bombay Committee for Public Health has adopted few victims for sustained care and support. In a significant move, citizen for peace in solidarity with several civil society organisations have organised peace meetings on August 6, 2008 at Mumbai to strengthen ongoing endeavour to build a cohesive citizen's network to defeat the forces of hatred and terror. Broadly, this coalition has resolved the following against terror:

— By demanding better security and anti-terrorism measures from the state;

— By fostering greater anti-terrorism preparedness among citizens by refusing to participate in any backlash and by resisting those who spread hatred.

— By working actively towards building peace and harmony.

Besides, civil society organisations, media (both print and electronic) has also taken up vigorously devastating effects on terrorism, suffering of victims and their families and also community support to the victims of terror attacks. This acted as a pressure put on the government to implement police and legal reforms.

Concerned citizens in association with corporate sector have also raised money to provide financial support to the families of slain police officials (16 cops) during Mumbai terror attacks. This support is provided to the affected police families at the rate of Rs. 25,000 per month for five years.

It is pertinent to mention that the Taj Group of Hotels has set up a "Taj Public Welfare Trust Fund" to provide immediate relief to all victims of recent terror attacks including the families of those who were killed. The Trust will continue to discharge its mandate in the coming years, specially covering relief to victims of sudden acts of violence, natural calamities and other tragic events that inflicts damage to life and property.

Conclusion

There is justifiable criticism that the present criminal system is totally centered around the accused, ignoring the victims for whom the system purportedly exist and is supposedly operating. The UN has also acknowledged this indifference, to the victims of terrorism and called up on Member States to amend their laws and procedures, giving special rights to victims to participate in criminal proceedings and to claim compensation and other support irrespective of the outcome of the case.

It might be pointed out that although the General Assembly continues to debate the question of whether terrorism itself violates human rights, there is broad agreement that terrorism has a grave impact on individual's ability to enjoy their human rights. Indeed, UN system is paying increasing attention to the issues of human rights of victims of terrorism. The issue was addressed specially in the Outcome Documents 2005, World Summit and Security Council Resolution 1566 (2004), which called for the creation of a working group to consider the possibility establishing an international fund to compensate victims of terrorism acts and their families. In Security Council Resolution 1624 (2005), the Council expressed "its profound solidarity with the victims of terrorism and their families" and stressed the importance of assisting victims of terrorism and providing them and their families with support to cope with their loss and grief.

In addition, the question of rights of victims was also raised by the UN Secretary General as a key concern in a comprehensive counter terrorism strategy, however, at national level much attention was not given on this aspect while formulating strategy to counter terrorism.

The Committee on Criminal Justice Reforms recommended (2003) empowering of the victims of serious offences with the right to implead themselves as a party, right to be represented by counsel, right to produce independence evidence and cross-examine witnesses with leave of the court, right o be heard in the manner of bail, right to continue with the case of the prosecution sought withdrawal, and the right to advance arguments and to prefer an appeal against an adverse order. There may also be need for victim protection schemes in certain situations. The state should ensure rehabilitation of hapless victims of crime and violence.

The case for a nation-wide victim's compensation scheme and compensation fund has been acknowledged for a long time. It is clearly an obligation of the state both under international and national laws. The Criminal Procedure Code (Amendment) Bill, 2006 which is now under consideration of the President's accent does stipulate the state government to establish a Victim Compensation Fund and authorise the legal services authority to administer the compensation scheme. It will be a step in the right direction, much more, however, requires to be done to compensate the victims of crime promptly and satisfactorily, particularly in respect of victims of rape, communal violence, terrorism and other heinous crimes. The policy needs to be pursued and expanded with the intervention and support of the Union Government.

There have been special legislations like the SC/ST (Prevention of Atrocities) Act, Civil Rights Protection Act, Domestic Violence Act, Immoral Traffic (Prevention) Act etc. under which victims have been given special rights and privileges which signify the legislatures' concern for victims of crime. This policy also needs to be given a comprehensive and progressive push to restore the balance with the system badly needs.

Although the Malimath Committee has recommended that "the victim has a right to be represent by an advocate of his choice; provided that an advocate shall be provided at the cost of the state if the victim is not in a position to afford a lawyer, this fails to acknowledge that the present state of implementation of the statutory provisions concerning free legal aid in the criminal justice system leaves much to be desired. The reform of the criminal justice system as whole will have to be simultaneous with the reform of the legal aid systems before a victim of crime can be guaranteed an effective right of representation in a criminal trial.

The limitation of the resources of the State in making adequate provision in the form of a victim assistance fund ought not to be countenanced any longer. The attempt at devising a statutory scheme of witness protection will have to be preceded by a wide range of consultations by the law making body with not only victims of crime including terrorism but other statutory bodes like the National Human Rights Commission which are plagued with a rising number of complaints. The approach would also have to be multi-disciplinary involving, inter alia, academicians, social workers and professionals from the field of law and medicine etc. Given the endemic delays faced by litigants in the present legal system, it would be appropriate to implement legal reforms without diluting the need for providing fair and equal justice to victims of crime including terrorism. The United Nations resolutions on human rights of victims of terrorism will serve as a useful benchmark in reordering the State agencies to address the needs of victims of terrorism.

References

Govt. of India: Second Administration Reforms Commission. Eight Report on Combating Terrorism: Protecting by Righteousness June 2008; p. 3.

Although terrorism has yet to be authoritatively defined, States have already agreed on some of its core elements. On 9 December 1994, the General Assembly adopted the Declaration on Measures to Eliminate International Terrorism, in the annex to resolution 49/60. The Declaration stated that terrorism includes "criminal acts intended or calculated to provoke a state of terror in the general public, a group of persons or particular persons for political purposes", and further held that such acts "are in any circumstances unjustifiable, whatever the consideration of apolitical, philosophical, ideological, racial, ethnic, religious, or other nature that may be involved to justify them" – Digest of jurisprudence of the United Nations and Regional Organisations' on the protection of Human Rights while countering terrorism, New York and Geneva 2003.

CHRI 2007 Report on Stamping Out Rights: The Impact of Anti-Terrorism Laws on Policing, p. 53; Available at www.humanrightsinitiative.org

Para 164 of A More Secure World: Our Shared Responsibility – Report of the Secretary-General's High-level Panel on Threats, Challenges and Change, 2 December 2004. A/59/565. The full report is available at www.un.org/secureworld/report.pdf.

Ibid, para 160.

Now the Special Rapporteur of the Human Rights Council for the promotion and protection of human rights while countering terrorism.

Adapted from http://www.un.org/terrorism/strategy-counter-terrorism.shtml

Das, H.N. (2009): The Asian Tribune, July 02, 2009 (Editorial).

The Times of India, Mumbai, August 31, 2007; p.15.

Source: Country Report on Terrorism, 2008, US Department of State Publication, Office of the Coordinator for Counter-Terrorism, April 2009; pp. 144-146.

PUCL and others vs. Union of India, AIR 2004 SC 456-480.

The same criticism is raised in countries suffering from high crime levels, where human rights lawyers are accused of using the law to hobble police inquiries and protect criminals from prosecution, without regard for the suffering of crime victims. See International Council on Human Rights Policy, 2003.

The economic cost of terrorism is huge. For e.g. serial terror blast in Jaipur in May 2008 that claimed 64 lives, hit business hard leading to an estimated cost of Rs. two thousand crores. The walled city has 24 established markets including gems and jewelry, handicrafts, eatables and readymade garments. Jaipur's contribution accounts for about 65% State's annual turnover of Rs.Fifteen-thousand crores (Mumbai Mirror, May 17, 2008; p.14). Similarly, bomb blasts in Hyderabad in 2007 has resulted in loss of five thousand jobs. As a MNC decided to set up shop in Kuala Lumpur instead of Hyderabad. Special correspondent the Hindu, Chennai, 31st August 2007). The terror attacks on Bangalore, Hyderabad, Jaipur and Mumbai have been designed to keep foreigners away from India and hurt the economy besides infusing a web of fear and insecurity among the citizens.

Gaurav Choudhary and Sandeep Singh, New Delhi, July 2008, reported in the Hindustan Times, Mumbai, dated July 30, 2008; p. 11.

Viju, B, The Times of India, Mumbai, Insurance Companies Terror Cover is a big opportunity, July 30, 2007; pp. 1-8.

Times of India, 15 December, 2007.

Gaurav Chaudhary: 600 bills under screener for terror links, The Times of India, Mumbai, 4th October, 2007.

UNAFEI Newsletter No. 118, October 2005, p. 3.

A rights-based approach is founded on the conviction that each and every human being, by virtue of being human, is a holder o rights. Thus rights-based approach involves not charity or award of compensation, but a process of enabling and empowering those not enjoying their human rights to claim their rights. The process of staking a claim not only asserts an individual's ownership of his or her entitlement, it also helps define the right and raised awareness that what has been claimed is not a privilege or an aspiration but a right.

Parasuraman, S.: The Issue of State is the State's Legitimacy, DNA, Mumbai, December 7, 2008.

The Times of India, Mumbai, December 15, 2008.

S/RES/1624, Ninth Preamble Paragraph; similar language is used in the Outcome Document of the 2005 World Summit (A/RES/60/1, para 89).

Murlidhar, S. (2004): Rights of Victims in the Indian Criminal Justice System.

8

ON CRIMINOLOGY IN INDIA: STATUS AND SCOPE

G.S. Bajpai

Criminology is now too visible. One click of 'criminology' on any search engine on Internet would pour in well over fifty thousands entries. This abundantly signifies the fact that the growth of criminology as discipline and profession has grown noticeably in the recent past. The dismal feature of this scene is that the entries from India in this search are very few and far between. However, criminology as subject of teaching in India has a history of more than fifty years. The perception of even learned people about criminology in this nation are quite vague and misplaced. This requires a systematic stock taking.

In the U.S., it is almost a tradition that the address of the newly elect president of American Society of Criminology would make a thorough assessment of status and future directions in the subject. In one of the presidential addresses, Laub (2003) analysed the development of criminology in the U.S. and he used a 'life course framework' to identify the significant developments and turning points in the history of criminology. Similar exercise is perhaps needed in India to locate criminology in its correct positioning.

There has been hardly any substantial debate or effort to systematise the teaching, research and professional pursuits in the field of criminology. Scholars in India display considerable excitement to work on criminological issues but parallel keenness in the development of criminology as subject is rarely seen. There is a spate of conferences and seminars in the recent past devoting attention to the contemporary themes of criminological interests.

Invariably, these kinds of gatherings have seldom benefited the subject as profession or discipline. This paradox is misleading in the sense that it gives complacency to many that criminology as discipline is growing substantially. A proper shift would be undertaken into this situation subsequently. Let us look at the beginning of teaching of criminology.

Teaching of Criminology

The UNESCO Report in 1957 on teaching of Criminology provided required impetus to introduce this subject in teaching worldwide. This Report advocated the need of Criminology in reducing crime and develop theoretical understanding about crime not merely as judicial abstraction but as human act, a natural and social fact. The Canadian Committee Report (1956) is also considered a major initiative that endorsed the need to develop a professional understanding and practice in controlling crime. Many international fora, time and again, have been recommending the introduction of Criminology in the teaching framework of universities. Particularly, the International Penitentiary Congress (1890, 1925), International Congress on Penal Law, First International Congress on Criminology has stressed the need for developing Criminology as teaching discipline. Resultantly, Criminology as subject was started in various leading universities of the world. The researches in Criminology in these countries have been greatly utilised for policy purposes. Drastic changes have been planned on the basis of applied researches carried cut in these countries.

The beginning of teaching of Criminology did not start from academic institutions in this country. Jail officers training schools and many police training institutions in the country have incorporated criminological contents in their syllabi. Infact, a particular breed of criminology definitely owes a lot to criminal justice agencies and persons who carried out extensive writings on subject of contemporary criminological interests.

In the later years, University of Saugar became the first University in the country to have established the first full-fledged Department of Criminology and Forensic Science in the year 1959. Besides there were many institutes/universities that have partially or totally started focusing on criminology in their curriculum.

These include: Christian College, Indore (1950), Madras School of Social Work (1952, 1962) Tata Institute of Social Sciences Bombay (1954), Bhagalpur University, Bhagalpur (1956), Institute of Social Sciences, Agra (1957), University of Saugar, Sagar (1959), Kashi Vidya Peeth, (started in 1963 and discontinued now), Madras University, Chennai (1965), Karnataka University, Dharwad, (1970), Mysore University (college level) and so on have introduced the teaching of Criminology at various levels. Later, University of Lucknow, Banaras Hindu University, Varanasi and Bundelkhand University, Jhansi (2002), MS University, Thirunelveli (2003) and the National Institute of Criminology and Forensic science, Delhi in affiliation to Guru Gobind Singh Indraprastha University, Delhi (2004) have introduced post graduate level teaching in Criminology and Forensic Science. Amity, a private University in New Delhi, is also reported to have started teaching in criminology and Forensic science. The details are, however, not known. Besides these institutions, teaching of Criminology, at a very limited level (in the form of a special paper), was also being conducted in various departments of Law/Psychology/Sociology/Social Work/Anthropology etc. in many universities.

The teaching of criminology is available at two levels in India: (I) Academic Institutions (II) Training Institutions:

(I) In academic institutions, there are five levels of teaching in criminology in India:

(a) *Independent departments of criminology* : They are - Department of Criminology and Correctional Administration, Tata Institute of Social Sciences, Mumbai (1954); Department of Criminology, University of Madras, Chennai (1965) Department of Criminology and Criminal Justice, M S University, Thirunelveli (2003), Department of Criminal Justice, University of Andhra, Waltair. There is another category where the postgraduate courses in Criminology are conducted by other social sciences departments. The Department of Sociology, Banaras Hindu University, Varanasi and Department of Social Work, Univertsity of Lucknow are such departments.

(b) *Joint departments of criminology and Forensic Science* : Department of Criminology and Forensic Science, Dr. Harising Gour University (formerly University of Saugar), Department of Criminology and Forensic Science, Karnataka University, Dharwad, Institute of Forensic Science and Criminology, Bundel khand University and the National Institute of criminology and Forensic Science, Delhi.

(c) *Diploma Courses*: Faculty of Law, University of Luknow, Jaipur Law College, University of Rajasthan have these courses. More recently departments of law in Utkal University, Manipur University, Aligarh Muslim University, Panjab University, Chandigargh, Panjabi University, Patiala, University of Jammu, Guru Ghasidas University, Bilaspur, Jai Narayan Vyas University, Jodhpur have introduced diploma courses in Criminology.

(d) *Criminology as a special paper*: The post graduate departments of sociology, social work, psychology, law and National Law Universities in the country also have the subject of Criminology as a paper in the curriculum.

(e) *Distance education courses*: There are correspondence courses in Criminology. The Department of Criminology and Forensic Science, Dr Hari Singh Gour University (formerly University of Saugar) conducts a Post Graduate Diploma in Criminology and Police Administration. The Department of Criminology and Criminal Justice Administration, MS University also has a correspondence course in criminology and police science. The National Law Institute University, Bhopal and the Law School of IGNOU also started course in criminology and Forensic Science and criminal justice respectively.

(II) *Criminology in training institutions*: There are specific training institutions where criminology forms a part of the training programmes for the functionaries of criminal justice administration. They include: National Institute of Criminology and Forensic Science, New Delhi, National Institute of Social Defence, New Delhi, Indian Institute of Public Administration,

New Delhi, SVP National Police Acdemy, Hyderabad, State police academies, training colleges and schools, jail training schools and regional correctional institutes also have a fairly wide coverage of criminology.

Thus, scenario remains that only nine Universities/deemed Universities/Institutes of the country have postgraduate teaching in Criminology.

It emerges prominently that Criminology could not develop as an independent discipline in this country. Even where the teaching of Criminology is continuing as a separate discipline, various structural confusions regarding the scope of the subject, conceptual boundaries, thrust areas, methodology, applications are plaguing the development of this discipline.

(2) Professionalisation

More than its independent character, criminology in this country has developed as an integral part of the social sciences. The curriculum of sociology at post graduate level embraces criminological areas like sociology of deviant behaviour, juvenile delinquency, conflict, social disorganisation and the like. Contents of social problems segment of sociology curriculum also carry the issues of criminological relevance.

The interface of criminology with psychology and anthropology is quite significant. Psychology and anthropology contributed a great deal to the development of abnormal or criminal psychology and to the analysis of constitutional provisions. The interdisciplinary direction in criminology is a major characteristic of this discipline. Methodology used in criminological studies is basically sociological. In addition, psychological testing, anthropological measurements, and social work-specific field studies are also carried out as part of criminological research.

Professionalisation of criminology as subject is clearer in certain sectors. Criminological contents, for instance, form part of training of criminal justice personnel. Private security industry and detective services also rely on criminological inputs. However, this has not bolstered the subject, as end-users of criminology did not develop any direct channel of making use of trained manpower in this area.

One index of professionalisation of the discipline is formation of an Association of professionals and publication of journals devoted to a given speciality. In this regard, there are useful developments in Indian Criminology.

There is now a professional body named Indian Society of Criminology (ISC). The ISC publishes a refereed Journal – *Indian Journal of Criminology.* Indian Society of Victimology (1994) is another forum for criminologists. In 2003, a forum as R C 18 on 'Sociology of Crime and Deviance' has been constituted under the auspices of the Indian Sociological Society. The Indian Social Science Association has also supported work on criminology.

The National Crime Records Bureau, New Delhi brings out a Journal called *Crime in India* that contains crime statistics. The National Institute of Social Defence, New Delhi, also carries out many activities of criminological interest. This Institute publishes *Social Defence* that carries articles of criminological interest. The MS University, Thirunelveli started electronic on line publication namely, International Journal of Criminal Justice Sciences. As compared to past, the funding opportunities and publications avenues in criminology have surely expanded in India.

Studies

Some sporadic efforts have been made to assess the problems and issues in Indian criminology. Panakal (1973) Gupta (1974), Menon (1978), Jatar (1979, 1980), Shukla (1981) and Khan (1984), Srivastava (1987), Diaz (1990), Pande (1991), S. P. Srivastava (1995) have studied factors affecting the growth of Criminology in India.

So far there have been three efforts, in the frame of ICSSR Survey Reports in Sociology and Social Anthropology, to document criminological studies. The first trend report was part of 'Social Work Research' (Ranade, 1974) undertaken in the first ICSSR Survey in Sociology and Social Anthropology. The second effort was a trend report on 'Sociology of Deviant Behaviour' (1985) by K S Shukla undertaken in the second survey in Sociology and Social Anthropology. The third effort was a report on 'Crime, Delinquency and Correctional Methods' undertaken as part of the third survey in Sociology and Social Anthropology by D R Singh (2000).

The Second Survey Report on 'Sociology of Deviant Behaviour' covered the period 1969-79. This report presented not only an extensive range of works in criminology but also developed insightful arguments and observation unfolding the development of teaching and research in this area. This report brought forth the issues and areas affecting the growth of this subject in India. The scheme of classification of topics in this work was: deviance among men, women, juveniles, suicide, de-notified communities, drug addiction, youth unrest, correction. The report noted the dearth of doctoral and post doctoral works in criminology (ibid: 223), lack of sociological interpretation of the phenomena hindering the growth of this discipline and over reliance on foreign tool and techniques lacking indigenous methodologies (ibid: 224) are some of the factors affecting the development of criminology and sociology of deviance. The report, *inter alia*, suggested that crime and deviance need to be linked and seen in broader sociological framework connecting with mainstream sociological thinking. Social structural, functional, social change related perspectives should be used in the interpretation of crime and deviance. Longitudinal and interdisciplinary studies were also recommended to be undertaken in this area.

While the focus in the third survey report was on deviance, the fourth survey report by D.R. Singh focused on crime, delinquency and correctional methods. This report covered the works undertaken between 1979 and 1994. The set of problems and, as shown in this report, was quite changed as compared to the earlier report. Therefore several new areas like victimology, collective violence, organised criminality etc. were brought into this publication. Compared to the earlier survey report, this report refrained from specifically commenting or critically analysing the general scenario concerning teaching, research and practice of criminology. The report in the closing paragraphs (ibid: 51), however, concluded that '— the researches in the area of crime, delinquency and correctional methods are almost sketchy'. The report found the absence of theory building, monitoring and evaluation studies, time series and prediction studies in criminology. Lack of proper utilisation of research in policy purposes was also noted in this work. While this paper was being written, the fifth survey report was under preparation. The Fourth

Survey of the ICSSR has incorporated a chapter on 'Criminological studies' during post 1994 period.

Apart from ICSSR Surveys, Bajpai (2007) also carried out a major project titled 'Criminology in India in 2000 A.D.' It surveys the criminological literature produced in this country in the last one hundred years.

The Present Study

The present paper seeks to underscore the current issues and problems in the discipline of criminology specially in teaching research and pratice. The observations and statements presented at various places in this paper are based on a major research project 'criminology in India in 2000 A.D.' undertaken with the assistance of Indian Council of Social Science Research, New Delhi. The core objective of this project was to make a review of the research works and other publications on various aspects of criminology in India during 1979 to 2003. The premise was to explore the status and issues in Indian criminology. The idea was to assess the trends, priorities and key issues in the growth of criminological researches in India. To achieve the objectives stated above, some 833 studies carried out in a period of about 18 years were analysed. The Report produced plenty of information and data. The finer trends, specific direction and precise focus of the studies surveyed in the exercise are not possible to present here for want of space. The paper, however, discusses some key issues and trends in criminological researches in this country.

Several factors crucial to the growth of this discipline in the country were identified in this study. Firstly, criminology is yet to be extricated from its embryonic state to emerge as a major independent discipline, though the subject is more than fifty years strong in this country. Secondly, the subject initially grew as an adjunct to major social science discipline, even later it remained dependent on the academicians hailing from parallel discipiines. Thirdly, the subject could not be started extensively in many universities. As a result, trained manpower and students in this area were very few and far between. Fourthly, this position has also restricted the possible employment avenues in this discipline. The vicious circle, hence, continued. Fifthly, as Shukla (1985) also noted, the teachers/faculties, who were initially instrumental in the teaching and research in this area, brought with them the concepts and methodology of their parent disciplines. They invariably utilised their background training in criminology. There were hardly any efforts to evolve basic and foundational criminology with its own methodology. Sixthly, the syllabi of this subject in different institutions do not follow a standard pattern.

Trends

As many as 833 studies analysed in this paper have shown varying trends in researches in criminology. Broad trends as identified in this study can be summarised as below:

1. The researches surveyed in this study represent that most studies on subjects of criminological nature were conducted by researchers hailing from sister disciplines like sociology, psychology, Law, social works.

2. A sizeable amount of literature has also been produced by criminal justice professionals including police officials, lawyers and judges. The writings in this category remain invariably impressionistic.

3. The research projects sponsored by Government agencies have also been a major category. These studies were undertaken by social scientists.

4. A good number of criminological studies were those conducted by individual scholars at doctoral level.

5. The trend in research can also be seen in quantitative terms. Of the total 883 works surveyed in this exercise presents a varied picture. Studies in victimology were the most preferred choice (23.99 per cent) of many criminologists during this period. Almost half of these (12.33 per cent) focused on women victimisation. Considerable amount of researches (22.19 per cent) remained confined to various forms of crimes. Collective violence (9.3 per cent), drug addiction (4.2 per cent) and criminality by women (3.5 per cent) received greater attention. Several new forms of crimes forming a pattern were also seen to have escalated (12.33 per cent) considerably. Mounting interest of criminologists in human rights (12.10 per cent) has been a prominent trend during the period of this study Criminal justice, correction and crime prevention have also been adequately represented while the studies on juvenile delinquency have been relatively on a low priority (3.31 per cent) for criminologists.

Furthermore, most publications (35.3 per cent) were published in the Indian Journal of Criminology followed by the Indian Police Journal and Indian Journal of Criminology and criminalistics (15 and 12.4 per cent respectively). Out of 833 publications, the percentage of books was 35.1.

As many as 45 percent studies covered under this study were based on secondary data. An effort has also been made assess the approach adopted in these studies. The data reveal that most studies (48.0 per cent) were analytical or applied research (43.6 percent). The ratio of researches adopting historical method, fundamental research or action research ranged between 1 to 4 per cent. As regards disciplinary orientation of various studies, most studies (68.9) were uni-disciplinary while 30.7 per cent were in inter-disciplinary category. As many as 52.5 per cent studies applied descriptive research design while 42.7 per cent had exploratory research design.

The data collected in this exercise show that only 12 per cent studies had applications of some tools like scale or test. As regards application of methodology in studies 72.5 per cent studies were descriptive studies. It has been observed that studies did not apply advanced methods of data analysis frequently. Instead of relying on electronic data analysis, researchers mostly (89.9 percent) analysed their data manually.

The number of studies contributing to knowledge and information (26.3 and 49.3 respectively) was much higher than of others (Table1.15). Table 1.16 provides a broad view of the studies falling in various fields of criminology. Deviance and crime and police studies received greater attention of researchers in the period under review.

6. Thus, Criminologists have shown considerable interest in victimology in the recent times. A large number of studies in women victimisation is a remarkable development in Indian criminology.

7. Focus of researchers on human rights issues is an emerging trend in criminology.

8. Community policing and crime prevention has also started gaining attention in this decade.

9. Unlike the observations made in the second Survey of Research (pp. 223), the number of doctoral dissertations in the present survey has increased considerably.

(II) General Trends

1. Teaching of criminology at degree and post degree level is not extensively available as there are only a very few institutions providing teaching, research or practices in Criminology. The situation has resulted in many untoward outcomes. For instance, the academic openings and a broad network of academicians in criminology could not grow in India.

2. Criminology in India has not been able to foster a clear-cut beneficiary base. Linkages between practice and profession in Criminology are obscure and unexplored.

3. On account of being mainly associated with their parent disciplines, the researchers who made commendable contributions to criminology remained indifferent to the development of Criminology in India.

4. The basic researches in Criminology in India leading to the development of theories explaining the major problems of criminality in this country have been almost non-existent. Nor do the criminologists, in most cases, have been able to prescribe polices and programmes oriented research findings.

Issues

Some discernible features in this regard can be summarised as below:

1. The number of criminologists with basic orientation in terms of degree and affiliation in criminology is extremely low. A good amount of researches in criminological issues are conducted by sociologists, psychologists and legal scholars. This position has been both facilitating and impeding for the growth of this subject. On the one hand, the process resulted in making this subject a dynamic discipline with an interdisciplinary orientation and, on the other hand, criminology suffered in creating its own identity as independent and mainstream discipline, as happened in the west. The researches conducted by the scholars of the parallel subjects have invariably failed to connect their research with prevailing criminological theories and concepts. Resultantly, they

did not contribute to the theories in the subject. Besides, these scholars hardly have any direct academic commitment to criminology as they have been vacillating conveniently between criminology and their parent disciplines.

2. Researchers did not have much financial encouragement for research in criminology. Later, UGC and ICSSR have, however, started financing doctoral works/research projects in this area.

3. Until the advent of Indian Society of Criminology in1970 and Indian Society of Victimology in 1994, there were almost no national fora in this area. Recently (2003), a forum as RC 18 on 'Sociology of Crime and Deviance' has been constituted under the auspices of the Indian Sociological Society. The output of conferences/seminar did not seem to benefit the discipline of Criminology. In the recent past, no debate in any such fora was organised to review the status of Criminology in the country.

4. Researchers in Criminology had considerable discouragement due to difficult and daunting data collection conditions involving contacting of criminals, prisoners, visiting jails, police and other problem areas and persons.

Research Gaps

A brief account of research gaps as identified in the paper are presented below:

1. Although the studies in correction are rising but there are areas forming research gaps. For instance, little is known about impact of imprisonment, prison subculture, prison violence, privatisation of prisons, efficacy of prison personnel etc.
2. Similarly, there are unanswered and unexplored areas in Criminal Justice Administration. These include: process of criminal justice on a continuum, sentencing behaviour of judges, failure of prosecution, cost effectiveness of criminal justice, victim based justice, restorative justice, restitution and the like.
3. Research based understanding about organised crime, economic crimes, kidnapping, racketeering etc. is far from being satisfactory.

4. Violence in all forms is the order of the day in India. The subject has been under researched in terms of explaining its undercurrents and processes.
5. Research gaps are also visible in terms of connecting the findings with theories in criminology.
6. Researches, in many cases, followed superficial texture of the problem and subtle elements have not been brought forth prominently.
7. Considerable deficiencies are noticeable in methodologies of criminological studies. The advanced methods of data analysis and quantitative applications by using standard softwares are mentionable here. There are hardly any methodological innovations seen in criminological studies.
8. This study also noticed that senior researchers' expositions in criminology are more and more based on ideas and impressions and the tendency to visit field is getting deteriorated in them. Most researches involving field-based observations are in the form of doctoral works and conducted by young researchers.
9. There was a visible penury of research contributing to and evaluation of policies in Indian context.
10. The nature of research covered in this exercise shows that there has been hardly any study precisely contributing to theory formulation in criminology or evaluating any existing theory in criminology.
11. Despite escalating problems of violence and terrorism and other forms of criminality, there are absolutely no particular indigenous expositions, concepts and theories for our contexts.
12. Out of total works surveyed in this paper, the percentage of empirical works is hardly over 35 percent. Lack of empirical works in criminology has hindered the growth of this discipline in India
13. The presence of Indian criminology in terms of publications on the World Wide Web (www) or Internet is almost non- existent.

Criminology and Public Policy

The crisis concerning the status and scope of criminology has been in active debate in the U.S. as well where we find the subject flourishing very prominently. The American contributions to criminology theories, criminal justice practices, crime reduction and public policy issues have been greatly recognised. Initially, Criminology in the U.S. faced stiff reaction and resistance from mainstream social sciences but the significant contribution in selected spheres has eventually given this discipline a major status. This model needs to be viewed in India. Criminology will have to be made instrumental in responding the indigenous crime situations so that some direct applications of knowledge generated by criminological studies in India could be highlighted.

Future Concerns

Research priorities in academic discipline are relative and time specific. These need to be seen at two levels: one, at the international level to understand the trends and emphasis in research. This is significant from the standpoint of academic growth of the subject in the international context. Second, the discipline ought to address the indigenous problems of contemporary nature with possible contribution in policy and planning. Going by this, it would be logical to suggest that the research priorities in criminology must be guided by the gaps in research suggested in the preceding section. Following areas are worth considering as priorities in criminological researches:

1. Basic research contributing to indigenous understanding of major forms criminality
2. Evolving data base and information based on non government sources
3. Areas like victims of kidnapping, terrorism, organised crimes involving secondary victimisation, restitution, restorative justice, system as victim, political criminology unraveling nexuses, vulnerability of political processes for criminalisation, radical criminology, action criminology, pragmatic criminology, social tolerance of deviance, decriminalisation, economics of crime and justice, impact

of imprisonment, forensic psychology, environmental criminology including crime profiling, GIS applications and crime mapping, situational crime prevention, alternatives to imprisonment, community sentence, continuum of criminal justice process, fear of crime, victimisation survey, risk of victimisation are in need of systematic research attention and form priorities in research in criminology in the times ahead.

4. Need is also to make the criminological literature produced in India available on the Internet.
5. A look at the performance of criminology and concerned institutions abroad (viz., U.S., UK, Australia) can provide the needed insight in developing this subject in India as a vibrant discipline with amasing potential.
6. To grow and sustain, teaching and research in criminology need to be made widely available like any other social science subject.
7. Criminology in this country is required to link itself and contribute to broad disciplines of social and behavioural sciences. On the other hand it has to explore its own concepts, methods, scope, professional practices and areas of intervention. This would provide a standing and status to the subject. This would also discard the perceptional status of the subject as mere appendage of social or behavioural sciences. Criminologists pursuing researches have to carry this responsibility.
8. Pressing need on the part of criminologists is to demonstrate the potential of this discipline as problem solving instrumentality and its scope to contribute to the professions.
9. Criminology needs to be enabled to come out with some insight and solutions of crime and criminality being daily projected in the media.

Way Forward

To develop and sustain Criminology as a discipline of learning and applications, it is imperative to work on the gaps and problems identified in this paper. The ambit of criminology has diluted before its construction. Need of the hour is to construct hard-core criminology with its own precise focus, concepts and approaches. The part time romance of academicians and professionals with criminology need to be replaced with a committed cadre of full time criminologists working towards the larger objectives of public policy and community safety.

The Role of Indian Society of Criminology (ISC)

The ISC, since its inception, has been doing a great service to further the discipline of criminology. The ISC is more often guided by its constraints than the statement of its mission. The ISC should have a clearly laid down charter to develop core criminology. The American Society of Criminology had refused to shift its focus from core academic and pure criminology when criminal justice professionals tried to divert its direction towards making it mote administrative type.

The ISC has numerous constraints in being so bold. But some beginning is needed. The need is to encourage, promote and collaborate basic research in criminology. It is the basic research based on indigenous understanding that would give recognition to Indian criminology in the international community. It's a plain fact that only young scholars in this country are carrying out some empirical researches in the form of doctoral studies. They need to be given space and attention by the ISC forum. The ISC need to chalk out a five-year plan kind programme to make some contribution in research, training and consultancy in relevant areas. The members could be networked for this purpose.

The UGC, ICSSR and the institutions already working in this area are required to display greater concern for this subject. The UGC can think of establishing centers of excellence in criminology or a National University for Criminological studies. The matter can also be taken up with the Government agencies and organisation for considering the subject in their recruitment process.

The need is also to take up the matter with the UPSC for its inclusion in the Civil Services. The UGC or Ministry of Human

Resource Development can do the needful into this matter. The UGC and ICSSR may consider of greater and separate funds allocation for researchers in Criminology. The developing of standard syllabi in criminology may also be given attention to. Despite shortcomings found and expressed in the present paper, Criminology as a subject of learning and research has tremendous promise and potential for a country like India.

References

Bajpai G. S. (2006): *Criminology in India in 2000 A.D.*, a research project sponsored by the Indian Council of Social Science Research.

Bajpai G.S. (2006): 'Criminological studies' in Fifth Survey in Sociology and social Anthropology, ICSSR, New Delhi (in press).

Bajpai G. S. (2009): 'On Criminology in India: Demands and Directions', a theme paper presented at the 32nd All India Conference of ISC held at Bangalore University (Feb. 25-27, 2009).

Diaz S.M. (1995): 'Teaching of Criminology in Indian Universities, *Indian Journal of Criminology*, Vol. 18, No. 2, pp. 101-104.

Gupta, A. (1974): 'Education and Research in Criminology', *Indian Journal of Criminology*, No. 2.

Jatar D.P. (1979): 'Teaching and Research in Criminology in India', *The Indian Journal of Criminology*, Vol. 7, No. 2.

Jatar D.P. (1980): *Survey of Research in Criminology*, Dept. of Criminology and Forensic Science, University of Sagar, Sagar, (Mimeo).

Menon N.R. Madhava (1978): 'Towards Evolving a Research Agenda for Criminology and Related Criminal Sciences: A Preliminary Draft Proposal', *Indian Journal of Criminology*, Vol. 6, No. 2, pp. 67-76.

Laub John H.(2003): 'The Life Course of Crimnology in the United Sates: The American Society of Criminology 2003 Presidential Address, *Criminology*. Vol. 42, No. 1.

Panakal J.J. (1973): 'An Agenda for Criminology', *Indian Journal of Criminology*, No. 1.

Khan M Z (1984): Criminology in India: Problems and Prospects, *Indian Journal of Criminology*, Vol. 12, No. 2 July.

Pande, B B (1991): 'Criminology Research: Issues and Priorities', *Indian Journal of Criminology*, No. 2, pp. 72-78.

Ranade, S. N. (1974) : 'Social Work Research: A Trend report' in *Survey of research in Sociology and Social Anthropology*, Vol. 2, Bombay: Popular Prakashan, pp. 531-64.

Shukla K S (1985): ' Sociology of Deviant Behaviour' in *Survey of Research in Sociology and Social Anthropology*, Vol. III . pp. 197-246, New Delhi: Satvahan.

Shukla K.S. and Krishna K.P. (1981): 'Teaching of Criminology in India: Status and Scope', *The Indian Journal of Social Work*, Vol. XLII, No. 3, Oct.

Singh D.R. (2000): 'Crime Delinquency and Correctional Methods', M.S. Gore (Ed.),Third Survey of Sociology and Social Anthropology, Vol. 2, New Delhi, Indian Council of Social Science Research and Manak Publishers Pvt. Ltd., pp. 1-63.

Srivastava S.P. (1995): 'Expanding the Horizons of Indian Criminology-Toward Identifying Critical Concerns and Commitments', *Indian Journal of Criminology*, Vol. 23, No. 1, pp. 1-8.

Srivastava S.S. (1995): 'Towards a Rational Criminology in Indian Context', *Indian Journal of Criminology*, Vol. 15, No. 2, pp. 80-83.

UNESCO (1957) : *The University Teaching of Social Science-Criminology*, Paris: UNESCO.

9

DOING JUSTICE DIFFERENTLY: RESTORATIVE JUSTICE AND SOCIAL WORK

Hema Hargovan

Introduction

Growing and influential critique of criminal justice responses to community expectations about safety, the crisis of public confidence and rising public expectations fuels public demands for greater safety and more efficient institutions; not always accompanied by a realistic sense of the limited role that criminal justice plays in contributing to broader issues of safety and security. Perceptions that the criminal justice system is failing vulnerable groups, increased recognition of gender based violence, exploitation and abuse of children, secondary victimisation of victims by the criminal justice system and the rise of victim advocacy all contribute to growing support for reforms expanding the rights of victims. Coupled with these challenges, most developing countries face considerable restraints on the resources they are able to devote to criminal justice.

Worldwide recognition that greater allocation of resources to policing and prisons may not necessarily produce greater public satisfaction or even an increased sense of safety and justice clearly points to the need for more innovative and creative ways of increasing access to justice for all citizens. The relationship between criminal justice and prosperity cannot be denied, nor is the contribution to be made by criminal justice to transitional justice, especially in those countries whose economies are in transition and emerging from conflict. (Eleventh United Nations Congress on Crime Prevention and Criminal Justice, Bangkok, 18-25 April 2005).

One of the strategic goals of the Department of Justice and Constitutional Development (DOJCD)-the promotion of the rule of law and access to justice, includes building a restorative justice programme by adopting an integrated cluster approach to justice, crime prevention and security; necessitating the building of partnerships between state and non-state actors (government and civil society).

The cluster's main goal is to work towards a transformative approach to justice, crime prevention and security, 'by adopting a restorative justice approach, building and strengthening civil society organisations that promote, protect and advance human rights, particularly those giving special attention to the needs of the most vulnerable and marginalised' (DOJCD Policy Framework; DOJCD Medium Term Strategy Framework-2007-2013). In order to achieve the objectives outlined above, the department has adopted restorative justice as one of the 'result areas' under the theme 'Justice and the Rule of Law' where a whole host of strategic goals for the restorative justice sector are outlined such as; promoting community based alternative dispute resolution mechanisms to resolve civil disputes in communities, facilitating a protocol for engagement between justice and crime prevention cluster and civil society organisations working in the sector, facilitating education and training programmes in the field of restorative justice for communities and civil society, and facilitating programmes that will assist with building the capacity of civil society organisations.

Restorative approaches to justice have developed through practice, and will probably continue to do so. As a consequence, there is no single notion of restorative justice, no single type of process, no single theory (Ashworth, 2002:578). This paper provides and overview of areas of resonance between restorative justice and social work practice. Legal reform in South Africa has incorporated restorative justice approaches but is in many instances reliant on social workers for delivery of services pointing to the need for greater dialogue on the integration of restorative justice values, processes and outcomes into social work practice.

Restorative Justice and Social Work

Restorative justice is a flexible model varying from country to country and area to area depending on local needs and customs. Responses to crime that derive from restorative justice are usually embedded in a community context and of necessity involves individuals, families and community representatives in understanding the harm caused by the offending behaviour, the experiences of the victim, and together finding appropriate responses.

All forms of direct restorative communication between crime victims and offenders and facilitated by one or more third parties, fall under the umbrella term 'restorative justice conferencing' (Umbreit in Naude, 2006: 107). Shuttle mediation, a term adopted for indirect restorative mediation, opens up tremendous possibilities for victim impact panels, support groups, victim and offender empowerment and diversion. Consequently, the responsibility for seeking to repair harm and prevent future harm can be shared and includes the community; going beyond just the affected individuals.

Recent years have seen a plethora of policies, research initiatives, theorising, critical analyses and emerging restorative justice jurisprudence. One would therefore expect a great deal of involvement and commitment from all the relevant departments employing social workers (Department of Social Development, DOJCD and Department of Education) in the integration of restorative justice values into practice.

Common Values

Social work's dual focus-the well being of communities and individuals- makes it the ideal realm for the implementation of national policies and procedures relating to restorative justice. While social workers generally direct their activities towards innovative, creative initiatives and programmes that address the needs of people on the ground, core values of social work practice that resonate with restorative justice and include inter-alia: the role and importance of community, empowerment, social justice, service, respect for the dignity and worth of the person, human relationships and competence (van Wormer, 2003: 445).

Community

Sue King, in a paper presented to the Global Social Work Forum in 2004 highlighted the fact that while crime incidents may occur through the action and choice of individuals or small groups of individuals they nevertheless are 'shaped through a series of interactions within communities. Restorative processes provide an opportunity to focus not just on the isolated incident which caused the harm but also on the 'history and context of the incident'.

The term community in the restorative process refers to people who have been directly harmed by the offence. This 'community of care' includes anyone who feels connected, either directly or indirectly to the persons involved in the crime or the event itself (Schiff, 2007: 229). Micro-communities are networks of relationships in individual communities of care (not dependant on geography), comprising family members, friends and others with whom we have meaningful relationships. Macro-communities on the other hand, are groups not defined by geography or membership and have little or no significant emotional connection to any specific crime. From a micro-community perspective crime harms specific people where for example, the emotional pain experienced by family and friends can be intense):156-157 From the macro-community perspective crime creates aggregate harm and is not limited to specific individuals with the effect usually being a loss of public safety (McCold, 2004: 156-157).

Communities serve other important functions- by developing, communicating, influencing and upholding standards and norms of behaviour, including censuring of anti-social behaviour by those who fail to uphold the standards of collective living. Schiff (2007: 236) points out that this is difficult when members do not consider themselves as integrated members of any community and feel no obligation to live by its rules and regulations. Finally, communities are deemed to be responsible for developing a collective ownership of the problem of crime, by developing strong informal control mechanisms, sanctions and social support. Ultimately, this would require community members to build skills in responding to problems without relying exclusively on the criminal justice system. While agents of criminal justice (police, court, corrections) are trained to take responsibility for the preventing and responding to crime, it has inadvertently diminished the capacity of the community to handle its own problems.

However, critics argue that the individualised and privatised nature of contemporary industrial society makes it unlikely that interventions relying upon merely community based responses will be sustainable. Braithwaite's view is somewhat different.

...we consistently under-estimate the extent and variety of interdependencies in modern society. They exist, but are organised often on a non-geographical basis (Braithwaite in Newburn, 2007: 765).

Braithwaite and Daly's (1994: 208) 'domestic violence enforcement pyramid' assumes that communities will be condemnatory of the behaviour involved. In reality there is no guarantee that this will in fact be the case. Together with legal reforms that seek to address violence against women, other initiatives such as awareness raising and advocacy, female emancipation and the Bill of Rights has still not resulted in any significant drop in the rates of violence against women, whether in the private or public domain.

Even though restorative justice notions of community might be viewed simplistically, social work has a strong tradition with community work- viewing community not as a homogenous entity but rather as diverse and multi-plural. This places them in a strong position to engage in capacity building of communities. According to Walgrave (2002:75) community can be both 'a central resource in resolving conflict and at the same time be the focus for the exploration of causation of offending behaviour'.

Empowerment

In recent years governments have seen renewed interest in strengthening civil society and the belief that the best way to help vulnerable people is to empower them. The challenge for the practitioner is to overcome obstacles that arise from restorative justice interventions and meetings. This means taking the parties through 'an empowering process of consultation, discussion, venting and negotiation that eventually takes the parties to the point where reconciliation and healing' can happen. In the more difficult and serious cases the power of the restorative justice process is located in the ability to create and empower a community of caring supporters for both victims and offenders.

These will typically involves family members, friends, colleagues, neighbours, teachers, etc. (Barton, 2000:4)

Once involved, participants and their supporters can be empowered as a community to deal with both the causes and consequences of the incident in question and crime generally, thereby minimising the chances of recurring problems. Local problems are best addressed through local solutions. Braithwaite's book 'Restorative Justice and Responsive Regulation' offers a way of reconciling empowerment practice with coercion in which much social work takes place. The writer alludes to the regulatory pyramid where restorative justice practices form the basis of the pyramid with increasingly coercive, deterrent or incapacitating regulatory actions higher up. The role of the state is to constrain these self regulatory excesses in the community (harsh punishment) and safeguard the process.

Community empowerment can mean two things. Firstly, the community of primary stakeholders in the dispute-offender, victims, and their respective families, friends, neighbours, colleagues etc. and secondly, the community of secondary stakeholders refer to the wider community such as community representatives, and other professionals such social workers, polices officers, probation officers etc. Most restorative justice programmes consist of a mixture of participants from both categories.

Social workers may be directly or indirectly involved in court proceedings or may be in a position to influence legislation. Restorative justice is especially relevant in matters affecting children, parents and families' engagement with the criminal justice system but especially in matters affecting the well being of children.

However, the social work profession is not necessarily geared up or prepared for the dictates of the criminal justice system, especially since it often reinforces the view that somehow the victim is responsible for the crime having occurred in the first place (victim blaming). While the new emphasis redressing this imbalance has resulted in more vocal representation of victim's views, especially at the pre-sentence phase, families and communities that have been affected by the crime (secondary victims) have no voice at all.

Social Justice

Restorative justice has special relevance to the field of social work because social workers attend to cases where clients are invariably entangled with the criminal justice system. Two important and most commonly used restorative justice practices victim offender mediation and family group conferencing are widely used in situations involving youth and families. Strongly resonating with issues of social justice, restorative justice ideology is predicated on the principle of equal justice – just and fair treatment for both offender and victim. Traditional criminal justice processes invariably disempower or revictimise the victim with victims' interests being relegated to the periphery. The ethics of restorative justice can be undermined if there is bias towards any particular party; whether victims, offenders or communities. Victims may sometimes feel that they are being used instrumentally for example where restorative justice is part of a prison rehabilitation programme, or a diversion programme at the pre-trial stage. Other schemes might protect victims' rights but at the expense of offenders' rights. Hence it becomes imperative that all parties participate on an equal footing.

In the context of child justice, the role of social work is pivotal; not only during the arrest, assessment and preliminary inquiry phases but also prior to sentence and diversion. Social workers are called upon to facilitate family group conferences, prepare parties for the encounter, case follow-ups, monitor agreements, and develop and implement diversion programmes; all within a restorative justice framework. While countries use different criteria when it comes to referral of cases, proper screening and risk assessment are important to minimise risks involved and prevent offenders from exploiting the restorative justice process.

Restorative justice practices should ideally involve the use of trained facilitators/mediators. Usually mediators are drawn from a range of backgrounds, including justice, education and social welfare. However, social work practitioners who work at the interface between individual and community are especially well suited to utilise their skills not only as case workers and community workers to empower participants in restorative justice processes, but also to train community members outside disciplinary realms of social work practice on the goals and philosophy of restorative justice practice.

Key issues for social workers is the utilisation of co-facilitators; the nature and duration of follow-up victim-offender meetings; the use of victim-offender mediation for more serious offences including those where the offender has been incarcerated; facilitating victim offender mediation and community group conferencing prior to release from prison; and the implementation of victim-offender sessions in multi-cultural settings.

Dignity and Worth of the Person

The typically adversarial and combative atmosphere in a traditional court room stands in stark contrast to restorative justice meetings where parties are encouraged to maintain respect and dignity. Court ordered restorative justice processes at the post trial phase usually follows formal adjudication of guilt. At the pre-trial phase, the offender who acknowledges responsibility for his actions is able to engage in an informal, intense process which aims to delve into the wider, deep seated reasons for his offending behaviour, rarely occurring during a court process. The emphasis is on restoring the individual to the community. Most importantly the process gives victim a voice whereby concerns about personal safety are addressed.

Victim offender conferences and family group conferences, with their focus on truth telling and disclosure, are conducted with a primary focus on protection and support for the immediate and/or extended family unit.

Importance of Human Relationships

Restorative justice processes play and important role in drawing together young offenders and victims in a face to face setting such as a family group conference, where they are encouraged to participate which may in turn enhance the prevention of reoffending behaviour. Family group conferences or victim offender conferences include families and support persons with a facilitator/mediator to assist them. A great deal of emphasis is placed on the collaboration of key stakeholders: victim, offenders and community.

The family group conference brings together extended family members with professionals and others involved in the situation to assist the family in developing a plan to keep all its members safe. Partnership with the state allows for rights of participants to be protected and safeguarded while at the same time protecting the privacy of the family (Pennel and Burford, 2002).

The significance of restorative justice is especially relevant in the field of child welfare. The FGC with its unique 'social network-building aspects' is extremely well placed to make inclusive decisions which keep at the forefront the best interests of the child.

Competence

Social workers are considered extremely competent in their interaction with both victims and perpetrators. This is especially so in the context of vulnerable groups such as women, children, persons with mental illness and survivours of domestic violence.

Of particular relevance is the need for interdisciplinary teamwork whereby a holistic community based treatment plans may be devised. Community social workers are especially well placed to empower participants in restorative justice processes by 'widening their gaze from the individual to the social' (King, 2004:4).

Formal and informal helping

Recent literature on civil society and social capital, rebuilding neighbourhoods and communities and partnerships with families emphasise the importance of non-governmental organisations, social networks, trust and civic engagement for families, communities and democratic societies. There is indeed greater appreciation today of the incapacity of state institutions, including police and social workers, to provide for the support, care and empowerment needs of families and communities. Formal human services represent 'no more than a single strand in the complex web of relationships and services, formal and informal, statutory and non-statutory, which together provide care and control in the community. The overall effectiveness of provision depends not on one part of this network alone but on how well the whole is woven together' (Hadley et al in Burford, 2004: 2).

Pulled in different and competing directions restorative justice is largely shaped by the interests of government and non-governmental groups, professions, theories and ideologies. The overarching question facing practitioners is how to balance empowering processes with safeguarding the rights of individuals; and in turn allow for solutions to emerge from the participants themselves?

Recent South African Developments

African indigenous systems, which generally acknowledge and affirm elements of restorative justice, have greatly influenced the growth of modern restorative justice. The growing worldwide popularity of restorative justice coincided with the campaign for new child justice and child welfare legislation and creation of the new democratic South African state. This has allowed the principles of restorative justice to become embedded both within and alongside the criminal justice system (Skelton, 2007: 228).

Community based non-governmental organisations (NGOs), referred to as service providers, currently offer restorative justice programmes through partnership/collaborative agreements with the Criminal Justice System (Department of Justice, National Prosecuting Authority, Department of Correctional Services and Department of Social Development).

The Child Justice Act defines restorative justice as:

An approach to justice that aims to involve the child offender, the victim, the families concerned and community members to collectively identify and address harms, needs and obligations through accepting responsibility, making restitution, taking measures to prevent a recurrence of the incident...'

The Act provides for a restorative approach to be taken at one of two points: either as a means of diverting a child from the criminal justice process altogether at the pre-trial stage; or after conviction, as an alternative to a custodial sentence.

Probation Services Act 116 of 1991 (as amended by Act 35 of 2002) defines restorative justice as:

The promotion of reconciliation, restitution and responsibility through the involvement of a child, and the child's parents, family members, victims and the communities...

The Act details the powers, functions and duties of probation officers who are generally social workers appointed specifically to render probation services prescribed by this act or any other law; the establishment and implementation of programmes aimed at combating crime; and the rendering of assistance to and treatment of certain persons involved in crime and related matters.

Probation services are integral to the management of children in conflict with the law and play an important role in transforming the child justice system.

Not only are these services important once the child enters the criminal justice system; they are also critical to prevention of crime and recidivism among young offenders and have long term benefits for young offenders, their victims and communities, and society in general. It is the probation services that devise the most appropriate recommendations before the matter of an alleged child offender goes to trial, and then assist the child offender to become a rehabilitated and responsible citizen.

In the South African context then, for restorative justice interventions to be effective in the case of 'juveniles', strengthening of family and community bonds is a key factor. In addition to families, parents, communities and support persons, other surrogate regulators such as NGOs providing mediation and conferencing services, are extremely crucial to the child justice process.

The Children's Act 38 of 2005 contains a range of provisions relating to the protection of children including the identification of children in need of care, Children's Courts, and specific orders that may be made by these courts. Restorative approaches and processes, which are non-confrontational and 'conducive to conciliation and problem solving', are specifically favoured; keeping the best interest of the child, paramount. Only a brief description of some specifically 'restorative' provisions is discussed. Before deciding on a matter or issue, the court may order a lay forum hearing in an attempt to settle the matter or issue out of court (Section 49 (1)). Hearings may include mediation by a family advocate, social worker, social service professional or other suitably qualified person; a family group conference (S

70); or mediation (S 71); keeping in mind all the relevant factors, including the vulnerability of the child, the ability of the child to participate, the power relationships in the family, and the nature of the allegations made by the parties in the matter (Section 49 (2) (a-d)).

In line with the general principles above, child protection orders may include an order 'instructing a parent or care-giver of a child to undergo professional counselling, or to participate in mediation, a family group conference, or other problem solving forum (Section 46 (1) (h) (iii)).

Part 3 pays particular attention to various. restorative justice approaches, including; pre-hearing conferences, family group conferences, other lay forums (including a traditional authority), and settling matters out of court. However, pre-hearing conferences and other lay forums are specifically excluded for matters involving the alleged abuse or sexual abuse of the child (Section 69 (2) and S 71 (2).

Additional legislative safeguards relate to the holding of pre-hearing conferences and procedures regulating such conferences (Section 75 (1) (d); the holding and monitoring of family group conferences or other lay forums; procedures regulating such conferences and other lay forums (Section 75 (1) (e)); and the qualifications and experience of persons facilitating family group conferences, including special requirements that apply to persons facilitating in matters involving the alleged abuse of children (Section 75 (1) (f)).

Recommendations

Training

Good initial training is essential in evolving, refining and maintaining good practice. The onus is on those entrusted with the implementation of the programme to establish best practice and no one should be allowed to practice until they demonstrate minimum standards of competency in meeting preparation and facilitation. Social work curricula should be revisited to include the development of competency in mediation, conference specific facilitation techniques etc for those who opt for this career path. Policies and actual restorative justice interventions need to ultimately make a positive difference for the primary stakeholders.

There is currently substantial involvement of social workers, both state and non-state, in instances where offenders are diverted to restorative justice processes at the pretrial stage. The Department of Social Development (social workers) is an important role-player in the implementation of restorative practices in the courts. The duties of the social worker includes screening of cases, assessment, monitoring of non-custodial sanctions, setting-up and managing an accurate information management system, proper monitoring and evaluation of processes, and maintaining the link between the courts, victims, offenders and service providers.

Notwithstanding the important role social workers play in the domain of restorative justice, there is a critical shortage of social workers due to their paltry salaries and migration to other countries and the private sector. Burdened with innumerable social problems – from an increase in teenage pregnancies, abandoned children, growing number of AIDS orphans to an increase in substance abuse with a consequent a rise in domestic violence and crimes such as rape and theft, social workers have traditionally not placed much emphasis on restorative justice values, processes and outcomes as a paradigm to inform their practice (*The Sunday Times Newspaper*: *28 October 2007*).

Training and capacity building of social workers in the specialised interventions related to restorative justice remains a cause for concern. The current dependence on community based NGO service providers who make widespread use of volunteers, further emphasises the need for a broad based, dedicated training and capacity building agenda. It is recommended that a multi-disciplinary panel be set up to drive this process. The spectre of secondary victimisation of participants in cases where the process has not been properly managed is a possibility that cannot be ignored. As restorative justice processes become more 'popular' the likelihood of legal and constitutional challenges must be acknowledged.

The criminal justice system might be compelled to look elsewhere to increase their pool of facilitators/coordinators and mediators for restorative justice processes.

Additional human capital such as criminologists and paralegals can serve as an ideal group for the administration and management of restorative justice processes at the courts. Their functions could include; assessment and screening of potential participants, setting-up victim offender mediation or conferences and family group conferences, follow-up reports to courts on whether conditions and/or agreements have been adhered to, reports on compliance or non-compliance of conditions of non-custodial sentences, manage victim services and community participation services, provide information and court preparation to all court users, and liaise between victim, courts, and other stakeholders.

Mobilising Community and State

State-community partnerships would need to be strengthened for restorative approaches to criminal justice to be fully adopted. This can be achieved by developing and maintaining forums to discuss crime and its impact, identifying and communicating normative standards of collective living, conveying censure when norms have been violated, developing collective ownership of crime, engaging communities in a combined response to crime, creating safe environments, informing communities about services and resources for victims, developing collective capacity to resolve problems with or without government intervention and creating re-integrative strategies for both victims and offenders. To this end the participation of existing community or traditional structures may be considered over and above the usual media campaigns.

Specific state responsibilities under a restorative justice framework include addressing victims' needs irrespective of offender status (parallel justice mentioned above). Related to the greater use of referrals to restorative justice processes at various stages in the criminal justice process, is the need for the state to take responsibility for the following initiatives:

- Supporting offenders who take responsibility for their actions by the provision of appropriate programmes to prevent re-offending.
- Providing skills development and employment opportunities.

- Creating strong and consistent re-integrative resources for offenders.
- Strengthening resources for non-custodial sentences.
- Developing and accrediting mediation and conferencing programmes.
- Training of criminal justice and allied personnel in the use of these programmes and partnership working.
- Facilitating community partnerships and consultation.
- Researching and monitoring of new developments to inform their gradual improvement.
- Developing judicial oversight of processes, agreements and outcomes.
- Instituting complaints mechanisms for individual participants.
- Promoting public education to ensure an understanding of the reforms and their rationale.
- Initiating phased programmes to enable assessment, monitoring and evaluation and the formulation of minimum standards.
- Expanding the discussion on restorative approaches to sentencing.
- Longitudinal studies of those who have been through restorative justice processes with proper comparative controls with court processes cases.

Community policing forums can serve as the most appropriate structure to support and monitor the effective functioning of non-custodial sanctions, where community buy-in and participation is crucial, especially for the monitoring of these offenders.

What is needed is not simply to devolve responsibility to the community, 'but rather to transform the work of justice professionals from 'expert' service providers, to supporters of community and citizen driven restorative responses' (Schiff, 2007: 238). Criminal justice reform cannot proceed without the active support of the community. This is particularly true for reforms such as the greater use of diversion, alternate dispute resolution mechanisms and restorative initiatives in general. However, engaging the public would require a great deal of investment in awareness raising campaigns. The media can play an important role in influencing community and state involvement in restorative processes.

Conclusion

Community building, peace building and community participation are the overarching goals of restorative justice. An understanding of the needs of the communities as well as their assets can provide an important foundational component; especially relevant to many marginalised and victimised communities in need of healing. However, power hierarchies, political agendas and community dynamics will have to be considered carefully before fully involving community members.

Clearly the agenda for implementation and strengthening of restorative practices in the criminal justice system has to go hand in hand with services for victims, for which many policies already exist. There is no advantage in imposing a single centralised model from the outset, since the pace of development should be sensitive to the need for gradual readjustment in the mindset of criminal justice personnel and public attitudes.

The restorative justice agenda continues to be shaped by criminal justice due in part to the fact that the latter remains in control of case selection and case definition. While to date the focus has been on the processing of individual cases, restorative approaches present communities with a 'window of opportunity' to create and build local knowledge about the causes and conditions of crime and conflict thereby encouraging the development of ideas on how 'generic problems, collective disadvantages and issues of social inequalities can be approached'. A number of scholars lament the fact that restorative justice programmes 'show little concern for or have demonstrated little capacity to forge such a link between individual cases and more structural problems' (Froestad and Shearing, 2007: 537).

Ultimately, restorative justice requires a positive orientation- an open mind and an interest by victims, offenders and the community to engage in the process. Indeed, South Africa is a prime example where a 'more future-oriented transformative' would go a long way towards integration of restorative justice values, processes and outcomes into services for victims, offenders and communities.

References

Ashworth A (2002) Responsibilities, rights and restorative justice, *British Journal of Criminology*, (42), pp. 578-95.

Braithwaite J and Daly K (1994) 'Masculinities, violence and communitarian control', in Newburn T. and Stanki E. A. (eds.) *Just Boys Doing Business: masculinities and crime*, Routledge, London.

Burford G. (2004) Restorative justice, responsive regulation and social work, *Journal of Sociology and Social Welfare*, March 2004, accessed at http://findarticles.com/p/articles.

Crawford A. (2007) Situating restorative youth justice in crime control and prevention, *Acta Juridica*, pp. 1-21.

Department of Justice and Constitutional Development Policy Framework; DOJCD Medium Term Strategy Framework: 2007-2013.

Eleventh United Nations Congress on Crime Prevention and Criminal Justice, Bangkok, 18-25 April 2005 accessed at http://www.daccessdds.un.org/doc/UNDOC/GEN/VO5/809/79/PDF.

Froestad J. and Shearing C (2007) Conflict Resolution in South Africa: a case study, in Johnstone G. and Van Ness D. W. (eds.) *Handbook of Restorative Justice*, Willan Publishing, Cullompton.

King S. (2004) Paper presented to the Global Social work Conference, October 2004 accessed at www.restorativejustice.org/resources/docs/king.

McCold P. (2004) What is the Role of Community In Restorative Justice Theory and Practice in Zehr H. and Toews B. (eds.) *Critical Issues in Restorative Justice*, Criminal Justice Press, New York.

Naude B. Prinsloo J and Ladikos A (2003) 'Restorative Mediation Practices', Acta *Criminologica*, 16 (5) pp. 10-11.

Naude B. (2006) An International perspective of restorative justice practices and research outcomes, *Journal of Juridical Sciences*, 31(1): pp. 101-120.

Pennel J. and Burford G. (2002) Feminist praxis: Making family group conferencing work in Strang H. and Braithwaite J. (eds.) *Restorative justice and family violence* (108-127) New York: Cambridge University Press.

Pranis K. (2007) Restorative values, in Johnstone G and Van Ness D W (eds) *Handbook of Restorative Justice*, Willan Publishing, Cullompton.

Schiff M. (2007) Satisfying the needs and interests of stakeholders, in Johnstone G and Van Ness D. W. (eds.) *Handbook of Restorative Justice*, Willan Publishing, Cullompton.

Skelton A. (2002) Restorative justice as a framework for juvenile justice reform-A South African Perspective, *British Journal of Criminology*, 42: 496-513.

Skelton A. (2007) Tapping indigenous knowledge: traditional conflict resolution, restorative justice and the denunciation of crime in South Africa, *Acta Juridica,* 2007, pp. 228-243.

Van Wormer K. (2003) Restorative Justice: A Model for Social Work Practice with Families, *The Journal of Cotemporary Human Services* accessed at www.familiesinsociety.org on 30 December, 2008.

Walgrave L. (2002) From community to dominion: in search of social values for restorative justice, in Weitekamp E. G. and Kerner H. J., *Restorative Justice: Theoretical Foundations,* Portland, Oregan, Willan Publishers.

10

RETHINKING UNTHINKABLE TEACHING PRACTICES IN CRIMINOLOGY!

P. Madhava Soma Sundaram

In a time of rapid change, when global forces are re-shaping the ability of ordinary people to influence the decisions which affect their lives, Criminologists are challenged to learn new skills and competences, and to develop their capacities for learning through critical reflection on action. Those who think and see the world differently find it harder to make themselves heard, whilst institutions that claim to advance teaching and learning in turn become purveyors of information and propagators of knowledge that fits within existing paradigms (Taylor, Deak, Pettit and Vogel, 2006). Much 'learning' on offer in a formal way, for example in, colleges and universities, is didactic, rote, top-down and therefore does not lead to the kind of social change desired by the activists (Bawden, 2004; Mott, 2005).

Knowledge and the process of learning are shaped by power relations, and the institutions and forums where teaching takes place tend to reinforce the relationship between power and learning – a relationship that often is asymmetrical. Also the content of these learning experiences is often narrow – perhaps dealing with skills, methods or theory, but rarely integrating the personal, conceptual, organisational and methodological dimensions of learning. Many courses are not sufficiently action-oriented, do not consciously address solving issues, are disconnected from experience, or fail to explore the self in a deeply reflective way. Many learning experiences are not grounded within a sound conceptual understanding of social change processes, and the depth and scope for learning are limited. The purpose of this chapter is to re-examine some widely accepted ideas about conventional criminology teaching and learning and to question whether current organisational patterns in criminology education supports student learning and development in today's environment. The need to do so is clear: few of the social, economic, cultural, political, and pedagogical conditions and assumptions that framed the structures and methods of our modern universities remain unchanged.

One of the most enduring recommendations in learning literature about the teaching of evaluation is that students receive hands-on or practical experiences during their education. This recommendation has been periodically but consistently made since the early 1970s. For example, Hargreaves et al., (1978) recommend specialised training in community mental health evaluation that includes a strong component of supervised, practical evaluation experience for students.

Sanders (1986) suggest that hands-on evaluation experiences could be part of pre-service programmes in education, such as programs for the training of administrators, school counselors, and teachers. Chelimsky (1997) called for the realistic training of evaluators that includes hands-on experiences, in addition to didactic course work. While few details were offered in these recommendations, these ideas are part of a consistent theme in the teaching of evaluation: to include practical training for students.

The argument for this recommendation is that practical experiences should be part of the training for any practice-oriented field, like criminology and allied subjects (Altschuld, 1995; Fitzpatrick, 1994). These practical experiences provide students with exposure to the intricacies of conducting evaluation in real-world settings. Issues that can be experienced in practical training include:

- Negotiating within an organisation
- Handling incomplete data
- Dealing with clients who don't communicate well and
- Thinking creatively and flexibly because of resource, organisational, or political constraints (Chelimsky, 1997; Cronbach et al., 1980).

Proponents argue that understanding of and appreciation for these issues will more likely come from practical experience, rather than simply from reading about these issues in textbooks or discussing these issues in class (Chelimsky, 1997; Davis, 1986; Morris, 1994). Note that these issues include both technical (e.g., handling missing data) and non-technical (e.g., dealing with clients who don't communicate well) aspects of a profession. Trevisan (2002) argues that for non-technical issues in particular, practical experiences may be the only way for students to effectively learn, understand, and appreciate the challenges in such aspects of evaluation work.

Related to the argument for practical evaluation training experiences for students, are calls for these experiences based on findings from the adult education literature. This literature shows increased educational outcomes for adult students when they learn concepts and strategies within the context of practical experiences (Preskill, 1997). The reason is that adult students have accumulated experiences, work-related and other, and have often acquired the capacity and preference to learn through these experiences. Practical training that incorporates hands-on experiences capitalises on this phenomenon.

Teaching Criminology

Academic criminology is only the best-elaborated and most scientific sector of a discourse that includes everything from the working categories of penal institutions to the crime images that circulate in common sense, popular culture and news papers. Criminology is not just a creature of the academics. It is also located in other social and institutional settings and these other settings have shaped much of its development. To simplify a complex picture one could say that criminology is inscribed in three major social settings or matrices (Garland and Sparks, 2000). It is located in:

- The world of the academics—of social science and scholarly discourse,
- The world of government—of crime control and criminal justice, and
- The world of culture— including mass mediated popular culture and political discourse.

Since the expansion of the academics in the late 1960s, criminology has been a focal point for most of the intellectual currents of the last four decades: Marxism, feminism, post-structuralism, postmodernism, all the strands of sociology, social psychology and cultural studies, not to mention occasional incursions from life sciences, Bio-technology, genetics and neurobiology—incursions that will in all likelihood increase in frequency and insistence in the near future. It has seen grand theory and focused empiricism, radical critiques, consultancy work and policy-driven inquiries. Criminology is a 'rendezvous subject', as there has been a great crowd of varying types of people meeting up and passing through, sometimes establishing fruitful exchanges, sometimes merely rubbing shoulders in the crowded passages of textbooks and conferences (Garland and Sparks, 2000).

Contemporary criminology inhabits a rapidly changing world. The speed and profundity of these changes are echoed in the rapidly changing character of criminology's contents, it includes, in crime rates, in crime policy, and in the practices of policing, governance, prevention and punishment. If one looks beyond the immediate data of crime and punishment to the processes that underpin them—to routines of social life and social control, the circulation of money and persons, the organisation of families and households, the spatial ecology of cities, the character of work and labour markets, the power of state authorities—it becomes apparent that criminology's subject matter is centrally implicated in the major transformations at this time. There are now numerous works that summarise and analyse the competing schools of criminological thought (see, for example, Kornhauser, 1978; Cullen, 1984; Pfohl, 1985; Liska and Messner, 1999; Vold et al., 2002; Akers and Sellers, 2004; Cullen and Agnew, 2006; Lilly et al., 2006). This body of literature makes the invaluable contribution of tracing the formal intellectual linkages within and among theoretical traditions, of evaluating the consistency of each tradition's internal logic and of assessing how well theoretical assertions survive the scrutiny of available empirical evidence. In deriving their claims, however, the typical accounts of criminological frameworks suffer the limitations inherent in a research approach to theory that relies predominantly, if not exclusively, on the analysis of published works.

Imparting criminological knowledge to the students both at the graduate level and at the master's level is a difficult process.

Many Criminology programs, both at graduate and master's level, lack evaluation, relying heavily upon research methods or informal training. The few courses that are taught, however, often employ traditional instructional methods, such as lectures and reading lists. It is argued that these modes of teaching are not appropriate for building the skills necessary, nor do they foster deep understandings of theoretical perspectives. Moreover, many contemporary students prefer to develop knowledge through doing rather than sitting and listening. In such cases, doing typically refers to Participatory learning Methodology, where students learn experientially. This represents an intentional restructuring of the students' learning experiences to foster more explicit intellectual connections among students and between students and faculty. This is compatible with the adult learning literature in which it is noted "action begets learning" (Cavaliere and Sgroi, 1992). John Dewey's notion of learning by doing established a methodology of instruction promoted by adult learning scholars suggesting that social and intellectual skills come to the learner through situations characterised by interactivity, not isolation (Carr, 1992).

However, when teaching a theory course that takes place over a limited period of time (an academic year or semester), the approach of participatory techniques in curriculum presents limitations. For instance, there are time constraints and logistical concerns. Arranging appointments with experts (panel discussion), preparing students (role play), and multiple follow-up meetings to focus the evaluation can be enormously time consuming.

Adult Learning Principles

Transfer of knowledge, at the master's level, especially in subjects like criminology, involves understanding how adults learn best. Compared to younger children and teens, adults have special needs and requirements as learners. The field of adult learning was pioneered by Malcom Knowles (1990). He identified the following characteristics of adult learners:

- Adults are autonomous and self-directed. They need to be free to direct themselves. Their teachers must actively involve adult participants in the learning process and serve as facilitators for them. Specifically, they must get students' perspectives about what topics to cover and let them work on projects that reflect their interests. They should allow the participants to assume responsibility for presentations and group leadership. They have to be sure to act as facilitators, guiding participants to their own knowledge rather than supplying them with facts. Finally, they must show participants how the class will help them reach their goals.

- Adults have accumulated a foundation of life experiences and knowledge that may include work-related activities, family responsibilities, and previous education. They need to connect learning to this knowledge/experience base. To help them do so, they should draw out participants' experience and knowledge which is relevant to the topic. They must relate theories and concepts to the participants and recognise the value of experience in learning.
- Adults are goal-oriented. Upon enrolling in a course, they usually know what goal they want to attain. They, therefore, appreciate an educational program that is organised and has clearly defined elements. Instructors must show participants how this class will help them attain their goals. This classification of goals and course objectives must be done early in the course.
- Adults are relevancy-oriented. They must see a reason for learning something. Learning has to be applicable to their work or other responsibilities to be of value to them. Therefore, instructors must identify objectives for adult participants before the course begins. This means, also, that theories and concepts must be related to a setting familiar to participants. This need can be fulfilled by letting participants choose projects that reflect their own interests.
- Adults are practical, focusing on the aspects of a lesson most useful to them in their work. They may not be interested in knowledge for its own sake. Instructors must tell participants explicitly how the lesson will be useful to them on the job.
- As do all learners, adults need to be shown respect. Instructors must acknowledge the wealth of experiences

that adult participants bring to the classroom. These adults should be treated as equals in experience and knowledge and allowed to voice their opinions freely in class.

Kolb (1984) provides one of the most useful descriptive models available of the adult learning process.

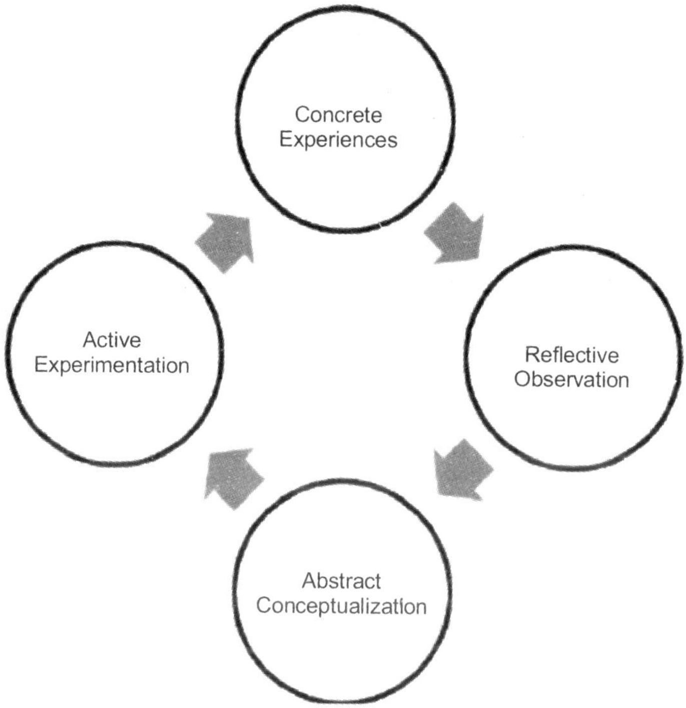

Fig. 1. Adult Learning Process.

—Adopted from Kolb (1984)

This suggests that there are four stages in learning which follow from each other: Concrete Experience is followed by Reflection on that experience on a personal basis.

This may then be followed by the derivation of general rules describing the experience, or the application of known theories to it (Abstract Conceptualisation), and hence to the construction of ways of modifying the next occurrence of the experience (Active Experimentation), leading in turn to the next Concrete Experience. All this may happen in a flash, or over a period of time, depending on the topic, and there may be a "wheels within wheels" process at the same time.

Honey and Mumford (1982) have built a typology of Learning Styles around this sequence, identifying individual preferences for each stage (Activist, Reflector, Theorist, and Pragmatist respectively); Kolb also has a test instrument (the Learning Style Inventory) but has carried it further by relating the process also to forms of knowledge. Learning styles mean that:

- At a minor level there is a need for adjustment between learner and teacher: sometimes their preferences are complementary, sometimes antagonistic, and ofcourse sometimes collusive if they both tend to go for the same stages in the cycle.
- At a major level, neglect of some stages can prove to be a major obstacle to learning.
- At a really serious level, teachers are easy to con with plausible clichés.

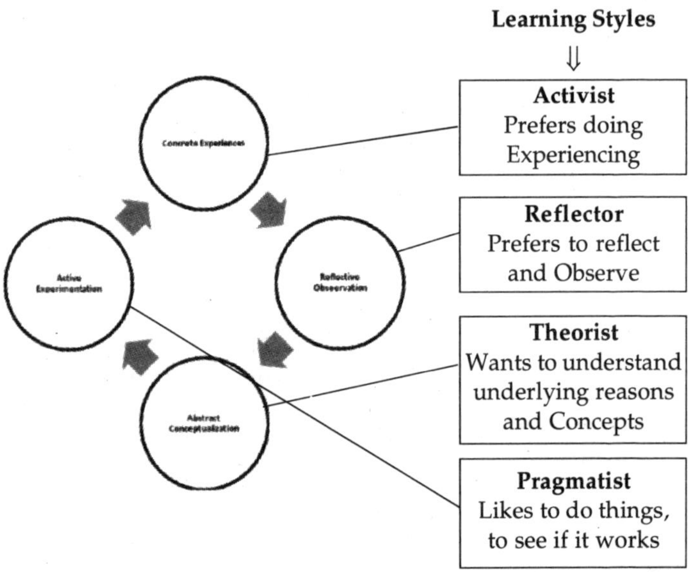

Fig. 2. Adult Learning Process.

— ***Adopted from Honey and Mumford (1982)***

The reasons most adults enter any learning experience is to create change. This could encompass a change in:

- Their skills
- Behavior
- Knowledge level or
- Even their attitudes about things

Motivation

Adults learn best when convinced of the need for knowing the information. This plays an important role in any learning situation. Many times, a life experience or situation stimulates the motivation to learn (O'Brien, 2004). Meaningful learning can be intrinsically motivating. The key to using adults' "natural" motivation to learn is tapping into their most teachable moments (Zemke and Zemke, 1995). Lieb (1991) described six factors which serve as sources of motivation for adult learning:

- Social relationships
- External expectations
- Social welfare
- Personal advancement
- Escape/Stimulation
- Cognitive interest

Providing a challenge to the learner without causing frustration is additionally important. Above all, provide feedback and positive reinforcement about what has been learned (Lieb, 1991).

Experience

Adults have a greater depth, breadth, and variation in the quality of previous life experiences than younger people (O'Brien, 2004). Past educational or work experiences may color or bias the student's perceived ideas about how education will occur. If successfully guided in the learning environment, former experiences can assist the adult to connect the current learning experience to something learned in the past. This may also facilitate in making the learning experience more meaningful. However, past experiences may actually make the task harder if these biases are not recognised as being present by the teacher. This would be an opportune time to address any erroneous or preconceived ideas.

Level of Engagement

Rogers (1969) illustrated that when an adult learner has control over the nature, timing, and direction of the learning process, the entire experience is facilitated. Adults have a need to be self-directed, deciding for themselves what they want to learn. They enter into the learning process with a goal in mind and generally take a leadership role in their learning. The challenge for teachers is to be encouraging to the learner but also reinforce the process of learning. The endpoint of learning cannot always occur quickly or on a pre-set timeline.

Adults learn best when:

- Their prior learning is appreciated and/or rewarded
- The subject matter is relevant to their needs (professional or other)
- Full of partial opportunity for self direction is provided
- They can employ critical reflection
- Mistakes are seen as opportunities to learn
- The instruction provides opportunity for interaction
- Dialog is part of the learning
- Practical/hand-on experience is part of the learning

Constructing Experiential Learning for Criminology Courses

Criminology teaching has always been through the teaching of subjects like, laws, policing, forensic medicine, forensic sciences, human rights, and contemporary forms of crimes. Generally, it includes the process of lecturing, by a teacher, for a fixed period. Audio visual methods may be used by the teacher, if available. Apart from this the students are taken on field visits to institutions that interface with the criminal justice system, like the police, prisons and the like. Some curricula's also provide for case studies and internship, by the students for a fixed time, where they work in institutions learning the nuances of the job.

Experiential learning methods like group discussions, role play are rarely used by teachers for imparting criminological inputs to their students. Participatory methods, when used among students, has electrifying effect on them, and they also contribute to the deliberations in the class, which otherwise will generally be non participative. Some of the experiential learning methods that can be adopted in criminology class rooms are:

- Lecture
- Chalk and talk
- Demonstration
- Dramatic Presentation
- Discussion
  - — Structured or unstructured
  - — Group or plenary
- Buzz Group
- Fish Bowl
- Brainstorming
- Mind mapping (similar to brainstorming specifying the most important/ priority issues Overview of Participatory Learning)
- Expert panel / panel discussion
- Role play
- Simulation
- Games
- Problem solving (Synchronous or asynchronous problem solving are valid approaches depending on the subject matter)
- Case study/Analysis
- Debate/Discussion
- Class room seminar/workshop
- Short Education tour
- Practical exposure
- Assignment
- Peer teaching
- Individual or group projects

Role Play and Criminology Training

Role plays could play an important role in criminology teaching. This technique brings out the cybernetics between the offender and the victim and the like. This method makes the students to understand the feelings of the victims at the emotional level. In capacity building sessions of criminal justice professionals, this method restructures the orientation of the individual, at the attitudinal level. Participants assume a "role", that is, they play a part (either their own or someone else's) in a specific situation/ scenario. "Play" means that the role is taken on in a safe environment where participants can express their views in creative ways. To further understand the definition of role-play, one should distinguish between role-play and simulation, although that some argue that such a fine distinction is unnecessary. The use of role-play as an educational or training technique is considered to be part of a wider set of techniques that have collectively become known as simulation. Simulations are complex, lengthy and relatively inflexible events, yet they always include an element of role-play. Role-play, on the other hand, can be a simple, brief technique, easily organised. Role-play is highly flexible, leaving much more room for the demonstration of individual variation, initiative, and imagination (Ladousse, 1987). Both, however, take an approach to learning that is fundamentally different from other teaching methods found in most institutions. The key difference is the emphasis on experiencing the course as opposed to simply being lectured to. Role-play promotes interaction in the classroom and peer learning, which increases motivation (Livingstone, 1983). Classrooms that utilise role-play tend to create environments that are less anxious and fearful. This, in turn, helps to create a classroom characterised by "community sharing" (Adams, 1973). That is to say, students more readily share their ideas and thinking. Because of the lack of anxiety and increased motivation, students tend to experiment more broadly. Instructors, also act as participants in role-play, rather than simply observing it. Thus, when role-play is a core element of a course, learning is more easily promoted.

Role-playing is most commonly used in situations dealing with attitudes and feelings, for example, to replicate the feelings of someone in a particular social situation. Role-play can also be a tool for cognitive development, although it is not used frequently in this manner. It is also used to develop skills such as coaching, listening and conflict resolution. In the context of teaching, the purpose of role-play in the course differs slightly from that of the theory course. A common aim of both is to train participants to think on their feet. For the procedures course, it is also to learn how to handle situations as they unravel—a useful dress rehearsal for real life. For the theory course, the aim is to move beyond the simple regurgitation of readings by developing advanced understandings of difficult theoretical notions through communication. Various forms of role play are:

> **Sequential role** plays allow the observing participants to tap a role player on the shoulder and step into that role. The action does not stop, but continues with one or more new players. Sometimes an observing participant will clap to indicate that he or she wishes to step into a role. Sequential role plays are often used in complicated situations where a quick resolution of an issue is not possible, or where a number of options might be considered.
>
> **Multiple role** plays allow all participants to practice at the same time. These are sometimes done in trios, with two participants playing the designated roles, and the third person being an observer. After a few minutes of action, the facilitator calls time, and the observer leads a discussion in the trio using questions provided. Roles are then rotated, and each person plays a different role. After the second discussion, roles are rotated one more time. After the final small group discussion, the whole group discusses the experience, with the facilitator bringing up key points.

Experimentation on Criminology Curriculum

Experiential Education in a criminology curriculum should be used to amplify academically related aspects with work experience. In addition to preparing students for examinations, criminology teachers are to prepare students for the complex issues they will encounter in their workplace. Keeping this in view, a draft syllabus with experiential inputs have been prepared for the Graduate course. This syllabus included such activities as practica, cooperative learning, and student teaching. It provides a bridge between learning in the classroom and learning on the job.

The syllabi included a brief note on experiential learning and certain useful information to the teachers, including a reading list on experiential learning. Some of the highlights of this syllabus were:

- The teaching methodology adopted for the course utilized participatory learning methods, like workshops, discussions, assignments, short education tours, seminars, peer teaching, and group work, apart from regular lectures.
- The syllabus indicated the type of teaching method, to be adopted for a particular topic, in the footnote of the same page.
- The method suggested was only recommendatory; the concerned course teacher had the option to use other methods or a combination of any other methods, to improve the quality of knowledge transfer and attitude building.
- Course teachers adopting participatory teaching methods were asked to take extra care on the following issues:
  - — To set a brief, clear task rather than lecturing
  - — To use hands-on, multi-sensory materials rather than rely only on verbal communication
  - — To create an informal, relaxed atmosphere
  - — To choose growth-producing activities Evoke feelings, beliefs, needs, doubts, perceptions, aspirations
  - — To encourage creativity, analysis, planning, and
  - — To decentralise decision-making

The following details of some contemporary techniques that may be followed by course teachers, for the criminology teaching were suggested.

Brainstorming

Brainstorming is a familiar technique in which the teacher asks a specific question or describes a particular scenario, and students offer many different ideas. These ideas are then usually written on a flipchart or chalkboard and considered for further discussion. One of the modified versions of this technique is called mind mapping.

Case Studies

A case study is a written scenario that usually involves an important community situation. Since it is written beforehand, it can be specifically created to address relevant local issues. Variations to this method include:

Best Practices: Often, case studies are not made up, but are drawn from real situations in the community or in similar communities. For example, case studies might involve a description of a programme that has been particularly successful or has met specific challenges in another area, so that participants benefit from the lessons learned.

Simulations: A more complicated version of the case study is a simulation. This activity is usually presented in steps—with participants receiving some information, working on the data, making decisions, and processing the findings. Then, the facilitator provides additional information or the next steps in a scenario, and the groups go back to work with these new data.

Demonstrations/Practical Exposure

A demonstration is a structured performance of an activity to show, rather than simply tell, a group how the activity is done. This method brings to life some information that you may have already presented in a lecture.

Dramatisation

A dramatisation is a carefully scripted play where the characters act out a scene related to a learning situation. It is designed to bring out the important issues to be discussed or messages to be learned.

Fish bowl

In a fishbowl discussion, most of the students sit in a large circle, while a smaller group of students sits inside the circle. The fishbowl can be used in two distinct ways:

- As a structured brainstorming session: Choose a specific topic based on the group's needs or interests. A handful of seats are placed inside a larger circle. Students who have something to say about the topic at hand sit in the center. Anyone sitting inside the fishbowl can make a comment, offer information, respond to someone else in the center, or ask a question. When someone from the outside circle has a point to make, he or she taps the shoulder of someone in the center and takes that person's seat. This continues, with people from the outside tapping and replacing people on the inside, as a lively brainstorm takes place. You will need to process the many ideas after the fishbowl exercise.

- For structured observation of a group process: Students in the fishbowl are given a specific task to do, while students outside the fishbowl act as observers of the group process. The inner group works on its task together, and the outer group is asked to note specific behaviours. To process the activity, ask the inner group to reflect on the group process, and ask the outer group to describe what they observed.

Games

Games are appropriate participatory tools when they are used to encourage students to take charge of their own learning, and to test and reinforce new knowledge or skills. Adapt a popular game to convey or test knowledge of a particular topic, or create a new game to test or reinforce learning. Divide the students into groups, if necessary, to play the games. Use games after information has already been shared using another method (e.g., lecturette, demonstration, jigsaw learning, etc.) or to assess students' knowledge at the start of a learning activity.

Jigsaw Learning

In a jigsaw activity, evenly divided groups are given a topic to learn (a piece of the puzzle to master). Once these small groups have mastered the content, the groups are reorganised so that each new group contains one member from each original group (now each group contains all essential pieces of the puzzle to put together). Each new group now contains an "expert" on the content that they have mastered in the original groups, and one at a time, each expert teaches the new content to the newly formed groups. The teacher then processes the activity and emphasises key learning.

Lecturette

A lecturette is a short, oral presentation of facts or theory. No more than 15-20 minutes in length, the goal of a lecturette is to impart information in a direct, highly organised fashion. The course teacher presents knowledge on a topic, sometimes using flipcharts, computer software presentations or other media to guide the discussion. Variations of this method include:

Best Summary: Each student prepares a summary of the main points at the end of a presentation. Teams of students switch their summaries and select the best summary from each set. To use this technique, the teacher stops the lecture at appropriate intervals. Ask students to write a summary of the content presented so far. Organise students into equal-sized teams. Redistribute summaries from one team to the next one. Ask each team to collaboratively identify the best summary among those given to them—and read it.

Essence: Students write several summaries of a lecture, repeatedly reducing its length. Ask students to listen carefully to the presentation and take notes. After the presentation, teams prepare a 32-word summary of the lecture. Listen to each team's summary and select the best one. Now ask teams to rewrite the summary in exactly 16 words, retaining the key ideas and borrowing thoughts and words from other teams' earlier summaries. Repeat the process three more times, asking teams to reduce the length of the summary to eight, four and then two words. Finally, ask each student to write an individual summary of appropriate length.

Interpreted Lecture: Lecturing is for about five minutes. The teacher pauses briefly and then randomly selects a student to repeat the essence of the lecture so far by "translating" the lecture into plain English (or the local language). After one student interprets, ask others to add any missing items. Repeat the procedure in approximately five-minute intervals. This method will be more effective if you explain the process and the expectations clearly before you start.

Press Conference: The teacher presents a short overview of the major topic and identifies three or four subtopics. Distribute index cards to students and ask them to write at least one question on each subtopic. Collect the question cards and divide students into as many teams as there are subtopics. Give each team the set of questions dealing with one specific subtopic. Team members organise the questions in a logical order, eliminating any duplicates. After a suitable pause, play the role of an expert and invite one of the teams to grill you for 5-10 minutes. The presenter responds to the questions in a press conference format. At the end of this press conference, ask members of each team to review their notes and identify what they consider to be the two most important pieces of information given in your answers. Repeat this activity with the other teams.

Superlatives: At the end of each logical unit of a presentation, ask teams to identify the most important, the most disturbing, the most surprising, or the most complex idea presented so far. Or, during your presentation, stop at some logical point and ask students to work in teams to identify the most important piece of information you presented so far. After a suitable pause, ask each team to share its decision. Now ask teams to select the most controversial (interesting, thought-provoking, etc.) statement that you made in your presentation. After teams respond, make the next unit of presentation. Repeat the teamwork procedure by specifying different types of information to be identified (such as the most radical, the most surprising, the most interesting or the most humorous).

Panel Discussions

This method usually involves the presentation of an issue by several teachers at a table in front of a group. Usually, each teacher speaks briefly on the topic and then a moderator solicits questions from the audience. The moderator introduces the presenters/ teachers, keeps the discussion on the topic and within time limits and summarises the discussion at the end. Each teacher typically speaks for a set period of time (for example, five minutes). After all teachers have spoken, the moderator invites questions from students. At the end of the session, the moderator may summarise the discussion and thank the presenters for their participation.

Skit

A skit is an impromptu performance by students to demonstrate something they know. Skits can be created by students to show concerns they have about such things as peer pressure, victim issues in their community or lack of resources. Give students a topic, the maximum length of the skit and the amount of time they have to prepare (depending on the complexity, 30 minutes or an afternoon, for example).

Small Group Discussion

A small group discussion is a structured session in which three to six students exchange ideas and opinions about a particular topic or accomplish a task together. After the groups have had an opportunity to work together, they report the highlights of their work back to the large group, and the teacher helps the group process the activity. Begin the learning activity by briefly presenting a topic to the large group. Then, divide the group into smaller groups and set a clear task for the small groups to accomplish. Write directions, goals and time allotted for the task on a chalkboard, flipchart or handout. As groups are working, walk around and listen in briefly to each group. Many times individual members from one group can be transferred to another group, for "cross pollination of ideas". Keep groups focused by announcing the time remaining periodically. After the small group work, students typically reassemble in the large group and a representative from each small group shares their findings to the large group for a whole group discussion. Help the group process the activity to be sure the intended message was conveyed.

Group Report Out: In turn, a representative from each group stands in front of the room and reports its findings, usually guided by written flipcharts or other notes. Sometimes this report includes a brief question-and-answer session with the rest of the group.

Gallery Walk: Groups are instructed to write their information (or their drawings, community maps, etc.) clearly and legibly on flipcharts. Groups post their flipcharts around the room, and the facilitator invites everyone to take a "gallery walk"—to walk from one group's findings to another, reading the information and making note of important learning. After about 15 minutes (longer or shorter depending on the number of groups), the facilitator reconvenes the participant group and processes the activity, often beginning with basic questions about what the participants have noted in the gallery walk, what stands out, etc.

Sl. No.	*Technique (What is it?)*	*How Does it work?*	*Important Features*	*Suggested usage in Criminology*
1	2	3	4	5
1.	**Brainstorming** Brainstorming is a familiar technique in which a facilitator asks a specific question or describes a particular scenario, and students offer many different ideas. These ideas are then usually written on a flipchart or chalkboard and considered for further discussion.	Brainstorming can be used in any kind of group discussion when you want to encourage creativity and contributions from all members. Use this technique at the beginning of a session, class or meeting to ascertain students' knowledge about a topic or to set an agenda. Or, use brainstorming briefly in the middle of another learning activity, such as storytelling or dramatisation, to capture some of the ideas raised by the exercise. Similarly, leading a brief brainstorm at the end of a learning activity captures important "take-away" points.	• Ideas are called out randomly and freely from any student. • No idea is silly or unimportant. • Usually, no discussion or comments on the ideas are allowed during the brainstorming phase, except for purpose of clarification. This keeps the flow of ideas coming quickly. • The person recording the ideas should write them down as he or she hears them, without modifying them. • Plan to do something with the list generated. Brainstorms are energizing and thought-provoking, but it can be frustrating to students to make a list and take no action on it.	• Biological and Constitutional Schools • Introduction to Internet • Impact of corruption on democracy • Fundamental Rights • Factors of Delinquency causation.

1	2	3	4	5
2.	**Case Studies** A case study is a written scenario that usually involves an important community situation. Since it is written beforehand, it can be specifically created to address relevant local issues.	Typically, the facilitator distributes the case studies, and students can work on them individually, in pairs or in small groups. After students read, reflect upon, and discuss the case studies, the facilitator leads a large group discussion about the issues raised in each scenario.	• Be clear about the learning objectives. What is to be conveyed with the case study? Construct the case study so that these objectives can be met. • Ensure cross-cultural appropriateness, and check for the adequate inclusion of women and men. • Understand the learning needs of the student group, and construct the case study so that it will be challenging to the participant group, but still manageable. • Anticipate some of the questions participants will ask, and be ready with helpful answers. • Work through the data and descriptions you provide in the case studies carefully. You don't want the group spending most of their time	• Computer applications in Criminal Justice • Bhopal Gas tragedy • Portrayal of crime and Police in media • Crimes against women: Cruelty, Miscarriages, Rape, dowry deaths • Immoral traffic offenders

1	2	3	4	5
			trying to figure out confusing or ambivalent details.	
3.	**Demonstrations** A demonstration is a structured performance of an activity to show, rather than simply tell, a group how the activity is done. This method brings to life some information that you may have already presented in a lecture.	Model the activity slowly and clearly for students, answering questions after the demonstration to ensure understanding. Then, Students' practice the activity individually, in pairs or in groups, to reinforce the learning.	• Gather all materials and practice the demonstration by yourself before you do it in front of the group, to ensure that it is clear enough to make students feel comfortable to try it themselves. • Before demonstrating a technique, consider its suitability for the people, customs and economic constraints in the area.	• The structure of Computers • Internet • Scene of Crime • Memory • Fingerprints • Footprints
4.	**Dramatisation** A dramatization is a carefully scripted play where the characters act out a scene related to a learning situation. It is designed to bring out the	Present a dramatization at the beginning of a learning activity to raise issues that are then dealt with through other methods: lecture, large or small group discussion, and so on. The dramatisation may be	• Identify the message of the dramatisation first. Then, create a way to present the message through drama. • Keep the drama simple and on target, so that the messages are clear.	• Child Abuse and Violence • Violation of the rights of marginalised groups • Culture conflict • Sub culture

1	2	3	4	5
	important issues to be discussed or messagesto be learned.	designed by the teacher/ facilitator or by members of the participant group. It may be presented by co-facilitators, peer educators, or chosen participants who learn their parts and practice prior to presenting it to the target audience. Or, it may be the culmination of learning, with participants designing a dramatisation to carry messages to others, such as to other students, to groups in the community, or to the general public. Dramatisation combines learning and entertainment, and may involve puppets, and songs.		
5.	**Fishbowl** In a fishbowl discussion, most of the participants sit in a large circle, while a smaller group of	As a structured brainstorming session: Choose a specific topic based on the group's needs or interests. A handful of seats are placed inside a larger circle.	• When using the fishbowl as a structured brainstorming session, it is important to model how participants from the outside circle can	• White Collar Crime • Crime syndicates • Contract Killings • Child rights • Homosexuality

1	2	3	4	5
	participants sit inside the circle.	Participants who have something to say about the topic at hand sit in the center. Anyone sitting inside the fishbowl can make a comment, offer information, respond to someone else in the center, or ask a question. When someone from the outside circle has a point to make, he or she taps the shoulder of someone in the center and takes that person's seat. This continues, with people from the outside tapping and replacing people on the inside, as a lively brainstorm takes place. You will need to process the many ideas after the fishbowl exercise. For structured observation of a group process: Participants in the fishbowl are given a specific task to do, while participants outside the fishbowl act as	tap and replace people from the inside circle. Model this technique by choosing a simple topic for the fishbowl as a quick practice activity, so that participants are comfortable tapping and replacing before discussion of the real topic begins. • Ask one person to be the 'recorder' and jot down the main points that are raised during the activity for the group to discuss later. • Keep the activity on track by clearly defining the discussion topic or group task before beginning the fishbowl.	

1	2	3	4	5
		observers of the group process. The inner group works on its task together, and the outer group is asked to note specific behaviours. To process the activity, ask the inner group to reflect on the group process, and ask the outer group to describe what they observed.		
6.	**Lecturette** A lecturette is a short, oral presentation of facts or theory. No more than 15-20 minutes in length, the goal of a lecturette is to impart information in a direct, highly organized fashion.	The teacher presents knowledge on a topic, sometimes using flipcharts, computer software presentations or other media to guide the discussion. A question and answer period follows.	• There is important specific information to convey or new theories or skills to be learned. • An expert is available to share knowledge about a particular topic. • The lecture is presented dynamically and care is taken to include participants by allowing questions, soliciting comments or using one of the variations below. • The lecture uses personal	• International Environmental Policy • Beijing Rules • United Nations Declaration of Human Rights • Indian Community policing experiments • Code of conduct for the police

1	2	3	4	5
			stories or familiar examples to support theoretical points. Often, people remember stories more readily than theory. • The lecture is reinforced using another learning method, such as demonstrations, role plays and games.	
7.	**Panel Discussions** This method usually involves the presentation of an issue by several resource persons at a table in front of a group. Usually, each presenter speaks briefly on the topic and then a moderator Solicits questions from the audience.	The moderator introduces the presenters, keeps the discussion on the topic and within time limits and summarises the discussion at the end. Each presenter typically speaks for a set period of time (for example, five minutes). After all presenters have spoken, the moderator invites questions from participants. At the end of the session, the moderator may summarize the discussion	• Panel discussions are best used when one would like to present a number of different perspectives on the same topic. • Rather than having a series of lectures or longer sessions, you might gather people with the relevant experience or knowledge on one panel. • Consider preparing a guide for your panel guests, to help them prepare in	• Terrorism • The ragging Act • Salient Features of Constitution of India

1	2	3	4	5
		and thank the presenters for their participation.	advance and to ensure that your objectives are met.	
8.	**Role Play** Role plays are short interactions of participants playing specific, predetermined roles to explore issuesor practice skills. Roles are usually written out, and the facilitator may help students playing the roles understand "who" they are to be.	Role plays are generally used after a period of instruction or discussion. For example, if students are learning communication skills, groups can role play being assertive in typical situations (e.g., students in peer pressure situations, or people needing to access services in a clinic or office). Stop the role play periodically and discuss what behaviors worked and what was difficult and allow the group to brainstorm different choices of behavior/words. The role play may be done again, with the same person practicing or someone else trying.	• For best results, the role playing situation should be realistic, and the roles of anyone involved should be written out or described verbally to each player. • Younger people are often more willing to role play in front of a group than adults, but care must be taken not to embarrass participants. • Monitor the timing and process of the exercise so that the role play does not drag on, become silly or unrealistic. • At any time, stop a role play and lead a discussion. Open-ended questions such as: "What was effective in X's behavior?" "How did s/he counteract the behavior of	• Alcoholism • Spread of rumors • Stalking • Interview : Nature, definition, objectives and Interviewing technique • Rights of women, children, prisoners and dalits • Counselling; Reflection of feelings • Procedures to be followed while dispersing violent crowds • Surveillance • Difference between interrogation and Interview • Perception and learning • Feeling and Emotions • Conflict and Adjustment

1	2	3	4	5
			X?" can help involve the audience as well as the players. • Invite new participants to come and practice the role, using their own words and ideas for the situation. • It is important to process role plays after the activity. Ask participants open-ended questions such as: "How did you feel when...", "Why did you say..." or "What do you think went well?"	
9.	**Skit** A skit is an impromptu performance by participants to demonstrate something they know. Skits can becreated by participants to show concerns they haveabout such things as peer	Give participants a topic, the maximum length of the skit and the amount of time they have to prepare (depending on the complexity, 30 minutes or an afternoon, for example).	• The topic assigned needs to be "demonstrable"; that is, it should be fairly easy to determine how one might act it out. • The participants need to have the experience or knowledge to prepare the skit on the topic given.	• Trafficking and exploitation of Children • Barriers to effective counselling sessions • The Dowry Prohibition Act • Interactions in daily life relationship • Differential Association

1	2	3	4	5
	pressure, health issues intheir community or lack of resources. Skits may beused to demonstrate something learned, such as two styles of being a leader.		• Give participants adequate time to prepare the skit; they will want to think of the points they want to make, create a setting and characters, practice and get some props (potentially). • In most cases, a minimum amount of time to prepare is 30 minutes.	Theory • Migration
10.	**Small Group Discussion** A small group discussion is a structured session in which three to six participants exchange ideas and opinions about a particular topicor acco-mplish a task together. After the groups have had an opportunity to work together, they report the highlights of their work back to the large group, and the	Begin the learning activity by briefly presenting a topic to the large group. Then, divide the group into smaller groups and set a clear task for the small groups to accomplish. Write directions, goals and time allotted for the task on a chalkboard, flipchart or handout. As groups are working, walk around and listen in briefly to each group. Keep groups focused by announcing the time	• Set a clear task that can be accomplished within the time limit. • Make sure the task is interesting to participants and relevant to their learning goals. • Rehearse the instructions in your mind to be sure your directions are clear and complete. • Give instructions clearly, one at a time, especially if there are many steps. Giving	• Structure of Indian Police • Types of Punishment • Prisoner's rights • Aggression

1	2	3	4	5
	facilitator helps the group process the activity.	remaining periodically. After the small group work, participants typically reassemble in the large group and a representative from each small group shares their findings to the large group for a whole group discussion. Help the group process the activity to be sure the intended message was conveyed.	too many instructions at once can leave participants confused. • It is also crucial to devote as much energy to the reporting back and processing as to the small group work itself. • Groups that have spent time working on a topic may feel cheated if they are not given adequate opportunity to present their findings, and the entire group may miss key learning. • Most importantly, it is imperative to complete the learning cycle by processing the activity—the facilitator should guide a group reflection,	
11.	**Visualisation** In a visualisation exercise, the facilitator asks the group to imagine some	Invite participants to close their eyes and imagine a particular experience, place or situation in the future. Give	• Guiding a group through a visualisation exercise can be an incredibly powerful experience.	• Crime Trends • Decriminalisation • Crime prevention

1	2	3	4	5
	point in the future, often an ideal image of the future. The facilitator then guides the group through this image, asking them toimagine particular aspects of it. The exercise is designed to invite participants to explore the "big picture" and to tap into their deepest hopes and wishes.	participants permission to get as comfortable as possible. Guide the visualisation in a calm and slow voice. First, ask participants to make ncte of the particular scene and pause while they imagine. Pausing for a moment or two between directives, ask them to visualise a specific situation, the people or issues involved and their emotions at the time. Generally, visualisation usually lasts about five or 10minutes. Visualization might be followed by a deeper discussion of the images, or by the creation of a vision statement or another approach.	• Be clear and specific about your objectives before using a visualisation exercise and spend time before the activity practicing what you will say as you guide participants through their imagery.	• Crime victimization • Human rights violations • Prisonisation • After care
	Pictures Pictures can help to creatively involve participants in a	Create pictures around a particular topic with your co-facilitators or counterparts, and use those pictures to begin	• When using pictures to spark a discussion, ensure that the images are appropriate to the culture	• Crime scene Investigation • Human Rights violations • Child Rights • Perception

1	2	3	4	5
	discussion, and to engage the right-mode processing.	a group discussion. Bring in photographs, perhaps from the newspaper, or photos that you have taken yourself. Use these pictures to begin a discussion. Or, provide a topic and invite participants to draw a picture on that topic. After drawing the picture, participants stand and describe the image.	and the particular audience. • Check the background of photos and illustrations to make sure there are no unusual images that distract from the message you are exploring.	• Prison conditions • Child institutions

Each table adds an idea: If a number of groups have been working on similar tasks, guide the report by asking each table to share one idea. The group briefly discusses the idea, and then the next table shares a different idea, and so on, until all ideas have been shared

Some of the techniques which can be adopted for specific topics in a criminology curriculum are suggested:

Student Evaluation

The system of student evaluation, during the semester also needs restructuring. Evaluation during the semester, called the continuous assessment (CA) or, Internal Assessment (IA), is done by the course teacher. The purpose of this system is to get constant feedback from the students, on their understanding. The present system provides specific scores for tasks like assignments, seminars and sessional tests, which may add up to 40 or 50 marks, the rest forming the final test, to be conducted by the university/ institution in a centralised way.

The continuous assessment, alternatively, be changed, where each student can be allotted by the course teacher, 50 marks on the first day of the semester. Subsequently, depending upon the non participation of the student, in the learning activities during the semester, predetermined marks can be subtracted. For each deviance, predetermined, pre published, marks are to be deducted, from the 50 marks originally awarded. Some of the activities for which marks can be subtracted, is suggested:

Sl. No.	*Activities*	*Suggested Marks (to be deducted)*
1.	Initial marks allotted 50	
2.	Attendance (absence in each class)	0.25 marks
3.	Non submission of assignments	5 marks
4.	Not taking one sessional tests	10 marks
5.	Poor/Non participation in class room activities	0.5 marks
6.	Poor performance in seminars	0.5 marks

This system will put all students in the equal footing, at the beginning of each semester, and will motivate in participating in all the learning activities during the semester. The success of this system depends on the transparency and non biased attitude of the course teacher.

Experiential learning challenges students to think in new ways, explore new ways of problem solving, and raise critical questions about their learning and service. It enhances student academic experience through participation that reflects the complex issues of students' future workplaces. Students get the opportunity to wrestle with complex issues right in their own communities and to become a part of the solution. These solutions are shared. Introduction of this methodology at institutions of higher learning is an ideal method to create a bridge between academic learning and community service. It gives individuals a chance to share knowledge and learn more about how to use each methodology while connecting with community partners and "filling the needs" they may encounter. Students can also potentially build long-lasting community partnerships that they will use when they enter their profession full-time.

Students learning are enhanced by providing multiple opportunities for practice and reflection. This same reflection is valuable in guiding students as they address community concerns. Students add to the richness of the dialogue by influencing the direction the dialogue will flow, sorting key ideas for deeper discussion, and focusing on key points. The learning experiences allow students not only to sharpen the focus of their own instruction and learning but also to deepen their level of inquiry through questioning, making connections, and honoring multiple perspectives.

Notes

This author was part of the team that set up the syllabus for graduate level criminology teaching.

This syllabus was prepared for the B.Sc., in criminology, at the Manonmaniam Sundaranar University. The syllabus has been approved by the University and is presently used to teach undergraduate students.

The University also planned an orientation course for the teachers, who offered coursed using experiential learning.

The syllabi were implemented by the University, and there were no issues with the teachers and or with the students.

References

Adams, D.M. (1973). *Simulation games: An approach to learning*. Worthington, OH: Charles A. Jones Publishing.

Akers, Ronald L. and Christine Sellers (2004) *Criminological Theories: Introduction, Evaluation, and Application* (4th edn). Los Angeles, CA: Roxbury Publishing Company.

Altschuld, J. W. (1995). Developing an evaluation programme: Challenges in the teaching of evaluation. *Evaluation and Programme Planning, 18*, 259–265.

Bawden, R. (2004). *Engagement, reflexive scholarship, and the learning turn within the academy*. Paper presented at the ALARPM conference, South Africa, August.

Carr, D. (1992). Cultural institutions as structures for cognitive change. *New Direction for Adult and Continuing Education, 53*, 21–35.

Cavaliere, L., and Sgroi, A. (1992). Active learning: Perspectives on learning that leads to personal development and social change. *New Direction for Adult and Continuing Education, 53*, 5–10.

Chelimsky, E. (1997). The political environment of evaluation and what it means for the development of the fieid. In E. Chelimsky and W. Shadish (Eds.), *Evaluation for the 21st century* (pp. 53–68). Thousand Oaks, CA: Sage Publications.

Cronbach, L.J., Ambron, S.R., Dornbusch, S.M., Hess, R.D., Hornik, R.C., Phillips, D.C., et al. (1980). *Toward reform of programme evaluation*. San Francisco: Jossey-Bass.

Cullen, Francis T. (1984) *Rethinking Crime and Deviance Theory: The Emergence of a Structuring Tradition*. Totowa, NJ: Rowman and Allenheld.

Cullen, Francis T. and Robert A. Agnew (eds) (2006) *Criminological Theory: Past to Present—Essential Readings* (3rd edn). Los Angeles, CA: Roxbury Publishing Company.

Davis, B.G. (1986). Overview of the teaching of evaluation across the disciplines. In B.G. Davis (ed.), *The teaching of evaluation across the disciplines*. New Directions for Programme Evaluation, No. 29. San Francisco: Jossey-Bass.

Fitzpatrick, J.L. (1994). What should an evaluation programme look like?: Alternative models for structuring professional preparation programmes. In J. W. Altschuld and M. Engle (Eds.), *The preparation of professional evaluators: Issues, perspectives, and current status*. New Directions for Programme Evaluation, No. 62. San Francisco: Jossey-Bass.

Garland, David and Sparks, Richard (2000) *Criminology, Social Theory and Challenge of our times*, British journal of criminology, 40, 189-204.

Hargreaves, W.A., Attkisson, C. C., Horowitz, M. J., and Sorensen, J. E. (1978). The education of evaluators. In C. C. Attkisson,W. A. Hargreaves, M. J. Horowitz, and J. E. Sorensen (Eds.), *Evaluation of human service programmes*. San Francisco: Academic Press.

Honey P. and Mumford A. (1982) *Manual of Learning Styles* London: P Honey

Knowes M. S. (1990) *The Adult Learner: a neglected species* (4th edition) Houston: Gulf Publishing.

Kolb D.A. (1984) *Experiential Learning: experience as the source of learning and development* New Jersey: Prentice-Hall (0 13 295261 0).

Kornhauser, Ruth Rosner (1978) *Social Sources of Delinquency: An Appraisal of Analytic Models*. Chicago, IL: University Chicago Press.

Ladousse, G.P. (1987). *Role-play*. Oxford: Oxford University Press.

Lieb, S. (1991) Adult learning principles. Retrieved April 28, 2005, from http://honolulu.hawaii.edu/intranet/committees/FacDevCom/guidebk/teachtip/adults-2.htm.

Lilly, J. Robert, Francis T. Cullen and Richard A. Ball (2006) *Criminological Theory: Context and Consequences* (4th edn). Thousand Oaks, CA: Sage Publications.

Liska, Alan E. and Steven F. Messner (1999) *Perspectives on Crime and Deviance* (3rd edn). Englewood Cliffs, NJ: Prentice Hall.

Livingstone, C. (1983). *Role-play in learning language*. London: Longman.

Morris, M. (1994). The role of single evaluation courses in evaluation training. *New Directions for Program Evaluation, 62*, 51–59.

Mott, A. (2005). *University education for community change: A vital strategy for progress on poverty, race and community-building*. Washington, DC: Community Learning Project.

O'Brien, G. (2004). *Principles of adult learning*. Melbourne, Australia: Southern Health Organisation. Retrieved December 2, 2005, from http://www.southernhealth.org.au/cpme/articles/adult_learning.htm

Pfohl, Stephen J. (1985) *Images of Deviance and Social Control: A Sociological History*. New York: McGraw-Hill.

Preskill, H. (1997). Using critical incidents to model effective evaluation practice in the teaching of evaluation. *Evaluation Practice, 18*, 65–71.

Rogers, C.R. (1969). Freedom to learn. Columbus, OH: Merrill.

Sanders, J.R. (1986). The teaching of evaluation in education. In B. G. Davis (Ed.), *The teaching of evaluation across the disciplines*. New Directions for Program Evaluation, No. 29. San Francisco: Jossey-Bass.

Taylor, P., Deak, A., Pettit, J., and Vogel, I. (2006). *Learning for social change. Exploring concepts, methods and practice*. Brighton: Institute of Development Studies. Retrieved from: http://www.pnet.ids.ac.uk/docs/FLASC.pdf

Trevisan, M. S. (2002). Enhancing practical evaluation training through long-term evaluation projects. *American Journal of Evaluation, 23*, 81–92.

Vold, George B., Thomas J. Bernard and Jeffrey B. Snipes (2002) *Theoretical Criminology* (5th edn). New York: Oxford University Press.

Zemke, R., and Zemke, S. (1995, June). Adult learning -What do we know for sure? Training. Retrieved July 11, 2006, from http://www.msstate.edu/dept/ais/8523/Zemke1995.pdf

11

CONTEMPORARY APPROACHES TO THE PSYCHOLOGY OF CRIME, LAW AND JUSTICE

Mark Brown

Introduction

A century has passed since the eminent German experimental psychologist, Hugo Munsterberg, wrote *On the Witness Stand* (1908), a book widely credited as marking the origins of psychology's engagement with crime, law and justice. For Munsterberg, it seemed incredible that the field of law, so intimately concerned with human thought and behaviour, should not look to psychology for the solution of its problems. The aim of his book, he wrote, was 'to turn the attention of serious men to an absurdly neglected field which demands the full attention of the social community' (p. 12). But he also envisaged this engagement as part of a wider field within which a new science of applied psychology would be born: 'Applied Psychology will then become' he argued 'an independent experimental science which stands related to the ordinary experimental psychology as engineering to physics' (p. 9).

The present day status of teaching and research in psychological approaches to crime, law and justice, and indeed to the whole gamut of criminological concerns, is tied in important ways to Munsterberg's presumptions and goals. Overall, Munsterberg's desire to see a field of applied psychology has borne fruit. Most respectable psychology programmes in universities today teach educational psychology, organisational psychology and clinical psychology, and also recognise the status of other applied sub-domains such as sports psychology (where would Olympians be without it?) and human factors psychology (e.g., better understanding airline pilots' performance at the human-machine interface). Yet in the field of crime, law and justice the status of psychological research and the support for such research within psychology has had a chequered and uneven history. At the same time, few parts of applied psychology have received such widespread recognition of importance: think for example of psychologists' assessments of an accused person's capacity to stand trial or of the prediction of future dangerousness of a serious offender. Criminology too seems to have had an often cool and certainly uneven relationship with those who work on its psychological dimensions. On the one hand, clinically based work with offenders was central to the birth of early penal sciences (see Garland, 1985), yet there has remained a certain tension between the spirit and aspirations of criminologists trained within psychological and sociological approaches. The effect of this often has been to leave psychological research and teaching as a subsidiary, and some would say, secondary, sub-domain within the criminology discipline.

The aim of this chapter is to improve knowledge and understanding of psychological contributions to the study of crime, law and justice by providing a brief overview of the different 'schools' of psychology as they have developed their respective approaches to these topics and then to focus in on one area of great contemporary interest – the psychology of rehabilitation and desistance from crime – so that the reader may get an appreciation of the finer points that animate research, teaching and policy development in this area. The chapter therefore proceeds in three parts. First, though the aggregation of research into 'schools' is a necessarily rough and ready strategy it is nevertheless possible to identify at least four different approaches that, while necessarily overlapping, vary in important ways in respect of methodology, assumptions and implications for practice: here these will be separated into what may be termed (i) psychologies of crime causation; (ii) psychology and law; (iii) forensic psychology; and (iv) criminal justice psychology. The aim of Part One is to provide a schematic overview of these approaches: some are better developed than others and, equally, some more relevant than others depending upon the nature and characteristics of different legal systems.

Part Two of the chapter begins an expanded look at one important area of criminal psychology: research into rehabilitation of offenders and the process of 'giving up crime' that has been such a long standing concern for psychological criminology. This research straddles the divide of forensic psychology and criminal justice psychology and new work is shifting the emphasis from a medical model of rehabilitation to a more social approach to desistance from crime. Some key recent studies will be discussed to provide a sense of the direction of contemporary work in this area. Finally, Part Three will discuss how the teaching of the psychology of crime, law and justice might sit within a broad based education in criminology, albeit in recognition of the difficulty of ever specifying what should represent 'core' training in a discipline like criminology.

I. Four 'Schools' of Psychology

The grouping of research into 'schools' or 'approaches' reflects an effort to contain within one coherent body, or under one meaningful label, a variety of methodological approaches and topics of concern. Much like the factor analyses so favoured within certain areas of psychology, the aim is to distinguish groupings of items (in this case studies) that both cohere around one theme while at the same time distinguishing this overall theme from other themes (in factor analysis, the idea of orthogonality). All of this makes little difference to the researcher, but for the teacher attempting to make sense of psychological investments in the fields of crime, law and justice, it is necessary to find such explanatory templates. Though teaching will be discussed in detail in Part Three, it is worth noting at this point that courses differ to the degree they are situated within a school's approach or attempt instead to present to students a broad survey of the work and finding achieved across the whole spectrum of activity. Each of course has its own advantages and disadvantages that will be discussed below. For the moment, it will be appropriate to begin with an attempt to characterise these four so-called schools.

Psychologies of Crime Causation

The origins of this approach lie in individual differences psychology. The question asked is a deceptively simple one: *Is it possible to distinguish those who engage in delinquency, crime or antisocial behaviour on the basis of measurable individual differences?* Of course the simplicity of the question is matched only by the complexity of answering it.

Early approaches amount to what might be termed 'single factor' models. Studies in this mould have been undertaken to estimate whether measured criminal conduct varies with, to name a few: intelligence (Hirschi and Hindelang, 1977), impulsivity (Pulkinnen, 1986), self esteem (Rosenberg and Rosenberg, 1978) and moral reasoning (Palmer and Hollin, 1998). Howitt (2009) suggests that at least five broad explanatory models for violence may be found within psychology, each relating the application of an existing framework to the problem of crime. These include social learning theory, attachment theory, models of deficient social information processing, the idea of post-traumatic stress and the proposal for deficient emotional regulation. Each of these seeks to capture and locate the causes of crime within the individual offender.

The difficulty with sort of approach is that it implies that the single factor or process studied, be it intelligence or social information processing, will have some kind of pure unmediated effect upon an outcome variable that is itself highly social in nature: offending. Recognition of the need for more complex models of causation is reflected in work done on the links between personality and crime. Unlike moral reasoning, for instance, personality reflects a more whole of person approach the question of crime causation. One of the earliest and most notable attempts to link personality to crime was the work of Hans Eysenck (1960). Eysenck's thought was that certain constellations of personality traits might leave individuals more likely to break the law and that these personality features were partly biological in origin. His concepts of extraversion-introversion and psychoticism-neuroticism have been quite influential, stimulated much research, but in the end have been found lacking in explanatory power (Farrington, Biron and LeBlanc, 1982). Nevertheless, the ideas of conditioning and of the influence of environmental factors on socialisation, key to his work, remain important.

Since the 1980s attention has turned increasingly to models of crime causation that trace change and development through time. These are termed pathway or life-course models and theories and constitute, at the present, perhaps the most powerful and well supported body of psychological work on the causes of crime (see generally, Farrington, 2008; Piquero and Mazerolle, 2001). One of the more influential theories in this respect is a dual track taxonomy proposed by Terrie Moffitt (1993). Moffitt proposes that aggregate levels of offending, and particularly the known association of crime with age (participation peaks in the teenage years) can be explained by the presence of two sorts of offenders. Life-course-persistent offenders represent the 5% or so of offenders who begin early (<10 yrs of age) and commit crime throughout the life course. Their presence was established in early cohort studies (e.g., Wolfgang, Figlio and Sellin, 1972) and Moffitt argues that they provide the models of independence and stature that form part of the explanation for her second group, adolescence-limited offenders, dabbling in crime as they make the transition from late childhood and adolescence to adulthood. This group engage in crime because it provides social rewards, but as they complete the transition to adult life roles these reinforcing factors (e.g., the risk taking associated with committing crimes) shift in their interpretation, such that they no longer present social value. At this point young people migrate back into the pro-social world, hopefully without having incurred any significant costs (e.g., a criminal record), leaving the bulk of adult offending to the life-course-persistent group and those of their compatriots who have become snagged in the criminal lifestyle by the costs associated with apprehension and punishment (e.g., imprisonment and cultures of criminality that go with it).

Psychology and Law

With a few exceptions within Europe, the field of psychology and law is a largely American endeavour, reflecting the special characteristics of American life and law. The totem around which this field is organised is the American Psychological Association's Division 41 journal *Law and Human Behaviour*. The aims of this school have been brought down almost intact from Hugo Munsterberg's (1908) *On the Witness Stand* described earlier. That is, to render the problems of law into terms suitable for psychological analysis. The broad assumption underlying this field is that the terrain of law is, after all, but the terrain of cognition and behaviour – of *mens rea* and *actus reus* – and the science that will render such cognition and behaviour understandable is psychology. Thus, though recognising the embeddness of law in social order, the psychology and law approach takes as it's *a priori* that many of the assumptions of law (e.g., that jurors understand judges' instructions) and problems faced by law (does deterrence really have an effect?) can be solved by science and thus by psychology (see generally, Brewer and Williams, 2005).

The topics addressed within this field are as broad as the law itself. They include topics such as the veracity of eyewitness testimony and the nature of confession evidence, both of which were concerns of Munsterberg. Also considered are a variety of issues around the interviewing and taking of evidence from children, such as the extent to which different interviewing approaches introduce suggestion and the susceptibility of children to these devices. In the wake of media interest and law suits during the 1980s and 1990s over the claim of recovered memories of child sexual abuse, psychologists conducted extensive research on the way memories may be extracted, whether or not apparently 'genuine' memories may have been primed in the process of recovery and recall, the way memories of trauma are formed and stored, and so on (Loftus and Ketcham, 1994).

Since the field of civil litigation and criminal cases involving jury trials is so much larger in the United States than elsewhere a whole industry of trial consulting has developed, supported by a wealth of research on juror attitudes, effects of pretrial publicity on jurors' judgements, jurors' capacities to deal with different types of evidence and the relationship between different types of juror characteristics and an equally varied set of outcome decisions (see generally, Kassin, 1988; Lieberman and Sales, 2006). In another approach to juries, through a series of studies using what are termed 'high fidelity' conditions – real jurors from the jury pool using real trial evidence – Nancy Pennington and Reid Hastie (1993) worked to understand how jurors integrate evidence in a trial and arrive at one of the legally available options (guilty, not guilty). Their story model indicates that, rather than functioning in a mathematical fashion in terms of 'balances of evidence' as had previously been suggested, jurors in fact construct narrative stories in order to make sense of evidence. This theory of a narrative cognitive structure that allows jurors to integrate new facts and reallocate the position and significance of older ones has been validated in respect of a variety of crime types, including sexual harassment (Huntley and Costanzo, 2003) and has implications for the way trial lawyers construct and present their cases to juries.

Forensic Psychology

Definitions of forensic psychology are varied and the field has considerable cross-over with the psychology and law school. Nevertheless, a useful rule of thumb and one that will be used here to divide forensic psychology off from other approaches to law, and indeed from other approaches to criminal justice processes and goals (such as rehabilitation), is that it emerges from and can be understood as a branch of clinical psychology. Forensic psychology is thus concerned with matters that lie on the boundary between normality and abnormality, which is, of course, the terrain of clinical psychology. These include: matters at law, such as the fitness or capacity of an individual to stand trial based upon assessments of their mental state; the delicate ground of legally defined insanity; the effect of certain syndromes upon behaviour, including Battered Woman's Syndrome or Post Traumatic Stress Disorder; clinical assessments of children, such as in relation to possible sexual abuse or child custody decisions; clinical assessments of offender behaviour, such as stalking or arson; assessments of reoffending risk, dangerousness and psychopathy as they relate to offenders and thus to prognoses of future behaviour; the design and conduct of clinical interventions around problem behaviours such as violent or sexual offending, gambling addictions, or drug and alcohol addiction; juvenile offending and more (see generally, Roesch and McLaughan, 2007).

Perhaps the longest standing relationship between psychologists (and psychiatrists, including their nineteenth century predecessors known as alienists) and the law lies in discussion around criminal responsibility. Many jurisdictions around the world use a variant upon the McNaughten Rule, formulated in 1843, to determine if an individual may be held responsible for a crime, or if they should be exculpated on grounds of being insane at the time of the offence. Although psychologists emphasise that the term insanity is a legal term and not a psychological one, the idea of disease of the mind is at the heart of the rule itself. It states: a person shall not be held responsible in respect of a criminal act if 'at the time of committing the act, the party accused of the act was labouring under such a defect of reason, from disease of the mind, as not to know the nature and quality of the act he was doing; or if he did know it ... he did not know he was doing what was wrong' (*McNaughten*, 1843; cited in Bartol and Bartol, 2005). Psychologists of the time reacted strongly against the idea that insanity was a purely intellectual defect and indeed that it was something that might be ascertained by laypeople and judges alone. Their desire to prise the concept of insanity from its legal setting and subject it to psychological expertise began what is now a long tradition within psychology to query the adequacy of non-scientific approaches to questions of mind and behaviour.

More recently, however, the expertise of forensic psychologists has become central to a new set of legal determinations concerning risk of violent and sexual offending. In the United States, there has emerged a whole new field of civil commitment statutes directed toward what are termed sexually violent predators (Janus, 2000). The idea lying behind these new laws is something akin to quarantine: they provide for the removal from society of those who threaten community safety in some acute way, or to some excessive extent. Similar laws have recently appeared in Australia and New Zealand, and forensic psychologists have been central to their operation. The psychologists' role has been to assess the relation between background aetiological factors and the likelihood of future offending. The rationale of the laws is that for those who pose a high risk to community safety, continued post-sentence detention will be necessary (Brown, 2009).

Criminal Justice Psychology

Researchers and practitioners of criminal justice psychology vary widely in their interests and concerns. They are distinguished by an interest in crime, law and justice that aims neither to (i) re-frame the law in psychological terms, nor (ii) apply principles of clinical psychology to solve problems of cognition or behaviour in the field of crime and justice. Research in this area covers a broad swathe of territory, but is among the most interesting and most important within the whole domain of applied psychology.

Criminal justice psychology engages with key issues in policing, such as crisis management, hostage negotiation, critical incident debriefing and police recruitment on the one hand, and critical understandings of police conduct, such as interviewing and interrogation techniques, on the other. It investigates the effects of new or innovative punishment strategies, looking for instance at the impacts and psychological effects of long periods of solitary confinement that have become a feature of supermax prisons (Haney, 2005). And it looks to understand criminal behaviour from a developmental and social psychological perspective, focusing upon the way crime emerges through processes like social learning and differential association experiences (Andrews and Bonta, 1998).

Some of the most powerful social psychological experiments ever undertaken belong to this field. In Palo Alto, California, in the summer of 1971 an experiment was undertaken in the basement of the psychology department at Stanford University. In what became known as the Stanford Prison Experiment, Philip Zimbardo, assisted by some of his graduate students, recruited psychologically normal young males to engage in a study of the effects of people's roles upon their behaviour. The two week experiment randomly allocated participants to guard or prisoner roles. But these roles proved so powerful, and the psychological impacts upon prisoners so debilitating, that the two week experiment was called off after just six days. The implications of the study, including the development of sadistic behaviour among guards and feelings of helplessness and anxiety among prisoners, have been crucial in helping understand the causes of recent prisoner abuse scandals in Abu Ghraib prison in Iraq. There, it will be recalled, U.S. soldiers were found to have committed a wide range of atrocities, including forms of torture, upon Iraqi detainees. Official military responses suggested these soldiers were merely 'bad apples' within an otherwise morally upstanding military culture and environment. However, the results of the Stanford experiment suggest otherwise, indicating the powerful effects of roles and the culture of permissiveness that allows abuse to occur. Zimbardo in fact testified as an expert witness in the defence of one of the handful of low ranking soldiers who faced trial over the abuses (see Zimbardo, 2007).

II. Contemporary Debates in the Psychology of Offender Rehabilitation

The presence of criminal behaviour in society creates an impetus and demand for its mitigation. In a perfect world, criminal penalties would deter potential offenders, yet the model of the rational, calculating, offender has long been recognised as little more than a chimera. In the absence of perfect deterrence, society is left to rely upon the blunt instrument of incapacitation to hold offenders at a distance, or to hope that strategies of reform and rehabilitation might 'cure' offenders of their criminal instincts or propensities. The goal of offender rehabilitation has thus been a central point of engagement between the discipline and its practitioners and the bureaucracies of law and justice.

But questions surrounding offender rehabilitation have also, in recent years, become something of a battleground within criminal psychology itself. A deep schism has been developed between those who would apply a traditional medical model to rehabilitation and others who argue for a greater recognition of offenders' social context and the impacts this has upon behaviour. The aim of this section is to give the reader some insight into the way this debate has moved and evolved, and thus a sense of some of the key problems that animate contemporary western research on and work with offenders. Perhaps the best place to begin is with a brief description of what has come to be the dominant model under which offending behaviour is understood and responded to in Australia, Canada, New Zealand, the United Kingdom and parts of the United States. This is what is known as the risk-need model (Andrews and Bonta, 1998; McGuire, 1995).

In fact, the term risk-need is something of a shorthand, for the approach identifies five principles of 'effective' intervention with youthful and adult offenders and proposes that these principles should guide rehabilitation intervention. Empirical research underpins the four main principles and this forms both a key strength and a key weakness of the approach. Before describing how this is so, however, it is worthwhile briefly outlining the five principles themselves. First is the *risk principle*, which proposes that: (i) interventions with high risk offenders produce greater impacts on subsequent offending than with low risk offenders; (ii) that intensive interventions with low risk offenders may be counterproductive (increasing offending); and thus (iii) that intensity of intervention should be matched to risk level. Risk itself is marked by a number of established statistically derived 'risk factors' which may be divided into those that are static, or unable to be changed (such as age at first conviction), and those that are dynamic and thus may be manipulated (such as attitudes, associates or employability). A second principle, the *needs principle*, proposes that dynamic risk factors should be understood as 'criminogenic needs' and should be the target of intervention programs. How they are targeted is determined by the *responsivity principle*, which recognises that people learn and respond differently and so proposes that interventions should take account of factors such as age, gender, ethnicity and so on, all of which can affect individuals' capacity to engage effectively with intervention programs. The quality of these programs is secured by an *integrity principle*, which proposes that programs should be delivered in exactly the way they were intended, so that effectiveness is not diluted by poor implementation or failure to comply with key theoretical principles. Finally, a *professional discretion principle* recognises that the preceding principles should not be implemented in a mechanistic or overly programmatic way, but should be guided by the professional judgement of those implementing the framework. The question of precisely what intervention programmes should do is answered by meta-analytic research. This is a methodology that allows data from multiple studies to be pooled and thus conclusions to be drawn across the entire group in a statistically meaningful way.

Problems with the Approach

In recent times dissatisfaction with this model has grown. The reasons for this lie in a confluence of three forces: firstly, significant confusion and incoherence within the model itself around the pivotal notion of 'criminogenic need' (see below); secondly, increasing dissatisfaction among practitioners with a singular reliance upon cognitive-behavioural programs as the 'gold standard' approach, combined with increasing evidence of minimal or even negative impacts when these programs are rolled out more widely (Gorman, Gregory, Hayles and Parton, 2006); and finally, increasing recognition that 'stopping offending' is less an event than a process, and that the risk-need model's *treatment rehabilitation* presumption may be less appropriate than some form of a *process of desistance* model that is currently taking shape within criminology (see below). This chapter is not the place for a thorough going review of these problems, but an attempt will be made below briefly to sketch the contours of the first and then to suggest how alternative approaches to offenders and offending behaviour are beginning to take shape.

Defining Offender 'Need'

There are a number of logical and theoretical difficulties inherent in the idea of criminogenic need and in the subsequent criminogenic/non-criminogenic needs distinction introduced in this model (Ward and Brown, 2003, 2004; see also Ward and Stewart, 2003). On this view, the main failings lie in two areas. First, it simply makes no sense to re-label statistically derived risk factors as needs. The term need has well recognised meaning: it connotes an essential element of life and both common knowledge and psychological theory alike have long sought to describe these basic building blocks of individual and social existence. So to label lack of stable employment, or prevalence of crime conducing attitudes, as needs is both wholly inappropriate and confusing. Instead, it might be better that statistically derived dynamic risk factors (which the model re-labels 'criminogenic needs') should be demoted from their current position as primary intervention targets and should, instead, be connected with a comprehensive theory or account of their relationship to the fundamental needs that shape human life and conduct; the needs for autonomy, relatedness and competence. Of course, opening up these broad human needs as targets of attention would also open up a space in which a variety of complementary intervention types, beyond cognitive-behavioural programming, could also be brought to bear upon the problem.

Secondly, the implication contained in the risk-need model's principles that so-called criminogenic needs such as (un)employment, anti-social attitudes and anti-social associates provide any guidance at all as to the *nature* of the problems faced by an offender should be challenged. As Ward and Brown (2003: 352) have put it: 'the current crop of empirically derived criminogenic needs are for the most part little more than range riders – they tell you that there is a problem but they do not tell you what to do or how to go about it'. Thus, programs that seek to target, for instance, pro-crime attitudes, do so in a conceptual and theoretical vacuum, since there is nothing underpinning the risk-need model that would link these sorts of attitudes to the fundamental needs that animate human thought and action. In practice, the approach works by setting negative goals (identifying things to get rid of) and attempting to suppress offender characteristics or capacities (such a bad attitudes or friends) rather than working with the person in a positive, developmental and forward moving fashion.

Reframing the Problem: Rehabilitation vs Desistance

The risk-need framework sits squarely within the classical medical disease model. The four conceptual elements around which it revolves are: disease (criminogenic needs to be eliminated); treatment (allocation to, ideally, a cognitive-behavioural program); dose (notionally e"100 hours = completion; otherwise, non-completion); and cure or rehabilitation (no further offending; otherwise, reconviction). Additional principles such as *risk* and *integrity* govern the distribution and application of elements within the framework. As Palmer, McGuire, Hounsome, Hatcher, Bilby and Hollin (2007) noted, the model's combination of assessment, treatment selection and treatment dose are aimed to produce what they term a 'completers effect' (p. 10), and failure particularly to achieve target dosage, will, as we are told about courses of antibiotics, both fail to cure the disease and possibly also aggravate its symptoms. Criminologists trained in the sociological tradition have long regarded this individual disease model as woefully inadequate and pernicious. Yet their basic point, that offending cannot be de-contextualised and all responsibility for it sheeted home to individual deficits, is broadly in line with modern psychology even if the sociologists and psychologists might differ as to the relative weight to be accorded internal and external factors.

The eminent American psychologist Craig Haney, whose career began working on the Stanford Prison Experiment described earlier, has noted the irony of individualistic psychologists propounding programmes that are out of step with a modern psychology that has moved increasingly toward greater contextualisation of action and toward placing ever greater weight on the power of situational factors (2005, cited in Carlen and Tombs, 2006). As a measure of the distance between the individualistic risk-need medical model and current thought, it is worth considering Haney and Philip Zimbardo's conclusion that '[v]irtually all sophisticated contemporary accounts of social behaviour now acknowledge the empirical and theoretical significance of situation, context and structure.' They go on to add that '[i]n academic circles at least, the problems of crime and violence – formerly viewed in almost exclusively individualistic terms – are now understood through multilevel analyses that grant equal if not primary significance to situational, community and structural variables.' (Haney and Zimbardo, 1998: 720). Indeed, Haney (2002) suggests that psychological research and theory would point our attention toward what he terms 'criminogenic social contexts' (p. 33) rather than criminogenic needs residing in the offender. The strength and direction of research here completely undermines the rhetoric of 'choice' and 'responsibility' underpinning conceptions of both the rational legal actor and the diseased body of the offender as it is constructed within the risk-need approach. 'By demonstrating the various ways in which deviant behaviour arises from a psychologically potent combination of traumatic social histories and criminogenic social circumstances' Haney argues, 'this literature casts doubt on the normative framework used to structure existing doctrines of responsibility.' (p. 34).

The reconfiguration of thinking proposed here by Haney is currently taking place is in the developing field of theory and research around the idea of desistance. Desistance may be thought of as both an end state (when something has stopped) and as a process leading to that state (Mulvey, Steinberg, Fagan, Cauffman, Piquero, Chassin, Knight, Brame, Schubert, Hecker and Losoya, 2004). While the former is that which we strive towards, it is the latter, the idea of a process of stopping, that is capturing much of the current attention and research effort. The desistance model aims to take account of those five key domains identified by Haney – psychological, historical, situational, local and structural that each impinge upon and shape the behaviour of all people at all times. Proponents of desistance often cite the process of recovery from alcoholism as an analogy: it does not occur over night, it will have a wide variety of variables influencing the final outcome which, itself, is always a contingent and often difficult state, and so on. A further analogy is also useful, which is of the process of education. One reason is that there are clear similarities between becoming educated and stopping offending: a student is not miraculously 'educated' by exposure to a course at school or university, for instance. Rather, education is a series of steps forward where not every step renders positive results. This more nuanced and socially grounded approach thus seems to offer real improvements over the idea of rehabilitation as cure that has been so central to psychological work with offenders for so long.

III. Locating psychology within the curriculum of criminology

It will be hoped that the forgoing sections have illustrated the breadth, depth and relevance of psychological research on crime, law and justice. And of course also, the extent to which these ideas remain fluid and subject to spirited debate. The development of such research in criminology is really a matter of choice for individual criminologists in the way they wish to shape and pursue their own research agenda. But for teaching, this body of work presents challenges of a rather different sort: how should students be introduced to this approach and to its engagement with the problems of criminology and law? It seems appropriate to conclude this chapter with three short observations on this question.

Psychology in the Curriculum

Much debate has occurred within Britain and Australia over what might constitute a 'core' of criminological knowledge and whether or not, or even how, that core might best be reflected in teaching. At the University of Melbourne, which is Australia's oldest criminology program and the third oldest among western nations (following the Oxbridge programs and that at U.C. Berkeley), focus has shifted in recent times toward a narrower and tighter undergraduate 'core' and 'capstone' series followed by advanced disciplinary training at the two-year masters course level, plus of course advanced research training via the Ph.D. The context to these developments is the recognition that undergraduate education should ideally be broad in character so that students receive exposure to a wide range of thinking, models and approaches across a variety of disciplines, including some outside their degree area (thus, exposure of science, commerce or engineering students to arts and social science programmes, and vise versa). Given the complexity of the modern world, the old ideal of specialist training in a discipline being achievable within a three year undergraduate programme seems unattainable. In this context, undergraduate programmes should aim to provide a broad survey of the contours of a discipline, while specialisation will be provided at the masters level and through higher degree research training (M.A. by thesis and Ph.D).

Given the centrality and importance of psychological research on crime, law and justice to the history and present shape of criminology, an ideal program might include a large segment on criminal psychology in first year, followed by a dedicated subject in second or third year. Within the masters programme, important exposure to psychological work may be achieved either through contribution to advanced theory subjects or through subjects focusing upon specific issues, such as punishment or desistance.

Teaching by Textbook or Collected Papers

One of the key questions facing teachers concerns resource materials for students. A number of excellent textbooks exist, both for lower and upper level teaching. These include Bartol and Bartol (2005), Howitt (2009), McGuire (2003, 2004) and Wrightsman and Fulero (2005). But a number of these are very expensive, and it is not entirely clear that texts written for British or American students are suitable for students in other places, be that Australia or India. At the University of Melbourne the practice has been to create 'reading packs' of photocopied articles and chapters (duly registered with the appropriate copyright authority) for distribution as an educational resource. The experience with these packs has been that they provide better focus to the particular way in which a teacher wishes to present a subject, but at the same time require greater effort on the part of that teacher to lead (particularly undergraduate) students through the reading and interpretation of textual sources.

Critical Criminology and Psychology

Much of the foregoing account has presumed an approach to

criminology that is best described as mainstream. Yet there are powerful currents within contemporary criminology suggesting the discipline has become overly conservative, administrative and intellectually unchallenging. To the extent that psychological research on crime, law and justice finds a place within criminology, it tends to do so within a model of this 'old criminology' (see Taylor, Walton and Young, 1973; Walton and Young, 1998), largely because psychology itself has been resistant to the intellectual challenges that have reshaped most disciplines since the 1970s and that are reflected in these new visions of criminology. Much of what is vigorous, challenging and boundary pushing in contemporary criminology falls within what is now being termed critical criminology (see generally, Anthony and Cunneen, 2008; Carrington and Hogg, 2002) and it is perhaps ironic that once standard texts like Steven Box's (1973) *Deviance, Reality and Society* must now have their main arguments framed for the new generation of students as a form of 'radical criminology' (Lynch and Michalowski, 2006).

This is not to say that psychological approaches are unable to engage with the new currents of thinking in criminology, currents that take in feminism, post-structuralism, masculinities, post-colonialism, culture, edgework, surveillance, globalisation and the like. Rather, it is that teachers who take on the task of presenting such work to students will need to tap into a literature on psychology that stands outside its own mainstream. This might include work such as Ian Hacking's (1995) *Rewriting the Soul: Multiple Personality and the Sciences of Memory*, an analysis of psychological modes of discovery and invention and the way new forms of pathology are regularly conjured up by the discipline to meet and reflect contemporary forms of social anxiety. Thus, a critical criminological approach to the nexus of psychology with crime, law and justice might conceivably look quite different to one focused on the traditional forms and frames through which these issues have been resolved within both psychology and indeed within criminology itself.

References

Andrews, D.A. and Bonta, J. (1998) *The Psychology of Criminal Conduct*, 2nd ed. Cincinnati, OH: Anderson Publishing.

Anthony, T. and Cunneen, C. (eds.) (2008) *The Critical Criminology Companion*. Annandale, NSW: Hawkins Press.

Bartol, C. and Bartol, A. (2005) *Criminal Behaviour: A Psychosocial Approach*, 7th Edition. Upper Saddle River, NJ: Pearson Education.

Box, S. (1971) *Deviance, Reality and Society*. London: Holt, Reinhart and Winston.

Brewer, N. and Williams, K. (2005) *Psychology and Law: An Empirical Perspective*. NY: Guilford Press.

Brown, M. (2009) 'Toward a new economy of suspended rights: sex offenders and post-sentence confinement and control.' In *Proceedings of the 25th Annual Law and Society Conference of Australia and New Zealand*, University of Sydney. (available at: http://hdl.handle.net/2123/4007)

Carlen, P. and Tombs, J. (2006) 'Reconfigurations of penality: The ongoing case of the women's imprisonment and reintegration industries' *Theoretical Criminology*, 10, 337-60.

Carrington, K. and Hogg, R. (Eds.) (2002) *Critical Criminology: Issues, Debates, Challenges*. Cullompton, Devon: Willan Publishing.

Eysenck, H. (1964) *Crime and Personality*. London: Routledge and Kegan Paul.

Farrington, D., Biron, L. and LeBlanc, M. (1982) 'Personality and delinquency in London and Montreal', in J. Gunn and D. Farrington (Eds.) *Abnormal Offenders, Delinquency and the Criminal Justice System*. Chichester: John Wiley.

Farrington, D. (2008) *Integrated Developmental and Life-Course Theories of Offending*. Piscataway, NJ: Transaction Publishers.

Gorman, K., Gregory, M., Hayles, M. and Parton, N. (Eds.) (2006) *Constructive Work with Offenders*. London: Jessica Kingsley Publishers.

Hacking, I. (1995) *Rewriting the Soul: Multiple Personality and the Sciences of Memory*. Princeton, NJ: Princeton University Press.

Haney, C. (2002) 'Making law modern: Toward a contextual model of justice' *Psychology, Public Policy and Law*, 8: 3-63.

Haney, C. and Zimbardo, P. (1998) 'The past and future of US prison policy: Twenty five years after the Stanford Prison Experiment' *American Psychologist*, 53: 709-27.

Haney, C. (2005) *Reforming Punishment: Psychological Limitations to the Pains of Imprisonment*. Washington, D.C.: American Psychological Association.

Hirschi, T. and Hindelang, M. (1977) 'Intelligence and delinquency: A revisionist review', *American Sociological Review*, 42: 571-87.

Howitt, D. (2009) *Introduction to Forensic and Criminal Psychology*, 3rd Edition. Harlow: Pearson Education.

Huntley, J. and Costanzo, M. (2003) 'Sexual harassment stories: Testing a story-mediated model of juror decision making in civil litigation', *Law and Human Behavior*, 27: 29-51.

Janus, E. (2000) 'Civil commitment as social control: managing risk of sexual violence', in M. Brown and J. Pratt (Eds.) *Dangerous Offenders: Punishment and Social Order*. London: Routledge.

Kassin, S. (1988) *The American Jury On Trial: Psychological Perspectives*. NY: Taylor and Francis.

Lieberman J. and Sales, B. (2006) *Scientific Jury Selection*. Washington, D.C.: American Psychological Association.

Loftus, E. and Ketcham, K. (1994) *The Myth of Revressed Memory : False Memories and Allegations of Sexual Abuse*. NY: St Martins Press.

Lynch, M. and Michalowski, R. (2006) *Primer in Radical Criminology: Critical Perspectives on Crime, Power and Identity*, 4th Edition. Monsey, NY: Criminal Justice Press.

McGuire, J. (ed.) (1995) *What Works: Reducing Reoffending: Guidelines from Research and Practice*. New York: Wiley.

McGuire, J. (ed.) (2003) *Offender Rehabilitation and Treatment: Effective Programmes and Policies to Reduce Re-offending*. NY: Wiley.

McGuire, J. (2004) *Understanding Psychology and Crime*. Maidenhead: Open University Press.

Moffitt, T. (1993) 'Adolescence-limited and life-course-persistent antisocial behaviour: A developmental taxonomy', *Psychological Review*, 100: 674-701.

Mulvey, E., Steinberg, L., Fagan, J., Cauffman, E., Piquero, A., Chassin, L., Knight, G., Brame, R., Schubert, C., Hecker, T. and Losoya, S. (2004) 'Theory and research on desistance from anti-social activity among serious adolescent offenders', *Youth Violence and Juvenile Justice* 2: 213-36.

Palmer, E. and Hollin, C. (1998) 'A comparison of patterns of moral development in young offenders and non-offenders', *Legal and Criminological Psychology*, 3: 225-35.

Pennington, N. and Hastie, R. (1993) 'The story model of juror decision making', in R. Hastie (ed.) *Inside the Juror*. Cambridge: Cambridge University Press.

Pulkinnen, L. (1986) 'The role of impulse control in the development of antisocial and prosocial behaviour', in D. Olweus, J. Block and M. Radke-Yarrow (Eds.) *Development of Antisocial and Prosocial Behavior: Research, Theories and Issues*. NY: Academic Press.

Roesch, R. and McLaughlan, K. (2007) *Clinical Forensic Psychology and Law*. Aldershot: Ashgate.

Rosenberg, F. and Rosenberg, M. (1978) 'Self esteem and delinquency', *Journal of Youth and Adolescence*, 7: 279-91.

Taylor, I., Walton, P. and Young, J. (1973) *The New Criminology*. London: Routledge and Kegan Paul.

Walton, P. and Young, J. (Eds.) (1998) *The New Criminology Revisited*. Houndmills, Basingstoke: Macmillan Press.

Ward, T., and Brown, M. (2003) 'The risk-need model of offender rehabilitation: A critical analysis' in Ward, T., Laws, D. R., and Hudson, S. H. (eds.), *Sexual Deviance: Issues and Controversies*. Thousand Oaks, CA: Sage.

Ward, T. and Brown, M. (2004) 'The good lives model and conceptual issues in offender rehabilitation' *Psychology, Crime and Law*, 10: 243-57.

Ward, T. and Stewart, C. (2003) 'Criminogenic needs and human needs: A theoretical model' *Psychology, Crime and Law*, 9, 125-43.

Wolfgang, M., Figlio, R. and Sellin, T. (1972) *Delinquency in a Birth Cohort*. Chicago: University of Chicago Press.

Wrightsman, L. and Fulero, S. (2005) *Forensic Psychology*. Belmont, Calif.: Thomson Wadsworth Learning.

Zimbardo, P. (2007) *The Lucifer Effect: Understanding How Good People Turn Evil*. NY: Random House.

12

CRITICAL PERSPECTIVES IN CRIMINOLOGICAL DEVELOPMENT IN !NDIA

Mridul Srivastava

"The field of criminology lacks a sense of its own history."
John H. Laub

In the last 50 years, an array of theories have appeared in criminology, many generated by the discipline of sociology. With so many competing models surfacing, it is difficult to determine if theory growth is occurring in criminology. The question of growth is important to resolve because criminology, if it is truly a progressive form of social science, should be producing theories that are contributing to the accumulation of knowledge. The theory growth is occurring in two different ways within criminology. First, there is evidence of traditional scientific theory accumulation in which new theories build upon the foundations of their forerunners. Second, it was found that perspectives are blended, and this fusion produces unique criminological theories.

Although contemporary definitions vary in the exact words used, there is considerable consensus that criminology involves the application of the "scientific method" to the study of variation in criminal law, the causes of crime, and reactions to crime. This combination of method and substance evolved over time with the expectation for a scientific methodology in place by the late 19th century, and acceptance of the broad, tripartite, substantive focus established by the middle of the 20 century. Criminology is an inter-disciplinary field of study, involving scholars and practitioners representing a wide range of behavioral and social sciences as well as numerous natural sciences.

Sociologists played a major role in defining and developing the field of study and criminology emerged as an academic discipline housed in sociology programmes. However, with the establishment of schools of criminology and the proliferation of academic departments and programmes concentrating specifically on crime and justice in the last half of the 20 century, criminology emerged as a distinct professional field with a broad, interdisciplinary focus and a shared commitment to generating knowledge through systematic research. One ultimate goal of criminology has been the development of theories expressed with sufficient precision that they can be tested, using data collected in a manner that allows verification and replication. The theoretical dimension of criminology has a long history and ideas about the causes of crime can be found in philosophical thought over two thousand years years ago.

Criminology is a field rich in theoretical imagination. Criminology was developed primarily as a tool for imperialist domination and it continues to operate largely as a repressive technology. Other technologies of domination crafted by imperialism, such as police and the prison have been generally appropriated by neo colonial regimes around the world. Criminology initially considered to be a discipline which only study crime and criminals. The study was limited to causes related to crime but now the focus has changed and now more focus is on the crime, criminal law and the criminal justice administration. In my opinion, without integration of all the three aspects of crime, criminal law and criminal justice administration the study of criminology is incomplete. A criminal incident will be followed through the system from detection to apprehension of the offender to the end of any formal or informal disposition. The study of factors involved in the discretion, decisions and practices of the entire system, including statutory and voluntary agencies are necessary before coming to any conclusion.

Crime is a social and economic phenomenon and is as old as the human society. Crime is a legal concept and has the sanction of the law. Crime or an offence is "a legal wrong that can be followed by criminal proceedings which may result into punishment." The hall mark of criminality is that, it is breach of the criminal law. Hart in his work "The Concept of Law" has said "human beings are vulnerable so rule of law is required to protect them." The law of crimes took birth alongwith our civilisation. As soon as people grouped themselves into an organised society, the need for criminal law was immediately felt. The purpose of criminal law is to punish the criminals and to prevent recurrence of crime. Before the emergence of modern political state it was an individuals' own responsibility to protect himself. Sir Henry Mayne has called the ancient criminal law as the law of wrong. After political states came into being they shouldered the responsibility for maintenance of peace and order in society.

Because of the recent changes in communication, transportation and commerce, crime has become a global phenonmenon. Given that assumption, criminology itself must become global in its scope. This means that criminology at all levels should be comparative in nature.

Criminology in India

The Aryans settled first in India as wandering farmers. In course of time they made their own laws for their good government. The Hindu law of crimes, especially the law of punishment, is of immense importance. Of the leading codes of ancient India, the code of Manu is the complete digest dealing with law, religion, custom and usages then prevalent, assault, battery, defamation, theft, robbery, gambling and cheating, trespass were the main offences of that time and the punishment prescribed for them was based on scientific principles and the highest prescribed punishment was the death sentence. Before punishing the offenders, the social status, caste etc. of the accused plus factors leading to the commission of crime were to be kept in view. The criminal jurisprudence of old times was not free from bias. From the times of Yajnavalkya and Brahaspati the rigour of punishment was lessened and softened and fines came to be the ordinary punishment for many crimes. People in those days realised that systematic penal law was necessary for their existence in society. In order to combat the crime a well defined and systematic criminal law was developed in ancient India.

The muslims in India also imposed criminal laws which is known as Shara. This was based on the the Quran and believed to be of divine origin. Since laws of Quran were inadequate to meet the entire requirement, so certain rules of conduct, called sunna, were introduced. All offences for punishment were classified under four broad principles:

1. Qisas (Retaliation) – Qisas applied specially to offences against a person, willful killing and grave injury and the injured party had a right to inflict like injury on the offender.
2. Diyut (Blood Money) - In certain cases where no retaliation was allowed, the injured party had a right to demand only blood money known as diyut.
3. Hadd (Fixed Penalities) – in the case of Hadd, the law prescribed and fixed the penalities for certain offences, e.g., zina (illicit intercourse), drinking of wine, theft, highway robbery and accusing a married woman. In case of theft hands were cut off and for docoity and robbery the maximum punishment was death.
4. Tazir (Discretionary Punishment) – Due to harshness and severity of punishments the proof of the crime alleged was made very essential. Where no punishment was prescribed it was at the discretion of the Judge to give any sort of punishment. As such there was no uniform system of administration of criminal justice.

Many provisions in the Muslim criminal law were not in conformity with good government, natural justice and common sense. That is why the British introduced certain reforms from time to time. The first step was taken after the passing of the Regulating Act, 1773 which established one criminal court in each district which consisted of a Kazi, a Mufti and two Molvis. There was a Court of Criminal Revision composed of a Chief Kazi, a Chief Mufti and three Molvis. In 1793 European judges were appointed in these courts and four appellate courts were set up at Calcutta, Decca, Patna and Murshidabad. Then there was the Supreme Criminal Court at Calcutta known as Sardar Nizamat Adalat. The British then began to refer to English Law of crimes for their guidance but each presidency had a system of its own. As a result contradictory judgements on the same point were delivered by them. The rule of precedent was unknown to them. In the meantime the Charter Act of 1833 introduced the system of single legislation for the whole British India. In order to bring uniformity throughout India the First law Commission appointed under the chairmanship of Lord Macaulay prepared the draft penal code which was revised twice by subsequent Commissions. The final draft code was presented in the Legislative Council in 1856 and then in 1857 and was finally passed and received the Governor General's assent on October 6, 1860 in order to enable the people, judges, administrators, etc., to know the provisions of the new Penal Code, its enforcement was deferred till January 1, 1862.

After that in Independent India many developments took place. So many research studies were conducted by the Law Commission of India, Prison Advisory Committees, Criminal Justice Reform Commissions and Administrative Reform Commissions. It was surprising that every report is somewhere influenced by the western model of criminology and Criminal Justice Administration. Due to the globalisation and liberal trade policies the nature of crime has changed and it effected the local dynamics and control system of society which was existing in the villages of India.

At the beginning of the 20th Century, Criminology was primarily limited to explaining the behaviour of those who committed crimes. Since then criminologists have examined the characteristics of societies, the clash between cultural values, family characteristics and a variety of social factors. Studies of prisons initially focused on individual inmates. For most criminologists, criminal behaviour is now viewed as something integral to a complex society rather than as something inherent in individuals. Recently criminologists have started looking into the police, court and other aspects of social control system, as well as white collar crimes and crimes without victims, e.g., drug use and prostitution.

Study of Criminology in India

Although the importance of criminology discipline was realised in India long back. The establishment of Jail Training School before independence in 1940 and the opening of a separate criminology department in Sagar, Madhya Pradesh shows the willingness of the early criminologist. Soon after the course has started in some universities like University of Madras, Lucknow University, Tata Institute of Social Work, in many Universities of Karnataka and Tamil Nadu, Bundelkhand University etc. But the unfortunate thing with the criminology scholars is that there is a great scarcity of the jobs in the field of criminology.

Criminology Text

The criminological theories can be conceptualised into four major categories of thought:

1. Theories focusing upon individual, group and/or environmental origins of crime
2. Theories focusing upon the role of social control agencies in creating, perpetuating or intensifying crime
3. Theories connecting crime to the social, political and economic conditions reflected in India's society
4. Theories that attempt to integrate several other individual theories in an effort to provide a more compelling explanation of crime.

In India the curriculum covers the theories of individual differences in offending, theories of variation in offending through the lifecycle, theories of diversity of crime rates among social entities, and theories of differences among social situations in criminal outcomes.

Some theories explain two or more categories simultaneously, but they are discussed within the categories reflecting their main focuses. Theories explaining how and why some acts are illegal, why there is differential enforcement of law, why there are differences in offending between males and females, and theories about numerous other phenomena are included in the study of Criminology.

Any intellectual account can be regarded as a theory. However, efforts range from simple one statement principles focused on specific events or phenomena to elaborate, intricately interwoven explanatory systems applying to wide ranges of different phenonmena.

In India there the course of criminology is taught at these different levels.

1. Undergraduate levels

2. Post graduate levels
3. Diploma and Certificate programmes and
4. Ph.D. programmes

The whole course structure of Criminology and Criminal Justice syllabus covers these following topics:

1. Introduction to the Criminal Justice System
2. Comparative Justice Systems
3. Introduction to Policing
4. Historical Perspectives in Criminal Justice
5. Introduction to Public Security
6. Introduction to Criminology
7. The Indian Legal System
8. Introduction to Corrections
9. The Police and the Community : Problems and Issues
10. Problem Management in Criminal Justice
11. Psychological Explanations of Criminal Behaviour
12. Sociological Explanations of Criminal Behaviour
13. Youth and Crime, Drug Abuse, Terrorism, Cyber and Newer forms of Crime
14. Research Methods in Criminology
15. Restorative justice
16. Human Rights and Civil Liberties

Apart from these some universities are running the criminology programme based on the study of criminal behaviour and society's response to it, including the analysis of those policies and systems designed to control criminality. Through the in-depth exploration and study of both theoretical and empirical research drawn from the behavioural, legal, and social sciences students learn about many aspects of crime as a social phenomenon, including the correlates of crime and criminal behaviour, the tools and methods used to study and prevent crime, and the institutions involved in the processing of criminal offenders. The department seeks to achieve this mission through its curriculum that emphasises the development of critical thinking and problem solving skills with respect to each of the following:

(1) the structure and organisational behaviours of the justice system;

(2) the theories underpinning normative socialisation and both formal and informal social control;

(3) the roles policing, courts, corrections, and laws play in contributing to social control;

(4) the practical and ethical complexities of the roles of justice professionals;

(5) macro and micro level criminology theories regarding the etiology of crime, criminality, and delinquency;

(6) the measurement, detection, and prevention of crime, criminality, and delinquency;

(7) the research, planning, and evaluation methods used to expand knowledge in the field;

(8) the international variations on criminal justice systems and social control and comparative criminology;

(9) the development and refinement of communication skills both orally and in writing with particular emphasis on persuasive argumentation supported by logic, legal precedent, and scholarly research; and

(10) the practical application of all of this knowledge in ways that promote active leadership that effectuates positive change in the agencies of law, law enforcement, rehabilitation, governmental service, academia, and research.

Future aspects of Criminology and Criminal Justice Systems: Critical Concerns and Core Issues

There is an extensive literature on the crisis of Criminal Justice System. All these explain the manifold problems besetting Criminal Justice System. Criminal Justice System is an often idea, philosophy and a mechanism. It is a thoughtfully designed system.

The idea, philosophy and mechanism is not part of law school syllabi.

However – all these three characterise features have not been fully put into practice.

Broadly speaking there are 6 key constituents of the system:

1. Public (Citizens of the country for whom the system is meant.)

2. Legislators
3. Enforcement Executives (Police Functionaries)
4. Prosecutors/ defense lawyers
5. Judicial officers (Magistrates/ Judges)
6. Correctional Administrators (Prisons, Observation Homes etc.)

However – the first two are generally excluded when the system concept is operationalised/formalised.

Criminal Justice: Reflections of Realities

1. Judged on the standards of justice our Criminal Justice System fails miserably and hence, it has too many critics and only few judgments reflect the spirit of law and larger welfare of the society.
2. The system seems to be analysed and is in a state of crisis.
3. Many times Criminal Justice System functionaries says that it is a criminal system and not a criminal justice system.
4. It is true that Criminal Justice system is fast losing its credibility and is getting increasingly unpopular.
5. The worst part is that the system is falling in the esteemation of the people as also many by people who manage it.
6. The system, is on the verge of breakdown and hardly has any features to be proud of.

Some of the critical concerns of the system are:

1. It is a non system because its components police, prosecution, courts and corrections instead of working in harmony, often work at cross purposes.
2. It suffers from
   (a) goal confusion
   (b) fragmentation
   (c) lack of coordination
   (d) outdated knowledge base
   (e) internal/external resistance to change
   (f) anti –poor orientation

Four Issues

1. First and foremost is the honest understanding of the peoples perception of criminal justice–court, police, corrections
2. Second issue of critical significance is reforming an archaic, obsolete and antiquated model of Criminal Justice System
   (a) National Policy for Criminal Justice
   (b) The Criminal Justice Act
3. The third issue is of cost, complexity and cumbersomeness of the Criminal Justice System
4. The last issue is corruption and abuse of authorities and the culture of insensitiveness towards the concerns of criminal justice

Random Reflections

Core Characteristics of Criminology and Criminal Law

1. It characterises statism rather than dynamism.
2. It has not progressed along with progressions in the contemporary ideas of justice and the contemporary realities of crime.
3. Its basic feature is obsolesce wraped and rooted in conservatism.
4. It is of ancient vintage, archaic and amachostic.
5. Its three Bibles (IPC, CrPC and Evidence Act) are hardly conscious of the modern strides in criminal jurisprudence and do not articulate the current thoughts of criminal justice.
6. Up till now, we have made only cosmetic changes.
7. Besides being obsolescent it shares in large measure the myth of legislation, which the British legacy which we have inherited and refused to discover.
8. It is concluded in such technical terms/concepts, some of which are not tenable today, and confuse the common man.
9. I suspect it is meant for the classes not the masses.

10. The real beneficiaries are indeed its creators
11. For all the evils of the Criminal Law we are blaming the British for giving us a colonial jurisprudence WHO STOPPED US?

    "Inefficient law is worse than no law, for it undermines the faith of the people in the rule of law itself".

    —Justice Krishna Iyer

    — Given the pervasive climate of lawlessness and weakened rule of law, people generally tend to believe that rule of law is cliché for the protection for the fortunate few.

    — In a given scenario, wherein the law forms the rich and resourceful, Justice Iyer coins terms as "Lawless laws"- "Lawful Illegality".

He sums up the travails of criminal law when he observes: "At a time when the credibility of criminal law is severely contested, it is only the criminal law that is on trial".

The whole problem with the criminology discipline in India is that the theories of crime and criminals are not applicable in totality when it comes to the ground realities. It is a divorced discipline with criminal justice and criminal law. Unless efforts have not been made for expansion of the subject and its practical importance is not proved, the criminology discipline will never be nourished and developed and may be criminology will vanish/abolish from the academic programmes of the country.

References

Akers, Ronalds L. "Criminological Theories: Introduction, Evaluation and Application, 3rd Edition, Los Angeles Roxbury Press, 2000.

Cullen T. Francis "Criminological Theory: Past to Present" 3rd Edition, Los Angeles Roxbury Press, 2006.

Gupta R.P. Das, "Crime and Punishment in Ancient India" Bhartiya Kala Prakashan, Delhi 1930.

Srivastava O.P. "Principles of Criminal Law" Eastern Book Company, Fourth Edition 2005.

Tannenbaum, F. "Crime and the Community", New York, Columbia University Press, 1938.

13

INTERVENTION IN SOCIAL WORK FOR CRIME PREVENTION—AN ACTION RESEARCH PAPER

Prateep V. Philip

The Social Justice and Human Rights Wing of Tamil Nadu's Police Department are formulating various modalities to prevent crimes proactive. One of the measures which is being adopted is by undertaking and motivating the various departments and through NGOs to take up various social measures by way of creating basic infrastructure facilities such as provision of drinking water, provision of street lights, provision of burial ground, pathway to burial ground, provision of link roads, provision of house sites and houses to the SC/ST habitations which are being the causes for creating the social tension. Another form of combating crime against SCs/STs is by way of proposing employment oriented welfare schemes in the untouchabliity/ atrocity prone areas. By proposing and implementing such schemes have not only helped the people by way of earning their livelihood but also improving their Social relationship by preventing crimes.

The trend analysis of crimes against SC/STs reveals that cases are being reported mainly based on motives such as petty quarrel, previous enmity, practice of two tumbler system in the tea shops, land dispute, caste/communal problems, monetary dispute, sexual jealousy, minor theft, Water/Irrigation dispute, political dispute, village festival, wage dispute, Eve teasing, burial ground problems, grazing of cattle etc. Initially, the Social Justice and human Rights Wing take preventive action only by collecting advance source reports. After the analysis of the crimes, it has been realised that the main cause for disputes are only the non-availability of basic amenities and poverty. Thereafter, this wing took various measures to provide basic amenities in the SC/ST habitations and by diverting the various socio-economic schemes of the Government for the benefit of the sections of the people particularly in the atrocity/dormant atrocity prone areas. The Government have also assigned high priority on the schemes proposed by this wing.

In addition to the above, the Social Justice and Human Rights wing of the Police Department has initiated a novel idea of conducting Social Justice Tea Parties in all the villages across the State. It is really heartening to note that this unique progranmme has become a great success. The Social Justice and Human Rights wings functioning not merely as a Police agency for effective enforcement of PCR and POA Acts but also as an "instrument of social change" in curbing inequalities in social system and redressing the grievances of SC/ST people. The tea party programme in villages has been labelled as "Mass Awareness Campaign".

The salient features of the campaign are as follows:

Synopsis

The project intend to create awareness on the constitutional safeguards, provisions of the Protection of Civil Rights act-1955, Scheduled Castes the Scheduled Tribes (Prevention of Atrocities) Act-1989 and its 'Rules in Tamil Nadu State by organizing Social Justice Tea Parties and on conducting interactive sessions on Equilibrium Thinking, an unique thought transforming process.

Genesis

The Social Justice and Human Rights Wing of the Police Department, has attempted to blend the activism of the Boston Tea Party and the ideology of the Justice Party to promote a movement against the practice of untouchability from the very same tea shops that have been characterised as a mean to impose social divide in the villages.

Need for the Awareness Campaign

There was a spurt in the activities of NGOs and the various SC/ST associations in the recent months, the news published in the papers and magazines on the prevalence of two tumbler system in general all over Tamil Nadu and in specific, they pointed out certain number of villages in Cuddalore, Salem, Coimbatore, Erode, Perambalur, Madurai, Virudunagar and other districts. But, the Police verification of the places jointly with the NGOs and others proved that the messages propagated by them are false, motivated and with the ulterior motive for political gains. This has projected a distorted image on the Government.

In these circumstances, it was felt that the Social Justice and Human Rights wing of the Police department should initiate mass campaign to create awareness among the various sections of the society and there by reducing the number of incidents and create mass awareness for social transformation.

Objectives

The objectives for the mass campaign are as follows:-

(i) To highlight on how the Acts and Rules are effectively enforced by the Police;

(ii) To promote confidence among the members of SCs/STs;

(iii) To sensitise the society on eradication of untouchablity and atrocities against the members of SCs/STs;

(iv) To promote harmony among the caste Hindus and SCs/STs and

(v) To create awareness on the nature of offences and it's gravity to the non-SC/ST people.

Organisation and Participants

It is proposed to organise the mass awareness campaign on the following 2 tier basis throughout Tamil Nadu covering about 40-50 per cent of the villages:

(a) At the District Level

There are 29 police districts and 6 police commissionrates. The District Level Campaign will be inaugurated by the concerned District Collector. The Commissioner of Police/Superintendent of Police will preside over the district level campaign. Other participants likely to be involved for the campaign are Police/ Revenue officials, Special Public Prosecutors, SC/ST Association leaders, Local leaders (Political and Non-Political), Friends of Police, Non-Governmental Organisations, the members of the District Level Vigilance and Monitoring Committee and others such as school and college students, publics. The Social Justice Rally will be arranged for the participants at the end of the campaign.

(b) At the Village Panchayat Level

There are 81,787* habitations/villages in 12,618* Village Panchayats in 29 districts in Tamilnadu. It has been proposed to cover 37,854 habitations/villages at an average of 3 villages in each Panchayat. The percentage of coverage is 46. At Village Panchayat Level, the Inspector of Police, SJ and HR is in-charge of organising the awareness campaign under the supervision of DSP, SJ and HR. The participants are Special Prosecutor/Public Prosecutor/prominent Lawyers, SC/ST Association leaders, Local leaders (Political and Non-Political) and Academician, Members of Non-Governmental Organisation, Friends of Police and others.

Project Cost

The total estimated cost for the proposed Social Justice Tea Party and Awareness Campaign will be Rs. 70 Lakhs at the rate of Rs. 2 Lakhs per Police District/Cities. The detailed estimate cost for the district level and village level campaign is worked out as below:

(a) At the District Level

The estimated expenditure for conducting awareness campaign with **SOCIAL JUSTICE RALLY** at the district head quarter level for 500 participants is worked out to Rs. 8,75,000 at the rate Rs. 25,000 per district/Commissionarates. At all the centers, there will be a presentation on the provisions of Act and rules, demonstrations on various forms of untouchablity/atrocities against the SCs/STs and their repercussions in the society, video and audio presentation etc., followed by a lunch on as in the case of Samabandhiboojanam.

(b) At the Village Panchayat Level

The estimated expenditure for conducting awareness campaign at the village panchayat level is worked out to Rs. 56,79,000 at the rate of Rs. 150 per village to cover 37,854 villages in 12,618 panchayats. There will reserve cash of Rs. 4,46,000 to meet out the unforeseen expenditure.

Implementing Agency

The programme is implemented by the Inspector of Police, Social Justice and Human Rights wing in the districts/cities and by the Dy. Superintendent of Police in the zones. The Inspector General of Police, Social Justice and Human Rights and Deputy Inspector General of Police, Social Justice and Human Rights, Chennai guide and supervise the implementation of the programme.

Duration of the Awareness Campaign and Publicity

The Awareness Campaign Programme is being implemented during a period of 12 months from the date of sanction. The tempo of the campaign is maintained in such a way that the public will keep alive the memory of the message of the Awareness Programme during the period of implementation through news and publicity in the local vernacular newspapers.

Proposed Coverage of Mass Awareness Campaign

The mass awareness campaign at the district and village levels will definitely have a ripple effect in the society. The campaign covers 29 police districts headquarters, 6 city police headquarters and 37,354 villages. It is more than 46 per cent of the total habitations in the State. If the message of the Social Justice Tea Party and Awareness Campaign is carried over to at least to 10 persons by each participant, the message will spread to at least among TWO CRORES POPULATION as per the assumption worked out below:

At the District Level : 500 Participants x 10 Persons x 35 Towns = 1,75,000 persons.

At the Village Level :50 Participants x 10 Persons x 37,854 Villages = 1,89,27,000 persons.

Total number of persons to whom message reached = 1,91,02,000 persons.

This ample coverage of town/villages would certainly bring an enormous awareness about the existing discriminatory practices in the society and would enlighten other caste people about the importance of advocating Social Justice. This will pave way for greater social change in the near future.

Proposed Impact on Implementation of Mass Awareness Campaign

The following are the anticipated ramifications of the mass awareness campaign:

(i) The Social Justice Tea Party and Awareness Campaign would definitely axe the discriminatory and evil practices against the deprived sections of the society in temples, buses, streets, burial grounds, restaurants, public places and in all walks of life;

(ii) The Social Justice Tea Party and Awareness Campaign would certainly bring down the crime rate against the SCs and STs; The Social Justice Tea Party and Awareness Campaign would surely stimulate the social system to render Social Justice at all the levels in the society;

(iii) The Social Justice Tea Party and Awareness Campaign would promote positive attitude among the public towards the SCs and STs. This will in turn accelerate the socio - economic status of the SCs and STs and promote smooth relationship with other castes;

(iv) The Social Justice Rally and Awareness Campaign would bring transformation in mindset among the youth, students and others;

(v) The Social Justice Tea Party and Awareness Campaign would bring absolute impact among the non-SCs by way of understanding each others;

(vi) The Social Justice Tea Party and Awareness Campaign would act as an instrument to bring the required change in the existing social structure and

(viii) The Social Justice Rally and Awareness Campaign would stress the need for communal harmony and peaceful co-existence in the rural areas.

First Time in India

It may be noted that such an innovative campaign on a war footing has been conceived and initiated for the first time in the whole country and would have spill over effect in all states in due course. This Mass Awareness Campaign will definitely promote equality, brotherhood and solidarity among all castes in the villages and eradicate all social inequalities against the members of SCs/STs.

Project Sanction

This project proposal was forwarded to the Secretary to Govt., Adi-Dravidar and Tribal Welfare Department on 03.10.2007 and the same was sent to the Ministry of Social Justice and Empowerment, Government of India seeking the entire cost of the project. But, the Ministry of Social justice and Empowerment, Government of India had readily sanctioned the 50 per cent of the project cost i.e Rs. 35.00 lakhs in Letter No. 11014/2007 – PCR (Desk) dated 11. 01.2008 of the Under Secretary to Government of India, Ministry of Social Justice and Empowerment. The Adi-Dravidar and Tribal Welfare Department of Government of Tamil Nadu have sanctioned the remaining cost of the project i.e. Rs. 35 lakhs in G.O M.S. No. 49, Adi-Dravidar and Tribal Welfare Department (POA) dated 10.04.2008.

The expenditure incurred in implementing this project is audited and statement of expenditure given for all 35 units (districts and commissionrates) in Tamil Nadu.

Benchmark Survey to Assess the Present Level of Awareness on the Various Constitutional Safeguards, PCR, POA Acts and IT's Rules

It is assumed that on the implementation of the project, it will create awareness among 19,10,200 persons directly and 2 crores population indirectly. In addition, the project aims at:

(i) to axe the discriminatory evil practices in temples, buses, public places etc.

(ii) to bring down the crime rate against the SC/ST;

(iii) to stimulate the social system to render social justice at all levels;

(iv) to promote positive attitude among the public towards the SC/ST and accelerate the socio-economic status of the SC/ST and

(v) to bring transformation in the mindset among the youth, students and others.

Objectives of Bench Mark Survey

The level of present awareness and other objectives before the implementation of the project has to be assessed, so that, the definite impact after the implementation of the scheme can be accurately measured. Therefore, the Inspector General of Police/ Deputy Inspector General of Police, SJ and HR have decided to organise a bench mark survey before the implementation of the project to assess the present level of awareness on the provisions of the acts, rules and constitutional safeguards to SC/ST among the public.

Sample Size

The bench mark survey was conducted on a sampling basis. Survey was conducted in all the 169 police sub-divisions in the districts except in cities, at the rate of 2 villages per sub-division. In each village, 10 respondents were interviewed and survey schedules filled up by the SJ and HR unit Statistical Officers/ Investigators. They were instructed to ensure that the 10 respondents were from SC/ST and other castes in more or less equal number.

Questionnaire

A format had been designed with questionnaires and circulated to all the Social and Human Rights units in the districts. The questionnaire was related to:

(i) Nature of relationship between SC/ST and other castes;

(ii) Existence of discriminatory practices in tea shops, in temples, in public places etc.;

(iii) Problems regarding the non-availability of burial ground and pathway to burial ground;

(iv) Level of awareness regarding the provisions of PCR Act and POA Act;

(v) Level of awareness about the various concessions and financial assistance extended by the Government;

(vi) Level of awareness about the monetary relief sanctioned by the Government to victims of atrocities;

(vii) Level of awareness about the functioning of NGOs in the selected villages;

(viii) Availability of basic amenities in the selected villages;

(ix) Number of persons who want mass awareness campaign to be conducted on the provisions of Acts and others;

(x) Enrollment of members of all communities in Self Help Groups;

(xi) Availing of educational concessions by members of respective communities and

(xii) Awareness regarding the Friends of Police.

The Inspectors of police and Statistical Inspectors were requested to organise the survey. The Statistical Inspectors, who are working in the SJ and HR units, are on deputation basis to this department from the Department of Economics and Statistics. The Statistical Inspectors are professionally experienced and therefore, the data to be collected is accurate and error free.

Organisation of Survey

The survey was organised by the Inspectors of Police and Statistical Inspectors. The survey work was supervised by the Zonal Deputy Superintendents of Police and also by the Economist and Sociologist of SJ and HR wing.

This survey was completed in April – May, 2008. Overall, the survey was conducted in 338 villages in 169 police sub-divisions ie., at the rate of 2 villages in a sub-division. The investigators contacted 3380 respondents of all age groups. This is at the rate 10 respondents per village. Among the 3380 respondents, 1789 (53 per cent) were from SC/ST communities and 1591 (47 per cent) were from other castes.

Findings of the Benchmark Survey

- GOI and GOTN have sanctioned Rs. 70.00 Lakhs to organise Mass Awareness Campaign on the constitutional safeguards on SCs/STs, provisions of PCR, POA Acts and Rules on 50:50 basis;
- Objectives of the Benchmark survey is to assess the present level of awareness regarding various aspects of the enforcement of the above acts and related matters;

- Survey was organised on the orders of the IGP/DIG, SJ and HR and carried out by the Statistical Inspectors of SJ and HR Units;
- Survey covered all the police sub-divisions in Tamil Nadu except the ranges/sub-divisions in the Commissionerates;
- Questionnaire was designed in such a way that it will reflect the general awareness on the Acts and other related SC/ST matters;
- Survey was organised on sampling basis by selecting 2 villages in each police sub-division by contacting 10 respondents in each village consisting of both SC/ST and other caste people;
- In the survey, the coverage of 3380 respondents from SC/ST and other castes in 338 villages spread over 169 police sub-divisions i.e at the rate of 2 villages per sub-division and 10 persons in each selected village;
- Among 3380 respondents, 1789 (53 per cent) are SC respondents and 1591 (47 per cent) are from other castes;
- Among the 3380 respondents 98 per cent of them have revealed that the relationship between the SC/ST and other castes/communities is cordial and only 2 per cent of them have informed that their relationship with other castes is strained;
- Regarding the existing discriminatory practices in tea shops, temples and public places, the survey reveals that 99.6 per cent of the 3380 respondents stated that there are no discriminatory practices in their villages; 0.4 per cent respondents from the districts in South Zone alone have said that there are discriminatory practices against SCs;
- 95 per cent of the respondents said that they have no problem regarding availability of burial ground and pathway to burial ground; 5 per cent of the respondents said that there is no burial ground and pathway to burial ground;
- Awareness on the provisions of the PCR, POA Acts and Rules among the respondents is enormous. 76 per cent out of 3380 respondents said that they are aware of the Acts and Rules but not in detail of the provisions; only

24 per cent of them said that they are not aware of the Acts and Rules. This 24 per cent of the public is our target group, for whom, we are organising the Mass Awareness Programme;

- Regarding various concessions and financial assistance provided by the Govt., 78 per cent of the respondents are aware of the concessions and assistance extended by the Govt. and the remaining 22 per cent are not aware of the concessions and assistance extended by the Govt;
- Monetary Relief is being sanctioned to the SC/ST victims of atrocities under SCs/STs (POA) Rules. This provision was known to 62 per cent of the respondents and not known to the 38 per cent of the respondents;
- Regarding the awareness about the functioning of NGOs in the sampled/surveyed villages, only 23 per cent of the respondents are aware and 77 per cent are not aware;
- 86 per cent of respondents said that the available basic amenities are adequate and 14 per cent of the respondents said that it is inadequate;
- One of the major outcome of the survey is that 94 per cent of the 3380 respondents felt that it is necessary to conduct Mass Awareness Campaign on the provisions of Acts and Rules and other matters and only 6 per cent have said that the campaign is not needed;
- Regarding the enrollment of members from all communities in SHG (Self Help Group), 53 per cent of the respondents said that the SCs/STs are enrolled and 47 per cent of the respondents said that the enrollment of the SCs/STs has to be increased;
- On availing of educational concessions by the members of all communities, 95 per cent of the 3380 respondents said that they are availing benefits and 5 per cent of them replied in the negative and;
- Regarding awareness of the FOP, 68 per cent of the respondents said that they are aware of the functioning of FOP and 32 per cent were not aware;

A major finding of this survey is that the erstwhile ubiquitous "Two Tumbler" practice as well as other forms of discrimination has been virtually eradicated and only 0.4 per cent of respondents from Southern Zone perceive that there is discrimination against the SC/ST. The conduct of Mass Awareness Campaign has become necessary because as many as 94 per cent of the individuals interviewed have felt that it is necessary to organise such a campaign. The survey findings indicate that 76 per cent of the persons interviewed were aware of the Acts and Rules but not the details of the provisions of the Acts; the remaining 24 per cent are not aware of the existence of the Acts.

Implementation of the Project

This scheme was implemented from 03.07.2008 in all the police districts in the State. In the first phase, a sum of Rs. 10 lakhs had been released to all the districts and the campaign/social justice tea parties have been conducted in 6,667 villages across the State. For the 2nd phase, again a sum of Rs. 10 lakhs had been released on 3.11.2008 and the campaigns have been conducted in 5000 villages. In the coming year, the Mass Awareness Campaign will be carried out in the remaining 26,187 villages. A large number of news reports about the ***Mass Awareness Campaign*** were published in the local vernacular newspapers as well as English news papers and TV media. The message of the Mass Awareness Campaign has been reached to about 6 lakhs people directly and 60 lakhs people indirectly so far in 11667 villages in 29 districts and 6 Commissionerates in addition to 3 lakhs students in 315 schools and colleges in all the districts and cities. In the months of May – June, 08 with the help of Statistical Inspectors of SJ and HR wing, a benchmark survey was conducted in all 169 Police Sub-Divisions of the State. 94 per cent of 3380 people of all castes/communities and districts polled were of the view that such a Mass Awareness Campaign is the need of the hour.

This is the very first time Social Justice Tea Party under the Mass Awareness Campaign is being conducted in the whole country to eliminate all types of social disparities and discrimination between social groups from the village to the urban centers.

Impact Analysis of Feedback

1. Out of Rs.70.00 lakhs sanctioned, Rs.10.00 Lakhs was released as the first instalment to conduct Mass Awareness Campaign in 6667 villages;

2. Campaign was organised from 30.06.2008 to 24.10.2008 and completed in all the 6667 villages. In the campaign, 3,55,993 persons participated. Among the participants, 2,22,231 (62 per cent) were male and 1,33,762 (38 per cent) female.
3. In order to assess the impact of the Mass Awareness Campaign, a minimum of 10 per cent of the villages were instructed to cover by enlisting the opinion of the participants in the campaigns consisting of both SC/ST and others;
4. Format for filling up the feedback information/opinion on the Mass Awareness Campaign was designed in such a way to enlist the views and opinions of the participants;
5. On the whole, 5724 participants in 1064 villages (16 per cent) were contacted both from SC/ST and other castes and their opinions were collected on the usefulness/ otherwise of the campaign;
6. Among the total participants of the campaign, 2264 (40 per cent) respondents belonging to SC/ST and the remaining 3460 (60 per cent) belonging to other communities;
7. Among the total participants, 5563 (97 per cent) persons opined that Mass Awareness Campaign was very useful to them;
8. 46 per cent of the total participants stated that Mass Awareness Campaign was instrumental in reducing the discriminatory and evil practices in the society;
9. 18 per cent of the total participants said that Mass Awareness Campaigns promoted positive attitude towards the SCs/STs;
10. 27 per cent of the total participants said that Mass Awareness Campaigns have changed the present social situation in their villages;
11. 73 per cent of the total participants felt that Mass Awareness Campaigns promoted communal harmony and peaceful co-existence in their villages;
12. 52 per cent of the total participants stated that they have come to know the provisions of the SCs/STs (POA) Act and its rules;

13. 51 per cent of the participants opined that they have come to know on the various welfare schemes and concessions sanctioned to SCs/STs by the Government and also about the monetary relief paid to the victims;
14. In general, both the SC/ST participants and others have felt that the campaign was very useful and if such campaigns are organised frequently, the social disparity among SCs/STs and others will disappear in the near future.

Recommendations of the Survey

1. An integrated multimedia centre called Social Justice Multimedia Development Centers may be established in the hub of atrocity prone/dormant atrocity prone villages at a cost of Rs. 10.00 lakhs each with the infrastructure including building, electronic library, and computer with internet connection etc. To start with, these centers may be opened in all the districts at the rate of one each in 169 police sub-divisions on an experimental basis. These centers will be manned by a person belonging to SC/ST community who has been trained in computer operation whose honorarium may be fixed at as consolidated Rs. 5000 per month. The total cost works out to Rs.18.00 crores with the non-recurring cost of Rs. 16.90 crores and recurring cost of Rs. 1.05 crores annually. Each multimedia Social Justice center may have an attached games/sports facility like a gymnasium, volley ball court etc. These centers will have CDs carrying details of various Governmental schemes to benefit weaker sections of society. The expenditure may be shared with the Central Government on 50:50 basis.
2. Survey reveals that there is existence of strained relationship between SC/ST and non- SC/ST (2 per cent (61) of 3380 respondents) in some villages in Kancheepuram, Villupuram, Krishnagiri, The Nilgiris, Thanjavur and Theni districts. The reasons for the strained relationship in these villages have to be identified and action taken to resolve the issues between them. The Superintendents of Police concerned may be instructed.
3. Outcome of the survey shows that 0.35 per cent (12) of

3380 respondents i.e., 1 from Arunthavapuram in Thanjavur district and 11 from Kanniservaipatti, Rasakanayakanpatti and Samanthipuram village in Theni district have stated that there are discriminatory practices in tea shops, temples and public places. The Superintendents of Police and District Collectors concerned may be requested to identify the problems and take necessary action.

4. In spite of the continuous efforts of the Government to provide burial ground and pathway to burial ground to SC/ST, the survey discloses that there is still demand for provision of burial ground and pathway to burial ground. 5 per cent (175 SC/ST and 5 non-SC/ST) of the interviewed respondents in Cuddalore (10), Vellore (30), Thiruvannamalai (10), Coimbatore (10), Pudukottai (7), Thanjavur (25), Nagapattinam (10), Dindigul (14), Theni (56), Madurai (2), Tirunelveli (2), Thoothukudi (1) and Kanyakumari (3) said that there is non-availability of burial and pathway to burial ground in their villages. It shows that there are many villages which are in need of this facility and the Government have to take action for providing a common burial ground to all the villages under the schemes in implementation. The Government may issue instructions to all District Collectors in this regard.
5. Findings of the survey on the awareness about the PCR, POA Acts and Rules highlights that there is still 24 per cent (798) of 3380 respondents unaware of the Acts and Rules. Therefore, there is a need to take the message to these sections of the people.
6. Survey reveals 38 per cent (1269) of the 3380 respondents are not aware about the monetary relief sanctioned to the SC/ST victims of the atrocities by the Government. Particularly, in the West (49 per cent), Central (48 per cent) and South Zones (40 per cent), the percentage of people not aware are relatively high. This is again pointing out the need for creating more awareness among the public. The Mass Awareness Campaign currently underway will address this.
7. Number of NGOs are working for the social, economic

and political upliftment of SCs/STs. But, the survey reveals that only 23 per cent are aware of the functioning of NGOs. It is to be considered that the people friendly NGOs who gained confidence among the public may be motivated to work for the cause of the SCs/STs by the Government.

8. As per the survey, 14 per cent (482) of the 3380 of the respondents have informed that the basic amenities such as drinking water, street lights, burial ground, pathway to burial ground, roads, drainages etc., which are now available in the villages are reported to be inadequate. 482 persons who have spoken about the inadequacy of basic amenities are spread almost in all the districts. All the District Collectors may therefore be addressed by the Government to ensure that all the villages have to be provided with the basic amenities.
9. 94 per cent (3182) of the 3380 respondents affirmed the need to conduct the mass awareness campaign programme. It is implicit that the awareness campaign now initiated by the Government through the Social Justice and Human Rights wing of the Police Department is the need of the hour.
10. 47 per cent (1582-755 SC and 827 others) of the respondents are of the opinion that the members of all caste/ communities are not enrolled in Self Help Groups. This shows that the members of SHGs are not representative of all castes/communities. Since, about 50 per cent of the respondents are of the above opinion, the Government have i) to review the membership pattern of SHGs ii) to find out whether the people from all castes/communities are active members of the SHGs and iii) to issue instructions down the line to ensure that people willing from all caste are enrolled as members of SHGs. Multi-caste self help groups should be encouraged with more bank financing.
11. 5 per cent (185) of the 3380 respondents informed that they have not availed any educational concessions. They are from Kancheepuram, Vellore, Namakkal, Dharmapuri, Coimbatoe, Erode, Trichy, Dindigul, Theni and Madurai districts. This may, perhaps, be due to the difficulties

experienced by them in availing the educational concessions provided by the Government. The difficulties, in general, may be ascertained and so ensure that all the eligible students irrespective of caste are provided with educational concessions. In this regard, general instructions may be issued to all concerned.

12. Role of Friends of Police (FOP) in the transformation of the society need not be stressed at this juncture. However, 32 per cent (1090) of the 3380 respondents are still not aware of the role of Friends of Police. To improve the image of the Police and its significant role in assisting public in all walks of life, so that the entire public will be aware, FOP may be further strengthened as ordered by the Hon'ble Chief Minister in the August, 2007 Superintendents of Police and Collectors conference by a series of measures.

Though the number of cases under POA has increased to the highest ever 1545, the percentage of grave crimes like murder, rape, arson have declined by 28 per cent.

14

CYBERCRIME MANAGEMENT—AN IT GOVERNANCE APPROACH

K. Rama Subramaniam

Studying cybercrime management from an IT governance perspective requires a good understanding of both IT governance and cybercrimes. Governance has been the subject matter of a number of position papers and discussion notes; mostly at the business level, starting with the Cadbury Committee Report that laid the foundations for understanding corporate governance though it was skewed towards the financial aspects of corporate governance. Drawing on the foundations of corporate governance, IT governance emerged and matured to a point where it is now well defined and has validated measurement metrics to determine its maturity level. IT governance continues to guide many large corporate investments in security products and services that are aimed at combating cybercrimes; *albeit* at corporate level. A general framework of IT governance for the purposes of this paper can be drawn in the form of aligning management action to stake holder expectations. Good IT governance is based on four key questions, also popularly referred to as the 'Four Ares' that are addressed while seeking to evaluate the degree of maturity of governance process from the point of view of the stakeholders:

- Strategic question: Are we doing the right things?
- Architecture question: Are we doing them the right way?
- Value question: Are we getting them done well?
- Delivery question: Are we getting the benefits?

This paper uses the Four Ares to build a framework for understanding the processes and challenges that face successful management of cybercrimes.

In contrast to the good degree of understanding obtained in studies related to IT governance, cybercrime continues to beg a rigorous conceptual framework and it may remain so, for more time to come. The absence of such a framework arises, *inter alia*, from usage of the term 'cybercrime' more emotively rather than on a consciously developed definition that has stood the test of scientific scrutiny. As an example, we have media reporting as cybercrime the case of an e-mail used to send out a threatening mail. All that had happened in this case is that a non-traditional means had been used for communicating a message whose content is offensive. The crime is the offensive content but because it was delivered through an electronic media, it got mis-classified as cyber crime. This is analogous to seeking to classify offensive contents as postal-delivery crimes, courier delivery crimes, telegram delivery crimes etc. when each of these delivery mechanisms had been used to deliver an offensive message. Misconceptions like this and the consequent search for a precise definition of cybercrime resulted in Wall opining that cybercrime has no specific reference point in law. The confusion in the usage of the word cybercrime has resulted in some authors wondering if there are indeed such things as cybercrimes. Attempts have also been made by scholars to determine if there is a need to understand cybercrimes differently from other forms of crimes and warrant evolution of a new set of criminological theories; or can the existing theories of Criminology be used to understand cybercrimes.

As with any process of search for a rigorous definition, an inquiry into the etymological derivation of the word "cyber" leads us to the inherent governance attribute in this term. Cyber appears to be the root of the word 'govern' as found in the 1830 French usage of the word *cybernetique* meaning 'art of governing.' One of the earliest usage of the word 'cyber' in the English language can be traced to Norbert Weiner whose epoch making work defines Cybernetics as "the entire field of control and communication theory, whether in the machine or in the animal." Later writers used the word cyber as the base to evolve such terms as cyberspace, cyber highway, etc. Interestingly both the French usage of the word cyber and its first known English usage point to its close relationship with the concept of controls, which is the cornerstone on which all governance edifices are built.

Loosely speaking, cybercrimes have been understood as having something to do with technology; more particularly the Internet. Summarising the impact of the Internet on criminal activities and behaviour, Wall articulates on the three different ways in which Internet has transformed criminal opportunities. These three different ways become important as they determine the contour of the technological domain within which the IT governance dimension of cybercrimes will be discussed in this paper. First, Internet has emerged as a fast and cost-effective vehicle for communication across the globe and is also used to disseminate knowledge of harmful activities. The dissemination of information about the manufacture and distribution of harmful drugs over the internet, as cited by Schneider, is a good example of the harmful utilisation of an otherwise technologically useful contribution of the Internet.

Second is the contribution of the Internet to the process of creating transnational opportunities for perpetrating harmful activities that is already covered by existing civil or criminal laws. Newman and Clarke identify deception in Internet auctions as a good example where the already criminal activity of deception in auctioning is expanded to a transnational level *via* the Internet.

Third is the characteristic of the virtual world in which the Internet has transferred economic value from physical property to intellectual property. A number of researchers including Barlow, Williams and Marshall have provided numerous examples of such value shifts in their works that deal with changing geo-social relationship between time and space in an Internet driven economy.

The above three attributes of the Internet are also misinterpreted to mean that the Internet has heralded lawlessness where disorder reigns and encourages the onset of social entropy. Despite such popular misconceptions presented by popular technology media projecting the Internet as the wild west of lawlessness, there have been well thought out perceptions that the Internet is governed by an assemblage of good governance practices that have shaped the behaviour of players in the virtual world along the lines of acceptable practices that is commensurate with the nature of transactions happening over the Internet. Further research have brought out the assemblage of heterogeneous contributors to the governance on the Internet though the relationships between such heterogeneous contributors do not extend to anything beyond such contribution. In this context, we seek to address the Four Ares of IT governance, referenced earlier, from the point of view of cybercrimes.

The Strategic question if we are doing the right things, can be broken into four sub-questions:

- Is it in line with the vision on cybercrime management?
- Is it consistent with the underlying principles of criminal justice system?
- Does it contribute to reaching strategic objectives in the area of crime prevention?
- Does it provide optimal value at an affordable cost within acceptable level of risk?

Responses to the above four questions, in the context of cybercrimes, leave much to be desired at the framework level, at the policy level and at the operational level. The gaps arise from the difficulty in working towards a reliable knowledge base about cybercrimes from a criminological stand point. On the one hand we continue to take the position that the Internet, which is arguably the most commonly used platform for commissioning of criminal activities, is not a lawless aggregation of disjointed hosts. On the other hand, we need to seek a response to the question if it is at all possible to create and validate reliable data streams on cybercrimes in the same way we have done in the case of other crimes.

Any attempt to create a comprehensive framework for understanding and managing cybercrime is stifled by four factors; the first being media sensationalisation. Media likes to report on crimes that have an Internet interface since they constitute what is referred to as "newsworthy copies." The skewed reporting and sensationalisation of Internet related crime stories result in situations where even a single case can whip up public anxiety and shape public opinion.

The second factor is more social than technological. As the Internet reaches out to millions of users eager to benefit from the power of information that flows through it, many groups have begun to see the benefits of controlling cyberspace. This power play, dubbed by some as "intellectual land grab" has significantly influenced the understanding of deviant behaviour on the Internet, which does not fall into traditional frameworks of deviant behaviour.

The third stifling factor is response by victims to cybercrimes. It is a frequently heard complaint that most victims of cybercrimes do not report it even to their inner circle of friends, colleagues and supervisors; much less do they report it to law enforcement. A number of factors have been stated as contributors to the lack of reporting including the opinion that the police may not be competent to handle technology crimes. Further, unlike the traditional forms of crimes where the victim is perhaps the first to feel the impact of the victimisation process, most cybercrime victims do not realise that they have been victims, for a long period of time. This also adds to the delay and ineffectiveness in the process of reporting cybercrimes.

The fourth factor contributing to the delays in creating a comprehensive framework for understanding the strategic dimensions of cybercrime is the interest of private enterprises when dealing with cybercrimes. Private enterprises against which cybercrimes have been perpetrated do not deal with it as they would deal with other forms of crimes. They generally seek to handle it internally as a matter of control weakness and put in place more stringent information security and control mechanisms thus distorting the availability of statistics on the *modus operandi* of cybercrimes. Cyber criminals are now focusing more on business enterprises due to the economic benefits arising from successful attacks on corporate information systems. This is in contrast to cybercrimes of yesteryears when it was done mostly for gratification of one's desire to obtain recognition as an expert or a geek. This disturbing trend needs urgent analysis and action to arrest it before it becomes a commonplace phenomenon.

The responses to these strategic questions remain unclear since there are impediments in the creation of a cybercrime management cycle as discussed above though there is a strong felt need to overcome these impediments and move on.

The Architecture question if we are doing the things in the right way can be broken into four sub-questions:

- Are cybercrime management processes in line with robust technology that can be validated?

- Are solutions and approaches in line with good technological principles that have the right degree of acceptance by all stake holders?
- Are cybercrime management processes in a position to contribute to the entire population of the users of Internet based distributed information systems?
- Are solution initiatives consistent with other efforts in this direction so that they create the required degree of synergy?

Crime prevention and crime control processes have to be well established in the case of cybercrimes as we have done in the case of conventional crimes. Given the high degree of technology content in the cybercrime process, there is a strong need for implementing technology driven solutions to address the above four sub questions constituting the Architecture question.

An important first step is to make the technological environment robust enough so that success rates of cybercrimes drop sufficiently to discourage those who may want a path of least resistance while perpetrating a cyber infraction. This has been done by corporate managers handling information assets as part of their good IT governance practices which warrant raising the risk-bar in respect of information assets. Risk, in this context, is understood as a function of five variables: asset value, threats, vulnerabilities, exploit path and countermeasures or controls. The primary aim of this response to crime prevention is to put in place a structured risk management framework that will remove the threats, where possible; eliminate or minimise vulnerabilities; remove or obstruct exploit paths and finally increase the effectiveness of controls. This process requires both technological and behavioural response to technology driven threats and vulnerabilities in information networks.

The second approach is to integrate security mechanisms or crime prevention mechanisms into the technology or product architecture. This approach can succeed provided the process of such integration of crime detection and prevention technologies into commonplace appliances and processes like encryption do not conflict with the rights and liberties of users and does not add to the processing overheads. The attempt by the US security protagonists to promote LEAF (Law Enforcement Access Field) in crypto systems and the idea of 'Clipper Chips' did not find favour with public and policy makers as they apparently were in conflict with the rights of citizens and in violation of the First Amendment to the US Constitution. The requirements under the Information Technology Act in India to respond to a Government demand for assistance to decrypt messages that is suspected of not being in the interest of the state, is questionable since it may be grossly misused against citizens. Attempts to use embedded security devices into information systems and processes have not been successful in any part of the world.

The third approach is to redefine the security stance of the information systems that contain valuable data. In contrast to the first approach in which the elements constituting the risks that envelope the information systems are sought to be managed, here the environment is itself being modified. The modification can happen by using a combination of many possibilities available in today's network architecture. An example could be redefining the perimeter of the trusted network and where required, modify it through positioning of demilitarised zones to host common applications and databases so that the overall impact of an attack is minimised. Proactive technology solutions like anti-phishing applications, spam filters and malware controls all add to the arsenal of the managers mandated to protect information assets. While most of these are proactive, none can eliminate the risks arising due to a zero day attack on the systems. This approach endeavours to minimise the risk but can never result in total elimination of the risk of a successful cybercrime being perpetrated on the information systems.

All the three approaches discussed above are essentially preventive controls implemented to minimise the risk and impact of cybercrimes on information assets and are mostly implemented within well defined contours of corporate information networks. The fourth approach will be to implement a detective control mechanism that will come into force should the preventive control mechanism fail. The developments in digital evidence mechanisms, the implementation of honeypots and honeynets have all added up against cyber criminals. These technologies are very important in bridging the gap in the desire to identify the perpetrators of crimes in the cyber world and the ability of such perpetrators to hide using the enormity of anonymity available while using Internet as a conduit to commit crimes. We still do not have clearly decided positions in law on the acceptability and relevance of digital evidence due to a number of factors but there is a slow but steady growth in the number of owners of information assets who see value in collection, preservation, analysis and interpretation of digital evidence.

Each of the above four approaches effectively adds to the architecture of solutions and processes for combating cybercrimes but it must be recognised that most of such technology driven responses to control and prevention of cybercrimes have to be implemented at an enterprise level intant when it is not possible to have a national level technology driven cybercrime management programme. Even at an enterprise level, this technology driven crime control architecture can lead to conflicts while balancing between privacy and security. As Hughes would put it, all users of information systems are affected by an "antisocial criminology of everyday life" though the offending behaviour is demonstrated by only a few individuals.

Another dimension to automating the solutions for securing information systems is what Levi and Wall calls the "drain the swamp and catch the snake" attitude to crime prevention and response. This attitude is particularly evident in all that is happening in the aftermath of the unfortunate events of 9/11 and has resulted in resistance to what is regarded as a clear intrusion into privacy, in the name of security and crime prevention.

Unlike the lack of clarity that had remained at the end of discussing the first of the Four Ares, there is good scope to use the second of the Four Ares to architect technology driven solutions to manage cybercrimes though technology alone will not provide a panacea to all ills of cybercrime.

The third and fourth key questions arising from an IT governance perspective can be addressed together since the need to keep these two questions separate does not appear to be relevant while looking at cybercrime control and prevention. The value question viz., are we getting them done well; and the delivery question viz., are we getting the benefits are to be handled separately when looking at a corporate information security system which is the focal point around which IT governance is woven but when we transpose these questions in the context of cybercrimes, they are better addressed together since value and delivery are invariably seen together in a broader social context which is more appropriate to cybercrime control and prevention.

While we will address both the value and delivery questions together, we still need to look at the sub-questions that arise from these two key questions that are part of the 'Four Ares' approach that we had considered when structuring this paper to use the IT governance model to understand cybercrimes better. The sub questions are:

- Are the expected benefits of implementing a cybercrime management system well understood by all stake holders and do they share a common belief about its utility?
- Is accountability established for realising the benefits from the various initiatives for controlling and preventing cybercrimes?
- Are measurement metrics established to determine the value proposition arising from crime control and prevention initiatives?
- Are there channels established to identify, communicate and realise all benefits of the initiatives
- Is a disciplined management process established to look at all aspects of crime control and prevention?
- Are resources used to manage cybercrime prevention and control process competent and reliable?
- Do the crime management resources have a process in place to update their knowledge, skills and attitude appropriate to the initiatives currently implemented?

The delivery and value dimensions of IT governance that is ported to the process of creating and sustaining initiatives for control and prevention of cybercrimes can be better understood only when we look at two key players involved in the initiative, *viz.* the police and judiciary. While judiciary plays a very important role in value and delivery of any cybercrime management initiative, the role of police is more pronounced as they are among the earliest in the delivery chain of any process to control and prevent cybercrimes.

As mentioned earlier in this paper, Internet is not considered as a lawless state in our conceptualisation of the governance driven cybercrime management. At the same time it must also be understood that there are clear instances of resistance to the governance of Internet and governance of initiatives aimed at better management of cybercrimes where the Internet is used as a conduit for commission of the crime and delivering the value accumulation arising from successful infractions of information assets. Attempts have been made by researchers to find if the resistance is outside the framework of the Internet or inside it and, predictably, there is no finality on this matter.

Developments in information and communication technology is so ubiquitous that it is very hard for the law enforcement and judiciary to create watertight compartments or silos which will look at cybercrimes and non-cybercrimes separately from a purely technology usage perspective. We have argued earlier that only because technology is involved in some parts of the crime process, a crime may not automatically qualify to become a cybercrime. On the contrary, it is equally correct to state that the process involved in what is strictly not cybercrimes; be it the committing of the crime or the gathering of evidence or the interpretation of evidence cannot be kept totally out of technology. Should we make this dichotomy between cybercrimes and other crimes that use technology in the crime management cycle? Establishing such a dichotomy becomes relevant since the application of the principles of IT governance to establish a crime management process will not be possible in traditional crimes however much its technological contents may be. This is because the IT governance process, the Four Ares, IT governance maturity models and metrics are all built around the usage of information technology as a means of delivering business value and it is the value proposition that is embedded in the governance phenomenon that has enabled us to relate it to the cybercrime management cycle.

Returning to the value and delivery questions that arose from the IT governance framework, we have some scenarios where the same technology that is used by the cybercriminals are also the technologies that empower the police in their investigative process. As Clarke would state, it is the 'dataveillant' quality of the Internet that had brought about this rather ironical situation. In addition to the attribute of dataveillance that has been introduced into the Internet access and usage cycle, the availability of records of every Internet transaction that takes place, though with differing degree of detail, has resulted in a fear that we will reach a stage referred to 'disappearance of disappearance.' While it may look fine to have data on every single transaction carried out *via* the Internet, at some point in time the enormity of such data will raise questions of archiving which in turn will raise question of its admissibility as evidence since it may not be regarded as having been 'generated in the normal course of business.' We do not have significant judicial pronouncements on this aspect of evidence as of now and it would be interesting to know what the judiciary has to say when archived data is used as evidence with its inherent propensity to be challenged in terms of integrity. The integrity guaranteeing technologies of today may work up to a certain size and when the archived data sizes move beyond terabytes and enter the realm of pentabytes, it is doubtful if they can be handled by today's technology for demonstrating integrity in a rigorous court room examination.

Assuming that the technology development that affects the Internet is concurrently available to the police force, it still does not always mean that the police force will use all that is available to it. Police, like other agencies that constitute the criminal justice system, is a deeply conservative institution that has deep rooted time tested traditions and hence will continue to be slow to respond to technological changes that, by their very nature, happen rapidly. It is doubtful if the stake holders in the cycle of cybercrime management would agree to a response by the police to be slower than the rate at which technology demands that they change. Also, it is quite clear that the issue of accountability will be hotly debated when the police response to cybercrimes is stifled because of the inability of the institution to adapt to the changing and growing demands of technology. Preventing usage of technology will not be a solution even worthy of consideration and such attempts have miserably failed in countries that had been reluctant to permit permeation of the Internet and Wireless driven technologies.

The lackadaisical response of police to the rapidly growing technology driven crime scenarios is not without reason. In most cases, resource availability could be the first stumbling block since, like every other economic decision, police funding also looks at optimizing the returns on money spent on policing, perhaps even at a local level. In addition to this limitation, police also have serious reservations about focusing on cybercrime management since they involve trans-jurisdictional issues. Since most cybercrimes span across multiple jurisdictions, police seek to determine if it would make sense to expend their local jurisdictional resources on the investigation, except where the cybercrime has trappings of sensationalisation by the media or where it is too heinous and therefore will carry a strong public resentment if the case is not handled in the best possible manner. For instance, in cases involving child pornography, cyberstalking etc, where the visibility of the case is glaring and public opinion is clearly galvanised towards seeking swift and decisive action, police will get in and do the needful even cutting across jurisdictional issues by invoking appropriate procedures and processes. Where the case does not attract public or media attention, handling trans-jurisdictional cases is not the best of the situation where the police want to find itself. In cases like these where the perceived value addition is low and the value delivery process is inefficient, police will tend to ignore the governance requirement of value addition to stake holders *via* efficient delivery cycle.

Another angle to the trans-jurisdictional issue arises from differences in the criminal justice process that has resulted in prosecutors shopping around to find the best place to prosecute the offender since in any case the offence can be treated as having been committed across many jurisdictions. This happens because it is still not very clear as to which location has exclusive jurisdiction over cybercrimes committed using the Internet as a conduit. In the well discussed case of United States of America *vs.* Robert A Thomas and Carleen Thomas, the prosecutors choose to proceed with the case in Tennessee instead of the original plan to prosecute them in California since the forum of prosecutors believed that the changed location offered greater likelihood of conviction.

Another challenge that has to be met while using the IT governance model to create and implement a cybercrime management cycle relates to the cultural stance of police. One set of police officers see the Internet as a technology manifestation that is characterised by risks of meeting pedophiles, fraudsters, hackers and extortionists. They are attempting to use their long used methods of handling such criminals in non-technology environment and end up being frustrated. All police jurisdictions have made significant progress in creating awareness of technological advances amongst members of their force but that does not seem to have created significant impact in their response to technology intensive crimes. This has been best brought out by Sussman who discusses the cultural disquiet between demands from traditional policing and the demands created by technology driven crime management systems with the result that many police officers still believe that cyberspace is like a neighborhood without a police department.

This paper was an attempt to understand cybercrimes from an IT governance perspective in the hope that the success reached in implementing IT governance structure in business enterprises may contain seeds of lessons to be learnt in implementing a structured response to cybercrimes. The process of enforcing security in enterprise information systems have a lot in common with enforcing crime prevention processes while managing cybercrimes. As could be seen in our earlier discussions, there is something common between enterprise IT governance and cybercrime management; at least at a strategic level. Therefore there is a strong reason to take this line of thought forward and determine how best to leverage on the lessons learnt from successful IT governance implementation while architecting cybercrime prevention and management systems.

References

Cadbury, Sir Adrian (Chair) *(1992) Financial Aspects of Corporate Governance,* LSE and Financial Reporting Council, London, UK.

IT Governance Institute (2006) *Enterprise Value: Governance of IT Investments, The Business Case,* Rolling Meadows, IL.

Thorp, John (2003) *The Information Paradox - Realizing the Business Benefits of Information Technology,* McGrawHill, Rev Ed.

Wall 05(2005) "The Internet as a Conduit for Criminals" in Pattavina A (Ed) *Information Technology and the Criminal justice System,* Sage, Thousand Oaks, CA.

Brenner S (2001) "Is there such a thing as virtual crime"? *California Criminal Law Review,* 4(1), p. 11.

Jones R (2003) Review of Crimes in Digital Age, *Internationa/Journal of Law and Information Technology,* 11, p. 98.

www.wordo.rigins.org, accessed on the 2nd of January, 2010.

Weiner N (1948) *Cybernetics: Or Control and Communication in the Animal and the Machine.* Librairie Hermann and Cie, Paris, France and MIT Press, Cambridge, MA.

Wall DS (2003) "Mapping out Cybercrimes in a cyberspatial surveillant assemblage" in Webster, F and Ball, K (Eds) *The Intensification of Surveillance: Crime, Terrorism and Warfare in the Information Age,* p. 122-138, Pluto, London.

Schneider J L(2003) Hiding in plain sight: An exploration of the illegal (?) activities of a drugs newsgroup, *Howard Journal of Criminal Justice,* 72 pp. 372-384.

IMewman G R and Clarke R V (2003) *Superhighway Robbery: Preventing e-commerce crime,* Willan Publishing, Cullompton, UK.

Barlow J P (1994) *The Economy of Ideas: A framework for rethinking patents and copyrights in the digital age,* Wired 2(3) p. 84.

Williams M (2003) *Virtually Criminal: Deviance, harm and regulation within an online community,* PhD thesis, University of Cardiff, UK.

Marshall L (2002) Metallica and Morality; The rhetorical battleground of the IMapster wars, *Entertainment Law,* 1(1), p. l.

Lebihan R (2000) *Is the Internet the Wild West of Lawlessness* in http://www.zdnet.com.au/news/soal/Is-the-Internet-the-Wild-West-of-lawlessness-/0,139023165, 120106763,00.htm last accessed on 2nd January, 2010.

Newman G Rand Clark R., *op cit.*

Walker C and Akdeniz Y (1998) The Governance of the Internet in Europe with special reference to illegal and harmful content, *Criminal Law Review (Special Issue on Crime, Criminal Justice and the Internet),* p. 5-18.

Haggerty Kand Ericson R (2000) The Surveillant Assemblage, *British Journal of Sociology,* 51, pp. 601-622.

The term 'assemblage' is used here in the same context in which it was used by Haggerty and Ericson *(op.cit)* and giving due credit to the concept of 'assemblage' as found in the works of Michel Foucault in his critiques of social system and prisons, denoting more than a mere 'disjointed assembly of ideas.'

Gabrosky P N and Smith R G (1998) *Crime in the Digital Age: Controlling communications and cyberspace illegalities,* Transaction Publishers, New Burnswick, NJ.

Boyle J (1996) *Shamans, Software and Spleens: Law and the construction of the Information Society,* Harvard University Press, Cambridge, MA. This power struggle is also well discussed in the works of Marshall L (op. cit). See also CareyM and Wall DS (2001) MP3: More beats to the byte, *International Review of Law, Computers and Technology* 15, pp. 35 -58.

Subramaniam, R K (2006) *Cybercrime: Criminological, Victrimological and Legal perspective,* Unpublished Ph.D thesis, University of Madras.

There are a number of factors that have resulted in the victims not realizing that they are victims of cybercrimes. These include the intangible nature of information assets; their ability to have value in multiple copies and forms; lack of understanding of complex technology, etc.

The term 'conventional crime' is used here to distinguish it from cybercrimes for want of a better term to bring out this distinction clearly.

The long felt need for a comprehensive framework for risk management that is vertical neutral can be found in ISO-31000.

Effectiveness of controls and their measurement has been a contentious issue among control professionals. While we still do not appear to have a clear solution to this, some headway is made by such initiatives as TCSEC (Orange Book) and 1TSEC.

Behavioural contribution to creating and sustaining a secure information environment has gained significant momentum in the recent years with best practice frameworks such as ISO-27001 clearly emphasizing the need for inculcating a high degree of security awareness among all users of information assets.

Post D (1995) Encryption vs. The Alligator Clip: The Feds worry that the encoded messages are immune to wiretaps, *American* / .oLvyer(Jan-Feb), p. Ill.

The question of relevance of detective control has been long discussed. While one school of thought believes that this can at best be a post-mortem and therefore all controls should be preventive in nature, another school argues for balancing controls vs. efficiency since every control implemented in an information network will add to processing overheads and therefore have an impact on throughout, latency and overall efficiency.

For more information on the Honeynet activities in India, visit www, h o n evnet.org,in

The acceptability of evidence is governed by more factors than their being technologically correct. For instance the need to have evidence gathered in the 'normal course of business' has been the subject of a number of interpretations in the electronic context. However, clear pointers towards consensus on these issues are quite visible.

Hughes G (2003) *The Future of Crime Reduction and the rise of the "new anti-social criminologies of every day life"—A Sociological Critique,* Meeting of the European Society of Criminology, Helsinki, Finland.

Levi M. and Wall D. S. (2004) Technologies, Security and Privacy in the post 9/11 European Information Society, *Journal of Law and Society*, 31, pp. 194-220.

Hermer J. and Hunt A. (1996) Official Graffiti of Everyday, *Law and Society Review*, 30, pp. 455-480.

Clarke (1994) Dataveillance in Green L and Guinery (Eds.) *Framing Technology: Society, Choice and Change*, Alien and Unwin, Sydney, Australia.

Haggerty and Ericson (2000), *op.cit.*

Wall D. S. (2005), *op.cit.*

Goodman M. (1997) Why the Police don't care about computer crime, *Harvard Journal of Law and Technology*, 10, pp. 645-694.

74 F.3d 701; US App Lexis 1069; Fed App 0032P (6th dr.), 1996.

Shearing C. and Ericson R. (1991) Culture as Figurative Action, *British Journal of Sociology*, 42, pp. 481-506

Sussman V. (1995) Policing Cyberspace, *World Report*, Jan. 23, p. 54.

15

CHILDREN IN CONFLICT WITH LAW: INTERNATIONAL AND NATIONAL INSTRUMENTS

M. Srinivasan

In November 1989, the General Assembly of the United Nations adopted a document, Convention on the Rights of the Child (UNCRC), with extraordinary implications for how children should be perceived and treated. The UNCRC is a set of universal standards for the protection and development of children. States that are party to the Convention are obliged to develop and undertake all necessary actions and policies to promote the best interest of the child. The rights enumerated in the Convention are the rights of all children everywhere. India ratified the Convention in 1992. Thus, we bound ourselves, morally and legally, to various principles laid down by the Convention. In India, much has been studied about the children in need of care and protection, but very little about juvenile offenders who are the truly neglected children. By and large, the state machinery keep them in institutions, where no outsider is allowed to visit those institutions, and as a result the children are left to their own devise with scant attention being paid to their well-being and rehabilitation. On completion of their sentence, they are sent out, and ill-equipped to handle life outside of the institution. Though the legislations relating to children recognise that juveniles in conflict with law also require care and protection, in reality the treatment meted out to juvenile offenders is most deplorable. The Juvenile Justice (Care and Protection of Children) Act, 2000, as did the Juvenile Justice Act, 1986 and the Children Acts before it, deal with both children in need of care and protection and juveniles in conflict with law, and as the title of the 2000 legislation suggests, it is both the categories that require "care and protection". Moreover, Article 12(2) of the UNCRC emphasises that the children should be provided the opportunity to be heard in any judicial and administrative proceedings affecting the child either directly or through a representative or an appropriate body, in a manner consistent with the procedural rules of national law. The whole article mandates the State Parties that the children who are in conflict with the law should be guaranteed in all judicial and administrative proceedings affecting them.

The present paper provides a bird's eye view on the provisions available in various national and international instruments to protect the rights of the children, including the rights of children in conflict with law.

Milestones in the History of Children's Rights

Initially, the international concern for children was linked with efforts aimed at women's welfare. This linkage is evident in the instruments on child labour and women's work adopted by the International Labour Organisation (ILO). The ILO's concern with regulating child labour commenced with the Convention on Night Work (1919). Since then the ILO instruments have recognised the exploitation of women and children in workplace and have attempted to humanise the workplace by laying down standards for the working environment. Furthermore, the early part of the twentieth century witnessed international concern about slavery and the protection of women and children from sexual exploitation, reflected in the Convention for the Suppression of the Traffic in Women and Children (1921) and the Slavery Convention (1926). These initiatives viewed women and children as weak members of the society in need of protection (Kumari and Brooks, 2004).

In 1924, in the aftermath of World War I, the Fifth Assembly of the League of Nations adopted a Declaration on Child's Rights. The above Declaration came about as a result of the pioneering efforts of Save the Children International Union. The Declaration establishes the rights of the children to the means for material, moral and spiritual development; freedom from economic exploitation; and an upbringing that instills a sense of social responsibility and so on (UNICEF, 2004).

In 1948, following the World War II, the United Nations adopted the Universal Declaration of Human Rights, in which the nations of the world acknowledged that children were entitled to special care and assistance. These instruments constitute an important foundation for upholding the rights of children along with all other members of society and continue to represent a comprehensive agenda for the protection of the full spectrum of children's rights (Kumari and Brooks, 2004).

After 1948 and before 1989, the United Nations also took other initiatives to protect the rights of the children. That is, in 1959 the UN General Assembly adopted the Declaration of the rights of the child. The United Nations declared 1979 as the international year of the child. The greatest achievement of the year was to set in motion a process of a much longer-term significance.

In 1989, the United Nations Convention on the Rights of the Child (CRC) was adopted by the United Nations' General Assembly. The Convention on the Rights of the Child was presented at the UN World Summit for Children convened in 1990 to consider how to guarantee children a better life. Perhaps, for the first time in history, the plight of children made it to the top of the world's agenda. Since, an unprecedented number of heads of state and national leaders gathered at the UN for this summit, the leaders promised to ratify the CRC by their respective states and also promised to achieve the goals of reducing child mortality, increasing immunisation coverage, delivering basic education, and many other measures by the year 2000 (Kumari and Brooks, 2004). Since then many other international tools and guidelines have come into being that operate in close conjunction with the CRC. Some of the international rules and guidelines includes the UN Standard Minimum rules for the Administration of Juvenile Justice (the Beijing Rules) of 1985, the UN Rules for the Protection of Juveniles Deprived of their Liberty of 1990, and the UN Guidelines for the Prevention of Juvenile Delinquency (the Riyadh Guidelines) of 1990.

The General Assembly adopted the United Nations Standard Minimum Rules for the Administration of Juvenile Justice in November 1985, also known as the Beijing Rules. The Beijing Rules provide a framework within which the National Juvenile Justice

Systems should operate and a model for States of a fair and humane response to children who may find themselves in conflict with law. The Beijing Rules were the first international legal instrument to comprehensively detail norms for the administration of juvenile justice with child rights and development-oriented approach. It is worthwhile to mention that the Beijing Rules operate within the framework of *two* other sets of rules governing juvenile justice: (1) the United Nations Guidelines for the Prevention of Juvenile Delinquency, also known as Riyadh Guidelines and (2) the United Nations Rules for the Protection of Juveniles Deprived of their Liberty (the JDL Rules). As stated by Van Bueren and Tootell (2007), these three sets of rules can be seen as a guidance for the three stage process such as: first, social policies to be applied to prevent and protect young people from offending (the Riyadh Guidelines); second, establishing a progressive justice system for young persons in conflict with the law (the Beijing Rules); and finally, safeguarding fundamental rights and establishing measures for social re-integration of young people once deprived at their liberty, whether in prison or in other institutions (the JDL Rules).

In an expert group meeting held in Vienna in 1997 drafted the Guidelines for Action on Children in the Criminal Justice System. The Guidelines are meant to assist States in the implementation of the provisions of the Convention on the Rights of the Child (1989), the Beijing Rules (1985), the United Nations Rules for the Protection of Juveniles Deprived of their Liberty (1990), and the Riyadh Guidelines (1990).

The links between the United Nations standards and norms in Juvenile Justice are emphasised in the texts of the instruments themselves. However, the Riyadh Guidelines refer to the Convention on the Rights of the Child, while the Beijing Rules, the United Nations Rules for the Protection of Juveniles Deprived of their Liberty and the Guidelines for Action on Children in the Criminal Justice System refer to all four instruments. Therefore, for all practical purposes, the criminal justice personnel should first look to the Convention on the Rights of the Child and then to the Riyadh Guidelines in seeking to prevent children from coming in to conflict with the law; secondly, they should look to the Convention and the Beijing Rules when dealing with children alleged as or accused of having come in to conflict with the law; and thirdly, the personnel of the criminal justice system should look to the Convention and the United Nations Rules for the Protection of Juveniles Deprived of their Liberty for dealing with children found to be in breach of the criminal law.

Having highlighted some of the important developments related to children's rights at the international level, it is worth delving further into the most important of these milestones — Convention on the Rights of the Child.

The United Nations Convention on the Rights of the Child

The Convention on the Rights of the Child was drafted by the United Nations Commission on Human Rights. On November 20 1989, the General Assembly of the United Nations adopted the Convention on the Rights of the Child. The Convention on the Rights of the Child is a set of international standards and measures intended to protect and promote the well-being of children in society. The CRC is the most universally accepted human rights instrument in history. As of 2003, 192 countries have ratified it, leaving only two member states of the UN those are not yet signatories. The two countries are the US and Somalia. The US has signalled its intention to ratify the CRC by formally signing the Convention, as has Somalia. However, the US now stands as the only industrialised country in the world yet to ratify the CRC. Somalia is presently without a recognised government. The Convention draws attention to four sets of rights for every child.

The Right to Survival

The Right to Survival includes the Right to life, the attainable standard of health, nutrition, and an adequate standard of living. It also includes the Right to a name and a nationality. These rights seek to ensure that children have nutritious food, potable drinking water, a secure home, and access to health facilities.

The Right to Protection

This right includes freedom from all forms of exploitation, abuse, and inhuman or degrading treatment. This also includes the right to special protection in situations of emergency or armed conflict. The aim is simple: to protect vulnerable children from those who would take advantage of them and to safeguard their minds and bodies.

The Right to Development

This right includes the right to be educated, to receive support for development and care during early childhood and to social security. It also includes the right to leisure, to recreation, and to cultural activities. This right seeks to ensure that children can study and play with whoever they want, practice their own religion and culture, and accept the uniqueness of other cultures and religions.

The Right to Participation

According to the Convention, the Right to Participation accords the child access to appropriate information and the freedom of thought and expression, conscience and religion. The aim here is to see that the children are able to develop their own set of values and principles and that they have the opportunity to express themselves and their opinions.

States that are party to the Convention are obliged to develop and undertake all necessary actions and policies to promote the best interests of the child. The rights enumerated in the Convention are the rights of all children everywhere. India ratified the Convention in 1992. Thus, we bound ourselves, morally and legally, to the various principles laid down by the Convention.

Constitutional Provisions for Children in India

India is committed to provide for the welfare of children. This commitment arises from certain Constitutional provisions, which are as follows.

- **Article 14** of the constitution provides — "The State shall not deny to any person equality before the law or the equal protection of the laws within the territory of India".
- **Article 15 (3):** enables the State to make special provisions for women and children.
- **Article 23 (1)** says — Traffic in human beings and beggary and other similar forms of forced labor are prohibited

and any contravention of this provision shall be an offence punishable in accordance with law.

- **Article 24:** provides that no child below the age of 14 years, shall be employed to work in any factory or mine or engaged in any hazardous employment.
- **Article 39:** requires the State, in particular, to direct its policy toward securing:
  (a) that the citizens, men and women, equally have the right to an adequate means of livelihood;
  (b) that the health and strength of workers, men and women, and the tender age of children are not abused and that citizens are not forced by economic necessity to enter avocations unsuited to their age or strength;
  (c) that children are given opportunities and facilities to develop in a healthy manner and in conditions of freedom and dignity and that youth are protected against exploitation and against moral and material abandonment.
- **Article 45:** The State shall endeavour to provide, within a period of 10 years from the commencement of the Constitution, for free and compulsory education for all children until they complete the age of 14 years.
- **Article 47:** The State shall regard the raising of the level of nutrition and the standard of living of its people and the improvement of the public health as among its primary duties, and, in particular, the State shall endeavour to bring about prohibition of the consumption except for medicinal purposes of intoxicating drinks and of drugs that are injurious to health.
- **Article 51 (c):** The State shall endeavour to foster respect for international law and treaty obligations in the dealings of organised peoples with one another.
- **Article 350 A:** Every State and local authority shall endeavour to provide children belonging to linguistic minority groups adequate facilities for instruction in their mother tongue at the primary stage of education. (Basu, 2003).

Milestones in the History of Juvenile Justice System in India

The early part of nineteenth century saw no substantial body of law relating to the liabilities, treatment and welfare of children. However, some of the following significant legislations were passed after 1850s.

- **Apprentice Act** was passed in 1850, sought to provide for better treatment of children between 10 and 18 years of age.
- Then came the **Reformatory Schools Act, 1876** and modified in 1897, which provided special courts, which could order 3–7 years detention and training instead of punishment.
- The first move to enact a **Children's Act** came from the Indian Jails Committee (1919–1920), which recommended special treatment for young offenders, to reform and rehabilitate them. The Children's Act in various states in the 1920s was the result of the recommendations of Indian Jails Committee.
- The **Madras Children Act, 1920** was the first Children Act to be enacted, closely followed by Bengal and Bombay in 1922 and 1924, respectively. Though the Bombay Children Act was enacted 4 years after the Madras Children Act, it was the first Children Act to become functional. In order to implement the provisions of Bombay Children Act within the municipal corporation limits of Bombay, a voluntary state-aided agency, namely, the Children's Aid Society was formed in February 1924.
- Legislations were passed in other states also to provide for separate procedure and institutions for the trial, custody, correction, and rehabilitation of delinquent children. Such State's Children Acts brought within its ambit two categories of children, namely, (a) youthful offenders, and (b) destitute and neglected children. The Juvenile courts handled both these categories of children. Throughout the World, during this period, children were dealt with under the "welfarism" mode. For both these categories of children, the well-being of the child was at the centre stage and adjudication of guilt was not stressed (Adenwalla, 2006).

- **In 1960**, the Government of India enacted the **Children's Act**, which is also applicable to the Union Territories, was conceived as a model piece of legislation (Barooah, 1992). The above act was to "provide for the care, protection, maintenance, welfare, training, education and, rehabilitation of neglected or delinquent children and for the trial of delinquent children in the Union Territories." Under this Act, a child was a boy below 16 years if age and a girl, below 18 years of age. The Child Welfare Board handled neglected children, and the children's court delinquent children (Section 2(e) of the Children Act, 1960 quoted by Adenwalla, 2006). The Children Act, 1960 was a precursor to the Juvenile Justice Act, 1986.
- **The Juvenile Justice Act, 1986:** Prior to the enactment of the Juvenile Justice Act, 1986, the State Governments had enacted their own legislations for children. But the provisions contained in each State's Children Act were varied. For example, the definition of the "child" differed from state to state. Under these circumstances, the Supreme Court in Sheela Barse vs. Union of India: (1986) 3 SCC (Cri) 352; 1986 Cri LJ 1736 (SC) observed that instead of each State having its own Children's Act different in procedure and content from the Children's Act in other States, it would be desirable if the Central Government initiates Parliamentary Legislation on the subject, so that there is complete uniformity in regard to the various provisions relating to children in entire territory of the country. The Children's Act which may be enacted by Parliament should contain not only provisions for investigation and trial of offences against children below the age of 16 years but should also contain mandatory provisions for ensuring social, economic, and psychological rehabilitation of the children who are either accused of offences or are abandoned or destitute or lost. Moreover, it is not enough merely to have legislation on the subject, but it is equally, if not more, important to ensure that such legislation is implemented in all earnestness and mere lip sympathy is not paid to such legislation and justification for non-implementation is not pleaded on ground of lack of finances on the part of the State. The greatest recompense which the State can get

for expenditure on children is the building up of powerful human resources ready to take its place in the forward march of the nation. The Juvenile Justice Act (JJA) came into effect in 1986, when Parliament decided to replace the Children Acts in different states and union territories with a single uniform piece of legislation. The above Act was to provide the care, protection, treatment, development, and rehabilitation of neglected or delinquent juveniles and for the adjudication of certain matters relating to, and disposition of delinquent juveniles.

Juvenile Justice (Care and Protection of Children) Act, 2000

The Government of India ratified the Convention on the Rights of Child on December 11, 1992. It became crucial for the Government of India to re-enact the existing law relating to juveniles bearing in mind the standards prescribed in the Convention on the Rights of the Child, the United Nations Standard Minimum Rules for the Administration of Juvenile Justice, 1985 (the Beijing Rules), the United Nations Rules of the Protection of Juveniles deprived of their Liberty of 1990 and all other relevant international instruments.

Keeping in view the above objective, the Parliament on December 30, 2000 enacted the Juvenile Justice (Care and Protection of Children) Act, 2000 to consolidate and amend the law relating to juveniles in conflict with law and children in need of care and protection. The above Act was aimed at providing for proper care, protection and treatment by catering to their development needs, and by adopting a child-friendly approach in the adjudication and disposition of matters in the best interest of children and for their ultimate rehabilitation.

The Juvenile Justice (Care and Protection of Children) Act, 2000 was brought into force on April 1, 2001. However, certain provisions of the above Act were challenged before the High Court of Delhi through a Public Interest Litigation. The High Court of Delhi also observed that some of the provisions of the above Act needed reconsideration. In the light of the observations made by the High Court of Delhi, it was proposed to carry out amendments in some sections of the above act. Accordingly, an amendment Bill was introduced in the Lok Sabha in July 2003. Thereafter, the Lok Sabha referred the amendment Bill to the Parliamentary Standing Committee on Labour and Welfare for examination and report. But, the Lok Sabha dissolved before the Standing Committee submitted its report and as a result the amendment Bill lapsed. Before re-introducing a fresh amendment Bill, the Government of India considered it necessary to revisit the amendment proposals again along with other suggestions received by the Standing Committee from various experts. The suggestions and views of all those concerned were obtained on the proposed amendments and based upon such suggestions and views it was proposed to make amendments in the provisions of the Juvenile Justice (Care and Protection of Children) Act, 2000, in addition to those contained in the earlier Bill. The amendment Act enacted by the Parliament in the Fifty-seventh year of the Republic of India (Act 33 of 2006) was notified on August 22, 2006.

Salient features of the Juvenile Justice (Care and Protection of Children) Act, 2000 and the Amendment Act of 2006

The Act ensures the use of languages in conformity to the high standards of human rights. The terminology of delinquent child was replaced by the word, child in conflict with law. Similarly, the term neglected child was replaced by the word, child in need of care and protection. The word arrest was substituted by apprehension. A few noteworthy features of the Acts are.........

(a) Juvenile Justice Board

1. The State Government may constitute one or more Juvenile Justice Boards for exercising the powers and discharging the duties conferred or imposed on such Boards in relation to juveniles in conflict with law. The Board shall consist of a Metropolitan Magistrate or a Judicial Magistrate of the first class, as the case may be, and two social workers of whom at least one shall be a woman, forming a Bench.

2. Sub-section (3) of section 4 states that no magistrate shall be appointed as a member of the Board unless he has special knowledge or training in child psychology or child welfare and no social worker shall be appointed as a member of the Board unless he has been actively involved in health, education, or welfare activities pertaining to children for at least 7 years.

(b) Juvenile in Conflict with Law

"Juvenile in Conflict with Law" means a juvenile who is alleged to have committed an offence and has not completed 18th year of age as on the date of commission of such offence. This sub-section is based on the amendment made in 2006.

(c) Criteria for fixing the Age

The date of commission of the offence is the criteria for fixing the age of the person. If a juvenile during the course of such inquiry ceases to be a juvenile, the enquiry shall be continued and the order may be made in respect of such person as if such person had continued to be a juvenile or a child. This provision is also applicable to children in need of care and protection.

(d) Apprehension of Juvenile in Conflict with Law

Upon apprehension of the Juvenile in Conflict with Law, he or she shall be placed under the charge of the special juvenile police unit or the designated police officer, who shall produce the juvenile before the Board without any loss of time but within a period of 24 hours of his apprehension excluding the time necessary for the journey, from the place where the juvenile was apprehended. Section 10(1) of the Act, provides that no case, a juvenile in conflict with law shall be placed in a police lockup or lodged in a jail.

(e) Bail of Juvenile

When a juvenile is accused of a bailable or non-bailable offence, and is arrested or detained or appears or is brought before a Board, he or she may be released on bail with or without surety. But he or she shall not be so released if there appear reasonable grounds for believing that the release is likely to bring him into association with any known criminal or expose him to moral, physical or psychological danger or that his release would defeat the ends of justice. According to sub-section (2) of section 12, when the juvenile having been arrested is not released on bail under sub-section (1) by the officer incharge of the police station, such officer shall cause him to be kept only in an observation home in the prescribed manner until he can be brought before a Board. Further, it is also stated under sub-section (3) of section 12, when a juvenile is not released on bail by the Board, it shall, instead of committing him to prison, make an order sending him to an observation home or a place of safety for such period during the pendency of the inquiry regarding him or her may be specified in the order.

(f) Information on the Arrest

The officer in charge of the police station or the special juvenile police unit, when a juvenile is arrested, may inform the parent or the guardian of the juvenile and the probation officer in such arrest.

(g) Inquiry by the Board

When a juvenile is produced before a Board, the Board shall hold the inquiry in accordance with the provisions of this Act and may make such order in relation to the juvenile as it deems fit (sub-section (1) of section 14). The above section also provides that an inquiry shall be completed within a period of four months from the date of its commencement, unless the period is extended by the Board having regard to the circumstances of the case and in special cases after recording the reasons in writing for such extension.

(h) Orders that may be Passed Regarding Juvenile

If a Board is satisfied on inquiry that a juvenile has committed an offence, then the Board may:

- allow the juvenile to go home after advice or admonition;
- direct the juvenile to participate in group counseling and similar activities;
- order the juvenile to perform community service;
- order the parent of the juvenile or the juvenile himself to pay a fine, if he is over 14 years of age and earns money;

- direct the juvenile to be released on probation of good conduct and placed under the care of any parent, guardian or other fit person for any period not exceeding 3 years; and
- make an order directing the juvenile to be sent to a special home for period of 3 years.

Sub-section (2) of Section 15 states that before passing an order, the Board shall obtain the social investigation report on juvenile either through a probation officer or a recognised voluntary organisation, and shall take in to consideration the findings of such report.

(i) Orders that may not be passed against juvenile

No juvenile in conflict with law shall be sentenced to death or committed to prison in default of payment of fine or in default of furnishing security. Sub-section (1) of section 16 also provides that a juvenile who has attained the age of 16 years and committed an offence which is of so serious in nature or that his conduct and behaviour have been such that it would not be in his interest or in the interest or other juvenile in a special home and that none of the other measures provided under this Act is suitable or sufficient, the Board may order the juvenile in conflict with law to be kept in such place of safety and in such manner as it thinks fit.

(j) Observation home and special home

1. State Government may establish and maintain either by itself or under and agreement with voluntary organisations, observation homes in every district or a group of districts, for the temporary reception of any juvenile in conflict with law during the pendency of any inquiry.
2. State Government may establish and maintain either by itself or under an agreement with voluntary organisations, special homes in every district or a group of districts, for reception and rehabilitation of juvenile in conflict with law.

The above overview of the international and national instruments shows that children in conflict with law require care and protection. Specifically, the provisions of Juvenile Justice (Care and Protection of Children) Act, 2000 emphasise the need for providing care and protection. However, in reality the rights of children in conflict with law are not protected during the judicial and administrative proceedings. The treatment meted out to them is most deplorable. The agencies concerned should make efforts to protect the rights of children in conflict with law in judicial and administrative proceedings. The agencies and institutions concerned should also ensure the participation of children in conflict with law in matters of apprehension, pre-trial and post-trail enquiries and opportunities to express their views in disposition.

References

Adenwalla, M. (2006). Child protection and juvenile justice for children in conflict with law. Mumbai: Child Line India Foundation.

Barooah, P. P. (1992). Hand book on child: With historical background. New Delhi: Concept Publishing Company.

Basu, D. (2004). Constitutional law of India. New Delhi: Wadhwa Publications.

Government of Tamil Nadu. (2002). Juvenile Justice (Care and Protection of Children) Act, 2000 (No., 56 of 2000). Chennai: Government of Tamil Nadu.

Government of Tamil Nadu. (2002). Juvenile Justice (Care and Protection of Children) Act, 2000 as amended by Act No. 33 of 2006. Chennai: Government of Tamil Nadu.

Kumari, V., and Brooks. L. S. (2004). Creative child advocacy global perspective. New Delhi. Sage Publication Incorporation.

United Nations (1985). United Nations Standard Minimum rules for the Administration of Juvenile Justice (the Beijing Rules) (Resolution No. 44/33 of 29 November 1985).

United Nations (1989). United Nations Convention on the Rights of the Child. (Resolution No. 44/25 of 20 November 1989).

United Nations (1990). UN Guidelines for the Prevention of Juvenile Delinquency (the Riyadh Guidelines). (Resolution No. 45/112 of 14 December 1990).

United Nations (1990). United Nations Rules for the Protection of Juveniles Deprived of their Liberty (JDL Rules). (Resolution No. 45/113 of 14 December 1990).

UNICEF (2004). The state of the world's children-2005. New York: UNICEF House.

Van Bueren, G., and Tootell, A. M. (2007). United Nations Standard Minimum Rules for the Administration of Juvenile Justice (Beijing Rules). Retrieved 12/4/2007 from http://www.child-abuse.com/childhouse/childrens_rights/dci_be29.html.

16

WOMEN AND CRIME—A SOCIOLOGICAL STUDY

R. Shankar,
S. Vedapurieswaran

"Violence against women and girls continues unabated in every continent, country and culture. It takes a devastating toll on women's lives, on their families, and on society as a whole. Most societies prohibit such violence — yet the reality is that too often, it is covered up or tacitly condoned."

—*UN Secretary-General Ban Ki-moon, 8 March 2007*

Crimes against women is a global phenomenon. In Indian society the problem of crimes against women is not new. Indian society has been bound by culture and tradition since ancient times. The patriarchal system and the gender stereo-types in the family and society have always shown a preference for the male child. Every year March 8 is celebrated as "International women's day" through out the world. From birth to death, the position of women in the society was deplorable. They were subjected to all sort of humiliation inflicted on them by men. Even manu dharma, the sacred Hindu code, does not permit the woman to decide her liberty. It states that a woman's father protects her in childhood, her husband protects her in youth, her son protects her in old age and a women is not allowed to be independent. In ancient India women enjoyed equal status with man in all fields of life, she received the same education like man, many Hindu religious books like Vedas, Upanishads, Ramayana, Mahabharata have mentioned the names of several women who were great scholars, poets, philosophers of that time. Now a days, a large number of girls go out of their homes for their study or work. Once outside their home, they are less protected and more exposed to dangers in society and exploitation. Compared to boys, young girls are in greater danger of exploitation. The women victims of crime became the subjects of public humiliation and their continued life in society become difficult for many of them. If a victim of rape was not married, several ugly stories may be propagated against her. This social attitude had repelled many women to keep away from police action and court procedures. Even today, the social attitude towards women-victims of crime had not changed much. Data on different types of crime in India, put together from police records by the NCRB, are being published on an annual basis since 1953.

Since 1971, the NCRB has been providing data on rape and culpable homicide not amounting to murder. Data under other crime heads such as dowry deaths, molestation, sexual harassment, cruelty by husband or relatives were added to the crime list only in recent times, since 1995. From 1995 to 1997, the publication Crime in India has been providing data relating to women-specific crime categories. An analysis of women victimisation by the National Crime Records Bureau in India shows that there is a rape every 29 minutes, a molestation every 15 minutes, a kidnapping and abduction every 23 minutes, an act of sexual harassment every 53 minutes, a dowry death every 77 minutes, a Cruelty by Husband and Relatives every 9 minutes and a Crime Committed against women every 3 minutes.

These are some of the most alarming and horrifying facts registered by the National Crime Records Bureau, Ministry of Home Affairs, Government of India in 2005. Development along with its progressive changes in personal life style, living standards varied economic growth caused by urbanisation and changes in social ethos contributes to a violent attitude and tendencies towards women which has resulted in an increase in crimes against women.

Violence: Violence is an often heard term, hence before we progress any further, one question that needs to be discussed is: What is violence? How should it be conceptualised? The focus of those researching violence towards women has mainly been to describe the most obvious forms. However, feminists are extending both their empirical range and their conceptual framework to embrace activities and personnel not previously included in the literature of the subject. The term 'gender stratification' underlines the unequal power relationship between men and women in both the public and private spheres. The analysis of violence, including the threat and fear of violence, demonstrates some of the mechanisms through which that domination and subordination is maintained and reproduced. Current feminist research reveals, therefore, the existence of a complex social structure where power, inequality and oppression operate along socially constructed gender lines. In 1978, Hanmer argued for the first time that not only should a definition of violence be based on the perspective of the victim, but that women's definitions covered a wide spectrum of abuses:

> *"A sociological definition of violence needs to include both the use of force and its threat to both compel or constrain women to behave or not to behave in given ways."*

Violence and its threat, in various forms, are common and inhibiting features of most women's lives. Jill Radford's piece, based on research conducted in the London borough of Wandsworth, is significant both for including non-white women in its respondents (a serious omission in so much of the literature) and for the coverage given to women's experiences of and feelings about the police response to violence against women. (Although the women involved in the Wandsworth survey reported a high incidence of male violence, they were very reticent of going to the police and critical of the latter's response when an incident was reported to them). Similarly, although the women in Liz Kelly's research were aware of the threat of violence and most had experienced forms of sexual harassment, they had learnt to 'cope' with this rather than feeling it could be dealt with directly.

The work of Jill Radford and Liz Kelly (1992) demonstrates some of the ways in which feminists have developed alternative research strategies for the study of violence against women. Both are concerned with what women themselves define as violence, rather than some objective measure of it; both are concerned to let women speak for themselves; both are concerned to extend the range of women included in gender and violence studies.

In the article by Caroline Ramazanoglu's wherein she uses personal experiences and observations to study the sexual politics of academic life, she quotes the following definition of violence by Quaker Pinthus:

> *'Violence should be understood as any action or structure that diminishes another human being'.*

This seems to aptly summarise the nature of problems that are dealt with at the AWPS as these problems are often not physically violent in nature but are violent in as much as it stems from the fact that women experience these due to their particular positions affected by the triple yoke of class, caste and gender. The problems that are dealt with at the AWPS reflect the fact that they are in power relationships even within the micro unit of society – the family and which are reflected in the larger fabric of society too.

In exploring the relationship between women's oppression and the state, different analyses were developed, some stressing the class nature of the state and others stressing its gendered nature. The former was associated with Marxist-feminists and the latter with radical feminists. Marxist-feminists conceptualised the state as a class state upholding women's oppression because it served the interests of capitalists. This was ensured by state support for a family form in which the main breadwinner (male) supported his dependent wife and children at home. His job was to create surplus value in the public world of production; hers was to create labor power in the private world of reproduction (Wilson, 1977). Thus women were oppressed by a capitalist state, not because that state was patriarchal but because women's domestic labor within the family was the cheapest way of reproducing labor power. Women's oppression was in the interests of the capitalist class (gender neutral) rather than men (Mclntosh, 1978). This argument has been criticised for being too functionalist, for being ethnocentric, for conceptualising the state as a monolithic entity and for ignoring the benefits men as men gain from a system, which ensures that they have many of their needs are met by the domestic labor of women (Walby, 1990; Sim, 1988).

A very different analysis emerged from radical feminism (Hanmer, 1977; 1978). The state was conceptualised as representing 'the interests of the dominant group, *i.e.,* men, rather than as representing class interests. Male control of women (and hence male dominance) was dependent on force; the state therefore supported male violence against women (Hanmer, 1978). In this analysis the state is regarded as essentially patriarchal. It is a gendered state reinforcing heterosexual relations, which embody men's power over women; male violence towards women is an expression of this power (MacKinnon, 1989).

Later analyses have accepted the radical feminist contention that the state is gendered but also attach importance to a variety of practices in its maintenance. Thus Walby argues for the existence of a patriarchal mode of production, which is located in the domestic sphere where the husband exploits the domestic labor of his wife. Patriarchal social relations are reinforced by practices at other levels of society such as in paid employment, in culture, by male violence and so on. Walby makes an important point about male violence towards women. Weber argued that one of the distinctive features of the state is its monopoly of the legitimate use of force. Walby suggests that this analysis is gender blind because it leaves out of account the violence perpetrated by men on women, often in the name of the state, which is legitimated by the state in so far as the state does nothing effective to end it (Walby, 1990).

The social and cultural construction of gender is institutionally and valuationally mediated. There is universality about such construction although there are variations in their manifestations and expressions. In ultimate analysis, women experience deprivation, powerlessness or inequality of opportunity and treatment compared to men. Even when she works more and her work brings greater economic value, the social structures and cultural patterns relegate her contributions to the background. In Africa, 70 per cent of agricultural production is in the hands of women. There are tribes in India where women work and men laze around. In upper classes, where wealthy women do not work and enjoy the luxuries provided by male family members, she is a loser on two accounts. Firstly, her creative potentials are curbed as her freedom gets repressed through male definition of her space of movement wherein her potential 'contemporaries' who are located in outer spaces, are not within the relational bounds. Her family kin network makes her 'consciates' who are part of her immediate interactional matrix. Secondly, she is denied power, which is largely in the public domain. The golden chain ties her down and she lives a life of luxurious-slavehood.

Even the development plans related to poverty alleviation do not take into consideration that in matters of food, health care and clothing, the woman is at a disadvantage in poor families as well. The benefits of getting above poverty line accrue to men in real terms. Thus, the gender hierarchy cuts across classes, castes, races and nations. The intention of putting women at the centre of developmental efforts had very little to do with their own development. In population control programs, women in the Third World countries became the targets of coerced family planning drives.

Crime against Women can be broadly classified under two categories:

(I) Crime under the Indian Penal Code (IPC)

(*i*) Rape—Section 376 IPC

(*ii*) Kidnapping and Abduction—Section 363 – 373 IPC (for different purposes)

(*iii*) Torture (both mental and physical)—Section 498A IPC

(*iv*) Molestation—Section 354 IPC

(*v*) Eve-teasing—Section 509 IPC

(*vi*) Infanticide or attempts – act done with intent to prevent child being born alive or to cause it to die after birth, causing death of quick unborn child by act amounting to culpable homicide, expose and abandonment of child under twelve years, by parents or persons having care of it, concealment of birth by secret disposal of dead body – Section 315 to 318 IPC.

(II) Crimes under the Local and Special Laws

With regard to specific social problems existing in the country some special laws have been enacted, primarily with a view, to safeguard the women. The laws falling under this category are:

(i) Dowry Prohibition Act, 1961.

(ii) Immoral Traffic (Prevention) Act, 1978.

(iii) Indecent Representation of Women (Prevention) Act, 1986.

(iv) Commission of Sati (Prevention) Act, 1987.

Rights of Women

Woman, just like man, should be allowed to enjoy all rights to live a dignified life. She has the right to claim equal opportunities in all walks of life. She could not be treated like a second grade citizen not only at home but also in the society. She has the right to life, liberty and security, the right to education, the right to undergo any training, the right to do any job, the right to enjoy all social, economic and cultural benefits and the rights to be free from torture. In short, every woman is eligible to enjoy all rights and freedoms set forth in the Universal Declaration of Human Rights (DHR), 1948 without distinction of any kind such as race, colour, sex, language, religion, political or other opinion, national or social origin, property, birth or other status (Karthikeyen, 2005).

However, women are treated as child bearing machine. They are not allowed to have any say even in the matter of conceiving a child. Cases of female foeticide, female infanticide and sexual abuse of children have become a common phenomenon throughout the world. Traficking in women has assumed alarming proportions. Gender bias and gender apartheid exist even in the developed world. Women have suffered much under the oppressive, socio-political and economic systems. Many customs and traditions have neglected women to the status of second class citizens. Most of such victims, however, are from Asia, Africa and South America (Veer, 2000).

Though offences against women are a global phenomenon, the Indian women seem to be exploited from cradle to grave. As a girl child, she is bargained for a bridal price, as a grown-up girl, she is looked upon as a supplier of dowry and as a widow, she is expected to immolate herself on her husband's pyre or condemned to spend her days in a state of living death.

Devi (2005) points out that in Indian society the problem of violence against women is not new. The ever present fact of violence, both overt and covert, physical and non-physical has an alarming influence on the status of women. Violence against women causes more deaths and disabilities among women than any other illness. By 2010, the growth rate of crime against women is likely to be higher than population growth. Further, she explains that low income families suffer severe malnutrition. But low income boys fare better than low-income and upper-income girls. Adult women suffer more than men from malnutrition from iodine deficiency, anaemia and stunting caused by protein-energy malnutrition. In most poor countries, pregnancy complications are the large single course of death among women in their reproductive years. An African woman is 180 times more likely to die from pregnancy complications than a Western European Woman.

Veer (2004) reveals that women are a soft target for the criminals and anti-social elements. He studied all areas and aspects of the world of crime against women. The crime against women include molestation, sexual abuse, forced labour, victimisation, physical and mental torture and all sorts of exploitation. In other words, women are subject to all sorts of torture and violence.

Seehon (2003) explains that the way they are being tortured, dehumanised, forcibly married, sold off, murdered and paraded naked through the streets speak volumes about the degradation and victimisation of our weaker gender in a male dominated traditionally sick society. The law seems toothless, the legislation ineffective and the authorities indifferent.

Kahol (2003) states that women have been neglected for centuries. Everywhere the women are the victims, always vulnerable to violence and exploitation. Women accept atrocities against them with light hearts. They are confined to the child bearing and rearing. Child marriage is still prevalent in many parts of rural India. Wife abuse is perhaps the most prevalent form of the atrocities in family life. Today, in our society, women are vulnerable to all sorts of exploitation, molestation, violence and even fatal assaults.

Mishra (2002) explains that violence affects the lives of millions of women worldwide, in all socio-economic and educational classes. It cuts across cultural and religious barriers, impeding the right of women to participate fully in society. Violence against women takes a dismaying variety of forms, from domestic abuse and rape to child marriages and female circumcision. All are violations of the most fundamental human rights.

Violence against women is a global phenomenon. Cases of female foeticide, female infanticide, sexual abuse, child prostitution, molestation, rape, wife-beating and bride burning have become a common phenomenon all over the world. Women have borne the brunt of this violence and discrimination. All the social institutions and the moral codes are favourable to men and throw open possibilities of suppressing women all over the world.

Habib (2008) cites the study conducted by the Social Science Research Council of the Planning Ministry in support of his view. It is revealed that more than 90 per cent of adolescent girls and women in Bangladesh were being sexually-abused in their workplace, but many of the cases are not reported.

Sethi (2008) explores the various kinds of systemic violence that women face even in developed countries. In United States, for instance, wife battering is the prime cause of injury to women. Over 4,000 women yearly get beaten to death. Every nine minutes a woman gets raped in Mexico. Every 10 days one woman is beaten to death in Sweden.

Shadnazkhan (2005) proves that acid throwing is one of the most alarming and horrific forms of violence targeted at woman. Unfortunately, Bangladesh has the highest incidence of such attacks in the world. Despite increased public awareness and efforts of the government and Non Government Organisations (NGOs) to tackle the problem, the number of acid attacks in the country is on the rise. Acid throwing has a devastating effect on the victims. It inflicts lifelong suffering on them.

Malhotra, M., (2004) explains that women in Pakistan are constantly being harassed, at work place and on other public places. But, they do not report these incidents for fear of being restricted in their movements. Women also fear retaliation, stigmatisation, and the uncooperative and humiliating attitude of officials and law enforcers. The Pakistan Penal Code prescribes punishments for sexual harassment offences, often policemen turn a blind eye even when they are approached by women. Women in Afghanistan have suffered a catastrophic assault on their human rights during regime of the Taliban.

Women Right Violation in India

In Indian Society, the problem of violence against women is not new. Indian Society has been bound by culture and tradition since ancient times. The patriarchal system and the gender stereotypes in the family and society have always shown a preference for the male child. Cases of female foeticide, female infanticide, sexual abuse, child-prostitution, molestation, rape, wife-beating and bride burning have become so common in India.

Kapadia (2007) studied the occurrence of physical violence experienced by young married women at the hands of their husbands. This study also examines linkages between gender role expectations and physical violence in two low-income settings in Maharashtra. Their analysis of two low-income settings indicate two patterns of initiations of physical violence in young married women, i.e., within six months of marriage and after the birth of the first child. Their study highlights a critical social construct as a main trigger for physical violence against women. Sarode (2006) explains that an average Indian woman is bound by all the social constraints that men are not bound by. She is brought up with the values, to live a chaste and righteous life.

Devi and Prema (2006) bring to light that Indian society has been bound by culture and tradition since ancient times. The patriarchal system and the gender stereo types have always preferred a male child. Sons are regarded as a means of social security. Throughout life, a woman remains under male domination; subject to the confines of her home. Due to her subordinated position, she has, suffered years of discrimination, exploitation and subjugation. She has become the victim of several social evils like child marriage, stati, polygamy, purdah system, female infanticide and restriction of widow-remarriage. The gender discrimination and violence against women have had a profound effect on the sex ratio in India. The child sex ratio (number of females per 1000 males (0-6 years)) shows a decline from 945 in 1991 to 927 in 2001.

Shankarjha (1998) explains that even today, various forms of violence against women have manifested themselves directly in foeticide, female child killing, bride-burning dowry-murder, wife battering, abduction, eve-teasing, verbal abuses or verbal rebukes. Women on many occasions are victimised by all sorts of discriminations, deprivations and obstructions. It was upheld by Bhambri (1997).

Banerjee (1993) states that molestation and rape, sexual harassment and wife abuse, bias against the girl child are a global phenomenon, and India is being no exception. Male characteristic milieu has reduced her status to a plaything of men's whims and fancies. Gang rapes and custodial rapes, molestation, eve-teasing, bride burning, child and sexual abuse, prostitution, dowry, wife battering, domestic bias and social injustice take a heavy toll on Indian women. Sexual harassment outside the house is of the major atrocities. When she complains of harassment, no one believes her, then the second thing she encounters is the doubt cast on her moral character.

Sahay (1991) highlights that as young girls, they are loaded with the albatross of guilt about being female. Much of our folk music and dance and Hindi films perpetuate the theme that a girl child is a burden to be got rid of.

Jesudasan (2008) briefs that most people think of violence as physical assault or using guns and bombs. But, workplace violence has a broad spectrum i.e. from prejudice, discrimination, bullying, oppression, to acts in which a person is abused, threatened, intimidated or assaulted and to rumour mongering, gossiping and bitching behind someone s back. Workplace violence also includes threatening behaviour such as shaking fists, Glamming doors, destroying property or throwing objects verbal or written threats, harassment, behaviour that demeans, embarrasses or humiliates person, swearing, insulting or using condescending language and of course physical attacks. Women most commonly face many problems, especially sexual harassment. There is a shocking revelation of a report that nearly about sixty per cent of working women have faced sexual harassment at some point of time in their working lives.

Verma (1997) states that a tremendous sociological change has taken place. Even then, Indian woman has no sense of individuality – working only for her household. Indian society has always been a male-dominated society. Today's woman, who is committed to her job equally, is divided between her work and home. Her day starts early in the morning with many responsibilities on her shoulders before going to her work place. She is subject to various kinds of exploitation just because she is a female. Another major problem which a career woman confronts is the so-called high and mighty ego of her husband.

In the wake of Raja Ram Mohan Roy's movement against women's subjugation to men and British influence on Indian culture and civilisation, the position of women had once again undergone a change. However, it was only under the enlightened leadership of Mahatma Gandhi that they re-asserted their equality with men. In response to the call of Gandhi they discarded their veil and came out of the four walls of their houses to fight the battle of freedom shoulder to shoulder with their brothers. The result is that the Indian Constitution today has given to women the equal status with men. There is no discrimination between men and women. All professions are open to both of them with merit as the only criterion of selection.

As a result of their newly gained freedom, Indian woman have distinguished themselves in various spheres of life as politicians, orators, lawyers, doctors, administrators and diplomats. They are not only entrusted with work of responsibility but also they perform their duties very honestly and sincerely. There is hardly any sphere of life in which Indian women have not taken part and shown their worth. Women exercise their right to vote, contest for Parliament and Assembly, seek appointment in public office and compete in other spheres of life with men. This shows that women in India enjoy today more liberty and equality than before. They have acquired more liberty to participate in the affairs of the country. They have been given equality with men in shaping their future and sharing responsibilities for themselves, their family and their country.

Women's contributions in politics and social services have also been quite significant. We cannot fail to mention the name of Indira Gandhi who shone so brilliantly and radiantly in the firmament of Indian politics. She ruled this country for more than a decade and took India, victorious out of Pakistan-war which resulted in the historic creation of a new country, Bangladesh. In the field of social service Indian women have also done some excellent jobs. They have not only served the cause of the suffering humanity but have also brought highest laurels for the country. The name of Mother Teressa cannot but be mentioned. She brought the Nobel Prize for India by her selfless services to the poor, destitute and suffering people of our country in particular and the needy and handicapped people of the world in general. Today, we need the services of the educated women who can tour throughout the country and help in removing human sufferings. The Government is alarmed at the rapid growth of population in the rural areas in particular. Women volunteers can more easily take up the task of canvassing the advantages of family planning among the rural womenfolk. They can, more easily than men, carry on propaganda against hazards of unhygienic conditions under which the villagers live. In urban areas they can efficiently take up the task of visiting and teaching the orphans and the helpless widows in the orphanages and the widow welfare centres. They can train them in sewing, knitting, embroidery and nursing in which women by nature excel. They can also train them in the art of music and dancing.

Legislations for Women: Social legislation as a means for effecting an improvement in women's position, removing their legal disabilities and ensuring a parity of status and equality of rights had for long been an accepted norm for Indian reformers, nationalists and activists of women's organisations. The specific demand for a Hindu Code reforming areas of personal law (such as marriage and inheritance) appears to have been articulated from the closing years of the third decade of the present century. The efforts of a small but distinguished group of liberal reformers such as H.S. Gour, H.B. Sarda and C.D. Deshmukh in the Legislative Assembly and eminent members of the legal profession such as V.V. Joshi—a High Court pleader from Baroda—appear to have initiated the process concerning reform of women's legal incapacity which ultimately culminated in the demand for a Hindu Code that would improve women's rights in marriage and inheritance. Women's organisations were, of course, enthusiastic and strong supporters of social legislation for enhancing women's status, and as early as 1934 the All India Women's Conference had passed a resolution for enactment of a Hindu Code ensuring a variety of reforms. Also in 1939-40, the Congress had appointed a National Planning Committee, under the formal direction of Nehru, and one of the 29 sub-committees established was on "Women's Role in Planned Economy". Nehru appears to have taken keen personal interest in the deliberations and report-formulation of this sub-committee which ultimately made several recommendations concerning personal law reform regarding disabilities that women faced in Hindu Law and even "called for a uniform civil code, optional during a transition period, to replace the separate personal laws of the various religions".

The participation of women in national problems on such a large scale was no doubt a novel and unique phenomenon in the history of the country. During the movement, they did not remain passive onlookers but actively participated in it and made important contributions. Gandhi laid foundations of a new tradition, which enabled the Indian women to play a significant role in the social and political life of the country. He was an acknowledged saint and the purity of his character added a magic to his personality. People of the country had reposed great faith in his leadership. "The menfolk knew that the honour of their women was safe in a non-violent struggle guided by Gandhiji. They, therefore, had no hesitation in allowing their women to participate in the freedom fight". Gandhi had great respect for women and was, in return, greatly respected by them. It was only this mutual faith in each other and respect for each other that made possible this active participation of women in the freedom movement at the national level.

Policies and Planning: Within the framework of a democratic polity, our laws, development policies plans and programmers have aimed at women's advancement in different spheres. From the Fifth Five Year Plan (1974-78) onwards has been a marked shift in the approach to women's issues from welfare to development. In recent years, the empowerment of women has been recognised as the central issue in determining the status of women. The National Commission for Women was set up by an Act of Parliament in 1990 to safeguard the rights and legal entitlements of women. The 73rd and 74th Amendments (1993) to the Constitution of India have provided for reservation of seats in the local bodies of Panchayats and Municipalities for women, laying a strong foundation for their participation in decision making at the local levels. India has also ratified various international conventions and human rights instruments committing to secure equal rights of women. Key among them is the ratification of the Convention on Elimination of All Forms of Discrimination Against Women (CEDAW) in 1993. The Mexico

Plan of Action (1975), the Nairobi Forward Looking Strategies (1985), the Beijing Declaration as well as the Platform for Action (1995) and the Outcome Document adopted by the UNGA Session on Gender Equality and Development and Peace for the 21st century, titled "Further actions and initiatives to implement the Beijing Declaration and the Platform for Action" have been unreservedly endorsed by India for appropriate follow up.

The Policy also takes note of the commitments of the Ninth Five Year Plan and the other Sectoral Policies relating to empowerment of Women. The women's movement and a widespread network of Non-Government Organisations which have strong grass-roots presence and deep insight into women's concerns have contributed in inspiring initiatives for the empowerment of women. However, there still exists a wide gap between the goal enunciated in the Constitution, legislation, policies, plans, programmes, and related mechanisms on the one hand and the situational reality of the status of women in India, on the other. This has been analysed extensively in the Report of the Committee on the Status of Women in India, "Towards Equality", 1974 and highlighted in the National Perspective Plan for Women, 1988-2000, the Shramshakti Report, 1988 and the Platform for Action, "Five Years After-An assessment". Gender disparity manifests itself in various forms, the most obvious being the trend of continuously declining female ratio in the population in the last few decades. Social stereotyping and violence at the domestic and societal levels are some of the other manifestations. Discrimination against girl children, adolescent girls and women persists in parts of the country. The underlying causes of gender inequality are related to social and economic structure, which is based on informal and formal norms, and practices. Consequently, the access of women particularly those belonging to weaker section including Scheduled Castes/Scheduled Tribes/Other Backward Classes and minorities, majority of whom are in the rural areas and in the informal, unorganised sector-to education, health and productive resources, among others, is inadequate. Therefore, they remain largely marginalised, poor and socially excluded.

Forms of Crimes against Women

Special forms of crimes committed against women because of their sex, their limited capacity to resist due to weakness and their economic dependence on men and due to the prevalence of unfair customs and practices of the society for the exploitation of women are generally categorised as crime against women discussed here cover a wide range: domestic violence including dowry deaths, rape, widow immolation *(sati)*, child marriage, female infanticide and foeticide, forced prostitution including temple prostitution, eve-teasing, sexual harassment in public places by lewd remarks, pinching, pawing, etc., and pornography. There are other social evils also due to which Indian women suffer. The three types of violence which are culture specific to India are *sati* (This custom is prevalent in India since a long time. Although it is prohibited as per law, no case was registered under **Sati Prevention Act-1987** in 2009 as against one case reported from Chhattisgarh in 2008.), deaths related to dowry demands, Devdasi (girls in their childhood are made Devdasi's to serve God in the temple and they have to leave their home and stay in the temple complex. These girls grew up in the shelter of priests in the temple and when they are grown up, most of them are compelled to stay and live as kept. Even today dedications of temple girls are a rampant practice in some part of Karnataka and Maharastra and the use of sex determination tests for female foeticide.

Domestic Violence Against Women

This form of domestic violence is most common of all. **The UN Declaration on Elimination Violence against Women** affirms that "Violence Against Women is a manifestation of historically unequal power relations between men and women, which have led to domination over and discrimination against women by men to the prevention of the full advancement of women, and that violence against women is one of the crucial social mechanisms by which women are forced into subordinate position compared with men".

According to the Beijing Platform for Action adopted at the Fourth United Nations World

Conference on Women in 1995, Violence against Women is an obstacle to the achievement of the objectives of equality, development and peace. Violence against women both violates and impairs or nullifies the enjoyment by women of their human rights and fundamental freedoms. The long-standing failure to protect and promote those rights and freedoms in the case of violence against women is a matter of concern to all States and should be addressed.

Violence in Domestic Relationship

Domestic violence is the most common form of violence against women within the home. It is a global issue reaching across national boundaries as well as socio-economic, cultural, racial and class distinctions. Domestic violence is a serious problem in India. Women's real life experiences show that they face violence in the form of physical, mental, verbal, psychological, sexual and economical. The social, cultural and religious fabric of our country including the institution of family is pre-dominantly patriarchal contributing extensively to the subordinate status of women. Thus it increases their vulnerability to all sorts of violence in the family. The girl children, young girls, married women, old aged women are all victims of different forms of domestic violence. Women in India are socialised to accept, tolerate, and even rationalise domestic violence and to remain silent about such experiences. This makes domestic violence more systemic and epidemic.

The UN Declaration on Elimination of Violence Against Women defines 'Domestic Violence' as those violence which includes physical, sexual and psychological violence occurring in the family, including battering, sexual abuse of female children in the household, dowry-related violence, marital rape, female genital mutilation and other traditional practices harmful to women, non-spousal violence and violence related to exploitation.

A study published by the WHO in 2005 on the basis of data collected from 24000 women in all regions of Tamil Nadu reveals that between 55 to 95 per cent of women who had been physically abused by their partners had never contacted NGOs, shelter or the police for help.

A **nationwide survey by the International Centre for Women's Research** shows that 52 per cent of women suffer at least one incident of physical or psychological violence in their life. A 2006 **UNICEF report** says that 69 million children witness violence within homes in India.

According to **United Nation Population Fund Report (2005)**, around two-third of married Indian women are victims of domestic violence and as many as 70 per cent of married women in India between the age of 15 and 49 are victims of beating, rape or forced sex.

According to a report published on 2nd March 2009 in the **British medical journal, The Lancet,** over 100,000 young women were killed in fires in India in a single year, a symptom of the gravity of domestic violence. Young Indian women are more likely to be killed by fire. The victims were mainly 15 to 34 years old. The study estimated that out of the 163, 000 fire-related deaths in 2001 (6 times higher than those in police records), 106,000 (65 per cent) were women.

The **National Family Health Survey – 3 (NFHS-3) survey 2005-2006**, for the first time, documented the widespread spouse violence and 'culture of silence' observed by the victims.

Violence within Marriage

State	*Emotional Violence*	*Physical Violence*	*Sexual Violence*	*Physical or Sexual Violence*	*Physical or Emotional or Sexual Violence*
Tamil Nadu	16.8%	41.9%	3.2%	41.9%	44.1%
India	15.8%	35.1%	10.0%	37.2%	39. 7%

Source: National Family Health Survey-3.

In Tamil Nadu, 44.1 per cent of married women are victims of some form of physical or sexual or emotional violence by their husbands, which is higher than the national average of 39.7 per cent. The percentage of violence is the highest among the uneducated (52.9 per cent) having no schooling and 52.3 per cent amongst women having less than 5 years of schooling. The prevalence is the least amongst women (24.6 per cent) who have completed 10 years of schooling. The data shows that the most common form of violence is physical violence. All the women who are subjected to sexual violence are also victims of physical violence in Tamil Nadu.

Marriage, Divorce, Widowhood and Suicides

As per NFHS-3 (2005-06), 44.5 per cent of the recently married women were married by the age of 18 yrs. (28.1 per cent-urban, 52.5 per cent- rural) whereas 29.3 per cent of the recently married men were married by 21 yrs. (16.7 per cent-urban, 36.5 per cent-rural). The Urban–Rural gap in both cases is very significant.

The share of married females aged less than 18 yrs in the total female population of the same age group is 2.51 per cent whereas, the share of married males aged less than 21 yrs. in the total male population of the same age group is 2.73 per cent. At all India level, in 2004, the mean age at effective marriage for those females who married < 18 years is 16.3 yrs.

The incidence of crime under the Child Marriage Restraint Act has shown an increase of 32 per cent in 2005 (number of cases-122) vis-a-vis number of cases (93) in 2004. There are 342.9 lakhs (34.29 miilion) widows in India. Of them 72.75 per cent live in rural areas. The widowed/divorced/separated female population constitutes 7.38 per cent in the all India female population.

NFHS-3, (2005-06) reported that at all India level, 37.2 per cent of ever married women have experienced spousal violence. In 2006, 42410 females committed suicide which is 35.91 per cent of the total suicides committed in the country. The age group witnessing highest number of female suicides in 2005 is 15-29 yrs. (45.88 per cent) followed by 30-44 yrs. (30.39 per cent).

Incidence of crime against women cases from 2007 to 2009 in Tamil Nadu

Sl. No.	*Heads*	*2007*	*2008*	*2009*
1.	Rape	523	573	596
2.	Dowry Death	208	207	194
3.	Molestation	1558	1705	1242
4.	Sexual Harassment	875	974	501
5.	Cruelty by Husband and his Relatives	1976	1648	1460
6.	Kidnapping and Abduction of Women and girls	1097	1155	1133
7.	Dowry Prohibition Act	368	262	207
	Total	**6605**	**6524**	**5333**

Source: State Crime Record Bureau.

Proportion of Crime against Women (IPC) towards total IPC crimes

Sl. No.	*Year*	*Total IPC Crimes*	*Crime Against Women (IPC cases)*	*Percentage to total IPC crimes*
1.	2005	18,22,602	1,43,523	7.9
2.	2006	18,78,293	1,54,158	8.2
3.	2007	19,89,673	1,74,921	8.8
4.	2008	20,93,379	1,86,617	8.9
5.	2009	21,21,345	2,03,804	9.2

A total of 2,03,804 incidents of crime against women (both under IPC and SLL) were reported in the country during 2009 as compared to 1,95,856 during 2008 recording an increase of 4.1 per cent during 2009. These crimes have continuously increased during 2005 - 2009 with 1,55,553 in 2005, 1,64,765 cases in 2006, 1,85,312 cases in 2007, 1,95,856 cases in 2008 and 2,03,804 cases in 2009.

Incidence of Crimes Against Women within marriage at the national-level During 2000 – 2009

Crime Head	*Year*									
	2000	*2001*	*2002*	*2003*	*2004*	*2005*	*2006*	*2007*	*2008*	*2009*
Offences under the Dowry Prohibition Act	2876	3222	2816	2684	3592	3204	4504	5623	5555	5650
Dowry Death	6995	6851	6822	6208	7026	6787	7618	8093	8172	8383
Cruelty by husband and relatives (Sec 498A **IPC)**	45778 (32%)	49170 (34%)	49237 (34%)	50703 (36%)	58121 (38%)	58319 (38%)	63128 (38%)	75930 (41%)	81344 (42%)	89546 (43%)
Total No. of Crimes Against Women	141373	143795	143034	140601	154333	155553	164765	185312	195856	203804

Source: National Crime Record Bureau

The above table shows that the 'matrimonial cruelty' incidents continuously increase in all these years and accounted for a large share of the total crimes against women. Within matrimonial cruelty, the 'dowry death' incidents in 2009 have increased by 20 per cent over 2000. There is a significant increase of 65 per cent in 'cruelty' incidents under 498A in the year 2009 when compared to 2000 in spite of Dowry Prohibition Act, 1961 being in force.

In the case of Tamil Nadu, there is a significant increase in the number of registered cases under Sec 498A from 620 in 1999 to 1462 in 2009, an increase of 235 per cent. It only shows that both the national figures and the state figures regarding offences of cruelty under sec 498A is on the rise, which only proves the vulnerable position of the women in the matrimonial homes. The situation really calls for a deliberation to reverse the observation of the Courts to make the provision bailable and compoundable.

Statistics from the Kilpauk Medical College reveals that out of 1277 cases of fatal burns in 2008, 68 per cent (869) were female victims. These were cases from Chennai City and adjoining districts like Thiruvallur, Kancheepuram and Chengalpattu. Dr. R. Selvakumar, Professor of Forensic Medicine said that: "There have been numerous instances when we have been told that the woman got burnt while cooking because the stove burst. If this is the case, then the woman should have suffered burns only on the front portions of her body. Her back would have been spared. If a woman has set herself on fire while standing, then her soles would still remain unaffected." He further said that by assessing the distribution of burns suffered by the victim, we can classify whether the fatal burns is accidental, suicidal or homicidal. A senior professor of the Department said: "In my opinion, less than 5 per cent of fatal burns cases are caused by dowry harassment. Abetment of suicide forms another 50 per cent. The rest of the cases are suicidal". (Only 207 dowry death cases were registered in Tamil Nadu in 2008.)

Honor Killing: This form of violence against women involve killing of a girl by her own family. Whenever a girl tries to marry a boy from other caste, religion or a class, parents or relative of the girl attempt to kill the girl and dramatise the incidence as a suicide attempt. Recent "Honor Killing" case involves murder of a journalist allegedly by her mother.

Remarriage of widows: For long Hindus believed that Hindu widows once married were incapable of contracting a second valid marriage, and the offspring of such widows by any second marriage were held to be illegitimate and incapable of inheriting property. The Widow Remarriage Act was passed in 1856, prohibiting enforced widowhood practised mainly among Brahmins and a few other castes such as Rajputs, Banias and Kayasthas. The law was also designed as a relief for child widows whose husbands died before consummation. The Act was further amended in 1956 to incorporate certain provisions in favour of second marriage. This was done with a view to promoting good morals and to ensure the public welfare. All rights and interests which any widow may have in her deceased husband's property by way of maintenance, or by inheritance to her husband or to his lineal successors would cease on her re-marriage. Yet the problem of young widows in India has not vanished.

Sexual Harassment at Workplace: Sexual harassment is a common problem affecting all women in this world irrespective of the profession that they are in, but legal system is sleeping and so they fail in providing them security. It's not all, women living in those countries having developed legal system faces other problems like being fired out of work, ridiculed, societal pressure or promises of desired promotion, etc. that makes them left with no words. Sexual harassment is about male dominance over women and it is used to remind women that they are weaker than man. In a society where violence against women is posed just to show the patriarchal value operating in society, these values of men pose the greatest challenge in curbing sexual harassment.

India is a democratic country. All citizens have the fundamental right to live with dignity under article 21 of the constitution of India. But there is no law specifically dealing with sexual harassment. Laws are not able to provide justice to the victims. There are various cases brought before the supreme court of India but all cases were not successful in laying down new laws for sexual harassment.

Sexual harassment the law: According to the law in India, sexual harassment violates the women's fundamental right of gender equality and life with dignity under article 14 and article 21 respectively. Although there are no specific laws for curbing sexual harassment at the workplace in India, but certain provisions are there in other legislation like Indian Penal Code, which provides protection against women's sexual harassments such as in IPC:

- Section 294 deals with obscene acts and songs at public place.
- Section 354 deals with assault or criminal force against women.
- Section 376 deals with rape.
- Section 510 deals with uttering words or making gestures which outrages a women's modesty.

There is another act passed by legislature for protecting women's interest namely, Indecent Representation of Women, Act (1997). This act has not been used in cases of sexual harassment but there are certain provisions in this act which can be used in 2 ways:

(1) If a person harasses another by showing books, photographs, paintings, films, etc., containing indecent representation of women than he will be liable with minimum 2 yrs. imprisonment.

(2) Section 7 of this act punishes companies, if there is indecent representation of women like showing pornography.

The harassed women can also go to civil courts for tortious actions like mental anguish, physical harassment, loss of income in employment of victim, etc.

Sexual harassment can be distinguished on two basis, one of them is quid pro quo in which a woman gets sexually harassed in exchange of work benefits and sexual favours this also lead to some retaliatory actions such as demotion and making her work in difficult conditions. Another is 'hostile working environment' which imposes a duty on employer to provide the women worker with positive working environment and prohibits sexist graffiti, sexual remarks showing pornography and brushing against women employees.

Bill to Prevent Sexual Harassment

After few years of the guidelines set by the Supreme Court, the first attempt was made to frame suitable draft legislation with considerable involvement of and pressure from women's organisations. This was called "the protection against sexual harassment of women bill, 2005". However, that too gathered dust till it was replaced by "the protection of women against sexual harassment at workplace bill, 2007" which focused specifically on SH at the workplace, the reason presumably being that the 2005 bill was too wide ranging and hence difficult to implement. This 2007 bill was not in the spirit of Vishakha because it defines aggrieved women as "...any female/persons whether major or minor, who allies that she/they have been subject to sexual harassment..." This bill is also silent on third party harassment and is emphasising only on harassment within the workplace. This bill treats sexual harassment as a civil dispute whereas the Vishakha guideline has provided criminal proceedings for the same. A recent amendment in the draft bill is section 12 (1) which states that "if the allegations of sexual harassment are found to be false, the complainant can be punished for it". This provision will create a new space for employers to manipulate the evidence to stand up against the women. It will abstain women from registering any complaints against the wrongdoer due to the fear that employers can take negative action against them so this part needs to be deleted.

Eve teasing is a euphemism used in India, Bangladesh and Pakistan for sexual harassment or molestation of women by men. Considered a growing problem throughout the subcontinent, eve teasing ranges in severity from sexually suggestive remarks to outright groping. Some guidebooks to the region warn female tourists that eve teasing may be avoided by wearing conservative clothing, though eve teasing is reported both by Indian women and by conservatively-dressed foreign women.

In recent years the Indian government has made some efforts to round up eve teasers. The deployment of plain clothed female police officers for the purpose has been particularly effective. The death of a female student (Sarika Shah in Chennai in 1998, caused by Eve teasing, brought some tough laws to counter the problem in South India. After this case, there has been about half-a-dozen reports of suicide that have been attributed to pressures caused by Eve Teasing. Many other cases go unreported for fear of reprisals and exposure to public shame.

In 1997, in a landmark judgment, the Supreme Court of India took a strong stand against sexual harassment of women in the workplace. The Court also laid down detailed guidelines for prevention and redressal of grievances. The National Commission for Women (NCW) subsequently elaborated these guidelines into a Code of Conduct for employers. National commission for women in its report: " A decade of Endeavour" rightly states that " sexual harassment of women at work places, as an antithesis to the basic human and fundamental rights, not only violates the sense of dignity of a woman but also vitiates the whole work environment and inter-personal relationship, resulting in low level of efficiency and productivity. "women victims need to be treated with sensitivity. Victims of sexual crime suffered from a sense of shame, self-guilt, fear and feel humiliated, abandoned, traumatised and stigmatised. In case of domestic crime offences were committed. In case of domestic crime, offence were committed in the privacy of home, by a person on whom the woman was emotionally and economically dependent. Moreover even though she was a victim, she was compelled to live with the assaulter as she had no other alternative. In such cases the role of the police was not one of an interrogater but of a facilitates and empathiser".

Conclusion

The General Assembly of UNO designated 25 November as the International Day for the Elimination of Violence against Women, by resolution 54/134 of 17 December 1999, and invited all concerned to organise activities to raise public awareness of the problem. Historical evidences show that three Mirabal sisters were brutally assassinated by the political activists in the Dominican Republic, on orders of Dominican ruler Rafael Trujillo in 1960. Since 1981, woman's activists have marked 25th November as a day against the violence targeted towards women. The General Assembly adopted declaration on the Elimination of Violence against Women on 20 December 1993.

The National Commission for Women was set up as statutory body in January 1992 under the National Commission for Women Act, 1990 (Act No. 20 of 1990) to review the Constitutional and legal safeguards for women, to recommend remedial legislative measures, facilitate redressal of grievances and to advise the

Government on all policy matters affecting women. The Commission is under the administrative control of the Ministry of Women and Child Development. The worth of a civilisation can be judged by the place given to women in the society. Of the several factors that justify the greatness of India's ancient culture is the honorable place granted to women.

Indian women are very patient and to be tolerant. However, their patience and tolerance is subject to newer ways of testing by the male dominated society. Women have borne the brunt of this violence and discrimination. The religious practices, rituals, scriptures and some historical forces have pushed women into a secondary status in the Indian society. All the social institutions and the moral codes are favourable to men and throw open possibilities of suppressing women all over the world. Globalisation and education, we have failed to eliminate the violence against the women. We worship woman as a Goddess, regard her as a mother, love her as a wife and she is most affectionate to us as a daughter but still we commit violence against her.

New technology has made woman more prone to blackmail. Use of spying camera, mobiles equipped with camera and other cheaply available devices have made it convenient to make MMS clip or video clip and thereafter conversion of these into CD or DVD's. The Constitution of India guarantees equality to women, prohibits all sorts of discrimination towards women, prescribes special measures for maternity and childcare, and provides for reservations in Panchayati Raj.

A number of laws aimed at protecting and promoting the interests of women have been enacted from time to time. A large number of programmes and schemes having the objective of development and empowerment of women have been launched. Despite all this, women continue to remain weak and vulnerable, being subjected to various kinds of violence. Women routinely put up with the discrimination family laws, segregation and isolation in society, gender bias in a patriarchal society, discrimination at work, pshychological and physical weakness, family violence and gender wage gap these factors are the main cause for the crime against women.

In the Indian society, women had been considering fit to be inside their home and they were not allowed to go outside the home alone or to express themselves in the public. If any of the crime against women was reported to the police, it might be publicised through the media. But women themselves did not want to give undue publicity to the offenses committed against them. "Suffer in silence" rather than "publicise the incidence" has been the policy adopted by women and men alike. But now a slight change has taken place and educated women come forward and report the cases before the police. The social consequences of such reporting are often very damaging to the victims of crimes. Remedy appears to be worse than the crime.

The women victims of crime became the subjects of public humiliation and their continued life in society become difficult for many of them. If a victim of rape was not married, several ugly stories may be propagated against her. This social attitude had repelled many women to keep away from police action and court procedures. Even today, the social attitude towards women-victims of crime had not changed much.

Most crime against women goes unreported for understandable reasons: attached social stigma, distrust in legal mechanism fear of retaliation and so on. Studies are needed to determine why the prevalence of rape and physical assault varies significantly among women of different caste backgrounds. Development and crimes go together. Crimes committed against women are a universal phenomenon prevalent in every region and society in one form or the other, irrespective of the social or economic class to which the women belong. Since Independence, the government of India has promulgated many laws to protect women's rights. In general, however, application of many laws are weak. There is a gap between policy and practice." Lack of proper moral education, marital male adjustment and legal causes like inefficiency of the legal machinery, and various compulsion which are contributory factors for the increasing crimes against women.

References

Ahuja, R. (1994). *Indian social system*, Jaipur: Rawat Publications.

Ahuja, R. (1997). *Social Problems in India*, 2nd edition, Jaipur: Rawat Publications.

Arora, J.C. Mishra and Surat. (1983). *Crime against women,* New Delhi: Bureau of Police Research and Development.

Arya, A. (2000). *Indian Women: Education and Empowerment,* 2, New Delhi: Gyan Publishing House.

Atray, J.P., *Crimes Against Women,* Vikas Publishing House, New Delhi, 1988.

Bajpai, A and Bajpai, P.K. (2000). *Female Criminality in India.* Jaipur : Rawat Publications.

Banerjee, Argha Kumar (1993) "Atrocities on Women in India", *Competition Success Review.*

Dak, T.M. (1988). *Women and Work in Indian Society,* New Delhi: Discovery Publishing House.

Das, M.S, Gupta,V.K. (1995). *Social Status of Women In Developing Countries,* New Delhi: MD publications Pvt. Ltd.

David J. Marshall and Justine F. Andronici, *"Sexual Harassment Law: A Brief Introduction for New Practitioners"* http://www.kmblegal.com

Devi, K. Uma (2005): *Violence Against Women: Human Rights Perspective,* New Delhi, Serial Publications.

Devi, Kamala and Prema Pandey (2006) "Combating Violence Against Women: Some Initiatives", *Women's Link,* Vol. 12, No. 3, July-September.

Gondolf, E W and Fisher, E R (1988): *Battered Women as Survivours,* Lexington Books, Canada.

Goode, W.J. (1965). *The Family,* New Delhi: Prentice Hall of India Pvt. Ltd.

Green, K. (1995). *The Woman of Reason Feminism, Humanism and Political Thought,* UK: Blackwell Publishers Ltd.

Greer, G.(1999). *The Whole Woman,* Doubleday, London: Transworld Publishers Ltd.

Habib, Haroon (2008) "Workplace Abuse on the Rise", *The Hindu,* 2nd July.

Hanmer, J and Maynard, M. (1987). *Women Violence and Social Control, London: Macmillan Press.*

Haralambos, M. Heald, R. (1980). *Sociology themes and perspectives,* India: Oxford University Press.

Heise, L Lori, Jacqueline Pitanguy and Adrienne Germain (1994).*Violence against Women - The Hidden Health Burden,* The International Bank for Reconstruction and Development, Washington DC, USA.

Hudson, V. and A. Den Boer, Missing Women and Bare Branches: Gender Balance and Conflict, ECSP Report, Issue 11, 2005.

Jalna Hanmer. "Violence and the Social Control of Women," *Power and the State.* (London: Croom Helm, 1978).

Jesudasan, Usha (2008) "Rights, Violence", *The Hindu,* 22nd June.

Jill Radford, Melissa Friedberg and Lynne Harne (Eds) (2000). *Women, Violence and Strategies for Action: Feminist research, policy and practice.* Buckingham: Open University Press.

Jyostnhamishra, *Women and Human Rights*, New Delhi 1989.

Kahol, Yudhishtar (2003): *Violence Against Women*, New Delhi, Reference Press.

Karthikeyan, D.R. (2005): *Human Rights: Problems and Solutions*, New Delhi, Gyan Publishing House.

Kelly, L. and Radford, J. (1998) Sexual violence against women and girls: an approach to an international overview, in R.E. Dobash and R.P. Dobash (eds) *Rethinking Violence Against Women*. Thousand Oaks, CA: Sage.

Koenig, A. M., et al.. "Individual and Contextual Determinants of Domestic Violence in North India". American Journal of Public Health. 96(1)(2006), pp. 132-138.

Lachance, L (1994): 'Marital Violence in Canada - A Journalistic Report', Research Centre for Women's Studies, SNDT Women's University, Bombay.

Latika Sarkar *"A human rights versus a patriarchal interpretation"*, Indian journal of gender studies VI (1) (1994), p. 69.

Malhotra, Meenakshi (2004): *Dimensions of Women Exploitation*, Delhi, Isha Books.

Martin L. S. et al. 1999. Domestic Violence in Northern India. American Journal of Epidemiology. 150(4): 417-426.

Mcintosh, M. (1978) 'The State and the Oppression of Women', in KUHN and WOLPE (1978).

Mishra, Jyotsna (2002): *Women and Human Rights*, Kalpaz Publications, Delhi.

Mridul Eapen, "sexual harassment: not fitting the bill", Economic and political Weekly, Volume XLV, No. 34 (2010).

Mridul Eapen, "sexual harassment: not fitting the bill", Economic and Political Weekly, Volume XLV, No. 34 (2010).

Panda, P. and Agarwal, B. "Marital Violence, Human Development and Women's Property Status in India". World Development. 23(5)(2005): 823-850.

Rhoodie, E.M. (1989), *Discrimination against Women: a Global Survey of the Economic, Educational, Social and Political Status of Women*, Chapter 6, Mc Farland, Jefferson, NC.

Sahay, Ruchita (1991) "The Place of Women in Indian Society", *Competition Success Review*.

Seehon, (2003) "The Dehumanisation of Women", *Human Rights Solidarity*, Vol. 13, No. 4, July 5, September.

Sethi, Rumina (2008) "On Violence and Violation", *The Hindu*, 1st June.

Shadnazkhan (2005) "Acid Attacks Heinous Crimes Against Women", *Human Rights Solidarity*.

Shah, A.M, Baviskar, B.S and Ramaswamy, E.A. (1998). *Social structure and change. Religion and kinship*, 5, Thousand Oaks, Sage Publications.

Shankarjha, Uma (1998): *Status of Indian Women*, New Delhi, Kaniska Publishers.

Sharma, K.L. (1997). *Social Stratification in India: issues and themes*, Thousand Oaks, Sage Publications.

Sheba Tejani ,"*Sexual Harassment at the Workplace: Emerging Problems and Debates*" http://www.jstcr.org/stable/4415633.

Sims Feldstein, H. and S. Poats (eds.) Working Together: Gender Analysis in Agriculture, Volume 1, Kumarian Press, West Hartford, Connecticut, 1989.

Sushma Sood (ed.) (1990): Violence against Women, Arihant Publishers, Jaipur.

Veer, Udai (2004): *Crime Against Women*, Anmol Publications Pvt. Ltd., New Delhi.

Verma, Vibha (1997) "Trials and Trauma of Career Women", *Competition Success Review*.

Vishvanathan, N. (1997). *The Women Gender and Development Reader*, London: Zed Books.

Walby, S. (1990) *Theorising Patriarchy*. Oxford: Blackwell.

Walker, E Lenore (1979): The Battered Woman, Harper and Row Publishers, New York.

Wilson, E. (1977) *Women and the Welfare State*, London: Tavistock.

Workplace Harassment and Violence Report 2004 Centre for Research on Violence Against Women and Children.

Young Married Women", *Economic and Political Weekly*, 3rd November.

Reports

A Handbook of Statistical Indicators on Indian Women 2007.

Crime in India (2000 to 2009). Bureau of Police Research and Development, Ministry of Home Affairs, New Delhi.

Fifth report of the National Police Commission.

National Family Health Survey-III Report and NFHS-III Fact Sheets.

NCW-Report of the workshop on Gender and law enforcement, Bangalore, 2001.

Report, (1992). Law Commission of India, Eighty Fourth.

The Protection From Domestic Violence Bill. Government Bill. Bill No. 133 of 2001.

UNICEF. 2000. Domestic Violence Against Women and Girls. UNICEF Innocent Digest. 6: 1-29.

17

RECOVERING DEPENDENCE THROUGH NON-MEDICAL TREATMENT: NARCOTICS ANONYMOUS—AN ALTERNATIVE RECOVERY TECHNIQUE FOR DRUG DEPENDENCE

Syed Umarhathab

Introduction

Narcotics are one of the most abused drugs in the world (*Office of National Drug Control Policy, 2004*), it has become more acute with the development and use of powerful drugs which have harmful effects on the individual and have often proved to be fatal *(Glatt, 1977)*. Drug abuse or dependence has a negative consequence for individuals and society. Once started with willingly for no reasons later for any reason it is difficult to keep away the drug. At first, the substance seems to solve the problem or make life better, so it used more and more. It is wrongfully assumed by dependence that they lack moral principles or will power, that they could stop using drugs simply by choosing to change their behaviour (Jerome, 1954). In reality, drug dependence is a complex disease, and quitting takes more than good intentions. Dependence is progresses, getting and using the drug becomes more and more important and your ability to stop using is compromised *(Glatt, 1977)*. What begins as a voluntary choice turns into a physical and psychological need. The good news is that drug dependence is treatable. The good news is that there are many tools that can help you on your journey to sobriety. With treatment and support, you can counteract the disruptive effects of dependence and regain control of once life (*Rehm, Mathers, Popova, Thavorncharoensap,*

Teerawattananon, Patra, 2009). The data available on the treatment success is extremely unreliable, because success can be rated only with the individuals consciences. There are myth that one is medically treated they will successfully overcome the problem, but reality is different. According to help guide, an online advisor on drug abuse and dependence following are few of the importance myths includes.

Myths about Drug Dependence and Substance Abuse

Myth 1: Overcoming dependence is a simply a matter of willpower. You can stop using drugs if you really want to. Prolonged exposure to drugs alters the brain in ways that result in powerful cravings and a compulsion to use. These brain changes make it extremely difficult to quit by sheer force of will.

Myth 2: Dependence is a disease; there's nothing you can do about it. Most experts agree that dependence is a brain disease, but that doesn't mean you're a helpless victim. The brain changes associated with dependence can be treated and reversed through therapy, medication, exercise, and other treatments.

Myth 3: Addicts have to hit rock bottom before they can get better. Recovery can begin at any point in the dependence process- and the earlier, the better. The longer drug abuse continues, the stronger the dependence becomes and the harder it is to treat. Don't wait to intervene until the addict has lost it all.

Myth 4: You can't force someone into treatment; they have to want help. Treatment doesn't have to be voluntary to be successful. People who are pressured into treatment by their family, employer, or the legal system are just as likely to benefit as those who choose to enter treatment on their own. As they sober up and their thinking clears, many formerly resistant addicts decide they want to change.

Myth 5: Treatment didn't work before, so there's no point trying again; some cases are hopeless. Recovery from drug dependence is a long process that often involves setbacks. Relapse doesn't mean that treatment has failed or that you're a lost cause. Rather, it's a signal to get back on track, either by going back to treatment or adjusting the treatment approach (Help guide, 2011).

What Happens when Drug is Taken?

Drugs contain chemicals that tap into the brain's communication system and disrupt the way nerve cells normally send, receive, and process information. There are at least two ways that drugs cause this disruption: (1) by imitating the brain's natural chemical messengers and (2) by over stimulating the "reward circuit" of the brain *(Schur, 1962)*.

Why do some People become Addicted while Others do not?

According to the document of NIDA (2011) there is no single factor that can predict whether a person will become addicted to drugs? Risk for dependence is influenced by a combination of factors that include individual biology, social environment, and age or stage of development. The more risk factors an individual has, the greater the chance that taking drugs can lead to dependence. For example,

- **Biology**. The genes that people are born with-in combination with environmental influences-account for about half of their dependence vulnerability. Additionally, gender, ethnicity, and the presence of other mental disorders may influence risk for drug abuse and dependence.
- **Environment**. A person's environment includes many different influences, from family and friends to socioeconomic status and quality of life in general. Factors such as peer pressure, physical and sexual abuse, stress, and quality of parenting can greatly influence the occurrence of drug abuse and the escalation to dependence in a person's life.
- **Development**. Genetic and environmental factors interact with critical developmental stages in a person's life to affect dependence vulnerability. Although taking drugs at any age can lead to dependence, the earlier that drug use begins, the more likely it will progress to more serious abuse, which poses a special challenge to adolescents. Because their brains are still developing in the areas that govern decision making, judgment, and self-control, adolescents may be especially prone to risk-taking behaviours, including trying drugs of abuse.

The Disease of Dependence

The standard criteria for diagnosing dependence require that a person compulsively seeks and uses a substance despite suffering harmful consequences. Researchers have traced the etiology of this behaviour to drug-induced changes in brain structure and function. While each addictive substance has its own mechanism of action, studies have shown that they all produce feelings of euphoria by massively increasing the action of the neuro-chemical dopamine in the brain's reward system. With repeated exposures to these extreme drug-triggered dopamine surges over an extended period of time, the reward system loses its responsiveness to naturally satisfying activities, such as eating and sex, and all the things we normally do to enrich our lives. At this point, the individual is addicted, and the only thing he or she cares deeply about is getting and taking the drug (Am I an Addict?, 2000). Researches have also shown that dependence can be treated. Medication and behavioural therapies support abstinence and promote the restoration of normal tone in the brain's reward system. Although dependence is a chronic disease marked, like other chronic conditions, by alternating periods of recovery and episodes of relapse, long-term recovery and a normal, healthy life are achievable goals. National Institute of Drug Abuse (NIDA) research has generated and validated a variety of effective treatments for dependence, most them are medical model. We continue to seek to expand the treatment repertoire, with the ultimate aim of providing every patient with interventions that suit his or her substance of dependence, individual characteristics, and social and cultural situation (Volkow, 2007). Which means the success of the treatment both medical and non-medical rely on the individual's acceptance of the treatment and their desire to stop using drug or substances? The only medical treatment existing throughout the world with free of cost is NA a highly placed non medical treatment mode for recovering dependence.

Narcotics Anonymous—An Overview

NA groups conducts regular meetings for addicts who intend to stop using the drugs and charge no money, meetings are organised and conducted by those who call themselves the recovering addicts (i.e. people who were addict in past years), here dependents share their experiences with the Co-dependents how they got away from problem (includes all humanly problem) and help each other to solve their problem (*The Group, 1988).* NA have no professional therapists, no residential facilities, no clinics and no hierarchy or authority structure in spite it is a successful recovery techniques followed through the world (The Narcotics Anonymous programme, 1991).

NA is an international, non-profit, community-based fellowship of men and women for whom drugs have become a major problem, recovering addicts who meet regularly to help each other stay clean. NA members learn from one another how to live drug free and recover from the effects of dependence in their lives. Membership is open to anyone regardless of age, sex, religion, race, creed or class and the only requirement for membership is "desire to stop using drugs". In order to maintain its focus, N.A. has established a tradition of non-endorsement and does not take positions on anything outside its own specific sphere of activity. NA does not express opinions on any civil, social, medical, legal, or religious issues, nor does it take stands on secondary dependence-related issues such as criminality, law enforcement, or free-needle program. NA neither endorses nor opposes any other organisation's philosophy or methodology. NA does not even oppose the use of drugs. NA believes its sole purpose is to help drug addicts to stop using drugs by providing a platform for them to share their experiences and their recovery with other addicts. NA non-addict friends have been instrumental in starting NA in many countries and helping NA grow. Anonymity is one of NA most important traditions.

Definition: Anonymous

According the NA literature the word anonymous *is* defined as "The basic premise of anonymity allows addicts to attend meetings without fear of legal or social repercussions. This is an important consideration for an addict thinking about going to a meeting for the first time. Anonymity also supports an atmosphere of equality in meetings. It helps insure that no individual personality and or circumstances will be considered more important than the message of recovery shared in NA"

History of the Narcotics Anonymous

NA sprang from the Alcoholics Anonymous Program of the late 1940s, with meetings first emerging in the Los Angeles area of California, USA, in the early Fifties. NA was founded in Sun Valley in Los Angeles, U.S.A., by Jimmy Kinnon and other in July 1953 and is one of the oldest and largest organisations of its type in the world (Kinnon, and Bob, 1973). Started by group of narcotics addicts who tried the trick and was success later termed it as NA then came the organisation as full fledge fellowship. Following that first NA meeting in Los Angeles, the society grew slowly, spreading to other major North American cities and to Australia by the early 1970s. In 1978 an international delegate assembly called the World Service Conference was established to provide guidance to national committees and to translate NA literature, assisted by NA's World Service Office in Los Angeles (A history of N.A., 1999).

In 1982, after NA published its self-titled Basic Text, the subsequent growth of the fellowship was phenomenal. New groups sprang up in North and South America, Australia, Western Europe, with newly formed groups and NA communities scattered across the Indian Subcontinent, Africa, East Asia, Japan, Middle East, Europe and Eastern Europe. More than 28000 meetings take place in 113 countries each week. Each groups elect delegates to form Area Service Committees (A.S.C's). Area committees are run exclusively by volunteer NA members, who serve on a rotating basis (A Guide to World Services in N.A., 1994).

These service committees become responsible for:

1. The distribution of NA literature
2. Manning telephone help lines
3. Carrying out public information presentations for drug treatment centers, civic organisations, government agencies, the police, prisons and other correctional and residential institutions, colleges and schools providing up to date directories of NA meetings.

The Narcotics Anonymous Programme

NA is a completely voluntary organisation. Membership is open to anyone with a drug problem seeking help, ***regardless of what drug or combinations of drugs have been used***. No membership attendance records are kept. There are no dues or fees for membership. NA is entirely self-supporting and accepts no financial contributions from non-members. Most members regularly contribute small sum of money at group meetings to help cover expenses such as rent, literature, tea and coffee but contributions are not mandatory (The Narcotics Anonymous programme, 1991). The core of the NA programme is a series of twelve steps, adapted from the recovery programme of Alcoholic Anonymous. These steps include admitting to a drug problem, seeking help, self-appraisal, confidential self-disclosure, making amends where possible where harm has been done, achieving a spiritual awakening and supporting other drug addicts who want to recover. NA works with twelve codes of Tradition.

Twelve Traditions

1. Our common welfare should come first; personal recovery depends on NA unity.
2. For our group purpose there is but one ultimate authority – a loving God as He may express Himself in our group conscience. Our leaders are but trusted servants; they do not govern.
3. The only requirement for membership is a desire to stop using.
4. Each group should be autonomous except in matters affecting other groups or NA as a whole.
5. Each group has but one primary purpose – to carry the message to the addict who still suffers.
6. An NA group ought never endorse, finance, or lend the NA name to any related facility or outside enterprise, lest problems of money, property or prestige divert us from our primary purpose.
7. Every NA group ought to be fully self supporting, declining outside contributions.

8. Narcotics Anonymous should remain forever non-professional, but our service centres may employ special workers.
9. NA, as such, ought never to be organised, but we may create service boards or committees directly responsible to those they serve.
10. Narcotics Anonymous has no opinion on outside issues; hence the NA name ought never to be drawn into public controversy.
11. Our public relations policy is based on attraction rather than promotion; we need always maintain personal anonymity at the level of press, radio, and films.
12. Anonymity is the spiritual foundation of all our traditions, ever reminding us to place principles before personalities.

NA is a non-religious fellowship, encouraging each member to cultivate an individual understanding, religious or not, of a "spiritual awakening". NA believes one of the cornerstones of its success is the therapeutic value of addicts working with each other to achieve recovery. In meetings members regularly share their personal experiences with each other, not as professionals but as ordinary people who have discovered that sharing brings about solutions to their problems. The closest thing to an NA counselor is the ***sponsor,*** someone who has been free from active drug use for a number of years who gives informal support and assistance to newcomers and those with less experience of the programme. The primary service provided by NA is the local weekly meeting. Each group is autonomous, organising itself according to a series of 12 principles common to the entire organisation.

Twelve Principles

1. Hope gives us something positive to look for and move towards. We can admit our need for help as we begin to share in our common welfare.
2. Surrender to the things we cannot change through our own power is a way to get on with our lives. We seek a Higher Power of our own understanding and that becomes our ultimate guide and source of strength.

3. Acceptance allows evasion and denial to give way to reality and peace. With the care of God, we are granted the power to welcome new people and new ideas into our lives.
4. Honesty is the ability to match up our insides with our outsides. It allows what we don't care about to go away and what we really want to appear and develop in our lives.
5. Open mindedness is our bridge to the experience of others. It is the passageway out of loneliness into the life of the Spirit.
6. Willingness to try is the beginning of doing our part. However grand or humble that might be, it is a state of readiness replacing depression and anxiety.
7. Faith is the evidence of our trust in God. True faith is the result of surrender coupled with experience that God can and will do for us if we ask for help.
8. Tolerance is knowing the other person has the same spirit in them as us and being curious about what that spirit is trying to do.
9. Patience is taking time for things to move into place without force or breakage.
10. Humility is knowing the importance of doing our part well and being open to the many forms of help required for a full and abundant life.
11. Unconditional love is given where we sense our spirit in another human being.
12. Sharing and caring is the active and passive forms of love that keeps us alive and allowing God to use us as instruments.

Meetings, which take place in rooms rented from public, religious or other organisations, may be "open", meaning anyone can attend or "closed", meaning only for people who want to address their own drug problems. Other members may take part by talking in turn about their experiences of dependence and the recovery, strength and hope they've discovered through NA. The NA programme uses a simple, experience-oriented concept of dependence by defining it as a disease from which recovery is possible. NA does not qualify its use of the term ***"disease"*** in any medical or therapeutic sense, nor does NA attempt to persuade others of the correctness of its views or that recovering addicts can be cured. The NA fellowship simply asserts that its members have found that an acceptance of dependence as a disease is an effective way of helping them come to terms with their condition and finding recovery.

NA encourages its members to abstain completely from all drugs including alcohol because NA members have discovered that complete and continuous abstinence provides the best foundation for recovery and personal growth. NA however, takes no stand on the use of caffeine, nicotine, or sugar. Similarly the use of prescribed medication for the treatment of specific medical or psychiatric conditions is neither encouraged nor prohibited by NA. While recognising numerous questions in these areas, NA feels they are matters of personal choice and encourages its members to consult their own experience, the experience of other members, and the opinions of qualifies health professional to help them make up their minds about these subjects (Who, What, How, and Why, 2000). NA also recognises it is one of many organisations addressing drug dependence and does not claim its programme will work for all addicts under all circumstances or that its therapeutic views should be universally adopted (Welcome to Narcotics Anonymous, 2000).

How does Narcotics Anonymous Work?

Addicts helping each other recover are the foundation of N.A. Members meet regularly to talk about their experiences in recovery. More experienced members (known as Sponsors) work individually with new members. The Core Concept of the N.A. program is the 12 steps. These "Steps" are a set of guidelines outlining a practical approach to recovery.

Twelve Steps

1. We admitted that we were powerless over dependence, that our lives had become unmanageable.
2. We came to believe that a power greater than ourselves could restore us to sanity.
3. We made a decision to turn our will and our lives over to the care of God *as we understood him.*

4. We made a searching and fearless moral inventory of ourselves.
5. We admitted to God, to ourselves, and to another human being the exact nature of our wrongs.
6. We were entirely ready to have God remove all these defects of character.
7. We humbly asked Him to remove our shortcomings.
8. We made a list of all persons we had harmed, and became willing to make amends to them all.
9. We made direct amends to such people wherever possible, except when to do so would injure them or others.
10. We continued to take personal inventory and when we were wrong promptly admitted it.
11. We sought through prayer and meditation to improve our conscious contact with God *as we understood Him*, praying only for knowledge of His will for us and the power to carry that out.
12. Having had a spiritual awakening as a result of these steps, we tried to carry this message to addicts, and to practice these principles in all our affairs.

By following these guidelines and working closely with other members, addicts learn to stop using drugs and face the challenges of daily living. NA is not a religious organisation and does not mandate any particular belief system (The Step Working Guides, 1986). It does teach basic *spiritual principles* such as *honesty, open-mindedness, faith, willingness, and humility* that may be applied in everyday life. The specific practical application of spiritual principles is determined by each individual. Recovery in N.A. is not a miracle cure that happens within a given period of time. It is a process, ongoing and personal members make an individual decision to join and recover at their own pace.

Narcotics Anonymous Meetings

NA primary approach of recovery is its belief in the therapeutic value of one addict helping another. Most NA meetings are held regularly at the same time and place each week, usually in a public facility. Meetings vary widely in format. Some formats are: *Participation, Speaker, Question and Answer, Topic Discussion,* and some have a *combination of these formats.* The function of any meeting is always the same: It is to provide a suitable and reliable environment for personal recovery.

Frequently asked questions by a New Comer (For the Newcomer, 2000).

- Who are the members of the NA?

  Any one who has the desire to stop using drugs may become a member of NA. Membership is not limited to addicts using any particular drug. Those who feel they may have a problem with drugs, legal or illegal, including alcohol, are welcomed by NA. Recovery in N.A. focuses on the problem of dependence, not on any particular drug.

- Does any member have to pay some money (i.e. as fee/ Charges) to the organisation?

  None

- Where does a NA meeting happen?

  Either at premise of churches (rented room) or private rented hall at almost all the state capitals, district capitals, cities, town and even in villages.

- What are the basic functions of NA?

  Conduct regular meets, it may be once or twice or thrice in a week or even daily.

- Who is in charge of conducting meeting?

  There are people elected called as P.I. Chairman, who was an addict and member of the NA for at least two years.

- What is the procedure for admission?

  None, the one and only requirement for admission is "desire to stop using drug(s)"

- What is the age group of the attendees?

  Prominent age group is between 21-40 years, but members below 21 and above 40 years do attend the meetings.

- What is the economic condition of the attendees?

  People from all walks of life attend.

- What is the educational qualification of the attendees?

  Both literate and illiterate attend including professionals, businessman and even mason.

- What happens when a member is absent for a meeting?

  Nothing serious, may be some interested member may ask the reason for your absence or most of the time it is not.

- Are there some limits on membership in a particular group?

  There is no limit for membership.

- Are member of NA provided with professional experts like Psychologist, Counselor, Psychiatric Doctor, Social Worker?

  No.

- Does NA maintain the records of the recovered addicts?

  No, it does not. Members call themselves as recovering addicts, but there is one concept called rebirth day celebrated at completion of one year of the membership of a member and continues on the same day of the every year. During rebirth day celebration the member is complemented with the words, medals, books, and etc.

- What kind of service does NA provide to its members?

  None, except for the two type of meetings (Open and Closed)

- Does NA support/advise its member with financial matters?

  No.

- Are member of NA advised or send to medical treatment?

  No.

- What does the word fellowship mean which is often used in group meetings?

  Fellowship refers to any local groups meetings!

- What does the word Sponsorship mean which is often used in group meetings?

  Any senior member who act as leaning wall for some of the member by useful advice, suggesting the solution for the member and helping the member to attend the meets regularly.

Narcotics Anonymous in India

Although there is no proper literature to support exactly when and where did the first NA meeting happened in India. As of today NA groups are organised and conduct meeting regularly at all the State capitals, union territory, major cities and town even in villages. Apart from the above distinct places NA meetings are organised also in many hill station and villages of mountains.

Conclusion

Drug abuse and dependence have huge impact on the family's economy and carry social stigma. Also, it impacts the family members and their social values especially the growth of their children. Most of the time children of drug dependence are bought by single parent or develop deviant in them to exhibit their disinterest to the society. Finally, it develops more disorganised family in the society ultimate increasing the crimes (*Maurer, and Vogel, 1962). It involves huge cost not only to the families but also to the society at large.* Estimates of the total overall costs of substance abuse in the United States, including productivity and health- and crime-related costs exceed $600 billion annually. This includes approximately $181 billion for illicit drugs (*Office of National Drug Control Policy, 2004*), $193 billion for tobacco (*Best Practices for Comprehensive Tobacco Control Programs, 2007*) and $235 billion for alcohol (*Rehm, et al, 2009). It is not mere the socities suffer of economic cost of dependence; the treatment involves more money towards the treatment of dependence.*

NA is a successful method of recovery (rehabilitation) for drug dependence. In India, concept of NA and its work have not reached the all corners of the country only little dependents are interested or who desire to stop using, look for a treatment which involves lees or no money. Most of the Indian believe any treatment free of cost is unworthy. The success of NA in India is mostly through the counselors in the de-addiction centre who advice the recovering dependent continue the recovery by attending the regular NA meets. Government(s) of India shall take some step towards publicizing NA programme in the drug dependence prone areas so that it shall reach the un-reached dependents which shall benefit them. NA welcomes the co-operation of those in government, religious organisations and professional and voluntary organisations committed to helping recovering addicts and are happy to co-operate with such bodies interested in NA by providing contacts, information and literature about recovery through the NA fellowship. Although NA is a non-profit, international, community based organisation for recovering addicts active in over 120 countries. It requires to publicizing the information to reach the public greater success and continue their yeoman service non-stop for the society.

References

A Guide to World Services in N.A., *(1994). Conference Cycle 2004–2006.*

Edition, USA: Narcotics Anonymous World Services, Inc. pp. 1-5.

A history of N.A., (1999). USA: Narcotics Anonymous World Services, Inc.

Am I an Addict? - Revised, (2000). USA: Narcotics Anonymous World Services, Inc.

For the Newcomer, (2000). USA: Narcotics Anonymous World Services, Inc.

Glatt, M.M (ed), (1977). Drug dependence: Current Problems and Issues.

UK: MTP Press limited.

History and Origin, (2006). Narcotics Anonymous Way of Life. USA: N.A.

Foundation Group.

Jerome, E. (1954). These Drug Addicts Cure One Another. Evening post.

August 7, 1954, p. 22.

Help guide (2011). Retrieved on 21.01.2011 from http://helpguide.org/mental/drug_substance_abuse_dependence_signs_effects_treatment.htm on

Kinnon, J. *and Bob, B. (1973).* "Anniversary speech" *speaks on the 20th anniversary. Retrieved on 29.12.*2006 *from www.aa.org*

Maurer, D.V. and Vogel, V.H. (1962). Narcotics and Narcotics.

Dependence. USA: Carles C Thomas Publisher, Springfield.

NIDA, (2011). Retrieved on 21.04.2011 from

http://www.drugabuse.gov/infofacts/understand.html

Office of National Drug Control Policy (2004). The Economic Costs of

Drug Abuse in the United States (1992-2002). USA: Executive Office of the President (Publication No. 207303). Retrieved on 21.01.2011 from www.ncjrs.gov/ondcppubs/publications/pdf/economic_costs .pdf

Rehm, J., Mathers, C., Popova, S., Patra, J., Teerawattananon Y., Thavorncharoensap, M. (2009). Global burden of disease and injury and economic cost attributable to alcohol use and alcohol-use disorders. Lancet, 373(9682):2223–2233.

Schur, E.M. (1962). Narcotics Dependence in Britain and America- The impact of public policy. UK: Tavisstock publication.

The Group, (1988). USA: Narcotics Anonymous World Services, Inc.

The Narcotics Anonymous program, (1991). *Narcotics Anonymous (Basic*

Text), 5th edition. USA: Narcotics Anonymous World Services, Inc.

The Step Working Guides, (1986). USA: Narcotics Anonymous World Services, Inc.

Volkow, N. (2007). The journal of minor medical students- Special report 1.

Retrieved on 21.01.2011 from http://www.drugabuse.gov/pdf/Spectruminsert2.pdf

Who, What, How, and Why, (2000). Reprinted from the White Booklet.

Narcotics Anonymous. USA: Narcotics Anonymous World Services, Inc.

18

CRIME AND DELINQUENCY PREVENTION IN INDIA: AN OVERVIEW

S. Ramdoss

Introduction

Crime and disorder is a universal phenomenon. The law enforcement agency, i.e., the police is striving hard to control crime menace. However, this may not produce a good result always. Because, they are fighting the battle alone without the help of members of the community. Crime and disorder can be better controlled with the support of the community members. Though, crime and delinquency cannot be completely eradicated from the society, it can be controlled and reduced to a great extent by employing various methods of crime prevention. Crime and delinquency can be controlled and prevented through various stages or levels. The primary crime prevention attempts to prevent crime before it occurs. The secondary crime prevention identifies the potential places, persons and predicts crime and delinquency. Based on the past experiences of crime, criminogenic conditions such predictions can be made and subsequently suitable measures can be initiated to prevent the occurrence of crime and delinquency. The tertiary crime prevention attempts to reduce the recidivism rate of criminals. This level of crime prevention attempts to intervene in the lives of known offenders to make them responsible citizens by various correctional programs. Prevention of crime and delinquency is the kernel duty of police. However, the responsibility of preventing crime and delinquency lies on every responsible citizen. This is exactly the community policing and community crime prevention programmes are carrying out.

In all parts of the world, people have realised that in their best interests, unless they themselves come forward and organise effectively, for purposeful crime prevention and prevention of victimisation, the best results cannot be achieved. It is on a realisation of this, that many modern peoples' cooperation schemes have risen all over the world. In many city suburbs in U.K., U.S.A., and Canada, 'Neighbourhood Watch Groups' are doing good work in this direction. In India, our own people's ward patrols and village defence squads are stepping in the same direction. The policemen on beat and patrol duty, and the head constables on supervision, should coordinate their work with the people's effort. In the process, apart from the effective crime prevention in all areas occasional special information may also be received leading to the arrest of wanted criminals, and detection of many important crimes (Diaz, 2000).

Crimes committed by juveniles are often referred to as juvenile delinquency or delinquency. In the context of India, juvenile delinquency refers to any crime committed by a juvenile, girl or boy under the age of 18 years.

Crime Prevention

Crime prevention is defined as "the anticipation, the recognition, and the appraisal of a crime risk and initiation of some action to remove or reduce it". This is the definition generally accepted worldwide and that was developed by the National Crime Prevention Institute (NCPI) based in United Kingdom.

Different Stages/levels of Crime Prevention

Crime can be prevented and controlled in different levels or stages. There are basic three stages in which crime can be prevented viz., primary crime prevention, secondary crime prevention and tertiary crime prevention. The three stages of crime prevention are briefly given below.

Primary Crime Prevention

Primary prevention addresses the conditions in the natural environment that may lead to the development and prevalence of crime. Conditions—Lack of street maintenance, broken windows and abandoned buildings are a few examples of a disorganised society.

Newman (1980; 1996) reported on the effect of changes to the Clawson Point public housing complex in the Bronx. The complex was changed by reducing the number of pedestrian routes through the project, creating separate areas within the complex, improving lighting, and enhancing the surface appearance of the buildings. Newman (1996) reports a 54 per cent decline in the crime rate and a 62 per cent decline in the rate of serious crime (burglary, robbery and assault).

Wilson and Kelling's, (1982) *Broken Windows: The Police and Neighbourhood Safety* addressed three major points supporting the fundamental necessity for community-oriented policing programs (community policing discussed in later part of this chapter). Considered precursors to criminal activity, neighbourhood neglect and disorder were identified as crime-inducing attractions. It was reasoned, then, that elimination of minor problems would likely preclude the formulation of larger problems. Two, it was determined that certain neighbourhoods send out "signals" that disorderly behaviour is tolerated, thereby encouraging crime. And three, community-oriented policing is essential for fostering trust between the police and the citizenry. If police are to reduce fear and combat crime, they must have the support and assistance of citizens. Community-oriented policing offers contemporary society and police agencies many benefits such as (1) a more realistic acknowledgment of police functions; (2) a better understanding of the limited capacity of the police to accomplish their jobs on their own and of the importance of an alliance between the police and the public; (3) less dependence on the criminal justice system and more emphasis on new problem-solving methods; (4) more effective use of personnel; and (5) an increased awareness of community problems as a basis for designing more effective police response (Goldstein, 1987). Contemporary police are willing to accept community help in both setting priorities and carrying out operations in the best interest of the people (Sparrow, Moore and Kennedy, 1990).

Primary prevention attempts to alleviate these factors that may lead to crime. This is directed at stopping the problem before it happens. Primary Crime Prevention focuses on social and situational factors.

Social Crime Prevention

This addresses factors that influence an individual's likelihood of committing a crime, such as; Poverty, Unemployment, Poor health, Low educational performance etc. Examples of prevention include-School-based programmes (truancy initiative) and Community–based programmes.

Many research studies carried out on the various factors linking poverty and crime and delinquency revealed that there is an association between poverty and crime. Some of those studies include the following: poverty and property crime (Hooghe et al., 2011; Edmark, 2005; Oh, 2005; Hope et al. 2001; Kawachi et al. 1999); poverty and violent crime (Sabates, 2008; Hales et al. 2006; Kubrin, 2003; Ludwig et al. 2001); unemployment and crime (Hooghe et al., 2011; Ivan et al 2010; Lin, 2008; Arvanites and Defina, 2006); poverty, drug addiction and crime (Allen, 2005; Bennett and Holloway, 2004; Buchanan, 2004; Lupton et al. 2002; Pearson, 2001; Foster, 2000; Hammersley et al. 1990).

Secondary Crime Prevention

This attempts to prevent crime by focusing on at – risk offenders or potential opportunities that may foster criminal activity. The main tool used in secondary crime prevention is – Identification and Prediction. Once we are able to identify – Potential places, People, Situations, and Opportunities that are at – risk for criminal activity it may be possible to predict and prevent any future crime.

Examples may include the following:

— By reducing the potential opportunities to commit crime.

— Increasing the risks of the crime (target hardening) and

— By minimising the potential gain of the criminal act, it is likely that the criminal will not engage in such behaviour.

People can take individual steps to protect themselves from crime victimisation. For instance, to protect children from kidnapping the following may be useful.

— Teach your children to run away from danger.

— If someone tries to grab them, tell them to make a scene and make every effort to get away by – Kicking, Screaming and resisting.

— Their safety is more important than being polite.

— Never let your children go anywhere alone.

— Know where your children are and who they are with at all times.

— Talk openly with your child about safety.

— Have a list of family members or friends who can be contacted in an emergency situation.

— Be alert to and aware of your surroundings.

— Know your employees/domestic helps etc. Do background screening and reference checks on everyone who works at your home.

— Particularly those who care for your children.

— Take steps to secure personal data about yourself.

— Be discreet about your possessions and your family's personal habits and information.

— Report any suspicious persons or activities to police immediately.

Certain programmes viz. situational crime prevention allows citizens to individually participate in crime prevention. There are many techniques that are used in situational crime prevention. This focuses on preventing a specific type of crime and criminal behaviour. Secondary crime prevention seeks to change people, typically those at high risk of embarking on a criminal career. The focus can be on - Rapid and effective early interventions (e.g. Youth programmes) and High – risk neighbourhood (e.g. Neighbourhood dispute centres). Urban slum areas provide more opportunities for the individuals to indulge in criminal and delinquent activities. Programmes like Police Boys clubs and Friends of Police (FOP), *inter alia,* are found to be useful and effective in terms of motivating individuals in the urban slums to take part in the activities of these programmes.

The findings and outcome of several empirical studies conducted on a few community crime prevention programmes that are pertaining to secondary crime prevention are presented below.

Bajpai (2009) conducted a study on Situational Crime Prevention and Crime Reduction in the state of Madhya Pradesh, with the help of a sample survey (N=400). The findings revealed that in Bhopal, the police patrolling was mostly occasional (46 per cent) and in Sagar, in majority of instances, there was no police patrolling at all (76 per cent). The regular police patrolling was found to be in 21 per cent cases in Bhopal and 1 per cent cases in Sagar. Further this study revealed that more than half of the crimes occurred in the places where there was no police patrolling (53.7 per cent). Areas with regular police patrolling had lower crime occurrence (11.1 per cent).

Ramdoss and Karna (2008) conducted an empirical study on Police Boys' Clubs in Chennai City. The results indicated that the police boys clubs playing an important role in preventing juvenile crime and reducing the rate of juvenile delinquency in Chennai City. Moreover, the personnel associated with the management of the Police Boys' Clubs such as Inspector of Police, Scout Masters/ Coaches and Teachers also perceived that the activities of the Police Boys Clubs have reduced delinquency rate in the City of Chennai. Further, this study found that the Police Boys Clubs have contributed a lot in the personality development of the members of the clubs through various programmes. In the absence of police boys' clubs and such programmes, there is a greater probability that these boys could have embraced the path of deviance.

Philip (2006) conducted a study on Friends of Police (FOP), through the perception of members of the public, who are the consumers of the benefits of this service-oriented movement. The focus of the study is on three variables, namely, level of awareness, level of acceptance and level of involvement. The results reveal that the awareness among the general public about the friends of police movement, its goals and what it stands for has increased. Understanding the objectives and benefits of the movement, many youngsters enroll themselves as members of the friends of police movement. In the perception of the police, public and members of the Friends of Police, there has been a considerable increase in the percentage of crime control from 1996-2005. This has been proved by the fall in the crime rate after the inception of the Friends of police movement, namely, a decrease in offences against people, offences against property, offences against the State, and decrease in public disorder. The effectiveness of police personnel is also enhanced because of the presence of friends of polices in all parts of the state.

Meera (2004) conducted a study on Effectiveness of Police Boys Clubs in Chennai City. The findings of his study revealed that out of 100 respondents (members of the police boys clubs in Chennai) 97 per cent of them did not indulge in any delinquent activities after attending the programme of the boy's clubs. Further, he reported that the majority of the boys experienced a positive change in their behaviour after attending the programme of the police boys' clubs.

Tertiary Crime Prevention

This focuses on prevention after a crime has occurred. The focus is to reduce the recidivism rate of criminals. Ensure that steps are taken so that a victim will not be revictimised. The primary form of tertiary crime prevention in many countries is that of *incapacitation*. Although it does not prevent criminals from committing crimes once they leave prison; it does protect the larger population from present victimisation at the hands of the criminals.

Recidivism implies 'persistent indulgence in crime'. Recidivism is the reoccurrence of criminal behaviour by prior offender. The term also refers to a tendency to return to criminal behaviour by offenders previously in the criminal justice system.

Sutherland, a criminologist attributes two major causes for recidivism. (*i*) Social Psychology of the Offender and (*ii*) Inadequacy of Reformative Techniques.

Social Psychology

Urbanised regions are more prone to recidivism than rural areas; The congested dwellings (slums); High cost of living; Highly mechanised life in urban places offer sufficient opportunities for offenders to carry on their criminal activities undetected or unnoticed for years. Thus, criminality becomes a habit with them and makes them recidivists. On the other hand, living in rural areas is relatively cheaper and simple. Therefore offers lesser chances for criminality. Besides, almost no chances of escape from detection. This makes rural areas unsuited for crime and recidivism. Among recidivists, men are more in number; because of their dominating social status. The stigma of prisonisation makes him to avoid the normal society. Thus, he prefers a routine life of a prison to which he is well accustomed. Another psychological reason for non – adjustability of released inmate to normal life is that – he begins to feel that the law abiding members of society look at him with suspicion; distrust and doubt. Thus, he suffers from inferiority complex and in an anxiety to overcome this weakness he repeats crime. Recidivists are very loyal to their organisations; the offender who talks of reformation is ridiculed by his fellow men; sometimes, even aggressive and violent methods are used to prevent him from disassociating with the criminal group.

Inadequacy of Reform

A large number of failures in parole, probation and reformatories reflect the ineffectiveness of correctional methods. Due to the failures of the correctional programs, many released convicts relapse into criminality again and again.

Studies revealed that there are certain specific offences which are more likely to be repeated by recidivists than others. Most recidivistic crimes are- theft; robbery; burglary; and forgery. Whereas, homicide, assault, rape are not likely to be repeated. Whatever causes crime also causes recidivism. The only exception is that the nature of prior contact with criminal justice system may also influence recidivism.

Statistics on Recidivism

In India, the share of recidivists among all offenders has increased to 9 per cent during 2009 as compared to 7.7 per cent during 2008. The actual number of past offenders involved in repeating IPC crimes during 2008 was 2,22,085 whereas during 2009 it was found to be 2,56,049 indicating 15.3 per cent increase. Number of recidivists convicted in the past: In 2008 - Once – 1, 54,343; twice – 47,129; thrice or more – 20,613. In 2009- Once – 1, 79,384; twice – 51,349; thrice or more – 25,316 (NCRB, 2009). Those who were convicted for three times and more are called habitual offenders. By and large the habitual offenders are committing crimes against property than against persons. The statistics depicted above clearly indicate the failure of the tertiary crime prevention which has failed to reduce the recidivism rate of the criminals during this period.

Community Policing

It is not always possible for police to fight crime effectively without the support of the members of the public. Therefore, it is imperative to understand the concept of community policing and its advantages in terms of crime control and crime reduction. Community policing can bridge the gap between police and public thereby encouraging the members of the public to have healthy relationship with police and vice-versa. The motivated members of the community can send information regarding crime and criminals to the police without delay and such information is very vital in the process of crime control and prevention. This kind of synergy between police and public pose a greater challenge to the potential criminals.

Community policing is one of the most popular contemporary approaches to police work and has emerged in response to evidence that indicated that the police could not fight crime by themselves and increasingly conflictual relationships with minority ethnic communities. It can take various forms, for example 'team policing', 'foot patrol', 'problem oriented policing', 'neighbourhood policing', 'service based policing', and 'policing by consent'. It recognises that effective police work is a collaborative effort between the police and the community and involves identifying the problems of crime and disorder that concern the community and attempts to include all sections of the community in the search for solutions to these problems.

Problem oriented policing identifies the underlying causes of crime and disorder that the community feels most strongly about and constructs tailor – made strategies that have the support of the community. It also enables police officers and communities to alter the conditions and circumstances that encourage criminal and disorderly behaviour. Community policing holds out the promise of reduced levels of crime and disorder, improved quality of life for the community, enhanced relationships between the police and community, a supportive environment for police operations and greater job satisfaction for police officers. The long – term aim is to produce strong self – sufficient communities that have the ability to protect themselves from crime and disorder (McLaughlin and Muncie, 2001).

In most of the community crime prevention programmes, the police become the facilitators of the programmes, but the community must at a minimum participate for the programmes to remain viable and have any chance at success (Oliver, 2001).

Many community based crime prevention activities require little more than common sense to achieve their goals. For example, closing and locking the doors of home or car when they are unoccupied are almost certainly going to reduce the risk of thefts from them, and running interesting summer activities for bored youngsters on marginalised housing estates is almost certainly going to reduce the amount of vandalism and antisocial behaviour they get up to in their spare time (Shaftoe, 2004).

Neighbourhood Watch programmes, depending on where one lives, can have a variety of names. Some of the names used are Block Watch, Crime Watch, and Community Alert. However, all of these programmes have one thing in common: to have neighbours watch out for each other, to be alert to day – to – day happenings in the neighbourhood, and to call the police when anything suspicious occurs (Garofalo and McLeod, 1988).

The concept is known as community-oriented policing or problem solving policing or by any number of similar catch phrases. The operating details vary from place to place, but the philosophy is the same: Law enforcement officers can do a better job with the trust and help of the public. (Wrobleski and Hess, 2000). Proponents claim that a community orientation reduces crime and improves police/community relations, thereby creating more livable neighbourhoods. Many areas have reported significant declines in crime rates as a result of implementing these community policing philosophies. Furthermore, citizens report enhanced feelings of safety that has resulted in a better quality of life. As a result of its successes, it is routinely praised as the future of policing, but without active community involvement forming strong partnerships with the police, the success of community-oriented policing is limited (Moore and Trojanowicz, 1988).

Kandasamy (2003) conducted a research on the public opinion on community policing and also to understand whether they are willing to support the police in the prevention of crime. The findings revealed that a majority of the respondents supported the police in the prevention of crime and involved in the community policing programmes.

Community Crime Prevention Programmes in India

Though the practice of community policing was not new to India, the concept is gradually gaining momentum. Some of the community crime prevention programmes are briefly presented in this part.

Gunhegar Niyantran Jan Samithi Yojana is a quiet revolution in "Operation-Crime Prevention" was taking roots in the crime prone areas of Marathwada including Aurangabad. In early 1980 a few top police officials in the region discovered themselves a revolutionary strategy in fighting crime and protecting the community-the strategy of using "Jan Sakthi" (People's participation) in curbing crime before it occurs. The impact of the programme has so far been impressive. Initial results indicated almost 80 per cent decline in bootlegging, gambling and such other organised crimes. For the first time in four years hurt cases have shown a declining rate in Aurangabad (Menon, 1982).

Prahari – Community Policing in Assam was started in 1996, the goal of Prahari was to tackle social problems and bring the police and community closer. Aaswas is another initiative of the Assam police, to combat violence and insurgency and also to extend a gesture of affection to children and those who have undergone the trauma of facing violence.

Maithri – which was launched in 2000, by the Andhra Pradesh Police throughout the state. The mission of Maithri is to render courteous, compassionate and caring and responsive police service, and increase public confidence in them with respect to maintenance of peace and order and to develop a feeling of safety from crime. It rests on the belief that contemporary community problems require a decentralised and personalised police approach, which involves citizens, who learn how to police themselves.

The Delhi Police has pioneered several important steps in community policing in India. The institution of Special Police Officer has acted as a bridge between the police and the public for a long time and has played a very useful role in controlling property offences, and in educating the local public in various security measures to protect their lives and properties (Philip, 2006).

Janamaithri Suraksha Project is the name given to the Community Policing Programme adopted by the Kerala Police - *The Objectives:* prevention of crimes, Furthering co-operation and mutual understanding between police and the community, and furthering security-related mutual co-operation among citizenry (http://www.communitypolicingkerala.org).

In Orissa Surakhya Samiti was started in 1999 is the Kernel of the Community Policing Programme of the State Government which directs the Superintendent of Police/Range DIG. These samiti are constituted by volunteers from specified areas in the city/village through municipal bodies and Gram Panchayats in consultation with the magistracy. The preamble to the Home Department Resolution makes it clear that the objective is to associate citizens with the police in solving neighbourhood problems, in enforcing the law of the land, and in restoring order and peace in the community.

The Village Vigilance Committee (VVC) is the first community policing initiative in the state of Tamil Nadu. Mostly viewed as a crime prevention measure in the villages, the Village Vigilance Committees' effectiveness depended on the enthusiasm displayed by the Individual Station House Officer. Of late, it has become obsolete. The first and foremost community policing initiative in Tamil Nadu in the true sense of the term is the Friends of Police Movement (FOP) that began in the year 1993. In the two decade's time, it has grown and spread all over the state.

Friends of Police Movement, Tamil Nadu–it is an example of police-public partnership, according to which citizens have been empowered along with police. It also provides opportunities for ordinary citizens to effectively contribute to the prevention and detection of crime. Any member of the public, male or female, who is not involved in civil or criminal case, can become members of Friends of Police (FOP).

Beat Box System – prior to the initiation of community policing in Trichy, the crime rate was very high. There were inter-caste and religious conflicts, rioting, murder, mayhem and other anti-social activities. The police not only had to handle forces of fundamentalism and lawlessness, but also had to instill a sense of confidence amongst the people. To achieve this, some community policing strategies were introduced such as, (1) Beat Officers System (2) Complaint/Suggestion Box System (3) Wide Area Network (WAN) (4) Helpline for Women in Distress and (5) Slum Adoption Programme.

Area Committee – In Coimbatore Area Committees were formed which helped them to trace and resolve small local issues. Regular meetings were held with the committee members and this forum helped the police to discuss and solve current problems and also provided valuable information to the police on the movement of terrorists and criminals. City Vigilance Committees were formed to bring down the incidence of property crimes by providing regular information on the whereabouts of absconding terrorists. This effectively resulted in seizure of contrabands, explosives, detonators, lethal weapons, black money, sandalwood and drugs, etc. The Traffic Warden System and Crime Stoppers Control are the other programmes practiced in the state (Philip, 2006).

Gandhirajan (2005) highlighted the various efforts initiated as part of the community policing in Railways, Tamil Nadu viz., Railway Detective Vigilance Committee, Friends for Better Services, Non Governmental Organisations, Madras Station Vigilance Committee, Public Vigilance Council, Tamil Nadu, Watch Dog Committee, Police Help Booths, Child Line, Public Relation Officer in each Railway Station, Police and Community Joint Patrolling to prevent crime in Railways. As a result of these measures, crime rate has been significantly reduced.

Police Boy's Clubs – started in Tamil Nadu during the Second Five Year Plan. Three Boys' Clubs were started in Chennai and one in each district. The aim was to channelise the energy of children in economically backward area, especially in slums. But in due course, the clubs became defunct. During 2003, the concept was revived and rejuvenated with the Chief Minister sanctioning 64 clubs – 25 in Chennai city alone. Public spirited organisations like Lions Clubs, Rotary Clubs, Round Table, Aid-et-Action and big industrial business houses like Touchtel, TVS etc., have come forward to sponsor 53 clubs. In Chennai City, Police, all the 86 Police Stations have one club each. The emphasis of Boys Club's activities will span literacy and sports. Rehabilitation of dropouts, Child Labourers, vocational training, and adult literacy are well within its scope. While the library will impart knowledge to these boys, Gym, Volleyball, Cricket, Football, Badminton and indoor games take care of their physical activity. The boys are groomed as epitomes of responsible conduct and taught to look at the law enforcer as a friend. A beneficial spin-off of Boys' Clubs could be curtailment of crime, by encouraging the boys to become law abiding self-reliant citizens (www.chennaicitypolice.org).

Conclusions and Suggestions

The following are the conclusions and suggestive measures to contain and prevent crime and delinquency:

- There are basically three stages in which crime and delinquency can be controlled and prevented. The three stages such as primary crime prevention, secondary crime prevention and tertiary crime prevention.
- The crime problem and delinquency rate can be substantially reduced with the help and support of properly organised community crime prevention programmes such as Friends of Police (FOP), City and Village Vigilance Committees, Police Boys clubs etc.
- Community policing, problem oriented policing are addressing the disorder and other social problems which are actually the root causes for the emergence of crime and delinquency in society.
- In the backdrop of rapidly changing socio, political and economic dimensions, the present society is in great need of pro active policing. However, more impetus and thrust is always given to reactive policing, i.e., the present style of policing – initiate the process of apprehending the accused, once the crime is reported to police. Whereas, the problem oriented policing and community policing address the core problem that causes disorder, crime and delinquency. In other words, the conventional policing is incident driven policing and community policing is problem driven policing. The latter will have a positive impact on members of the community and police personnel as well. This will enhance the image of the police and policing substantially among the public.

- As part of the Modernisation of Police Force (MPF), both the Centre and State governments may take initiative to introduce the community crime prevention programmes (if not set up already) and increase the number of such community crime prevention programmes, according to the requirements (if already established).
- After creating community crime prevention programmes, there should be periodical assessment and monitoring of such programmes so as to improvise the programmes according to the changing requirements and needs.
- The law enforcement agency or the state may extend financial assistance to the academic institutions to conduct study on the working of community crime prevention programmes. The findings of such research work should be given due importance to implement the measures suggested to enhance the efficacy of such programmes.

REFERENCES

Allen, C. (2005). 'The Links Between Heroin, Crack Cocaine and Crime: Where Does Street Crime Fit In?', *British Journal of Criminology*, 45: 355–72.

Arvanites, T. and Defina, R. (2006). 'Business Cycles and Street Crime', *Criminology*, 44:139–64.

Available at: http://www.chennaicitypolice.org

Available at: http://www.communitypolicingkerala.org

Bajpai, G.S. (2009). Situational Crime Prevention and Crime Reduction. UGC. Major Project. National Law Institute University, Bhopal (M.P).

Bennett, T. and Holloway, K. (2004). *Drug Use and Offending: Summary Results of the First Two Years of the NEW-ADAM Programme*. Research Findings 179. London: Home Office.

Buchanan, J. (2004). 'Missing Links? Problem Drug Use and Social Exclusion', *Probation Journal*, 51: 387–97.

Diaz. S.M. (2000). Prevention of Crime – The First Concern of the People. *Indian Journal of Criminology*, Vol. 28(1), pp. 1-6.

Edmark, K. (2005). 'Unemployment and Crime: Is there a Connection?' *Scandinavian Journal of Economics*, 107: 353–73.

Foster, J. (2000). 'Social Exclusion, Crime and Drugs', *Drugs: Education, Prevention and Policy*, 7: 317–30.

Gandhirajan C.K. (2005). 'Community Policing in the Prevention of Railway Crimes', *Indian Journal Criminology*. Vol. 33, No. 1 and 2, p. 91-101.

Garafalo, James and McLeod Maureen (1988). Improving the Use and Effectiveness of Neighbourhood Watch Programmes. In National Institute of Justice/Research in Action.Washington D.C.: National Institute of Justice April 1988.

Goldstein, H. (1987). Toward community-oriented policing: Potential, basic requirements, and threshold questions. *Crime and Delinquency*, 33, 6-30.

Hales, G., Lewis, C. and Silverstone, D. (2006). *Gun Crime: The Market In and Use of Illegal Firearms*. London: Home Office.

Hammersley, R., Forsyth, A. J. M. and Lavelle, T. L. (1990). 'The Criminality of New Drug Users in Glasgow', *British Journal of Addiction*, 85: 1583–94.

Hooghe, Marc, Bram Vanhoutte, Wim Hardyns and Tuba Bircan (2011). Unemployment, Inequality, Poverty and Crime Spatial Distribution Patterns of Criminal Acts In Belgium, 2001–06. *British Journal of Criminology*, 51, 1–20.

Hope, T., Bryan, J., Trickett, A. and Osborn, D. R. (2001). 'The Phenomena of Multiple Victimisation: The Relationship between Personal and Property Crime Risk', *British Journal of Criminology*, 41: 595–617.

Ivan Y. Sun and Doris C. Chu and Hung-En Sung (2010). A Cross-National Analysis of the Mediating Effect of Economic Deprivation on Crime. *Asian Criminology*, 6:15–32.

Kandasamy V. (2003). A Study on The Role of Community in Crime Prevention in Chennai. An unpublished Dissertation submitted to the University of Madras.

Kawachi, I., Kennedy, B. P. and Wilkinson, R. G. (1999). 'Crime: Social Disorganisation and Relative Deprivation', *Social Science and Medicine*, 48: 719–31.

Kubrin, C. E. (2003). 'Structural Covariates of Homicide Rates: Does Type of Homicide Matter?', *Journal of Research in Crime and Delinquency*, 40: 139–70.

Lin, M.-J. (2008). 'Does Unemployment Increase Crime? Evidence from U.S. Data 1974–2000', *Journal of Human Resources*, 43: 413–36.

Ludwig , J., Duncan, G. J. and Hirschfi eld, P. (2001). 'Urban Poverty and Juvenile Crime: Evidence from a Randomised Housing-Mobility Experiment', *The Quarterly Journal of Economics*, 116 : 655 – 79.

Lupton, R., Wilson, A., May, T., Warburton, H. and Turnbull, P. (2002). *A Rock and a Hard Place: Drug Markets in Deprived Neighbourhoods*. Home Office Research Study No. 240. London: Home Office.

McLaughten, Eugene and Muncie, John (2001). Community Policing. The Sage Dictionary of Criminology. London: Sage Publications.

Meera, Kadhar (2004). A Study on Effectiveness of Police Boys Clubs in Chennai. An unpublished Dissertation submitted to the University of Madras.

Menon, Madhava N.R. (1982). The Aurangabad Experiment in Preventive Action: Prospects for a National Strategy on Crime Prevention. *The Indian Journal of Criminology*, Vol. 10, No.1, pp. 12-15.

Moore, M.H., Trojanowicz, R.D and Kelling, G.L. (1988). 'Crime and Policing', in Perspectives on Policing, June, No. 2, U.S. Department of Jusitce.

National Crime Records Bureau (2009). Crime in India 2009.

Newman, Oscar (1980). Community of Interest. Garden City, NY: Anchor Press.

Newman, Oscar (1996). Creating Defensible Space. Washington, DC: U.S. Department of Housing and Urban Development.

Oh, J.H. (2005). 'Social Disorganisations and Crime Rates in U.S. Central Cities: Toward an Explanation of Urban Economic Change', *Social Science Journal*, 42: 569–82.

Oliver, M. Willard (2001). Community – Oriented Policing – A Systemic Approach to Policing. New Jersey : Prentice Hall.

Pearson, G. (2001). 'Drugs and Poverty', in S. Chen and E. Skidelsky, eds, *High Time for Reform: Drug Policy for the 21st Century*. London: Social Market Foundation.

Philip, V. Prateep (2006). The Friends of Police Movement-A Roadmap for Proactive People Protection. Hyderabad. The Icfai Unviersity Press.

Ramdoss, S and Mahendra Simha Karna, S.M (2008). Police Boys' Clubs in Chennai City-An Empirical Study. *The Indian Police Journal* Vol. LV No. 3, July-September. pp. 68-78.

Sabates, Ricardo (2008). Educational Attainment and Juvenile Crime *Area-Level Evidence Using Three Cohorts of Young People. British Journal of Criminology*, 48, 395–409.

Shaftoe, Henry (2004). Crime Prevention – Facts, Fallacies and the future. New York: Palgrave Macmillan.

Sparrow, M., Moore, M., and Kennedy, D. (1990). *Beyond 911: A New Era for Policing*. New York: Basic Books.

Wilson, J.Q. and Kelling, G. (1982). Broken Windows: The Police and Neighbourhood Safety. *Atlantic Monthly* (March): 29-38.

Wrobleski, H.M., and Hess, K.M., (2000). *An Introduction to Law Enforcement and Criminal Justice* (Sixth Ed.) Belmont, CA: Wadsworth Publishing.

19

AGEING AND ELDER ABUSE IN INDIA

M. Priyamvadha

> *"It is not sufficient to add years to life but the more important objective is to add life to years"*
>
> *—WHO Slogan*

Every individual born to this world, during his life time, undergoes different phases of development. It starts at infancy and ends at old age. After old age, nobody expects another phase– but death. Old age is the last phase of human life. Although it is a hard task to determine and define the exact age where 'old age' starts, as some individual become more frail even before they attain 50 years of age while some others are highly active even after 70 years of age. It is generally accepted that a person reaches 'old age' when he or she becomes 60 years of age. The age at which 'old age' starts for a person is a debatable issue. It is widely recognised as 60 years as the minimum age required for a person to be considered as senior citizen (United Nations, 2010). In India many central and state government schemes for the welfare and protection of the aged are targeted for those who are 60+years. The recently passed Maintenance and Welfare of Parents and Senior Citizens Act, 2007, also lay down that 60 years as the minimum age requirement for senior citizen status. It is necessary for any civilised society to ensure every individual who reaches at this phase could pass through it without much suffering or trouble. But, the issues and problems confronting the older people and the prosperity of their lives increases and as their number increases these issues and problem become more and more critical for the human society.

Ageing: The Global Scenario

Today, the proportion of older people, both in absolute and relative terms, is rapidly increasing all over the world. This phenomenon or process, whereby older individuals account for a proportionally larger share of the total population, is termed as population ageing. It was a key demographic outcome during the twentieth century and will surely be the distinct trait of populations during the twenty-first century. Since 1950, the proportion of older persons has been rising steadily, passing from 8 per cent in 1950 to 11 per cent in 2009, and is expected to reach 22 per cent in 2050 (United Nations, 2010). That means every fifth individual in the world population will be an older person by that time.

Ageing in India

India is one of the most populated countries of the world. Even before 1950, India has one million elderly people in the population. Presently, with the declining fertility, coupled with the increase in life expectancy, the number of older persons in the population is expected to increase by more than double-from 76 million in 2001 to 173 million in 2026 – an increase in their share to the total population from 7.4 to 12.4 per cent (Registrar General of India, 2001). Continuous increase in life expectancy means that more people are now living longer.

Ageing and Elder Abuse

Population ageing is profound, having major consequences and implications for all facets of human life. Since old age is associated with a gradual deterioration in physical as well as psychological well being of an individual, it becomes unavoidable for the individual to be dependant. In other words, old age requires a lot of care giving and protection. And the physical and psychological frailty makes the older people more vulnerable. Old age is a more prone age for any kind of victimisation.

Abuse and neglect of older people has become a very prevalent phenomenon today. Irrespective of the development status of the country, whether it is developed, developing or under developed, reports on incidents of elder abuse come out everyday. Moreover this issue has attracted the attention of researchers and professionals world wide and several studies have already been made. The World Health Organisation has conducted a global study on elder abuse and neglect in 2002 and has recognised the need to develop a global strategy for the prevention of the abuse of older people.

Elder Abuse

The abuse of older people is certainly not something new for the twenty-first century yet it is not given the high profile which its incidence deserves. One of the reasons for this is that in some societies older people are not given much respect; they may be seen as an economic burden on society because they are no longer economically productive. In societies which emphasis youthful vigor, old age will tend to have a very negative image; consequently, younger people may come to fear growing old. Becoming frail, disabled or incapacitated are typical stereotypes of older people despite the reality that being old can bring new experiences and many new rewards. Another consequence of ageism is that if people do not want to think about the inevitability of old age, they may avoid interacting with old people and also avoid watching, listening or reading about the 'nasty things' which can happen to an older person. Thus, elder abuse is frequently swept under the carpet, both by professionals and by the public at large. Not surprisingly, therefore, elder abuse does not get the same media attention as child abuse.

The timeless phenomenon of inter-personal violence has, in the latter part of the twentieth century, been framed within age-specific compartments. Societally hidden, bit manifest in literature, child and wife abuse were the first to emerge. Both types of abuse were framed as family violence issues and were originally called baby battering and wife beating respectively. Eventually, the problem of elder abuse (which was initially called "granny battering") emerged. The abuse of older people was first described in British scientific journals in 1975 (Baker, 1975; Burston 1977). In the US, these reports were immediately viewed as a socio-political concern, and quickly led to legislative action. The growing world-wide focus on the abuse of older people since then has sought to parallel the focus upon human rights, gender equality and especially population ageing.

Violence against parents by young children or by adolescents is rarer than other forms of family violence. However, when the parents are elderly, parent abuse is not uncommon, nor is abuse by grand children or other members of the family. Estimates of the number of abused elderly each year range from one-half million to over two million cases annually, with at least 70 per cent of the perpetrators being family members. Approximately two out of each one hundred people aged 65 or older experience physical violence and most of the studies show that the majority of the abused elderly are women, as might be expected given their greater longevity.

Elder Abuse: Definition

Over the years, the term elder abuse has been defined in different ways. It is a single or repeated act or lack of appropriate action, occurring within any relationship where there is an expectation of trust, which causes harm or distress to an older person. The WHO Toronto Declaration on Elder Abuse defined elder abuse as 'a single or repeated act, or lack of appropriate action, occurring within any relationship where there is an expectation of trust, which causes harm or distress to an older person.' This wording concurs with the definition used by Action on Elder Abuse in the United Kingdom since 1994.

Elder Abuse: Types

Elder abuse can take several forms, often with more than one type of abuse occurring at the same time for individuals. National and provincial statistics indicate that the two most identified and reported types of elder abuse are as follows.

Psychological/Emotional/Verbal Abuse: This may take the form of verbal aggression, humiliation, isolation, intimidation, threats and inappropriate control of activities. In all cases, it diminishes the identity and self-worth of older people. It can also provoke intense fear, anxiety or debilitating stress. It can include: removal of decision-making power while the person is competent, withholding affection for manipulative purposes, refusing access to grandchildren, denying privacy in institutions, forcing older people to do degrading things, controlling activities, treating them like children, attacking their self-esteem, intentionally frightening them

Physical Abuse: Physical abuse is the use of physical force causing discomfort which may or may not result in bodily injury, physical pain, or impairment. Older persons who are subjected to rough handling or mistreatment are the victims of physical abuse. It can include: slapping, shaking, pushing, kicking, punching, striking with an object or weapon, deliberate exposure to severe weather, unnecessary physical restraint, forced confinement, failure to provide adequate health care.

Sexual Abuse: All unwanted forms of sexual activity, behaviour, assault or harassment to older persons are elder sexual abuse. It can include: verbal or suggestive behaviour, fondling, sexual intercourse, lack of personal privacy, being forced to commit degrading acts, unnecessary help with dressing/hygiene.

Financial Abuse: This is the misuse of an older person's funds or property through fraud, trickery, theft or force. It can include: frauds, scams, the misuse of money or property, convincing an older person to buy a product or give away money, stealing money or possessions, misusing bank or credit cards, misusing joint banking accounts, forging a signature on pension cheques or legal documents, misusing a power of attorney.

Neglect: This is the intentional or unintentional failure to provide for the needs of someone. Neglect can be active (intentional) or passive (unintentional) and has the effect of failing to provide older persons with basic necessities or care. It can include: failure to provide a safe, warm and comfortable place to live, denial of social contacts, failure to provide personal hygiene, failure to provide proper food or clean clothing, failure to provide aids for daily living, (hearing aids, walkers, canes, wheelchairs, etc.), failure to prevent physical harm, abandonment or desertion. Self-neglect, while not technically considered abuse, is also a significant concern. It involves cases whereby, older adults, by choice or ignorance, live in ways that disregard their health and well being.

Medication: This is the misuse of an older person's medications and prescriptions. It can include: withholding medication, overmedicating, sedation, not complying with prescriptions refills or other safety needs and can in some cases pose a hazard to others.

Constitutional and Legislative Framework in India

Article – 41 of the Constitution recognises the needs of the elderly and enjoys upon the state the responsibility of making effective provision for public assistance in the case of unemployment, old age, sickness and disablement and in other cases of underserved want. While welfare of the aged is a state subject, the nodal responsibility at the center is assigned to the Ministry of Welfare. Item number 9 of the State List and Items 20, 23 and 24 of the Concurrent List (that are part of the Constitution of India) relate to provisions of old age pensions, social security, social insurance, economic and social planning and relief to the disabled and the unemployed. The Government of India is committed to provide an enabling environment to secure the goals of economic and social security for the elderly population. The non-governmental organisations, citizens and the community have to be partners in the campaign towards securing a society for all ages. Article 41 of the Constitution of India is reinforced by section 125 of Code of Criminal Procedure, 1973 under which every person having sufficient means is required to maintain his parents if they are unable to maintain themselves.

Under the section 20(1) of the Hindu Adoption and Maintenance Act, 1956, an aged and infirm parent, if unable to maintain himself or herself, is entitled to maintenance. Muslim law also imposes an obligation to maintain needy parents, subject to certain circumstances.

Independent of the personal Law, the code of Criminal Procedure 1973 Section 125(1) (d) makes it incumbent for a person having sufficient means to maintain his father or mother who is unable to maintain himself or herself and on getting proof of neglect or refusal, a first class Magistrate may order such a person to make a monthly allowance.

The Himachal Pradesh Maintenance of Parents and Dependent Elderly Act, 2001 provides a simple procedure for maintenance to be given for parents being ignored by their children.

Maintenance and Welfare of Parents and Senior Citizens Act, 2007.

The Act on Maintenance and Welfare of Parents and Senior Citizens, 20 was passed by the Parliament on December 6, 2007 and has been notified on December 31, 2007 and came into effect in 2008. The Salient Features of the Act ensure Maintenance of Parents and Senior Citizens within their family; places a legal obligation on children and relatives to maintain their Parents; prescribes setting up of Tribunals for quick settlement of maintenance claim; avoids Cumbersome Legal Procedure and recommends setting up Old Age Homes in all disticts.

Policy and Programme Initiatives in India

The Ministry of Social Justice and Empowerment acts as the nodal agency with regard to ageing issues. It provides basic policy guidance, the roadmap for implementation of the same and also coordinates with stake holders such as the other Ministries of the Central Government and the State Government, NGOs, Civil Society Institutions etc.

National Policy on Older Persons (NPOP)

The Government of India announced a National Policy on Older Persons (NPOP) in January 1999. This policy provides a broad framework for inter-sectoral collaboration and cooperation, both within the government as well as between government and non-governmental agencies. In particular, the policy has identified a number of areas of intervention.

Financial Security

Financial security through coverage under Old Age Pension Scheme for poor and destitute older persons, better returns on earnings/savings of government/quasi-government employee's savings in Provident Fund, etc., creating opportunities for continued education/skill up-gradation ensuring thereby continued employment/self-employment and income generation and provision for pension scheme for self-employed, employees of the non-formal and non-governmental sector.

Health Security

The NPOP recognises special health needs of the older persons to be met through strengthening and reorienting the public health services at Primary Health Care level, creation of health facilities through non-profit organisations like trust/charity, etc., and implementing health insurance.

Recognising Shelter as Basic Human Need

The NPOP provides for earmarking 10 per cent of the houses/housing sites in urban as well as rural areas for older persons belonging to the lower income groups, special consideration to the older persons falling in the category of Below Poverty Line (BPL) and destitute in housing schemes and loans at reasonable interest rates and easy repayment instalments with tax relief for purchase of houses etc.

Information/Education Needs

Education/information needs of older persons too have got adequately reflected in the National Policy. Education/information material relevant to the lives of older persons should be developed and made available through mass media. Education, training and information being the important human requirement, the NPOP provides for proactive role in ensuring the same by disseminating knowledge about preparation of old age. It is also emphasised for schools to have programme on inter-generational bonding.

Welfare and Institutional Care

Institutional care has been provided for in the NPOP as the last resort. The care in non-institutional set up, i.e., within family and the community needs to be strengthened and encouraged. This apart, the state should also create infrastructure in partnership with voluntary organisations to provide for poor, destitute and neglected older persons whose care cannot be ensured within the family. This is to be ensured through old age homes and other such institutional facilities that would be needed. Voluntary efforts need to be encouraged for creating facilities for day care, out reach services, multi-services citizen centers, etc.

Protection of Life and Property of Older Persons

The state has to gear up security network to save older persons from criminal offence and police is required to keep friendly vigil. Early settlement of property/inheritance disputes is to be done, safeguards to protect them from fraudulent dealings in transfer of property through sale will are to be put in place and free legal aid and toll free helpline services are to be placed across the country.

Caring the Elderly and Prevention of Elder Abuse

According to the general legacy of human beings, the protection and care of the weaker sections of the society, namely, the children, the women and the elderly must be done by the capable members. This is how caring the elderly and preventing them from being abuse and neglected became fundamental duty for every individual in the society. Man has developed many measures throughout the development of civilised life in order to ensure more harmony, order and peace in the societal life. Provisions were included to ensure the well-being of the weaker members of the society, including the aged. Today, as we are living in era of modern nation-states, there are both formal as well as informal ways of protection and care of the elderly exists. While the government institutes new policies, programmes and legislative measures for the sake of elderly people, the good traditional values, morals and ethics still play a vital role in designing and controlling the behaviour patterns of the people towards the elderly like in other aspects of life.

Conclusion

Elder abuse is a complex phenomenon that causes untold suffering and pain. It stripes victims of their dignity, independence, and self-worth. Because of its emotional, physical, and financial impact, it often brings on early death. It is committed by those who older people mostly trust – their families and friends, caregivers, and advisors. It has no easy solutions, but with greater societal awareness, increased options, and improved responses, there is hope that the promise of "the golden years" can be realised. The elderly had contributed their youth and vigor to build up what the younger ones utilises today. Now it's time for them to retreat and the primary responsibility rests with the younger generation to ensure that the elders' final phase of life is peaceful and joyous. Towards this end, all of us have to try together and bring up the coming generations with adequate value orientation and humanitarian concern.

Bibliography

Baker, A. A. (1975) 'Granny battering.' *Modern Geriatrics* 5 (8): 20-24.

Bacon, F. (1617). *Reports*. 33-34.

Bennett, G., and Kingston, P. (1993). *Elder abuse: Concepts, theories and interventions*. London: Chapman and Hall.

Bristowe, E. and Collins, J. B. (1989). Family mediated abuse of noninstitutionalised frail elderly men and women living in British Columbia. *Journal of Elder Abuse and Neglect*, 7(1), 45-64.

Burston, G. R. (1977) 'Do your elderly patients live in fear of being battered?' *Modern Geriatrics*, 7 (5): 54-55.

Chokkanathan, S. and Lee, A.E.Y. Elder mistreatment in urban India: A community based study. Retrieved from http://www.scopus.com on 20 January 2010.

Department of Health (1992). *Confronting Elder Abuse*. London: HMSO.

ESHEL (2004). *The National Survey on Elder Abuse and Neglect in Israel*. Haifa: Author.

Families Commssion (2008). *Elder Abuse and Neglect: Exploration of Risk and Protective Factors*. Wellington: Author.

Geriatric Centre Nepal. (2010). *A Baseline Study on Reported Cases of Elder Abuse in Nepali Press–July 2008-July 2010*. Kathmandhu: Author.

Haralambos, M. and Heald, R.M. (2007). *Sociology: Themes and Perspectives*. Oxford: Oxford University Press.

Heisler, C. J. (2007). 'Elder abuse'. In R. C. Davis, A. J. Lurigio and S. Herman (Eds.) *Victims of Crime* (pp. 161-188). Thousand Oaks: Sage Publications.

HelpAge India. (2010). *Report on Elder Abuse in India*. New Delhi: Author.

Hickey, T., and Douglass, R. L. (1981). Neglect and abuse of older family members: Professionals' perspectives and case experience. *Gerontologist*, 27(4), 171-176.

Homer, A., and Gilleard, C. (1990). Abuse of elderly people by their carers. *British Medical Journal*, 301, 1359-1362.

Jamuna, D. (2005). Issues of elder care and elder abuse in Indain context. In Phoebe S. Liebig and S. Irudaya Rajan (Eds.) *An Aging India: Perspectives, Prospects and Policies*. Jaipur: Rawat Publications.

Krienert, Jessie L., Walsh, Jeffrey A. and Turner, Moriah. (2009). 'Elderly in America: A Descriptive Study of Elder Abuse Examining National Incident-Based Reporting System (NIBRS) Data, 2000-2005', *Journal of Elder Abuse and Neglect*, 21 (4): 325-345.

McDonald, L. andCollins, A. (2000). *Abuse and Neglect of Older Adults: A Discussion Paper*. The National Clearinghouse on Family Violence. Revised 19 June 2000. Retrieved from: http://www.hcsc.gc.ca/hppb/familyviolence/html/neglect/english

Mears, J. (2003). Survival is not enough: Violence against older women in Australia. *Violence Against Women*, 9 (12): 1478-1489.

National Centre for Social Research and The King's College. (2007). *UK Study of Abuse and Neglect of Older People*. London: Authors.

National Centre on Elder Abuse. (1998). *National elder abuse incidence study*. Wasington, DC: Author.

O'Malley, H. C., Segars, H., Perez, R., Mitchell, V., and Knuepel, G. M. (1979). *Elder abuse in Massachusetts: A survey of professionals and paraprofessionals*. Boston: Legal Research and Services for the Elderly.

Padmasree, V. (1991). *A Study on Incidence of Elder Abuse and Some Factors Related to Abuse*. Unpublished Masters Thesis. Tirupati: S.V. University.

Pillemer, K. and Finkelhor, D. (1988) The prevalence of elder abuse: A random sample survey. *Gerontologist*, 28:51–57.

Pillemer, K. (1985). The dangers of dependency: New findings on domestic violence against the elderly. *Social Problems*, 33(2): 146-157.

Pittaway, E., and Westhues, A. (1993). The prevalence of elder abuse and neglect of older abuse who access health and social services in London. Ontario, Canada. *Journal of Elder Abuse and Neglect*, 5: 77-93.

Podnieks, E. (1992). National survey on abuse of the elderly in Canada. *Journal of Elder Abuse and Neglect*, 4 (1/2): 5-58.

Podnieks, E., Pillemer, K., Nicholson, J.P., Shillington, T. and Frizzel, A. (1990). *National Survey on Abuse of the Elderly in Canada*. Toronto: Ryerson Polytechnical Institute.

Pritchard, J. (1995). *The Abuse of the Older People, 2nd Ed.* London: Jessica Kingsley Publishers.

Pritchard, J. (2001). *Male Victims of Elder Abuse: Their Experiences and Needs*. London: Jessica Kingsley Publishers.

Priyamvadha, M. (2008). Fading values and forgotten victims: A study on violence against elderly women (unpublished project report). Chennai: University of Madras.

Quinn, M. J., and Tomita, S. K. (1997). *Elder Abuse and Neglect: Causes, Diagnosis, and Intervention Strategies (Sec. Ed.)*. New York: Springer Publishing Company.

Registrar General and Census Commissioner (2001). *Census Report-2001*. New Delhi: Government of India.

Reinharz, S. (1986). Loving and hating one's elders: Twin themes in legend and literature. In R. Wolf and K. Pillemer (Eds.), *Elder abuse: Conflict in the family* (pp. 25-48). Dover, MA: Auburn.

Rokeach, M. (1972). *Beliefs, Attitudes, and Values*. San Fransico: Jossey-Bass.

Sonkin, D.J., and Durphy, M. (1982). *Learning to live without violence*. San Francisco: Volcano.

Staub, E. (2003). *The Psychology of Good and Evil: Why Children, Adults, and Groups Help and Harm Others.* Cambridge: Cambridge University Press.

Stearns, P.N. (1986). Old age family conflict: The perspective of the past. In R. Wolf and K. Pillemer (Eds.), *Elder abuse: Conflict in the family* (pp. 3-24). Dover, MA: Auburn.

United Nations (2010). *World Population Ageing 2009.* Department of Economic and Social Affairs, Population Division. New York: Author.

Whitbeck, B.S., Hoyt, R.D., and Huck, N.S. (1994). Early family relationship, intergenerational solidarity, and support provided to parents by their adult children, *Journal of Gerontology*, 49(2): 85-94.

Wolf, R.S., Godkin, M.A., and Pillemer, K. A. (1986). Maltreatment of the elderly: A comparative analysis. *Pride Institute Journal of Long Term Home Health Care*, 5(4), 1017.

World Health Organisation (2008). *A Global Response to Elder Abuse and Neglect: Building Primary Health Care Capacity to Deal with the Problem Worldwide: Main Report*. Geneva: Author.

Yan, E., and Tang, C. (2001). Prevalence and psychological impact of Chinese elder abuse. *Journal of Interpersonal Violence*, 16: 1158-1174.

Yan, E., So-Kum, C. and Yeung, T. D. (2002). No safe haven: a review on elder abuse in Chinese families. *Trauma, Violence and Abuse*, 3: 167-180.

20

A STUDY ON THE YOUNG OFFENDERS OF CYBER CRIME

G. Deepak Raj Rao

ABSTRACT

Children have the curiosity to learn and explore the unknown things. This is same when they handle the new technology devices like computers and Cell Phone along with Internet. The curiosity sometime makes them to learn wrong information and misuse this technology. There are different stages for a child to become a child against the law. The study analyses the different stages and the methods they use to learn to become a criminal in this technology based world.

Introduction

The present day Computers and Electronic gadgets are made so user friendly that it can be handle by all the users easily and even the children aged below 15 years can operate without any difficulty. When we talk of children they not only learn the operations of these devices very quickly but they also start experimenting with the extra and hidden operations of the particular device.

The fun from this experiment motivates the children to move further which some times results in actions which is against the law. Some of them stop here because of the awareness and the parental guidance but some go further to be punished by the law. The NCRB report of Crime in India 2008 say that there is a raise of 32.7 per cent in 2008 over 2007. It also says that the agewise profile of persons arrested in Cyber Crime cases under IT Act 2000 showed that 61.2 per cent of the offenders were in the age group 18-30 years (109 out of 178) of them 4 persons were below the age of 18 years.

The child becomes an offender of cyber crime when he crosses the few stages of fun and experiment along with the improper guidance.

Curiosity to Learn: Stage–1

Children learn the wrong side of technology and the means to misuse it from their friends or peer group. They also learn from unethical Gurus like their school seniors or elder relatives or the internet friends. These gurus don't have any awareness about the ill-effect of this knowledge or the crime that is involved with it.

First they learn is the tips and tricks of the operations of the devices. Through these tips and tricks they do some fun and play with others. The other attraction for them is to learn the methods of downloading. It all starts with the downloading of songs, movies or movie clips or games. Now they become well versed in browsing the internet. Till now every thing is known to the parents and other guardians.

No Proper Guidance: Stage-2

Restriction comes from their parents or guardians by locking the computer with password. Then the child does the first cyber crime activity that is to break the Password or hack the administrator user account. After that they learn to erase their foot prints from the PC. They also learn the methods to hide files from the view of parents. It is so simple for them to learn this using the search engine or view the working methods that are kept is video sharing website like Youtube.com, etc. Present day search engines are so helpful to these kids that they don't need good vocabulary. If they type any wrong spelling the site will correct the mistake and suggest the correct word. If there is no proper guidance by the parents or guardians then the child will move to the next stage which will teach them to master advanced crime and become a problem to the society.

Interest in Pornography: Stage-3

When they do the searching operation they also come across pornographic site which are linked with some downloading site. They also learn the method to search the porn site without any kind of help. Here they start downloading obscene material and store it in the PC or Cell Phone or other storing medium. They not only view it but also send it to others. While doing this they also become an attacker indirectly as they will implant some zombies in their own computer which will use the resource of their computer to attack a target computer. According to Crime in India 2008 report 63.9 per cent (90 out of 178) of the offenders arrested were under Obscene publication or transmission in electronic form of which 67.8 per cent (61 out of 90) were in the age group 18-30 years.

Need for Money: Stage-4

In order to get the full Pornographic movie they have to pay money to these sites. For this they do some advance Internet search and finds the hacking sites which will teach them not only to crack the software or games but also hack the data base and collect the others credit card information of others. By now they become the masters in doing crime and well versed in using the Internet for wrong purpose.

There are hacking site which give full details of hacking and share the database of the credit card holders of some other country. They motivate these children to use this database and get some percentage of amount they have utilised by them as commission. These web site also update regularly the different methods of misusing the computers and cell phone or other electronic devices. On the other hand they have some group of friends in there social networking sites who also share these information and they update them. All these, they get by free of cost without any restriction and efforts.

Becomes an Expert: Stage-5

Now they can do as they like and do as they want using Internet, Computer and other electronic devices. They don't affride to harass others and go against the law as they found some ways to hide their identity in internet. They have not only learned how to use the proxy server but also the chain of proxy servers which are not traceable easily. There are some servers in countries like Russia which don't maintain any log of its user and they allow others to use it freely. Finally they also have good knowledge to spoof the IP address or Email ID or Cell Phone No and do all kinds of illegal tricks.

They will only stop this activity when they are caught by their parents or guardians and their proper guidance or engaged with higher education or job which will make them very busy. If they are not controlled now, they will continue without any kind of fear until the Police arrests them.

Cyberethics for Parents and Educators

Parents must have proper control over their children after allowing them to use the modern electronic devices like PC, Internet and Cell Phone. They must have to update themselves about the latest development in the technology and create awareness in the minds of the children that some of the tricks are wrong and are subjected to punishment.

On the other side the Educators and friends must share only that information which is good and suitable to others especially to the children. They must not tell all the information which they have got through their study or experiment.

Cyberethics for Kids

Kids must follow the guidelines and advice of the parents. They have to a good Cyber Citizen by following certain ethics like not to download copy right software, games or other material from internet and not to interfere in others privacy or not to misuse the internet and computer for wrong purpose. There must be a lesson for kids in their curriculum how to use the computer and internet safely for the benefit of the individual and society.

Cyberethics for Web sites

Search Engines are one of the main sources for the children to reach certain uncensored information and unethical web sites. So they must allow the users to use according to the age group by filtering through the email id. Web site authors must have to follow some ethics as their information will harm the young mind so restrict the users accordingly. International Internet Governing Organisation and Central and State Governments must take steps in blocking these web sites which are not following the guidelines.

References

Crime in India 2008, Chapter 10, Juvenile Delinquency, National Crime Records Bureau, New Delhi.

Norton, Cyber Ethics 2007, Chapter 1, New York.

Parthasarthy Pati, Cyber Ethics, Legal Service India.

21

JUDICIAL ACTIVISIM: AN OVERVIEW

Mehraj Uddin

1. The Backdrop

Judicial activism is a sharp weapon with judicious teeth which has kept the authorities at the helm of affairs on toes to discharge their functions in the rightful and dutiful manner. The top ranking executives too have not been spared by this weapon. Even in the circumstances where the legislatures have entangled in conflict with each other or raised allegations or cross allegations against each on the floor of the house or outside the house or raised allegations against Governor, the courts have stepped in to address to the grievances of the aggrieved party. Moreover, till 1970's the Indian judiciary resorted to what is called as the 'hands off doctrine', but in the post 1970 era, the Indian judiciary could not afford to shut its eyes and ears, as to what was going on in the country.

It is a matter of fact that the Indian Constitution has demarcated the boundaries for each Constitutional entity of the State and they are expected to perform their functions within their respective domains and not encroach upon each other's periphery. It is also true that the Courts can't create law for implementation nor can Courts enter into the shoes of executive to perform their functions.

The Supreme Court bench comprising of *Justice A.K. Mathur* and *Justice Makandey Katju* maintained that Judges can't create law and seek enforcement. The Bench as stated by *Dhanajay Mahapatra,* derived strength from the recent speeches of two former Chief Justices of India *Justice J.S. Verma* and *Justice A.S. Anand* expressing anguish over the manner in which the judiciary has breached the thin line separating the functions of the three organs of democracy-Legislature, Executive and Judiciary. The Bench cautioned against judicial activism.

The Bench rather in an unprecedented confession criticised the three-judge bench judgement and admitted that the judiciary has erred in the recent past in exercising powers of the executive. Cautioning against the judicial activism, it said if the trend continued, politicians would step in and clip the judiciary's wings. The Bench observed:

> *"If the judiciary does not exercise restraint and overstretches its limits, there is bound to be a reaction from the politicians and others. The politicians will then step in and curtail the power or even the independence of the judiciary".*

The Bench pointed out that in order to maintain independence, of the judiciary, the judges have to exercise restraint and honour the separation of powers among the three wings of governance, as maintained by the constitution. The constitutional trade off for independence is that Judges must restrain themselves from the areas reserved for other separate branches, executive and legislature.

The Supreme Court's disapproval of the manner in which the Delhi High Court used its public interest jurisdiction in dealing with the matters 'exclusively pertaining' to legislature domain has raised questions about judicial interventions in issues affecting the public at large.

2. Controversial Issues

Judicial activism has become a subject of controversy. Attempts have been made and are being made to curb the power of the courts as well as access to them. Some of the issues which led to the controversy include;

(i) DMC Demolition Drive 2006

The Court in this case found that the things did not proceed as desired, therefore, it set into motion an innovative mechanism of Court Commissioners to monitor illegal buildings. Land worth Rs. 9000 crores has been reclaimed but the MCD and the Commissioners are of late on collision course with corporation dubbing the Court as "parallel administration."

(ii) ***Nursery Admissions 2002***

The Court in order to bring transparency in nursery admission policy asked school management to follow guidelines framed by the Government, but the Schools are not happy, hence the confusion continues.

(iii) ***Crackdown on Traffic Violations***

The Court took note of news reports on tremendous increase in the number of road accidents in Delhi and enhanced fines on all traffic violations. The executive could not digest this direction.

(iv) ***Blueline Menace***

The Court concerned over a spate of killings by Blueline buses, ordered their immediate phase out. At present Bench is overseeing smooth change over to alternative transport system.

(v) ***Free Seats in the Schools***

Delhi Government in the year 2003 leased out land to the School Managements on the concessional rates with a clear orders that the management they will provide free seats to the students from economically weaker sections, a condition in the lease deed 200 out of 397 schools are yet to comply with the order. The Court cracked down on such schools.

(vi) ***Regularisation of the Employees***

Judgment of the trial court and the High Court on regularising certain employees of a private golf course. The Supreme Court overturned the judgment of the High Court.

(vii) ***Free Beds in the Hospitals***

Land given to the private hospitals at the concessional rates on the condition that that 25 per cent free beds shall be reserved for the poor. The hospitals have not followed their commitment, hence the judicial intervention. Other cases are misuse of ambulance service, auto rickshaws, begging, pollution and monkey menace etc.

The other important instances of judicial activism quoted by the Bench include an interim order of the Supreme Court in the year 1998 directing a composite floor test as a solution to the ugly drama by contending claimants *Jagdampika Pal* and *Kalyan Singh* for Chief Ministership of Uttar Pradesh. There were allegations that the Governor *Romesh Bhandri* was playing a partisan role. In yet another similar situation in 2005, three-Judge Bench asked the Jharkhand assembly to hold trust vote on CCTV. In this case *Shibu Soren Soren* and *Arjun Munda,* both claimed majority to seek the chief ministership. The apex court directed for video recording of the house proceedings and also sought a report from the speaker. Lok Saba Speaker *Somnath Chatterjee* had criticised the Supreme Court for directing the *Jharkhand Assembly Speaker* to conduct the trust motion under the glare of CCTV. The Bench had no hesitation in declaring that the three-judge judgment in the *Jharkhand* case as well as in *Jagdamika Pal* case virtually snapped the fine thread that separated the domains of three organs legislature, executive and judiciary.

Further, there are many more cases from a number of States, where the State High Courts have issued directions to the State authorities. The Jammu and Kashmir High Court issued direction to LAWADA asking to demolish all the illegal constructions around the world famous dallake. The Hon'ble High Court also issued direction to the authorities to expedite the investigation in the *Sabina sex scandal* and bring to the book all the persons involved in the scandal. A division Bench of the Kerala High Court on 12th Dec. 7 directed *Pathanamthitta District Collector* to employ sufficient number of persons for removing waste that has started pilling up in Sabarimala and Pampa. The Supreme Court on 10th Dec. 7 ordered colleges across the country to clearly state in their prospectus that students indulging in ragging will be expelled.

3. Recent Directions

As per recent directions of the two-judge bench of the Supreme Court, the judges are expected to follow the following parameters while discharging their functions:

(a) Judges must have modesty;

(b) Judges must exercise judicial restraint. If the judges don't exercise restraint, politicians will step in and curtail down their powers and take away the independence of judiciary;

(c) Judges must exercise judicial wisdom and avoid to venture into the domain of the executive or legislative;

(d) Judges must know their limits and must not try to run the Government;

(e) Judges must restrain from the areas reserved for others.

4. Mixed Reaction

The judicial activism has a long history in India. *Krishna Iyer* has pointed out that the constitutional system created by our National Charter entrusts the judiciary with administration of justice, including adjudication of disputes and interpretation of laws between the state and citizens, states inter se and between Union and the state. The Courts are independent of the Executive and the Legislature and the judges are free under the constitutional guarantee.

It is true that the Courts are independent of the executive, but Courts are not independent of the Nation or the Constitution. All power, including judicial power, it is people's trust. That is why the goal of social revolution, assured by part-III which enunciates Fundamental Rights and Part–IV which articulates the Directive Principles of State policy, has to be shared, not shunned, by the judiciary.

There is a mixed reaction to the directions issued by the two-judge bench of the Supreme Court. Some are in favour of the judicial activism but some call it as judicial terrorism. In fact neither judicial activism nor critical reaction to it is new. The apex judiciary has based many controversial rulings on the interpretations that has no obvious support from history, text or authority. The supporters of judicial activism have been many, but others urge judicial restraint.

Politicians for the reasons best known to them are very happy on this judgment of two-judge bench of the Supreme Court. *Vice-President of the BJP, M.A. Naqvi* said the observation was 'good and in the interest of democracy'. He further said Parliament–judiciary conflict is neither new nor desirable in the democratic set up like ours. 'If the judiciary moves towards reforms on its own it is a welcome step. People have a lot of faith in the judiciary, it must tackle from within 'the question that is raised from time to time with regard to its functioning' *Naqvi* added. The Congress working Committee member and former *Additional Solicitor General Devinder Dwivedi,* while reacting to the judgment, in his personal capacity remarked as under:

> "Welcome the judgment. The judicial activism judgments receive popularity, but it is the Constitution and not the popular support which lends legitimacy to the judicial process."

The Left Front Revolutionary Socialist Party (RSP) *Chief Abani Roy* said observations of the Hon'ble Court are welcome, if the judiciary follows its own advice. He further remarked, that what they have said is good, if it is followed. The judgment of two-judge Bench criticising the larger Bench however, did not go down well with the Constitutional experts. Former *Attorney General Soli J Sorabjee* remarked:

> "A Bench may disagree with the coordinate Bench, but it will be in breach of judicial decorum for a two-judge bench to characterise a judgment of three-judge bench as deviation from the constitutional scheme of separation of powers."

Senior Advocate and former Law Minister *Arun Jaitley* agreed with *Sorabjee* and maintained that the principle of separation of powers no doubt is sacrosanct, but the Supreme Court must speak in one voice and not in conflicting tones. There may be mixed reaction to the judicial activism, some executives or legislatures may or may not like judicial activism or some judges under the banner of judicial activism may resort to what is called as judicial terrorism, but there are some basic issues which can't be ignored.

5. Key Issues

In the light of the parameters laid down by the two-judge bench of the Supreme Court, the key issues now arises as under:

(i) What is the domain and role of the judiciary ?

(ii) What about millions of the people who are denied equality before law and equal protection of laws ?

(iii) What about the people who are suffering or made to suffer for none of their fault ?

(iv) What about the persons who fall prey to the false encounters ?

(v) What about the people who have disappeared and their parents are going from pillar to the post ?

(vi) What about the women who are exploited almost every day at every front ?

(vii) What about the weaker sections of the society who don't get an opportunity of vindicating their rights ?

(viii) What about the people who are exploited by the politicians ?

(ix) What about the people who suffer due to the bureaucratic high handedness ?

(x) What about the corruption which has penetrated very deep in our society ?

(xi) What about the people who are not in a position to get the basic minimum needs ?

(xii) What about the people who are made to suffer because of the strong nexus between the underworld syndicates, executive and politicians?

(xiii) What about the victims whose cases are not even registered in the police stations ?

(xiv) What about the people who are languishing in the four walls for the crimes which they have never committed ?

(xv) What about the poor people who can't purchase justice ?

6. Judicial Approach

A constitutional Court is not bound by what was originally intended by the founding fathers but can interpret the Constitution in terms of what would have been intended under the circumstances that exist at the time of such interpretation. In the light of key issues raised above, the questions in respect of the functioning of the judiciary arise ?

(i) Should judiciary remain silent spectator as to what is going on in the judiciary ?

(ii) Should Judges close their eyes to the ground reality and maintain silence ?

(iii) What the Judges are expected to do ?

(iv) Is job of the Judiciary over with interpretation of the statutes and announcement of the judgment ?

It is an admitted fact that in any system of constitutional governance, the judiciary plays an important role of interpreting and applying the law and adjudicating upon controversies between one citizen and another, between citizens and the state, between the state and the state. In a country with the Constitution, the judiciary has the additional function of protecting the Constitution by interpreting and applying the provisions and keeping all the authorities within the four walls of the Constitution.

7. Judicial Terrorism

The supremacy of the rule of law symbolised by the Supreme Court and High Courts in the country has strengthened the sense of justice and resistance to the arrogance of power. Case law in India has made it clear that the administrative action cannot be arbitrary, thanks to the canons of natural justice the courts have invoked from time to time. Fair procedure is obligatory even in considering a passport or canceling a poll.

Today it is possible for any man, small or big, to move to the court and seek redress. Likewise, wherever and whenever any injury is inflicted, the law can be invoked and the writ of the Court will run in redressal. Democratic legality, in its egalitarian, connotation is the exclusive domain of higher judiciary.

The judiciary in a democratic setup has a vital role in every sphere of the society. The role becomes very important particularly when people continue to have faith in the judiciary. But at the same time we must be in a position to draw a distinction between judicial activism and judicial terrorism. The judiciary no doubt has to ensure implementation of the rules and regulations through the executive but at the same time judiciary is not expected to issue directions which do not fall within its domain, otherwise the judicial intervention shall be termed as judicial terrorism. In my opinion, if the Hon'ble Court directs the Municipal authorities to remove garbage from the Streets, which seldom they have not done on their own or asks the Hospital authorities to ensure that medical staff on duty roaster are available during duty hours or directs the University or education authorities to provide quality education to the students, conduct examinations within the scheduled time and also declare results with out any delay or directs any authority to ensure a accountable and transparent administration, all this may be termed as judicial activism and the Judiciary is within its rights. However, on the other hand, if the Hon'ble Court directs Municipal authorities not to demolish a illegally raised building or stops Hospital authorities from taking action against the erring official or Doctor, or directs the University or education authorities to grant admission to a candidate who is not otherwise eligible or conduct examination of a student who is not eligible to appear in the examination, the judiciary is not within its rights as it may be termed as Judicial terrorism.

The Judiciary is not expected to watch like a silent spectator nor can it be expected from the judges that they will close their eyes to the ground reality and maintain silence over infringement of any right or whenever duty as per law is not performed. Moreover, job of the judiciary is not over with interpretation of the statutes and announcement of the judgment, but judiciary has to ensure that the judgment delivered is translated into action, even if such an approach is termed as judicial activism, but at the same time judicial terrorism is to be avoided. The judiciary is not expected to enter into the shoes of legislature for law making nor into the shoes of executive for issuing executive directions. The Judiciary has to act like a watchdog and interpret rules and regulations in the right perspective and ensure their implementation with judicial wisdom.

The judiciary exists to safeguard the right to life and liberty of the people, irrespective of caste, colour or gender. The courts are there to protect people from the excesses of the executive or any other Institution that violate the Constitution. While maintaining a healthy distance from the executive and the legislature, the judiciary must ensure that neither institution acts in a manner that is detrimental to the interests of the individuals, society and nation.

The Supreme Court on 14th Dec. 2007 said that it would lay down guidelines for the courts in the country for entertaining PILs in view of the two judge-bench telling the Indian Judiciary not to indulge in 'judicial activism' to the extent of converting it into 'judicial adventurism'. Very recently Chief Justice of the Supreme Court *Justice K.G. Balakrishnan* observed that we will consider questions referred to us by two-judge bench and indicated that it would lay down broad guidelines and parameters for the apex court and High Courts to entertain public interest litigations.

Notes and References

- Mehraj Uddin 'A language Called Justice' Greater Kashmir Jan.10, 2008.
- *Ibid.*
- Dhanajay Mahapatra, *Times of India* Dec. 11, 2007 (Tuesday).
- Sathe, S.P: 'Curbs on PIL: UF Government's Evil Designs' *Economic and Political Weekly* 1st March 1997.
- *Hindustan Times*: New Delhi, Tuesday Dec. 11, 207.
- The Asian Age, New Delhi Dec. 11, 7 and *Hindustan Times*, New Delhi, Tuesday Dec. 11, 07.
- Judith A. Baer; 'The Fruitless Search for Original Intent' Judging the Constitution: Critical Essays on Judicial Lawmaking (1989) Michael W. McCann; Gerald L. Houseman p. 49.
- See *Hindustan Times*: New Delhi, Tuesday Dec. 11, 207; The Asian Age, New Delhi Dec. 11, 7 and *Hindustan Times*, New Delhi, Tuesday Dec. 11, 7.
- *Ibid.*
- *Ibid.*
- Sathe; S.P: Judicial Activism in India (2002) 27.
- Jain; M.P. Indian Constitution Law 1978 .
- Sharma; B.R. Constitutional Law and Judicial Activism (1990).
- Krishna Iyer; Justice and Beyond; (1982).
- *Ibid.*
- Supra note 12.
- The Bench consisting Chief Justice K.G. Balakrishnan, Justice R.V. Raveendran and Justice J. M. Panchal. [The Hindu, Chennai 15th Dec. 2007]. See also Deccan Herald, Bangalore Dec. 15, 2007.

22

AN OVERVIEW ABOUT THE PREVALENCE OF CHILD ABUSE: A GLOBAL PERSPECTIVE

M.D. Allen Selva Kumar

Introduction

Traditionally in India, the responsibility of care and protection of children has been with families and communities. A strong knit patriarchal family that is meant to look after its children well has seldom had the realisation that children are individuals with their own rights. While the Constitution of India guarantees many fundamental rights to the children, the approach to ensure the fulfillment of these rights was more needs based rather than rights based. The transition to the rights based approach in the Government and civil society is still evolving. Child abuse is the physical, sexual, emotional mistreatment, or neglect of children. In the United States, the Centers for Disease Control and Prevention (CDC) define child maltreatment as any act or series of acts of commission or omission by a parent or other caregiver that results in harm, potential for harm, or threat of harm to a child. Child abuse can occur in a child's home, or in the organisations, schools or communities the child interacts with. There are four major categories of child abuse: neglect, physical abuse, psychological/emotional abuse, and child sexual abuse.

Different jurisdictions have developed their own definitions of what constitutes child abuse for the purposes of removing a child from his/her family and/or prosecuting a criminal charge. According to the Journal of Child Abuse and Neglect, child abuse is "any recent act or failure to act on the part of a parent or caretaker which results in death, serious physical or emotional harm, sexual abuse or exploitation, an act or failure to act which presents an imminent risk of serious harm". A person who feels the need to abuse or neglect a child may be described as a "pedopath".

Definition of Child Abuse

The term 'Child Abuse' may have different connotations in different cultural milieu and socio-economic situations. A universal definition of child abuse in the Indian context does not exist and has yet to be defined. According to WHO.

Physical Abuse

Physical abuse is the inflicting of physical injury upon a child. This may include burning, hitting, punching, shaking, kicking, beating or otherwise harming a child. The parent or caretaker may not have intended to hurt the child. It may, however, be the result of over-discipline or physical punishment that is inappropriate to the child's age.

Sexual Abuse

Sexual abuse is inappropriate sexual behaviour with a child. It includes fondling a child's genitals, making the child fondle the adult's genitals, intercourse, incest, rape, sodomy, exhibitionism and sexual exploitation. To be considered 'child abuse', these acts have to be committed by a person responsible for the care of a child (for example a baby-sitter, a parent, or a daycare provider), or related to the child. If a stranger commits these acts, it would be considered sexual assault and handled solely by the police and criminal courts.

Emotional Abuse

Emotional abuse is also known as verbal abuse, mental abuse, and psychological maltreatment. It includes acts or the failures to act by parents or caretakers that have caused or could cause, serious behavioural, cognitive, emotional, or mental trauma. This can include parents/caretakers using extreme and/or bizarre forms of punishment, such as confinement in a closet or dark room or being tied to a chair for long periods of time or threatening or terrorising a child. Less severe acts, but no less damaging, are belittling or rejecting treatment, using derogatory terms to describe the child, habitual tendency to blame the child or make him/her a scapegoat.

Neglect

It is the failure to provide for the child's basic needs. Neglect can be physical, educational, or emotional. Physical neglect can include not providing adequate food or clothing, appropriate medical care, supervision, or proper weather protection (heat or cold). It may include abandonment. Educational neglect includes failure to provide appropriate schooling or special educational needs, allowing excessive truancies. Psychological neglect includes the lack of any emotional support and love, never attending to the child, substance abuse including allowing the child to participate in drug and alcohol use.

Working Definition of Child Abuse

Child abuse refers to the intended, unintended and perceived maltreatment of the child, whether habitual or not, including any of the following:

Psychological and physical abuse, neglect, cruelty, sexual and emotional maltreatment. Any act, deed or word which debases, degrades or demeans the intrinsic worth and dignity of a child as a human being.

Unreasonable deprivation of his/her basic needs for survival such as food and shelter, or failure to give timely medical treatment to an injured child resulting in serious impairment of his/her growth and development or in his/her permanent incapacity or death.

Physical abuse is inflicting physical injury upon a child. This may include hitting, shaking, kicking, beating, or otherwise harming a child physically.

Emotional abuse (also known as verbal abuse, mental abuse, and psychological maltreatment) includes acts or the failure to act by parents, caretakers, peers and others that have caused or could cause serious behavioural, cognitive, emotional, or mental distress/trauma.

Sexual abuse is inappropriate sexual behaviour with a child. It includes fondling a child's genitals, making the child fondle an adult's genitals, sexual assault (intercourse, incest, rape and sodomy), exhibitionism and pornography. To be considered child abuse, these acts have to be committed by a person responsible for the care of a child or related to the child (for example a baby-sitter, parent, neighbour, relatives, extended family member, peer, older child, friend, stranger, or a day-care provider).

Child neglect is an act of omission or commission leading to the denial of a child's basic needs. Neglect can be physical, educational, emotional or psychological. Physical neglect entails denial of food, clothing, appropriate medical care or supervision. It may include abandonment. Educational neglect includes failure to provide appropriate schooling or special educational needs. Psychological neglect includes lack of emotional support and love.

Causes

Child abuse is a complex phenomenon with multiple causes Understanding the causes of abuse is crucial to addressing the problem of child abuse. Parents who physically abuse their spouses are more likely than others to physically abuse their children However, it is impossible to know whether marital strife is a cause of child abuse, or if both the marital strife and the abuse are caused by tendencies in the abuser. Substance abuse can be a major contributing factor to child abuse. One U.S. study found that parents with documented substance abuse, most commonly alcohol, cocaine, and heroin, were much more likely to mistreat their children, and were also much more likely to reject court-ordered services and treatments. Another study found that over two thirds of cases of child maltreatment involved parents with substance abuse problems. This study specifically found relationships between alcohol and physical abuse, and between cocaine and sexual abuse. Unemployment and financial difficulties are associated with increased rates of child abuse. In 2009 CBS News reported that child abuse in the United States had increased during the economic recession. It gave the example of a father who had never been the primary care-taker of the children. Now that the father was in that role, the children began to come in with injuries.

Prevalence

According to the (American) National Committee to Prevent Child Abuse, in 1997 neglect represented 54 per cent of confirmed cases of child abuse, physical abuse 22 per cent, sexual abuse 8 per cent, emotional maltreatment 4 per cent, and other forms of maltreatment 12 per cent.

A UNICEF report on child wellbeing stated that the United States and the United Kingdom ranked lowest among industrial nations with respect to the wellbeing of children. It also found that child neglect and child abuse were far more common in single-parent families than in families where both parents are present.

In the USA, neglect is defined as the failure to meet the basic needs of children including housing, clothing, food and access to medical care. Researchers found over 91,000 cases of neglect in one year (from October 2005 to 30 September 2006) using information from a database of cases verified by protective services agencies.

Neglect could also take the form of financial abuse by not buying the child adequate materials for survival. The U.S. Department of Health and Human Services reports that for each year between 2000 and 2005, "female parents acting alone" were most likely to be perpetrators of child abuse.

Fatalities

A child abuse fatality is when a child's death is the result of abuse or neglect, or when abuse and/or neglect are contributing factors to a child's death. In the United States, 1,730 children died in 2008 due to factors related to abuse; this is a rate of 2.33 per 100,000 U.S. children. Child abuse fatalities are widely recognised as being under-counted; it is estimated that between 60-85 per cent of child fatalities due to maltreatment are not recorded as such on death certificates. Younger children are at a much higher risk for being killed, as are African Americans. Girls and boys, however, are killed at similar rates. Caregivers, and specifically mothers, are more likely to be the perpetrators of a child abuse fatality, than anyone else, including strangers, relatives, and non-relative caregivers. Family situations which place children at risk include moving, unemployment, having non-family members living in the household. A number of policies and programmes have been put into place to try to better understand and to prevent child abuse fatalities, including: safe-haven laws, child fatality review teams, training for investigators, shaken baby syndrome prevention programmes, and child abuse death laws which mandate harsher sentencing for taking the life of a child.

It has very clearly emerged that across different kinds of abuse, it is young children, in the 5-12 year group, who are most at risk of abuse and exploitation.

Physical Abuse

1. Two out of every three children were physically abused.
2. Out of 69 per cent children physically abused in 13 sample states, 54.68 per cent were boys.
3. Over 50 per cent children in all the 13 sample states were being subjected to one or the other form of physical abuse.
4. Out of those children physically abused in family situations, 88.6 per cent were physically abused by parents.
5. 65 per cent of school going children reported facing corporal punishment i.e. two out of three children were victims of corporal punishment.
6. 62 per cent of the corporal punishment was in government and municipal school.
7. The State of Andhra Pradesh, Assam, Bihar and Delhi have almost consistently reported higher rates of abuse in all forms as compared to other states.
8. Most children did not report the matter to anyone.
9. 50.2 per cent children worked seven days a week.

Sexual Abuse

1. 53.22 per cent children reported having faced one or more forms of sexual abuse.
2. Andhra Pradesh, Assam, Bihar and Delhi reported the highest percentage of sexual abuse among both boys and girls.
3. 21.90 per cent child respondents reported facing severe forms of sexual abuse and 50.76 per cent other forms of sexual abuse.
4. Out of the child respondents, 5.69 per cent reported being sexually assaulted.

5. Children in Assam, Andhra Pradesh, Bihar and Delhi reported the highest incidence of sexual assault.
6. 50 per cent abuses are persons known to the child or in a position of trust and responsibility.
7. Most children did not report the matter to anyone.

Emotional Abuse and Girl Child Neglect

1. Every second child reported facing emotional abuse.
2. Equal percentage of both girls and boys reported facing emotional abuse.
3. In 83 per cent of the cases parents were the abusers.
4. 48.4 per cent of girls wished they were boys.

The gravity of the situation demands that the issue of child abuse be placed on the national agenda. The Ministry on its part has taken measures such as the enabling legislation to establish the National and State Commissions for Protection of Rights of the Child, the Integrated Child Protection Scheme, the draft Offences against Children Bill etc. These are a few important steps to ensure protection of children of the country. But clearly, this will not be enough, the government, civil society and communities need to complement each other and work towards creating a protective environment for children. The momentum gained needs to enhance further discussion on the issue amongst all stakeholders and be translated into a movement to ensure protection of children of this country.

Child abuse Across the Globe

The UN Secretary General's Study on Violence against Children has given the following overview of the situation of abuse and violence against children across the globe.

- WHO estimates that almost 53,000 child deaths in 2002 were due to child homicide.
- In the Global School-Based Student Health Survey carried out in a wide range of developing countries, between 20 per cent and 65 per cent of school going children reported having been verbally or physically bullied in school in the previous 30 days. Similar rates of bullying have been found in industrialised countries.

- An estimated 150 million girls and 73 million boys under 18 have experienced forced sexual intercourse or other forms of sexual violence involving physical contact.
- UNICEF estimates that in sub-Saharan Africa, Egypt and Sudan, 3 million girls and women are subjected to FGM every year.
- ILO estimates that 218 million children were involved in child labour in 2004, of which 126 million were engaged in hazardous work. Estimates from 2000 suggest that 5.7 million were in forced or bonded labour, 1.8 million in prostitution and pornography and 1.2 million were victims of trafficking.
- Only 2.4 per cent of the world's children are legally protected from corporal punishment in all settings.

Child abuse in Asia

While certain child abuse and neglect issues are common in almost all countries at the global level such as physical abuse, sexual abuse, emotional and psychological abuse, abandonment and, increasingly, problems of street children, there are also many issues which are prevalent only in certain regions of the world. For instance, in Asia where population density is high, the issues of child labour and child sexual exploitation are also high. Political instability and other internal disturbances, including conditions of insurgency in many countries in Asia are also creating major problems, with increasing number of child soldiers, refugee children, trafficked children and children on the streets.

Prevention of child abuse and neglect is still an uncharted field in Asia. The largest population of children in the world live in South Asia and majority of these children lack access to proper health care, nutrition and education. This reflects the socio-economic reality of the developing countries of the Asian region. The main factors that contribute to the magnitude of the problem of child abuse are poverty, illiteracy, caste system and landlessness, lack of economic opportunities, rural-urban migration, population growth, political instability and weak implementation of legal provisions.

Mostly, the approaches for prevention and methods of treatment of child abuse do not cover the entire gamut of abuse.

Lack of reliable data on the incidence of child abuse and of knowledge of methods of prevention and treatment has been recognised and is being addressed by sovereign governments, national and international organisations e.g., UNICEF, Save the Children, Plan International, ISPCAN, etc.

Child abuse in India

Nineteen per cent of the world's children live in India. According to the 2001 Census, some 440 million people in the country today are aged below eighteen years and constitute 42 per cent of India's total population i.e., four out of every ten persons. This is an enormous number of children that the country has to take care of. While articulating its vision of progress, development and equity, India has expressed its recognition of the fact that when its children are educated, healthy, and happy have access to opportunities, they are the country's greatest human resource.

Critical Concerns

- Every fifth child in the world lives in India
- Every third malnourished child in the world lives in India
- Every second Indian child is underweight
- Three out of four children in India are anaemic
- Every second new born has reduced learning capacity due to iodine deficiency
- Decline in female/male ratio is maximum in 0-6 years: 927 females per 1000 males
- Birth registration is just 62 per cent (RGI-2004)
- Retention rate at Primary level is 71.01 per cent (Elementary Education in India Progress towards UEE NUEPA Flash Statistics DISE 2005-2006)
- Girls' enrolment in schools at primary level is 47.79 per cent (Elementary Education in India Progress towards UEE NUEPA Flash Statistics DISE 2005-2006)
- 1104 lakh child labour in the country (SRO 2000)
- IMR is as high as 58 per 1000 live births (SRS- 2005)
- MMR is equally high at 301 per 100,000 live births (SRS, 2001-03)

- Children born with low birth weight are 46 per cent (NFHS-III)
- Children under 3 with anemia are 79 per cent (NFHS-III)
- Immunisation coverage is very low (polio-78.2 per cent, measles-58.8 per cent, DPT-55.3 per cent, BCG-78 per cent (NFHS-III)

Effects

There are strong associations between exposure to child abuse in all its forms and higher rates of many chronic conditions. The strongest evidence comes from the Adverse Childhood Experiences (ACE's) series of studies which show correlations between exposure to abuse or neglect and higher rates in adulthood of chronic conditions, high-risk health behaviours and shortened lifespan a recent publication, Hidden Costs in Health Care: The Economic Impact of Violence and Abuse, makes the case that such exposure represents a serious and costly public-health issue that should be addressed by the healthcare system.

Psychological Effects

Children with a history of neglect or physical abuse are at risk of developing psychiatric problems, or a disorganised attachment style. Disorganised attachment is associated with a number of developmental problems, including dissociative symptoms, as well as anxiety, depressive, and acting out symptoms. A study by Dante Cicchetti found that 80 per cent of abused and maltreated infants exhibited symptoms of disorganised attachment. When some of these children become parents, especially if they suffer from posttraumatic stress disorder (PTSD), dissociative symptoms, and other sequelae of child abuse, they may encounter difficulty when faced with their infant and young children's needs and normative distress, which may in turn lead to adverse consequences for their child's social-emotional development. Despite these potential difficulties, psycho-social intervention can be effective, at least in some cases, in changing the ways maltreated parents think about their young children.

Victims of childhood abuse, it is claimed, also suffer from different types of physical health problems later in life. Some reportedly suffer from some type of chronic head, abdominal, pelvic, or muscular pain with no identifiable reason. Even though the majority of childhood abuse victims know or believe that their abuse is, or can be, the cause of different health problems in their adult life, for the great majority their abuse was not directly associated with those problems, indicating that sufferers were most likely diagnosed with other possible causes for their health problems, instead of their childhood abuse.

The effects of child abuse vary, depending on the type of abuse. A 2006 study found that childhood emotional and sexual abuse were strongly related to adult depressive symptoms, while exposure to verbal abuse and witnessing of domestic violence had a moderately strong association, and physical abuse a moderate one. For depression, experiencing more than two kinds of abuse exerted synergistically stronger symptoms. Sexual abuse was particularly deleterious in its intrafamilial form, for symptoms of depression, anxiety, dissociation, and limbic irritability. Childhood verbal abuse had a stronger association with anger-hostility than any other type of abuse studied, and was second only to emotional abuse in its relationship with dissociative symptoms. More generally, in the case of 23 of the 27 illnesses listed in the questionnaire of a French INSEE survey, some statistically significant correlations were found between repeated illness and family traumas encountered by the child before the age of 18 years. According Georges Menahem, the French sociologist who found out these correlations by studying health inequalities, these relationships show that inequalities in terms of illness and suffering are not only social. Health inequality also has its origins in the family, where it is associated with the degrees of lasting affective problems (lack of affection, parental discord, the prolonged absence of a parent, or a serious illness affecting either the mother or father) that individuals report having experienced in childhood.

Physical Effects

Children who are physically abused are likely to receive bone fractures, particularly rib fractures, and may have a higher risk of developing cancer. Children who experience child abuse and neglect are 59 per cent more likely to be arrested as juveniles, 28 per cent more likely to be arrested as adults, and 30 per cent more likely to commit violent crime.

The immediate physical effects of abuse or neglect can be relatively minor (bruises or cuts) or severe (broken bones, hemorrhage, or even death). In some cases the physical effects are temporary; however, the pain and suffering they cause a child should not be discounted. Meanwhile, the long-term impact of child abuse and neglect on physical health is just beginning to be explored. The long-term effects can be:

- *Shaken baby syndrome:* Shaking a baby is a common form of child abuse that often results in permanent neurological damage (80 per cent of cases) or death (30 per cent of cases). Damage results from intracranial hypertension (increased pressure in the skull) after bleeding in the brain, damage to the spinal cord and neck, and rib or bone fractures.
- *Impaired brain development:* Child abuse and neglect have been shown, in some cases, to cause important regions of the brain to fail to form or grow properly, resulting in impaired development. These alterations in brain maturation have long-term consequences for cognitive, language, and academic abilities. NSCAW found more than three-quarters of foster children between one and two years of age to be at medium to high risk for problems with brain development, as opposed to less than half of children in a control sample.
- *Poor physical health:* Several studies have shown a relationship between various forms of household dysfunction (including childhood abuse) and poor health. Adults who experienced abuse or neglect during childhood are more likely to suffer from physical ailments such as allergies, arthritis, asthma, bronchitis, high blood pressure, and ulcers.
- On the other hand, there are some children who are raised in child abuse, but who manage to do unexpectedly well later in life regarding the preconditions. Such children have been termed dandelion children, as inspired from the way that dandelions seem to prosper irrespective of soil, sun, drought, or rain. Such children (or currently grown-ups) are of high interest in finding factors that mitigate the effects of child abuse.

Prevention

April has been designated Child Abuse Prevention Month in the United States since 1983. U.S. President Barack Obama continued that tradition by declaring April 2009 Child Abuse Prevention Month. One way the Federal government of the United States provides funding for child-abuse prevention is through Community-Based Grants for the Prevention of Child Abuse and Neglect (CBCAP).

Resources for child-protection services are sometimes limited. According to Hosin (2007), "a considerable number of traumatised abused children do not gain access to protective child-protection strategies." It is argued that only when "lower-level violence" of children ceases to be culturally tolerated will there be changes in the victimization and police protection of children.

Treatment

A number of treatments are available to victims of child abuse. Trauma-focused cognitive behavioural therapy, first developed to treat sexually abused children, is now used for victims of any kind of trauma. It targets trauma-related symptoms in children including Post-Traumatic Stress Disorder (PTSD), clinical depression and anxiety. It also includes a component for non-offending parents. Several studies have found that sexually abused children undergoing TF-CBT improved more than children undergoing certain other therapies. Data on the effects of TF-CBT for children who experienced only non-sexual abuse was not available as of 2006.

Abuse-focused cognitive behavioural therapy was designed for children who have experienced physical abuse. It targets externalizing behaviours and strengthens prosocial behaviours. Offending parents are included in the treatment, to improve parenting skills/practices. It is supported by one randomised study.

Child-parent psychotherapy was designed to improve the child-parent relationship following the experience of domestic violence. It targets trauma-related symptoms in infants, toddlers, and preschoolers, including PTSD, aggression, defiance, and anxiety. It is supported by two studies of one sample.

Other forms of treatment include group therapy, play therapy, and art therapy. Each of these types of treatment can be used to better assist the client, depending on the form of abuse they have experienced. Play therapy and art therapy are ways to get children more comfortable with therapy by working on something that they enjoy (coloring, drawing, painting, etc.). The design of a child's artwork can be a symbolic representation of what they are feeling, relationships with friends or family, and more. Being able to discuss and analyse a child's artwork can allow a professional to get a better insight of the child.

Ethics

One of the most challenging ethical dilemmas arising from child abuse relates to the parental rights of abusive parents or caretakers with regard to their children, particularly in medical settings. In the United States, the 2008 New Hampshire case of Andrew Bedner drew attention to this legal and moral conundrum. Bedner, accused of severely injuring his infant daughter, sued for the right to determine whether or not she remain on life support; keeping her alive, which would have prevented a murder charge, created a motive for Bedner to act that conflicted with the apparent interests of his child. Bioethicists Jacob M. Appel and Thaddeus Mason Pope recently argued, in separate articles, that such cases justify the replacement of the accused parent with an alternative decision-maker.

Child abuse also poses ethical concerns related to confidentiality, as victims may be physically or psychologically unable to report abuse to authorities. Accordingly, many jurisdictions and professional bodies have made exceptions to standard requirements for confidentiality and legal privileges in instances of child abuse. Medical professionals, including doctors, therapists, and other mental health workers typically owe a duty of confidentiality to their patients and clients, either by law and/ or the standards of professional ethics, and cannot disclose personal information without the consent of the individual concerned. This duty conflicts with an ethical obligation to protect children from preventable harm. Accordingly, confidentiality is often waived when these professionals have a good faith suspicion that child abuse or neglect has occurred or is likely to occur and make a report to local child protection authorities. This exception allows professionals to breach confidentiality and make a report even when the child or his/her parent or guardian has specifically instructed to the contrary. Child abuse is also a common exception to Physician–patient privilege: a medical professional may be called upon to testify in court as to otherwise privileged evidence about suspected child abuse despite the wishes of the child and his/her family.

Organisations

There are organisations at national, state, and county levels in the United States that provide community leadership in preventing child abuse and neglect. The National Alliance of Children's Trust Funds and Prevent Child Abuse America are two national organisations with member organisations at the state level.Many investigations into child abuse are handled on the local level by Child Advocacy Centers. Started over 25 years ago at what is now known as the National Children's Advocacy Center in Huntsville, Alabama by District Attorney Robert "Bud" Cramer these multi-disciplinary teams have met to coordinate their efforts so that cases of child abuse can be investigated quickly and efficiently, ultimately reducing trauma to the child and garnering better convictions. These Child Advocacy Centers (known as CACs) have standards set by the National Children's Alliance. Other organisations focus on specific prevention strategies. The National Center on Shaken Baby Syndrome focuses its efforts on the specific issue of preventing child abuse that is manifested as shaken baby syndrome. Mandated reporter training is a programme used to prevent ongoing child abuse.

References

"Child abuse — definition of child abuse by the Free Online Dictionary, Thesaurus and Encyclopedia". Thefreedictionary.com. http://www.thefreedictionary.com/Child+abuse. Retrieved 2010-9-15.

Leeb, R.T.; Paulozzi, L.J.; Melanson, C.; Simon, T.R.; Arias, I. (1 January 2008). "Child Maltreatment Surveillance: Uniform Definitions for Public Health and Recommended Data Elements". Centers for Disease Control and Prevention. http://www.cdc.gov/ncipc/dvp/CMP/CMP-Surveillance.htm. Retrieved 20 October 2008.

Herrenkohl, R.C. (2005). "The definition of child maltreatment: from case study to construct". *Child Abuse and Neglect* 29 (5): 413–24. doi:10.1016/j.chiabu.2005.04.002. PMID 15970317.

http://en.wiktionary.org/wiki/pedopath

"Child Abuse and Neglect: Types, Signs, Symptoms, Help and Prevention". helpguide.org. http://www.helpguide.org/mental/child_abuse_physical_emotional_sexual_neglect.htm. Retrieved 20 October 2008.

A Coordinated Response to Child Abuse and Neglect: The Foundation for Practice, Office on Child Abuse and Neglect (HHS), USA, 2003.

Noh Anh, Helen (1994). "Cultural Diversity and the Definition of Child Abuse", in Barth, R.P. et al., *Child welfare research review*, Columbia University Press, 1994, p. 28. ISBN 0231080743.

Haeuser, A. A. (1990). "Banning parental use of physical punishment: Success in Sweden". *International Congress on Child Abuse and Neglect*. Hamburg.

"States with full abolition". Global Initiative to End All Corporal Punishment of Children. http://endcorporalpunishment.org/pages/progress/prohib_states.html.

"Child Sexual Abuse". *Medline Plus*. U.S. National Library of Medicine. 2 April 2008. http://www.nlm.nih.gov/medlineplus/childsexualabuse.html.

"Guidelines for psychological evaluations in child protection matters. Committee on Professional Practice and Standards, APA Board of Professional Affairs". *The American Psychologist* **54** (8): 586–93. August 1999. doi:10.1037/0003-066X.54.8.586. PMID 10453704. "**Abuse, sexual (child)**: generally defined as contacts between a child and an adult or other person significantly older or in a position of power or control over the child, where the child is being used for sexual stimulation of the adult or other person."

Martin J, Anderson J, Romans S, Mullen P, O'Shea M (1993). "Asking about child sexual abuse: methodological implications of a two stage survey". *Child Abuse and Neglect* **17** (3): 383–92. doi:10.1016/0145-2134(93)90061-9. PMID 8330225.

Child sexual abuse definition from the NSPCC.

Brown, Patricia Leigh (May 23, 2011). "In Oakland, Redefining Sex Trade Workers as Abuse Victims". *The New York Times*. http://www.nytimes.com/2011/05/24/us/24oakland.html. Retrieved May 24, 2011. "Once viewed as criminals and dispatched to juvenile centers, where treatment was rare, sexually exploited youths are increasingly seen as victims of child abuse, with a new focus on early intervention and counseling."

Roosa M.W., Reinholtz C., Angelini P.J. (1999). "The relation of child sexual abuse and depression in young women: comparisons across four ethnic groups". *Journal of Abnormal Child Psychology* **27** (1): 65–76. PMID 10197407. http://findarticles.com/p/articles/mi_m0902/is_1_27/ai_54422556/print.

Widom C.S. (1999). "Post-traumatic stress disorder in abused and neglected children grown up," *American Journal of Psychiatry*. 156(8):1223-1229.

Levitan, R. D., N. A. Rector, Sheldon, T., and Goering, P. (2003). "Childhood adversities associated with major depression and/or anxiety disorders in a community sample of Ontario: Issues of co-morbidity and specificity," Depression and Anxiety; 17, 34-42.

Journals.lww.com

Messman-Moore, Terri L.; Long, Patricia J. (2000). "Child Sexual Abuse and Revictimisation in the Form of Adult Sexual Abuse, Adult Physical Abuse, and Adult Psychological Maltreatment". *15 Journal of Interpersonal Violence* **489** (5): 2000. doi:10.1177/088626000015005003. http://jiv.sagepub.com/cgi/content/abstract/15/5/489.

Jpedhc.org

Whealin, Julia (22 May 2007). "Child Sexual Abuse". National Center for Post Traumatic Stress Disorder, US Department of Veterans Affairs. http://www.ptsd.va.gov/public/pages/child-sexual-abuse.asp.

Finkelhor, D. (1994). "Current information on the scope and nature of child sexual abuse". *The Future of Children* (Princeton University) **4** (2): 31–53. doi:10.2307/1602522. JSTOR 1602522. PMID 7804768. http://www.unh.edu/ccrc/pdf/VS75.pdf.

Crimes against Children Research Center.

Gorey, K.M.; Leslie, D.R. (April 1997). "The prevalence of child sexual abuse: integrative review adjustment for potential response and measurement biases". *Child Abuse and Neglect* **21** (4): 391–8. doi:10.1016/S0145-2134(96)00180-9. PMID 9134267.

"Child Abuse". The National Center for Victims of Crime. http://ncvc.org/ncvc/main.aspx?dbName=DocumentViewer and DocumentAction=ViewProperties& ocumentID=32313 and UrlToReturn=http%3a%2f%2fncv c.org and 2fncvc%2fmain.aspx%3fdbName%3dAdvanced Search&gclid= CJ_1q6m2oZ4CFcx25QodNG2_ow.

"Child Abuse and Neglect Statistics". National Committee to Prevent Child Abuse. 1998. Archived from the original on 1998-05-15. http://web.archive.org/web/19980515052303/http://childabuse.org/facts97.html.

Child Poverty in Respective: An Overview of Child Wellbeing in Rich Countries. UNICEF: Innocenti Research Center, Report Card 7.

"Sometimes They Can't Afford to Leave their Abusers", *Santa Ynez Valley Journal*, California, 22 October 2009.

Stats for 2000; Stats for 2001; Stats for 2002; Stats for 2003; Stats for 2004; Stats for 2005.

Child Maltreatment 2008, U.S. Department of Health and Human Services, p. 55.

Nationalcac.org

Nationalchildrensalliance.org

Hughes, Sandra (20 May 2009). "Child Abuse Spikes During Recession", CBS News.

Middlebrooks, J.S.; Audage, A.C. (2008). *The Effects of Childhood Stress on Health Across the Lifespan*. Centers for Disease Control.

Dolezal, T.; McCollum, D.; Callahan, M. (2009). *Hidden Costs in Health Care: The Economic Impact of Violence and Abuse*. Academy on Violence and Abuse.

Gauthier L, Stollak G, Messé L, Aronoff J (July 1996). "Recall of childhood neglect and physical abuse as differential predictors of current psychological functioning". *Child Abuse and Neglect* 20 (7): 549–59. doi:10.1016/0145-2134(96)00043-9. PMID 8832112.

Malinosky-Rummell R, Hansen DJ (July 1993). "Long-term consequences of childhood physical abuse". *Psychological Bulletin* 114 (1): 68–79. doi:10.1037/0033-2909.114.1.68. PMID 8346329.

Lyons-Ruth, K.; Jacobvitz, D. (1999). "Attachment disorganisation: unresolved loss, relational violence and lapses in behavioural and attentional strategies". In Cassidy, J.; Shaver, P. *Handbook of Attachment*. New York: Guilford Press. pp. 520–554.

Solomon, J.; George, C., ed (1999). *Attachment Disorganisation*. New York: Guilford Press. ISBN 1572304804.

Main, M.; Hesse, E. (1990). "Parents' Unresolved Traumatic Experiences are related to infant disorganised attachment status". In Greenberg, M.T.; Ciccehetti, D; Cummings, E.M. *Attachment in the Preschool Years: Theory, Research, and Intervention*. University of Chicago Press. pp. 161–184.

Carlson, E.A. (August 1998). "A prospective longitudinal study of attachment disorganisation/disorientation". *Child Development* **69** (4): 1107–28. PMID 9768489.

Lyons-Ruth, K. (February 1996). "Attachment relationships among children with aggressive behaviour problems: the role of disorganised early attachment patterns". *Journal of Consulting and Clinical Psychology* 64 (1): 64–73. doi:10.1037/0022-006X.64.1.64. PMID 8907085.

Lyons-Ruth K, Alpern L, Repacholi B (April 1993). "Disorganised infant attachment classification and maternal psychosocial problems as predictors of hostile-aggressive behaviour in the preschool classroom". *Child Development* (Blackwell Publishing) 64 (2): 572–85. doi:10.2307/1131270. JSTOR 1131270. PMID 8477635.

Carlson, V. *et al.* (1995). "Finding order in disorganisation: Lessons from research on maltreated infants' attachments to their caregivers". In Cicchetti, D.; Carlson, V. *Child Maltreatment: Theory and research on the causes and consequences of child abuse and neglect*. Cambridge University Press. pp. 135–157.

Cicchetti, D. *et al.* (1990). "An organisational perspective on attachment beyond infancy". In Greenberg, M.; Cicchetti, D; MCummings, M. *Attachment in the Preschool Years*. University of Chicago Press. pp. 3–50. ISBN 0226306291.

Schechter DS, Coates, SW, Kaminer T, Coots T, Zeanah CH, Davies M, Schonfield IS, Marshall RD, Liebowitz MR, Trabka KA, McCaw J, Myers MM (2008). "Distorted maternal mental representations and atypical behaviour in a clinical sample of violence-exposed mothers and their toddlers". *Journal of Trauma and Dissociation* **9** (2): 123–149. doi:10.1080/15299730802045666. PMC 2577290. PMID 18985165.

Schechter DS, Zygmunt A, Coates SW, Davies M, Trabka KA, McCaw J, Kolodji A., Robinson JL (2007). "Caregiver traumatisation adversely impacts young children's mental representations of self and others". *Attachment and Human Development* **9** (3): 187–205. doi:10.1080/14616730701453762. PMC 2078523. PMID 18007959.

Schechter DS, Myers MM, Brunelli SA, Coates SW, Zeanah CH, Davies M, Grienenberger JF, Marshall RD, McCaw JE, Trabka KA, Liebowitz MR (2006). "Traumatised mothers can change their minds about their toddlers: Understanding how a novel use of video feedback supports positive change of maternal attributions". *Infant Mental Health Journal* **27** (5): 429–448. doi:10.1002/imhj.20101. PMC 2078524. PMID 18007960.

Takele Hamnasu, MBA. *Impact of Childhood Abuse on Adult Health*. Amberton University.

"Study of Living Conditions 1986-1987" INSEE survey with a sample of 13-154 individuals, cf. Menahem G., "Problèmes de l'enfance, statut social et santé des adultes", IRDES, biblio No 1010, pp. 59-63, Paris.

Kemp AM, Dunstan F, Harrison S, *et al.* (2008). "Patterns of skeletal fractures in child abuse: systematic review". *BMJ* **337** (oct02 1): a1518. doi:10.1136/bmj.a1518. PMC 2563260. PMID 18832412. http://bmj.com/cgi/pmidlookup?view=long&pmid=18832412.

Fuller-Thomson E, Brennenstuhl S (July 2009). "Making a link between childhood physical abuse and cancer: results from a regional representative survey". *Cancer* **115** (14): 3341–50. doi:10.1002/cncr.24372. PMID 19472404.

Child Abuse Statistics

Morad Y, Wygnansky-Jaffe T, Levin AV (2010) Retinal haemorrhage in abusive head trauma. Clin Exp Ophthalmol 38:514-520.

Factsheet

Ellis, Bruce J.; Boyce, W. Thomas (2008). "Biological Sensitivity to Context". *Current Directions in Psychological Science* **17** (3): 183–187. doi:10.1111/j.1467-8721.2008.00571.x. edit

Child Welfare Information Gateway, History of National Child Abuse Prevention Month. 3 April 2009.

Presidential Proclamation Marking National Child Abuse Prevention Month. The White House - Press Room, 1 April 2009.

U.S. Administration for Children and Families. Department of Health and Human Services. Children's Bureau.

Hosin, A.A., ed (2007). *Responses to traumatised children*. Basingstoke: Palgrave Macmillan. p. 211. ISBN 1403996806.

Briere, John (1992). *Child abuse trauma*. Sage. p. 7. ISBN 080393713X.

Cohen, J.A.; Mannarino, A.P.; Murray, L.K.; Igelman, R. (2006). "Psychosocial Interventions for Maltreated and Violence-Exposed Children". *Journal of Social Issues* **62** (4): 737–766. doi:10.1111/j.1540-4560.2006.00485.x.

Schechter DS, Zygmunt A, Trabka KA, Davies M, Colon E, Kolodji A, McCaw J (2007). "Child mental representations of attachment when mothers are traumatized: The relationship of family-drawings to story-stem completion". *Journal of Early Childhood and Infant Psychology* **3**: 119–141. PMC 2268110. PMID 18347736.

Appel, J.M. (October 2009). "Mixed motives, mixed outcomes when accused parents won't agree to withdraw care". *Journal of Medical Ethics* **35** (10): 635–7. doi:10.1136/jme.2009.030510. PMID 19793945.

"Springfield man denies charges in infant assault", *Rutland Herald*, New Hampshire, 5 August 2008.

"Springfield Father Charged with Baby's Murder", *WCAX.com*, Vermont, 21 January 2009.

"Withdrawal Okay When Surrogate's Refusal to Consent Based on Wrong Reasons", *Medical Futility* (blog).

National Center for Youth Law. "Minor Consent, Confidentiality, and Child Abuse Reporting". http://www.youthlaw.org/publications/minor_consent/. Retrieved 29 December 2010.

23

TERRORISM IN INDIA: AN OVERVIEW

E. Prabhakaran

Introduction

The word terrorism and threats to National Security have so insidiously worked its ways into everyday vocabulary and perhaps become an essential part of any intellectual and academic discourse on security and strategic issues in India today. The terrorist acts of 9/11 and the attack against the heart of Indian democracy on Dec. 13, 2001 have opened a new dimension of threats to the world in general and India in particular from state-sponsored non-state entity. These events have provided a basis for a 'paradigm shift' in the perception of national and international security thinking in the country by and large. In many ways, the current face of cross border terrorism as seen in Jammu and Kashmir, and other parts of India appear to be a form of a 'new war without front'. Events of the last decade have taught terrible lessons to civilised societies throughout the world, no country on this globe is immune against the scourge of modern means of terrorism. The phenomenon of militancy and militarism has been around the world for decades. The developments for the past decade have brought to focus this phenomenon on the international strategic environment, despite the fact that, India has suffered the scourge of militancy and terrorism since the last three decades.

In India, the assaults on pillars of the State have shaken the nation and continue to affect the whole country. Profoundly, no matter how one looks at it. There are different perceptions of its national and global impacts, dimensions and consequences. And terrorism is not seen as a monolithic threat alone, this threat is being analysed from various angles like religious, ethnic, ideological, psychological, political and military and security dimensions. India as growing economy and emerging power needs to review its security apparatus. A reconstruction of policies, doctrine and perception is essential. "If iron is soft even rats will swallow" may prove to be a reality. India's borders are safe but how safe and secured or Indian citizen?. Is it possible to remove or contain various types of violence without addressing its root cause?

A comprehensive approach will demand a number of effective measures. It will require well co-ordinated and well-orchestrated effort with a strong will and resources to address the issue by the Indian government. It will be impossible for the State to evolve a successful strategy to combat terrorism without evolving a doctrine for internal security. Hence, this idea would be an attempt to elicit various scholarly opinions, analyses and observations for a better understanding of this contemporary issue.

Concept of Terrorism

Expression of dissent and resistance to the established order is an age-old phenomenon in human history. Individuals or groups who felt aggrieved or oppressed and could not achieve their aims by peaceful means have resorted to violence to achieve them. At the national level, it took the form of combat between dissidents and the state but when they failed to confront the state machinery in open combat, they exploited the technique of terror which later came to be known as 'terrorism'. Thus, terrorism as a concept is as old as the ability of human beings to inflict pain on their fellow beings. But with the passage of time, particularly with the rise of non-state actors in the international system, with the democratisation of international relations or and with the advent of modern technology, this phenomenon has acquired complexity and ambiguity and has become global. In other words from being an occasional aberration, the use of violence has become preferred option of individuals or groups to express their sense of oppression, injustice and exploitation.

The term 'terrorism' is widely used, sometimes to justify freedom movement, sometimes as a technique of Guerrilla warfare, sometimes as a mode of low intensity conflict, and sometimes as a weapon of the weak. It is a symptom of a malaise in the society but is different from other manifestations of violence (crimes, riots, group clashes, vandalism and hooliganism) and is a threat which is much more serious than all other threats combined together being faced by the humanity like that of global warming, population explosion, nuclear proliferation and depletion of earth resources. It is becoming more and more formidable either because organised efforts have not been made to contain it or because a civilized world has not taken this threat as seriously as it should have been.

The definition of terrorism lies in the grey area that exists between crime and war, although experts disagree as to its approximate position. Some professionals who have spent their careers closely following the various competing theories have resigned themselves to the conclusion that, terrorism resists classification. In any case, terrorism results from various causes that defy any clear distinction "between the political and criminal". Terrorism can also be defined as "the selective or indiscriminate use of order to bring about political changes by inducing fear". Terrorism is one of the methods to be used in a frequent manner by the future revolutionary. This particular form of terrorism is called 'agitational terror'. It has been defined as, the use of "systematic tactics of terrorist violence with the objective of bringing about a political revolution". This form of terrorism has four major characteristics. First, it is carried out by groups, rather than individuals, which have clear, defined leaderships. Second, it is driven by a clear ideology and intends to create new institutional structures. Third, the movement has a definite strategy involving the planned use of violence against victims who have been selected for their symbolic value for a wider audience. Fourth, the purpose of this violence is to cause a permanent change in the attitudes and behaviour of the people. Terrorism is not an option chosen by large groups, but rather a strategy adopted by small groups, to organise clandestine acts of violence. An insurgency occurs when an opposition movement combines violence with a political strategy to defeat and replace a government. Terrorism is however, inextricably linked with insurgencies. There are at least six different goals of insurgent movements: reform, secession, revolution, restoration, reaction, or maintenance of the status quo. Most terrorists are rebels and an understanding of why they use terror requires the knowledge of insurgent strategies.

History of Terrorism

Terrorism, as a practice, has been embedded in political calculations from times immemorial. It dates back to 'Satya Yuga' wherein the 'rakshasas' terrorized the people to get an easy supply of food. Many rulers of the ancient civilisations committed atrocities in their kingdoms to terrorise and subjugate their subjects. The Bible mentions assassination in several places; the zealots (Israel 100 A.D) fought Roman occupation with hit-and-run tactics, the Assassins (Iraq 1100 A.D) fought crusader occupation; the Spanish Inquisition (1469-1600) dealt with Heretics; the Luddites (1811-1816) destroyed machinery, a Serb terrorist (1914) started World War I; and Hitler's rise to power (1938) involved terrorizing the Jews. However defined, it is clear that terrorism has shaped human history. Countries like Ireland, Cyprus, Algeria, Tunisia, and Israel probably would not have become republics if not for terrorism.

Chanakya and Sun Tzu had also advocated use of armed civilians to fight the enemy. Sun Tzu's statement, "kill one, frighten ten thousand" made 2,500 years ago, exemplifies its doctrinal vintage. While terrorism was resorted to in the ancient period as a means of survival, the religious fundamentalists employed it to promote religion in the medieval period. Killing of innocents by Ashoka in Kalinga, by Cromwell in Ireland, the eight Holy crusades between the Christians and the Muslims in West Asia from (1095 to 1291) and the Shia-Sunni clashes are all testimony to the use of the 'holy terror' for promotion of religion. In twentieth century terrorism has emerged as a new strategy for attaining political objectives. It has grown remarkably in Post World War II era. Soviet Union and China promoted Marxist philosophy by application of revolutionary warfare theories, with terrorism as a means. After 1968, the year which marks the transition from rural to urban terrorism, number of terrorist movements came into existence simultaneously all over the world. Carlos Marghela's Brazilian Action Group, Tupamaros of Uruguay and Revolutionary Armed Forces of Guatemala started diplomatic kidnappings and violent activities in a bid to seize power. In the middle east, disillusioned by the defeat of the Arab armies in

Six-Day war (1967), the Palestinians turned to guerrilla and terror tactics, and moved their focus to targets which were outside Israel. Islamic fundamentalist groups re-surfaced in North -Africa, Middle East and Asia and by late 1970s these terrorist groups proliferated tremendously. These groups included the Black Panthers in America, the Angry Brigade in Britain, Baader-Meinhof in Germany, the Red Brigade in Italy, the United Red Army in Japan and the Irish Republican Army in Ireland and JKLF in Pakistan.

Causes of Terrorism: Theoretical Perspective

The phenomenon of terrorism is universal. It happens in developed and developing countries; in rich and poor nation-states; in democratic and less-democratic systems of governance; it occurs in the process of nation-building in the process of development and in the process of transition. Terrorists, on the other hand, could be well-educated, uneducated, employed, un-employed, rich, poor, psychotic and normal. He could be male or female and of any age. Thus there could be numerous situations and conditions which can help in provoking terrorism, and thus there are number of theories for analysing the causes and conditions of terrorism.

Individual and Group Levels of Analysis

Studies at individual level acknowledge the ultimate importance of the individual actor of terrorism (since the phenomenon is dependent on motivated individuals i.e., if there is 'No' terrorist, there is 'No' terrorism) and concentrates on such research questions as: Who are the terrorists? Is there any terrorist personality? Why individuals join terrorist groups? Why do they act the way they do? What is the group-dynamics of terrorist groups? In answering some of these questions available theories could be divided into two broad categories.

Psycho-pathological Theories: The basic assumption of such theories is that non-violent behavior is indicative of 'normal' individual, whereas he who engages in terrorist activities (extreme violent behaviour) is abnormal (Sinha 1982). These research have identified a distinguishable 'terrorist personality', labelled as 'spoiled', 'disturbed', 'cold and calculating', 'perverse', 'excited by violence', 'psychotic', 'maniac', 'irrational' and fanatic etc. (Sinha, et. al. 1983). This theory of a terrorist personality has been dismissed by other researches stating that, terrorists are not alienated and psychologically distressed people but they are psychologically healthy persons for the most part and are strongly supported by their families and their ethnic community (Robert P. Clart 1980, Turner, et. al. 1984).

Corrado (1981) has examined theories that regard terrorism in western societies as rooted in sociopathy, narcissism, death wish or physiological impairment (e.g., neurological disorders leading to anti-social behaviour). He concludes that, this 'mental disturbance' approach is lacking in clinical observation and in diagnostic criteria and suggests that terrorist is more likely to be a product of frustration with rational idealism. Rasch (1979), a psychiatrist, while analysing several members of West German terrorist organisations, have found no conclusive evidence for the assumption that a significant number of terrorists are disturbed or abnormal. Jerrold Post (1990) suggests that there is a special logic of terrorist reasoning, known as 'terrorist psychologic', which propounds that "terrorists are driven to commit acts of violence as a consequence of psychological forces and that this logic is constructed to rationalise acts they are psychologically compelled to commit."

These psycho-pathological causes of terrorism (that terrorism is pathological behaviour) is an attempt, (a) to de-politicise terrorism and (b) to divest it from the socio-economic and political conditions. In fact, several researches (Crenshaw 1981, Corrado 1981, Turco 1987, Heskin 1984) have concluded that, "the best documented generalisation is negative i.e., terrorist do not show any striking psychopathology". Few other studies (Asthana Sinha et. al. 1988) conclude that, the most outstanding characteristic of a terrorist seems to be their normality and terrorists are seen as being motivated by ideologies or values that justify the use of terrorism as a legitimate political tool.

Psycho-Sociological theories of the causes of terrorism, recognise that, (a) individual's behaviour is influenced by the environment in which he lives, (b) the theories of "violence for the sake of violence" are inadequate explanation of terrorism, and (c) terrorism cannot be explained by pure psycho-pathological explanations. These theories concentrate on the social context (including political, historical and cultural) of the terrorist's ideologies, his beliefs and his political motivations (Wilkinson 1990). Crenshaw (1990) and others have integrated both psychological variables and environmental factors at different levels. These studies conclude that "terrorism, initially, is a matter of individual motivation, i.e., his perception of social condition and his deliberate choice to join a terrorist group and to participate in acts of terrorism, till such times he likes to discontinue continue". Thus, these studies analysed the phenomenon in relation to the social context in which it occurs i.e., when and under what circumstances extremist organisation find terrorism useful.

Another group of researches concentrates on a thesis that 'the decision to employ terrorism is a result of failure of other channels of influence. Their assumption is that masses seldom rise spontaneously; therefore the decision to employ terrorism often follows the failure to mobilise popular support for a political program or the failure of non-violent means of struggle to address political grievances. They also give weightage to the variable of 'excitement of terrorism' in decision-making. They conclude that, successful terrorist attack, or the thrill of it, can inspire the belief among perpetrators that terrorism might be a short-cut to revolution and that it may act as a catalyst, not as a substitute for mass revolt. In revolutionary theories decision to use terrorism is based on fundamentalist ideologies. Other studies concluded that "agenda setting function of terrorist act" is another variable in decision-making, particularly after information revolution, and help perpetrators to perceive terrorism as a force multiplier, neutralising numerical inferiority.

'Windows of opportunity' theory advocates that "time constraints contribute to the decision to use terrorism because terrorist organisation may perceive an immediate opportunity to compensate for its inferiority vis-a-vis the government. The change in situation may alter the balance of resources (funding, climate and international opinion, etc.) available to both sides."

Stephen Stedman (1997), Atlas and Licklider (1999) in their studies on 'intra-state conflicts and peace process' have analysed 'the context of decisions to violate cease-fire and resume armed conflict' and have concluded that 'resumption of armed conflict' (terrorist activities) is a strategy used by terrorist groups to prevent progress in peace process (phenomenon frequently observed in Indo-Pak peace negotiations).

Psycho-sociological explanation of causes of terrorism could further be classified in relative deprivation and contagion theories. There are four basic models of 'relative deprivation' which tend to explain terrorist behaviour, (a) capabilities remaining static while expectations rise, (b) rising capabilities overtakes rising expectations, (c) capabilities keep pace with expectations for a period and then suddenly drops (J-Curve Situation), (d) expectations remaining constant while capabilities fall or decline.

The correlation between human frustration and political violence have long been recognised (Aristotle's theory of revolution) as a conducive condition for terrorism, which arises out of discontent with the state's ability to satisfy socio-economic, political and other needs and demands of its citizens. These theories correlate mobilisation of human aggression with political violence emerging out of social, economic and political circumstances (frustration-aggression hypotheses). Scholars have termed this gap, in other words, between expectation and satisfaction as relative deprivation (Yale Psychologists, Joseph Margolin, Gurr). This theory propounds that 'as nearer one approaches to his desired goal, the stronger becomes one's need of satisfaction'. In other words, 'curve of intensity of need' increases sharply as one approach towards his positive or negative objective. Thus, tension based on the perception of relative deprivation is the basic condition for participating in collective violence (Gurr 1970, Alexander and Singer 1980). Further, empirical studies of pattern of terrorism point to the fact that transnational flow of information and symbiotic relationship between mass media and terrorism, causes terrorism (Contagion Theory). This contagion theory of terrorism explains "the variance" in terrorist's decision to launch terrorist attack. Studies supporting this theory (Weimann and Brosius 1988) conclude that, (a) there is a clear trend of periodical cycle in the occurrence of waves of terrorism (frequency of terrorists activity), (b) there is no clear periodicity regarding the degree of victimisation, (c) process of contagion is related to other incidents of violence (domestic-political violence, racial disturbances and international terrorism). Mass-media is a key variable in explaining this theory as terrorism can be analysed in the framework of communication theory (Brian

Jenkins 1978, Engene 1998) consisting of four components: transmitter (the terrorist), intended recipient (target), message (cause) and feed back (response of the government). In fact rise in the frequency of terrorism is attributed to the introduction of new devices in the electronic media which brings live coverage of terrorist activities in the living rooms of millions of people (explains the desire of terrorist groups to guarantee newsworthiness (Hoffman 1998, Volgy, Inwalle and Corntassel 1998).

This symbiotic relationship between mass media (both print and electronic) and terrorism has also helped in the increase of 'lethality of terrorism' (Crenshaw 1983). Midlarsky and Yoshida (1980) and others have concluded in their studies that "the need for international recognition encourages transnational terrorism with escalation to more destructive and spectacular violence. As the audience grows larger, more diverse, and more accustomed to terrorism, terrorist go to extreme lengths of shock". The empirical evidence supporting the theory of contagion suggests, (a) that rise of intensity of terrorism is because of loss of state control over effective technologies of terrorism (Volgly, Inwalle and Corntasel 1997), (b) that occurrence of terrorism in one country often leads, directly or indirectly, to more terrorism, whether by the same organisation, or by 'second generation' groups, in other country.

These studies (Redlick 1979, Crenshaw 1984 and others) conclude that, information flows seem to benefit militants in several ways. The media coverage of the terrorist activities attracts the attention to the groups' cause and their specific tactics and strategies are communicated worldwide. Thus, roots of terrorism in a particular national context in one country may inspire imitation in another country. In the process, terrorist groups establish direct and physical contacts with terrorist groups of other countries and their collaboration may range between buying weapons, to finding asylum, to acquiring funds, to obtaining passports, to preparing false documents, and to rendering assistance in planning and execution of terrorist activities. Thus, this transnational links between groups with common objectives make terrorism to spill over in neighbouring states (terrorism in one state may lead to terrorism in another state). In addition, process of contagion, sometimes, becomes operative in the absence of physical contacts, when geo-politically distant terrorist organisations become models of imitation (Moohead Kennedy 1998).

In fact no single scientific theory of the causes of terrorism can explain all conditions of terrorism. It is however possible, from above researches, to identify few contributory causes of terrorism, which are constantly appearing in recorded history, they are: (i) ethnic conflict, hatreds, discrimination and oppression; (ii) religious and ideological conflicts; (iii) socio-economic relative deprivation; (iv) stresses and strains of rapid modernisation; (v) perceived political inequalities, infringements of rights and injustice; (vi) lack of adequate channels for peaceful communication of protests, grievances and demands; (vii) existence of a tradition of violence disaffection and popular turbulence; (viii) the availability of a revolutionary leadership equipped with a potentially attractive ideology; (ix) weakness and ineptness of the government, and its organs; (x) erosion of confidence in the system, its values and institutions; (xi) division within governing elites and leadership groups.

Problems and Effects of Terrorism in India

Asia holds the world's fastest-growing markets, fastest-rising military expenditures, and most serious hot spots which include the epicenter of international terrorism, and also accounts for 75 per cent of all terrorism casualties worldwide. Much of its terrorist violence is concentrated in its southern belt of Asia, which in the past decade emerged as the international hub of terrorism. This southern part of Asia, is wracked by terrorist, insurgent, militant and separatist violence in a manner unmatched elsewhere in the world. To be sure, the entire expanse from the Middle East to Southeast Asia is home to militant groups and troubled by terrorist violence, posing a serious challenge to international and regional security.

Terrorism has become a way of life in some areas of southern Asia. The only thriving democracy in this vast region is India, wedged in an arc of authoritarian or totalitarian regimes engaged in covert actions in breach of international law. These regimes either export narcotics and terrorism (Afghanistan, Pakistan, and Burma) or make illicit transfers of nuclear and missile technologies (China). In South Asia, there are a number of disputes, the causes of which are deeply rooted in its history. The partition of British India is considered as the core of conflicts, which had started driving both the 'Key players' on the path of confrontation.

India, in fact, is a sort of laboratory where major acts of terror are first tried out before being replicated in democracies in the West. The logic is that if India, the world's largest democracy, can be shaken, so can other democracies. India's own soft response to terrorism has emboldened international terrorists and their sponsors over the years. Pakistan has employed Afghan war veterans and its homegrown terrorists to bleed India as part of what it calls a war of "a thousand cuts."

Since independence, India has been battling against terrorism and insurgency. In the early 1950's, it struggled with an insurgency, it inherited from the British administration in parts of the Northeastern states. In the 1960's insurgency spread to other areas including Manipur, Meghalaya and Tirupura and in 1970's this conflict entered into Assam. Unfortunately, these conflicts have not only consolidated but also have become intense. This part of the country is lush and verdurous; India has waged most of its counter insurgency campaigns in jungle terrain and small villages, although some of these conflicts in northeast have certainly had urban or semi-urban components. However, the rapid natural urbanisation of India has meant that the state encounters with such insurgent elements in the northeast are occurring at an alarming rate in built-up areas. Unfortunately in India, counter insurgency measures have not brought the desired results either in minimising, control or eliminating this violence.

In the 1980's these events were completely overtaken by large-scale terrorist activities waged by Sikh separatists in the state of Punjab. The Khalsa elements were engaged in a sustained campaign of militancy to secure an independent Khalistan. This terrorist movement was exceptionally brutal and had claimed over 21, 469 lives, before it was effectively eliminated in mid 1990's. The case of terrorism in Punjab merits study and research for its intensity and lethality but also as one of the few insurgencies that have been systematically eliminated. The vast Indian experience with numerous terrorist and criminal organisations operating in urban areas offers rich lessons.

Problems associated with terrorism did not stop with the elimination of the Khalistan movement in Punjab. In 1990s India witnessed numerous attacks by the foreign terrorists in what was called as Cross Border Terrorism (CBT). The intensity and magnitude of this menace was often perceived as a low intensity war in Jammu and Kashmir. This was generated, planned and executed by the Pakistani establishment with the intention to paralyse Jammu and Kashmir. On the other hand, insurgency was on rise in northeastern parts of India. The rise of Bodo, ULFA, NSCN, many other local militant outfits called as 'Army' had unleashed violence in the region. The decade of 1990 also saw the rise of domestic terrorist outfits having close networks with foreign terrorist organisations. On the other hand Pakistan policy to destablise India with continued violence was clearly visible with terrorist attacks taking place in different parts of India placed at short intervals.

For long, India has been indifferent to the growing menace of terrorism. Groups that indulged in extremism were often treated kindly, at times were even provided with official political patronage, economic assistance and military supplies; terrorism in other countries was exploited to promote national interests. While international political violence became terrorism, similar acts in neighbouring countries were hailed or excused as jihad, freedom struggle or popular resistance.

In December 2001, terror had finally struck the heartland of India, the epitome of its democratic existence: the Parliament. Half a century of cross-border terrorism in the border regions of India had now spread to other parts of the country. The assault on the hallowed precincts of Parliament came as yet another wake-up-call. However, it is not clear how the security threat was perceived by our security managers. Since then the terrorist attacks have been taking place regularly at short intervals in places like, New Delhi, Ayodhaya, Bangalore, Varanasi, Nagpur, Mumbai, Malegaon, Hyderabad and Panipat. While in Jammu and Kashmir militant attacks are taking place on a daily basis. This indicates that there are serious loopholes within our domestic security apparatus that we almost never apprehended those who kill innocent citizens, shows lack of political will and lack of governance in the security establishment. The politicians and the bureaucracy are already pontificating about the need to reinvigorate security measures to counter these terror attacks.

Indian security apparatus and elite are largely indifferent or have shied away from formulating an internal security doctrine. Since independence there is no serious attempt to institutionalise mechanism, direction or assertive policy to deal with "internal threats". Interim, adhoc and incremental means have been favourite methods adopted by the successive governments since independence. There is virtually no means to define coherently "the enemy", the sources of threats, the appropriate instruments that are required to deal with the perceived enemy and political will to thwart enemy's design. Last two decades have been continuous assault on Indian citizen and their psyche. Pakistan's strategy of "bleed India with thousand cuts" seems to be working well. In absence of any well-defined and coherent internal security doctrine, India's security apparatus has failed to plug the reoccurrence of terrorist attacks. Intelligence fraternity too is groping in dark about the actual strength, source, capacity and logistics of enemy's next plan.

Unfortunately in India these terror attacks and militancy is seen as mere a "law order" concern and treated as subject of provincial state, whenever, political violence in a massive scale breaks out in a state, the police become the first responders. Police in India are trained, equipped and mentally conditioned to deal with civil disorders only. When confronted with serious threats to internal security like terrorism, insurgency and other proxy war situations, they find it difficult to respond effectively. In such a situation, States seek he expert assistance of paramilitary forces. As paramilitary forces, other than Central Reserve Police Force (CPRF) are raised, trained and equipped to meet a specific need of national security, when deputed to deal with large scale disorders and proxy war situations, they are required to quickly modify and reorient heir operational doctrines to meet the situation at hand. Though the Para military forces in India have equipped themselves well in handling internal security problems, much valuable time has been lost before successes are recorded.

There have been two major views on the reasons for the increasing intensity of terrorist activities in India. The first view, points out, that the presence of foreign terrorist groups particularly in Jammu and Kashmir has significantly raised the level of violence not only in the state but also in other theatres of conflict in India. This has happened not only through the support extended through materials and logistics to local militant groups but also by the export of terrorism to other parts of India. The consistent efforts to render communal overtones to the conflict in Kashmir may also be understood in this light. These foreign terrorist groups have also played the most destabilising role of inciting the locals to take up arms through inducements, or coercion, or threat.

Indian security apparatus and elite are largely indifferent or have shied away from formulating an internal security doctrine. Since independence there is no serious attempt on institutionalised mechanism, direction or assertive policy to deal with "internal threats". Interim, adhoc and incremental means have been favourite methods adopted by the successive governments since independence. There is virtually no means to define coherently "the enemy", the sources of threats, the appropriate instruments that are required to deal with the perceived enemy and political will to thwart enemy's design. Last three decades have been continuous assault on Indian citizen and their psyche. Pakistan's strategy of "bleed India with thousand cuts" seems to be working well. In absence of any well-defined and coherent internal security doctrine, India's security apparatus has failed to plug the reoccurrence of terrorist attacks. Intelligence fraternity too is groping in dark about the actual strength, source, capacity and logistics of enemy's next plan.

Strategies to Counter Terrorism

In order to meet the challenge of global terrorism, some nations have chosen the path of least resistance and adopted a general policy of acceding to terrorist demands for the release of prisoners or the payment of a substantial ransom in exchange for a kidnapped hostage. In general, these states have adopted a generous policy toward captured terrorists, sometimes freeing them on their own recognisance or meting out only limited prison sentences, which often are revoked subsequently. These goals will not be realised, however, until stronger and more resolute governmental action on an international scale convinces terrorist organisations that acts of violence do not advance their cause and will not result in political, financial, or propaganda gain. Until then, transnational terrorism will continue to pose a significant security problem for the international community.

Effective counter-terrorism must consist of several approaches, including reducing the grievances and other risk factors; limiting the ability of terrorist organisations to conduct attacks; physically "hardening" the facilities that are at high risk of attack; creating and maintaining effective intelligence services to detect terrorist threats in advance; and engaging in public diplomacy that is generally respectful of other nations and cultures.

Unfortunately, even if states take all of these countermeasures, terrorism is unlikely to disappear altogether. Terrorism has existed for millennia, and people will almost certainly continue to perceive their realities in ways that lead them to conclude that violence is the best means to achieve their goals. India and other countries affected by terrorism should therefore be as prepared as possible to face a threat that will accompany us into the future. Curbing terrorism wherever and whenever possible, rather than the unrealistic goal of eliminating terrorism altogether, should be the primary objective. Understanding its roots, however, must be the first step.

National strategy covers the complete gamut of activities of government and is not limited to military centric security alone. It has to govern various functions of the state. Hence, assessment of all micro-macro threats, its magnitude and its sources is necessary to build up a 'threat matrix'. National security strategy flows from overall national strategy and is a sub-set of the former which cannot be conceived in a vacuum. Thus, articulation of national security is paramount for the emerging power status of India.

The security apparatus in India has not yet been geared up with adequate modern means of intelligence surveillance and communication interception technology to either nab the terrorist or to foil their attempts. Unfortunately, the magnitude of the loss of life and loss of property due to these attacks are still considered a mere law and order problem and not as a problem of internal security. Even left-wing extremist groups with different names like Maoist Sena, Peoples War Group (PWG), Maoist

Communist Centre (MCC) and others have started looking for targets in metro and cities. Their perfect planning and execution has sent shock waves even in the police establishments.

As part of the integrated approach to combat terrorism in the state, the central government has been taking various measures to offset the adverse impact of terrorism on the general public in Kashmir with emphasis on planned and balanced regional development for building up physical and social infrastructure and in improving productive potential of the state. A standing committee headed by Cabinet Secretary/Home Secretary has been constituted to monitor the development programmes of the central ministries in the state. There are six sub-groups working under the standing committee to provide focused attention to the implementation of various central schemes and projects in the state. In order to give a further impetus to the developmental efforts in the state, the Prime Minster's comprehensive reconstruction and development plans include 67 projects (such as The Autonomous Hill Development Councils for Leh and Kargil, Special Recruitment Drive for Jammu and Kashmir Youth, Enhanced outlay for Rehabilitation Council) covering various aspects of development and security, with thrust on generation of new employment opportunities for the youth of Jammu and Kashmir. It provides assistance for psychological and economic rehabilitation for victims of militancy.

Prime Minister Manmohan Singh has given the right signal to start a brave new campaign for comity among India, Jammu and Kashmir and Pakistan. He suggested that the 'Line of Control' could become a 'Line of Peace' with free flow of ideas, goods, services and people. This will change the 60 years of civilian carnage, causalities and huge military investments. The peace initiatives could stop the dividends of human resource waste, tensions and annihilation. Hence, all must come together as a region of amity. This gesture ought to be supported by all, which stand for socialism, secularism, humanism and peaceful co-existence.

The multi-pronged strategy adopted by the state and central governments, including proactive tackling of cross-border terrorism, are based on concrete factors, such as better functioning of law enforcement agencies and the judiciary, re-establishment of peoples' day-to-day socio-economic routine, free flow of information, etc.

The need for a well co-ordinated security apparatus can hardly be over emphasised. It should include the police, the paramilitary forces, the army and the intelligence agencies. A composite special force on the lines of the National Security Guards (NSG) should be organised in all the states, even in those states where the internal security situation is not so serious. It is easier to deal with the problems at the initial stages, than later, when the state police is no longer able to cope with them.

Evolving and strengthening appropriate legislation and streamlining the process of judicial conviction of the fugitives is another area that needs some priority and attention. Creation of fast tract courts to avoid judicial delay and enactment of a deterrent anti-terror law would constitute an essential step forward. The need of the hour is to institutionalise, develop procedure and process that would boost inter institutional co-ordination, facilitate professional conduct of operations on a thorough professional policy analysis. Lack of professional mindset for informed debates, fierce expression of spite, bitterness and mutual political acrimony take place instead of constructive policy discussions. Our politicians are known for rhetoric penchant without substantive action or operation; this has eroded the credibility of such oft repeated statement.

India has a coastline of about 7,500 km running along nine States and four Union Territories. A constant threat to India's security has been the possibility of terrorists entering the mainland by exploiting the country's porous maritime borders and perpetrating undesirable activities. These concerns were brought to light yet again when the perpetrators of Mumbai terror attacks entered India by exploiting the weak maritime border security. Concerned with the nature of the porous maritime border and inadequate maritime security of the country, the Ministry of Home Affairs stated in 2008 that the Government of India had planned to enhance surveillance and patrolling of India's coastline to discourage infiltration attempts by terrorists through the sea lanes.

In light of these events and threats, the Central and State governments in the country now perceive the modernisation and up-gradation of the country's Homeland Security infrastructure as an area of priority. This includes modernisation programs for providing better equipment and training to the security forces deployed with the task of Homeland Security in India, creation of a centralised Comprehensive database called National Information Grid (NATGRID) by combining the individual databases of several government agencies, setting up of the Crime and Criminal Tracking Network and Systems (CCTNS) and several other such measures. Recently, the Ministry of Home Affairs has proposed to create a Multi-Agency Centre (MAC) that will work at both the center and State level to compile intelligence from and disperse intelligence to the participating agencies and set up a National Counterterrorism Centre (NCTC) which would be the nodal point for handling all aspects related to terrorism in India.

Over the last few years, significant progress has been made in India in terms of improving legislation, strengthening security forces and streamlining procurement. Mumbai terrorist attacks of 2008 invited increased public scrutiny of the country's current State of Homeland Security and led to a strong political backing for several much-needed reforms like broadening the definition of terrorist attacks in the Indian legal system and also expedited the acquisition of critical equipment and items to improve the national security infrastructure.

Conclusion

The landscape of terrorism has changed now. It is a low-cost, low-risk and high return proxy war by Pakistan which has been cloaked with an element of denial. India therefore needs to adopt a policy that includes eliminating the cause of militancy, resort to international diplomacy, and make it too expensive for Pakistan to exercise this option against India. India should also vigorously apprise the Pakistani population about the miseries brought on Indian population by military and political establishments through their support to the *'jihadis'* operating in Jammu and Kashmir to build public pressure on them and emphasizing on the people to opt for people's democracy as a panacea for the present ills.

The critical infrastructure of a country includes public and private assets that are of strategic importance to the economic, political or security interests of the country should be well guarded. The security requirements have to be met, but that does not mean giving the security agencies a free hand. Striking the right balance is the key to success in meeting these challenges effectively. In this endeavor, there are several areas which are critical to the Homeland Security of India and thus require specific focus. We need an effective comprehensive security policy that will be implemented at all levels. Complex security threats need effective security management. It is an urgent requirement to review and refurbish each and every element of the entire security apparatus across various wings of the central and state governments. While varied steps are required to improve governance on all fronts, certain administrative reforms, enactment of new laws and legal modalities are essential to ensure effective functioning of the security management apparatus. India is endowed with able and competent security managers who are capable of changing the landscape of comprehensive security in India. But whether there is a collective wisdom and political will to assert? Well, competency alone cannot provide results without ability to act. Thus, competency and ability both is needed to address comprehensive security issues in India. Moreover, terrorism can be uprooted with the help of mass support. Such support is possible only when there is a social cohesion, harmony, peace, prosperity and enjoyment of liberty and freedom by all sections of society. The inability of the government in terms of providing employment avenues is well identified by the terrorist organisations to tap the educated and unemployed youngsters to be part of their anti social and anti national activities. Therefore, it is very significant and essential to have social welfare measures to address the basic issues concerning the masses.

References

Corrado, R. (1981) "A Critique of the Mental Disorder Perspective of Political Terrorism", International Journal of Law and Psychiatry 4 (1981), pp. 293-309.

Dr. John Dollard's (1939) Theory of frustration - aggression has proved that human become violent only if they are frustrated in their efforts to attain a particular goal, i.e., frustration leads to anger and anger to acts of aggressive violence.

INDEX

U

V

W

Y

Z